PEARSON CUSTOM LIBRARY

ENGLISH
MERCURY READER

Bridge to College Reading
Compiled by Lisa B. Rosenthal
for College Reading Classes
Portland Community College, Cascade Campus
Portland, Oregon

PEARSON

Please visit our website at *www.pearsonlearningsolutions.com*.

Attention bookstores: For permission to return any unsold stock, contact us at *pe-uscustomreturns@pearson.com*.

Pearson Learning Solutions, 501 Boylston Street, Suite 900, Boston, MA 02116
A Pearson Education Company
www.pearsoned.com

Printed in the United States of America
V3NL

ISBN 10: 1-269-27756-1
ISBN 13: 978-1-269-27756-3

General Editors

Janice Neuleib
Illinois State University

Kathleen Shine Cain
Merrimack College

Stephen Ruffus
Salt Lake Community College

Table of Contents

Essays and Stories for College Readers

Studentship Skills

Active Learning

Learning Objectives

From this chapter, readers will learn to:

1 Be active learners
2 Identify and take advantage of individual learning styles
3 Improve concentration
4 Adopt successful college behaviors

Two Girls Reading (1934); Pablo Picasso. Oil on canvas. Private Collection/The Bridgeman Art Library.

From Chapter 1 of *Bridging the Gap: College Reading,* Eleventh Edition. Brenda D. Smith. Copyright © 2014 by Pearson Education, Inc. Published by Pearson Education, Inc. All rights reserved.

WHAT IS ACTIVE LEARNING?

Learning Objective 1

Be an active learner

Active learning is the purposeful use of attention, effort, strategies, and resources to achieve a learning goal. Active learning is not just a single task; it is a project with multiple components. You, your instructor, your textbook, and your classmates are all parts of the project. Learn to use all four effectively, and you are on the road to success.

Active learning requires concentration and attention to factors beyond academics. You must manage yourself, manage the assignment or learning task, and manage others who can contribute to or detract from your success. In this chapter, we discuss many factors that contribute to your ability to become an effective, active learner. First, however, let's consider what psychologists have to say about focusing your attention, thinking, and learning. Understanding these cognitive aspects is a part of managing yourself.

What Are Cognitive Psychology and Neuroscience?

Cognitive psychology is the body of knowledge that describes how the mind works, or at least how researchers think the mind works. Cognitive psychologists study how people process information from their five senses and how they think, learn, remember, express ideas, and solve problems. The ideas of cognitive psychology are frequently described as *models*, or comparisons with something else we understand. For example, for many years, the brain was likened to the central processing unit of a computer. The human brain is more complex than a computer, but this information processing model has been useful to our understanding of brain function. However, as research continues, new concepts are also being developed.

Neuroscience is the scientific study of the molecular and cellular levels of the nervous system and of systems within the brain. It includes the study of behavior produced by the brain. With the development of sophisticated medical imaging techniques, scientists can now view the changes that take place in the brain during cognitive, emotional, and physical activity. Research in neuroscience is providing increasing information about the biological aspects of learning.

How Does the Brain Screen Messages?

Cognitive psychologists use the word **attention** to describe a student's uninterrupted mental focus. Thinking and learning, they say, begin with attention. During every minute of the day, the brain is bombarded with millions of sensory

BRAIN BOOSTER

Medical imaging techniques, such as PET scans, fMRI technology, EEGs, and newly developing methods allow neuroscientists to "see" the brain as it works. These instruments have created an explosion of knowledge that helps us understand how we can make better use of our brains to attain our learning goals. Scattered throughout this text you will notice a feature called "Brain Booster." In these short pieces, you will find practical ways to keep your brain working at its best—all thanks to research in neuroscience. Look for boxes like this one for brain-boosting tips.

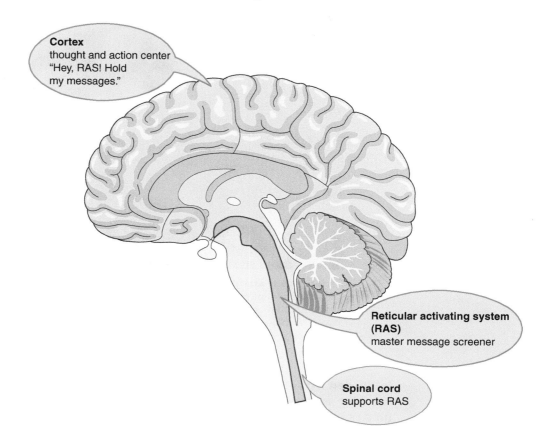

messages. How does the brain decide which messages to pay attention to and which to overlook? At this moment, are you thinking about the temperature of the room, outdoor noises, or what you are reading? With all this information available to you at the same time, how can your brain choose what's most important?

The brain relies on a dual command center to screen out one message and attend to another. Receptor cells send millions of messages per minute to your brain. Your reticular activating system (RAS)—a network of cells at the top of the spinal cord that runs to the brain—tells the cortex of the brain—the wrinkled outer layer that handles sensory processing, motor control, and memory storage—not to bother with most of the sensory input. Your RAS knows that most sensory inputs do not need attention. For example, you are probably not aware at this moment of your back pressing against your chair or your clothes pulling on your body. Your RAS has decided not to clutter your brain with such irrelevant information and to alert the cortex only when there is an extreme problem, such as your foot going to sleep because you have been sitting on it.

The cortex can also make attention decisions and tells your RAS to hold some messages while you concentrate on others. How well are your RAS and cortex cooperating in blocking out distractions so you can concentrate on learning?

Dividing your attention can have a cost. Researchers have found that the auto accident rate among people who drive while talking on the phone (including those texting or using headsets) is four times that of drivers who do not use the phone as they drive.
Arto/Fotolia

Is Divided Attention Effective? Is it possible to do two things at once, such as watching television and doing homework? Is it safe to drive and talk on a cell phone? In a 2002 study, researchers Rodriguez, Valdes-Sosa, and Freiwald found that dividing your attention usually has a cost.[1] You are more likely to perform one or both tasks less efficiently than if you were to concentrate on a single task. This corroborated, or made more certain, the earlier findings of two other scientists who tested the effectiveness of divided attention.[2] These researchers asked participants questions as they watched two televised sports events with one superimposed over the other. When participants were instructed to watch only one of the games, they successfully screened out the other and answered questions accurately. When asked to attend to both games simultaneously, however, the participants made eight times more mistakes than when focusing on only one game. Thus, this research seems to confirm the old adage "You can't do two things at once and do them well."

Can Tasks Become Automatic? Can you walk and chew gum at the same time? Does every simple activity require your undivided attention? Many tasks—walking, tying shoelaces, and driving a car, for example—begin under controlled

---

[1] V. Rodriguez, M. Valdes-Sosa, and W. Freiwald, "Dividing Attention Between Form and Motion During Transparent Surface Perception," *Cognitive Brain Research* 13 (2002): 187–93.
[2] U. Neisser and R. Becklen, "Selective Looking: Attending to Visually Significant Events," *Cognitive Psychology* 7 (1975): 480–94.

Are You Paying Attention?

Of course you are! Human brains are always attending to something. Perhaps the question should be, "What are you paying attention to?" Keeping our focus on a classroom lecture, a reading assignment, or a project is sometimes a struggle, but paying attention is critical to learning. Research tells us that two factors are most important to paying attention: meaning and emotion. So, think of a way to connect new information to something you already know. Recognizing your crazy Uncle Charlie in something you studied in psychology class will help you understand and remember it. Think of how you can apply a new concept at work or in your personal life. These are ways to give real meaning to what you're learning. Likewise, link emotion to new concepts with a funny story, an interesting case study, or a real-life concern. Studying or sharing a new idea with a friend also lends emotional energy to learning. Meaning + Emotion = Attention. Make the equation work for you!

*—Adapted from Patricia Wolfe, Brain Matters. ©2001
Association for Supervision and Curriculum Development: Alexandria, VA*

processing, which means that they are deliberate and require concentrated mental effort to learn. After much practice, however, such tasks become automatic. Driving a car, for example, is a learned behavior that researchers would say becomes an automatic process after thousands of hours of experience. You can probably drive and listen to the radio at the same time, but it may not be a good idea to drive and talk on a cell phone. Similarly, a skilled athlete can dribble a basketball automatically while also attending to strategy and position. Attention is actually not divided because it can shift away from tasks that have become automatic.

Automatic Aspects of Reading.   The idea of doing certain things automatically is especially significant in reading. As a first-grade reader, you had to concentrate on recognizing letters, words, and sentences, as well as trying to construct meaning. After years of practice and over-learning, much of the recognition aspect of reading has become automatic. You no longer stop laboriously to decode each word or each letter. For example, when you look at the word *child,* you automatically think the meaning. Thus, you can focus your mental resources on understanding the *message* in which the word appears, rather than on understanding the word itself.

College reading can be frustrating because it is not as automatic as everyday reading. College textbooks often contain many unfamiliar words and complex concepts that the brain cannot automatically process. Your attention to a book's message can be interrupted by the need to attend to unknown words, creating the dilemma of trying to do two things at once—trying to figure out word meaning as well as trying to understand the message. After the break in concentration, you can regain your focus, and little harm is done if such breaks are infrequent. However, frequent interruptions in the automatic aspect of reading can undermine your ability to concentrate on the message. Thus, mastering the jargon or vocabulary of a new course early on can improve your concentration.

COGNITIVE STYLES

Learning Objective 2

Identify and take advantage of your learning style

Do you learn easily by reading or do you prefer a demonstration or a diagram? Do you like to work with details or do you prefer broad generalizations? Many psychologists believe that people develop a preference for a particular style or manner of learning at an early age and that these preferences affect concentration and learning. These preferences are called **cognitive styles** or **learning styles.** Cognitive or learning style theorists focus on strengths and assert that there is no right or wrong way. These researchers believe that instruction and learning are best when they match the learner's particular preference.

Although knowing your preferences may not affect how your classes are taught, such knowledge can improve your attitude about yourself as a learner and enable you to build on your strengths.

Cognitive Style Preferences

One popular inventory that can be used to determine individual cognitive style preferences is the Myers-Briggs Type Indicator (MBTI). Based on psychologist Carl Jung's theory of personality types, it measures personality traits in four categories. The results are used as indicators for learning styles, teaching styles, management styles, career planning, team building, organizational development, and even marriage counseling. The inventory must be administered by a licensed specialist and is frequently given to entering college freshmen. The following descriptions of the four MBTI categories give an idea of the issues its proponents consider significant:

1. **Extroverted—introverted.** Extroverts prefer to talk with others and learn through experience, whereas introverts prefer to think alone about ideas.
2. **Sensing—intuitive.** Sensing types prefer working with concrete details and tend to be patient, practical, and realistic. Intuitive types like abstractions and are creative, impatient, and theory-oriented.
3. **Thinking—feeling.** Thinking types tend to base decisions on objective criteria and logical principles. Feeling types are subjective and consider the impact of the decision on other people.
4. **Judging—perceiving.** Judging types are time-oriented and structured, whereas perceivers are spontaneous and flexible.

Another test that uses the same type indicators as the MBTI is the Keirsey Temperament Sorter II. You can take this seventy-item personality inventory online and receive an extensive printout. However, experts do not consider it to have passed the same rigorous standards for validation and reliability as the MBTI. The Keirsey Web site (http://www.keirsey.com) provides background information about the test. It begins with a brief questionnaire and then provides a link to the longer Keirsey Temperament Sorter II.

Global Versus Analytical Preferences

Another popular cognitive style theory focuses on global and analytical preferences. Global learners absorb information more easily if they understand how it fits into "the big picture." They need to know how and when they can use the new ideas. Global learners quickly grasp the meaning of icons and symbols, but they can also be easily distracted from the task at hand. Analytical learners, however, are more interested in the details and favor learning one step at a time. They prefer words rather than symbols or drawings and respond well to clear, direct instructions. The analytical preference is sometimes referred to as a linear or sequential style.

Study Tips. Global learners should read the table of contents before reading a textbook chapter to better understand the entire topic. They will also benefit from a preview of the chapter headings and learning questions and a close look at pictures and graphic illustrations. Global learners should focus on how they can use the information they are learning. In mathematics, asking the instructor or referring to the textbook to find out how a formula or process fits into previously learned material will be advantageous. Annotating while reading will help to keep global learners focused. Previewing the headings and subheadings also aids analytical learners. They should look especially for steps in a process, parts of a concept, and details to support major ideas. They, too, will gain from carefully annotating as they read and then outlining to absorb the details. Analytical learners generally do well in mathematics, but they can benefit by "translating" formulas and problems into words.

Sensory Learning Styles

Other cognitive style theorists focus on sensory preferences. For example, some people find it easier to process information through visual input. Others are more attuned to auditory input—hearing. Still others need to touch and be physically active—tactile-kinesthetic input—to absorb information.

A simple test may help you recognize your strongest sensory style: How do you remember the name of a person you have just met? Do you picture the name and the person in your mind or need to see the name in writing? This indicates a visual preference. Do you need to hear the name repeated? This would suggest an auditory preference. Or do shaking hands and interacting with the person solidify the name in your memory? This indicates a tactile-kinesthetic preference. If you want to explore your sensory learning style in greater depth, a quick online search will yield more detailed assessments such as the Barsch Learning Styles Inventory.

College students who know their dominant sensory learning style have valuable information about themselves. They can plan their study activities so they learn and retain more but spend less time studying. Select the study methods that make the most effective use of your learning strengths, but remember that most people learn best with a combination of visual, auditory, and tactile-kinesthetic activities.

EXERCISE 1

Study Tips for Three Sensory Learning Styles

Read all of the descriptions and tips that follow. Highlight at least one study tip in each section that you do not already use. Highlight at least three tips suggested for your dominant style. Commit yourself to testing these new methods this semester and see if they yield good results for you. Your instructor might ask you to write down the methods you plan to try.

Visual Learner.   A visual learner needs to see, to *visualize*, in order to work and learn. He or she must keep the visual sense active. It is easy for him or her to learn by reading and to understand written directions. Reading, visualizing, and, then, learning are this person's most effective approach. Therefore, if you are a visual learner, you should try these strategies:

1. Definitely read, or at least preview, each textbook chapter before it is discussed in class.
2. While reading a chapter, examine each visual aid. Maps, pictures, charts, graphs, and tables are very important to your understanding of the subject.
3. After reading the chapter, highlight key points. Do not underline everything, only the important elements.
4. As the instructor lectures, focus on him or her. This will help you concentrate.
5. Again, as the instructor lectures, keep your textbook open. When your teacher discusses points from the book, look at the written words.
6. Take lecture notes. Writing notes enhances your memory.
7. Try to visualize your notes.
8. When combining the text material and your lecture notes, try to use visual forms—maps, outlines, or diagrams—to summarize important concepts. The more visual you make the ideas, the easier it will be for you to remember them.
9. Do not study with the television on. It will distract you.
10. Keep your study area free of clutter and distractions.

Auditory Learner.   An auditory learner needs to hear in order to work and learn well. However, he or she does not just hear on an unconscious level but listens actively with concentration and comprehension. This person learns easily from lectures and discussions; oral directions help, not hinder. Below are some suggestions for you to try if you are an auditory learner. As you study, use the ones that work best for you.

1. Be an active listener in every lecture classroom. Concentrate on the lecturer.
2. Definitely take written notes as you listen. If possible, tape the lecture so you can replay it at a convenient time.
3. When studying, read your notes out loud. Let your brain hear you say each idea.
4. When you cannot verbalize important material, at least lip-read it to mimic an auditory activity.
5. When possible, use recordings of assigned readings. Simultaneously read and listen to the material. This will increase your memory of it.
6. Study out loud with a friend. Ask each other questions, and listen to the answers.
7. Do not study with the radio playing. The noise, no matter how pleasant, is too great a distraction for you.

Tactile/Kinesthetic Learner.   A tactile/kinesthetic learner needs to *do* in order to learn. He or she needs touch and movement to participate in the learning process. Unfortunately, the typical classroom is not designed for tactile/kinesthetic learning. Therefore, this type of learner must devise ways to simulate a movement-oriented environment in a traditional classroom or to enhance those movements that are acceptable. Below are some suggestions for tactile/kinesthetic learners. Experiment with them; if needed, modify or discard them. Reading through this list may stimulate your own creativity and may push some long-dormant ideas of your own to the top. Try them out, too. When you discover a strategy that helps you learn, use it; use it repeatedly until it becomes an innate element in your learning process.

1. Writing is movement and touch; therefore, take copious notes while you read or listen to a lecture.
2. Rewrite and summarize key ideas.
3. Use a computer. Working with a computer is interactive, and it permits some movement.
4. Definitely try to choose lab courses and internship programs. Their structure enables you to learn by performing tasks.
5. Move around while you study. If movement helps you remember and concentrate, then walk around your room while you review notes or learn new information.
6. Tape your notes and listen to them while you jog by using your portable tape player.
7. Use your fingers to tick off a list of key elements as you review.
8. Do not try to remain still and study for long periods of time. Short, intense study sessions with a defined, limited goal work best for you.
9. Make outlines or concept maps of the information you need to learn. Make photocopies and cut them apart. Test yourself by putting them back together, being sure to match details with the right major labels. Check yourself by looking at the original notes.

Useful learning style inventories are available online.

Multiple Intelligences: There Is More Than One Way to Be Smart

During the 1900s, Western culture placed much emphasis on verbal and logical thinking, especially as measured by IQ (intelligence quotient) tests. Such tests were used to screen and assign positions to U.S. military recruits and to evaluate and place schoolchildren into classes. Although criticized for measuring only *schoolhouse giftedness*, IQ nevertheless remained the standard for assessing abilities for many years. However, in 1983, Harvard professor Howard Gardner changed the way many people think about being smart. Taking a much broader, more inclusive view of abilities, he developed a theory of **multiple intelligences.** According to this theory, there are eight different ways to be intelligent. Some people develop certain ways of being intelligent to a greater extent than they do others.

The following list describes Gardner's eight forms of intelligence with possible career choices for each. In which areas do you excel?

1. **Word smart.** *Linguistic* thinkers like reading, writing, and speaking. They become journalists, teachers, executives, and comedians.
2. **Picture smart.** *Spatial* thinkers like pictures, charts, and maps. They become architects, artists, and surgeons.
3. **Logical smart.** *Logical-mathematical* thinkers like to reason, sequence, and think in terms of cause and effect. They become scientists, accountants, bankers, and computer programmers.

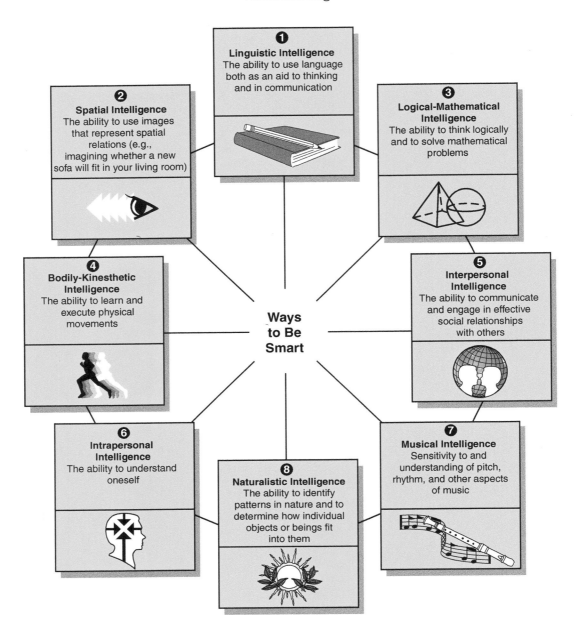

4. **Body smart.** *Bodily-kinesthetic* thinkers like to control body movements and handle objects skillfully. They become athletes, dancers, craftspeople, mechanics, and surgeons.

5. **People smart.** *Interpersonal* thinkers who work well with people can perceive the moods, intentions, and desires of others. They become networkers, negotiators, social service professionals, and teachers.

6. **Self smart.** *Intrapersonal* thinkers are introspective and meditative or can be self-disciplined, goal-directed independents who understand the inner self. They become counselors, theologians, and self-employed businesspeople.

7. **Music smart.** *Musical* thinkers with a "good ear" can sing and play in tune, keep time, and listen with discernment. They become musical audio engineers, symphony conductors, music educators, and musicians.
8. **Nature smart.** *Naturalistic* thinkers have expertise in flora and fauna, have "green thumbs," a knack for gardening, and an affinity for animals. They become landscapers, landscape architects, and veterinarians.

How does the multiple intelligences theory provide another way to look at strengths and weaknesses in learning? See for yourself. You may excel in several of these intelligences. Honestly rank yourself from 1 to 10 on each of Gardner's eight listed intelligences (with 10 being the highest agreement):

1. _____   2. _____   3. _____   4. _____

5. _____   6. _____   7. _____   8. _____

For a more scientific evaluation of your strengths, go to www.businessballs.com/freeonlineresources.htm. First, search the index for the "Human Resources" tab. Then, click on "Multiple Intelligences and VAK" for access to several assessments.

What If I'm Not a Verbal or Logical Learner?

Most college teaching is geared toward linguistic and logical-mathematical smarts. If those are not your strengths, how can you compensate? First, and most important, recognize the dilemma and be happy with your strengths, knowing that you have areas of high intelligence. Next, devise a few tricks to make the most of your strengths.

- For picture smarts, create diagrams and maps for study. Watch films on the subject.
- For music smarts, use rhymes and rhythms as memory devices, or *mnemonics,* to enhance memory.
- For people smarts, network and study with classmates.
- For body smarts, seek hands-on experiences to complement your tactile and kinesthetic abilities.
- For self smarts, reflect for self-understanding to enrich and guide your life.
- For nature smarts, relate learning to environmental issues.

In summary, cognitive psychologists offer many ways of looking at attention and learning by encouraging us to recognize our strengths and weaknesses. Use your strengths and be proud of them.

WHAT IS CONCENTRATION?

Learning Objective 3

Improve concentration

Regardless of your intelligences and the way you learn, knowing how to concentrate is critical to college success. Concentration is a skill that is developed through self-discipline and practice. It is a **habit** that requires time and effort to develop for consistent success. Athletes have it, surgeons have it, and successful college students must have it. *Concentration is essential for active learning.*

Concentration can be defined as the process of *paying attention*—that is, focusing full attention on the task at hand. Someone once said that the mark of a genius is the ability to concentrate completely on one thing at a time. This is easy if the task is fun and exciting, but it becomes more difficult when you are required to read something that is not very interesting to you. In such cases, you may find yourself looking from word to word and spacing out.

POOR CONCENTRATION: CAUSES AND CURES

The type of intense concentration that forces the RAS and cortex to close out the rest of the world is the state we would all like to achieve each time we sit down with a textbook. Most of the time, however, lots of thoughts compete for attention.

Students frequently ask, *How can I keep my mind on what I'm doing?* or they say, *I finished the assignment, but I don't understand a thing I read.* The best way to increase concentration is not by using some simple mental trick to fool the brain; rather, it involves a series of practical short- and long-range planning strategies targeted at reducing external and internal distractions.

External Distractions

External distractions are the temptations of the physical world that divert your attention away from your work. They are the people in the room, the noise in the background, the time of day, or your place for studying. To control these external distractions, you must create an environment that says, "This is the place and the time for me to get my work done."

Create a Place for Studying.   Start by establishing a private study cubicle; it may be in the library, at the dining room table, or in your bedroom. Wherever your study place is, choose a straight chair and face the wall. Get rid of gadgets, magazines, and other temptations that trigger the mind to think of *play*. Stay away from your bed because it triggers *sleep*. Spread out your papers, books, and other symbols of studying, and create an atmosphere in which the visual stimuli signal *work*. Be consistent by trying to study in the same place at the same time.

Use a Calendar, Assignment Book, or Smartphone.   At the beginning of the quarter or semester, record dates for tests, term papers, and special projects on some kind of planner, such as a print or electronic calendar, assignment book, or smartphone. Use your planner to organize all course assignments. The mere sight of your planner will remind you of the need for both short- and long-term planning. Assigned tests, papers, and projects will be due whether you are ready or not. Your first job is to devise a plan for being ready.

Schedule Weekly Activities.   Successful people do not let their time slip away; they manage time, rather than letting time manage them. Plan realistically and then follow your plan. After calculating the total study hours needed using the formula below, complete the weekly activity chart :

1. Enter your classes and all other fixed commitments such as work hours into the chart.

2. Calculate the number of study hours you should plan.

   Number of classes I'm taking: _____

   Number of hours each class meets each week: X _____

      Total hours in class each week   = _____

   Two study hours for each hour in class (some experts
   recommend three hours of study for each hour in class)   X   2

      Total number of study hours I should plan each week   = [____]

3. Distribute your total recommended study hours in reasonable places during the week. Make good use of time between classes as well as the longer blocks of time.

4. When you have a workable schedule, make copies of it.

Each week, make a list of the class assignments, divide them into small tasks, and write them into the schedule during the study hours you have already planned. Be specific about each task ("read first half of Ch. 8 in psychology, brainstorm research paper topic for English," for example). Always include time for a regular review of lecture notes.

Examinations require special planning. Many students do not realize how much time it takes to study for a major exam. Spread out your studying over several days, and avoid last-minute cramming sessions late at night. Plan additional time for special projects and term papers to avoid deadline crises.

Take Short Breaks. Even though it is not necessary to write this on the chart, remember that you need short breaks. Few students can study uninterrupted for two hours without becoming fatigued and losing concentration. In fact, research shows that studying in chunks rather than long spans is most efficient. Try the *50:10 ratio*— study hard for fifty minutes, take a ten-minute break, and then promptly go back to the books for another fifty minutes.

Internal Distractions

Internal distractions are the concerns that come repeatedly into your mind as you try to keep your attention focused on an assignment. You have to run errands, do laundry, make telephone calls, and pay bills. How do you stop worrying about getting an inspection sticker for the car or about picking up tickets for Saturday's ball game when you need to be concentrating completely on your class assignment?

Make a List. To gain control over mental disruptions, make a list of what is on your mind and keeping you from concentrating on your studies. Jot down on paper your mental distractions, and then analyze each to determine if immediate action is possible. If you decide you can do something right away, get up and do it. Make that phone call, write that e-mail, or finish that chore. Maybe it will take a few minutes

WEEKLY ACTIVITY CHART

Time	Monday	Tuesday	Wednesday	Thursday	Friday	Saturday	Sunday
7:00–8:00							
8:00–9:00							
9:00–10:00							
10:00–11:00							
11:00–12:00							
12:00–1:00							
1:00–2:00							
2:00–3:00							
3:00–4:00							
4:00–5:00							
5:00–6:00							
6:00–7:00							
7:00–8:00							
8:00–9:00							
9:00–10:00							
10:00–11:00							
11:00–12:00							

or maybe half an hour, but the investment will have been worthwhile if the quality of your study time—your concentration power—has improved. Taking action is the first step in getting something off your mind.

For a big problem that you can't tackle immediately, ask yourself, "Is it worth the amount of brain time I'm dedicating to it?" Take a few minutes to think and make notes on possible solutions. Jotting down necessary future action and forming a plan of attack will help relieve the worry and clear your mind for studying.

Right now, list five things that are on your mind that you need to remember to do. Alan Lakein, a pioneer specialist in time management, calls this a **to do list.** In his book, *How to Get Control of Your Time and Your Life,* Lakein claims that successful business executives start each day with such a list. Rank the activities on

To Do List	Sample
1.	1. *Get hair cut*
2.	2. *Do rough draft of essay*
3.	3. *Revise rough draft*
4.	4. *Finish Math homework*
5.	5. *Pay phone bill*

your list in order of priority, and then do the most important things first. Some people even make a list before they go to sleep at night.

Increase Your Self-Confidence.   Saying "I'll never pass this course" or "I can't get in the mood to study" is the first step to failure. Concentration requires self-confidence. Getting a college degree is not a short-term goal. Your enrollment indicates that you have made a commitment to a long-term goal. Ask yourself, "Who do I want to be in five years?" In the following space, describe how you view yourself, both professionally and personally, five years from now:

Five years from now I hope to be _____

_____

_____

Sometimes, identifying the traits you admire in others can give you insight into your own values and desires. Think about the traits you respect in others and about your own definition of success. Answer the two questions that follow, and consider how your responses mirror your own aspirations and goals:

Who is the person that you admire the most? _____

Why do you admire this person? _____

_____

_____

Improve Your Self-Concept.   Have faith in yourself and in your ability to be what you want to be. How many people do you know who have passed the particular course that is worrying you? Are they smarter than you? Probably not. Can you do as well as they did? Turn your negative feelings into a positive attitude. What are some of your positive traits? Are you a hard worker, an honest person, a loyal friend? Take a few minutes to pat yourself on the back. Think about your good points, and list five positive traits that you believe you possess:

Positive Traits

1. _____

2. _____

3. _____

4. _____

5. _____

What have you already accomplished? Did you participate in athletics in high school, win any contests, or master any difficult skills? Recall your previous achievements, and list three accomplishments that you view with pride:

Accomplishments

1. _____

2. _____

3. _____

Reduce Anxiety.   Have you ever heard people say, "I work better under pressure"? This statement contains a degree of truth. A small amount of tension can help you direct your full attention on an immediate task. For example, concentrated study for an exam is usually more intense two nights before, rather than two weeks before, the test.

Yet too much anxiety can cause nervous tension and discomfort, which interfere with the ability to concentrate. Students operating under excessive tension sometimes "freeze up" mentally and experience nervous physical reactions. The causes of high anxiety can range from fear of failure to lack of organization and preparation; the problem is not easily solved. Some people like to go for a run or a brisk walk when they feel overly stressed. Sustained physical activity can change the blood chemistry and improve mood, increasing the odds of focusing successfully on what needs to be done.

Another immediate, short-term fix for tension is muscle relaxation exercises and visualization. For example, if you are reading a particularly difficult section in a chemistry book and are becoming frustrated to the point that you can no longer concentrate, stop your reading and take several deep breaths. Use your imagination to visualize a peaceful setting in which you are calm and relaxed. Imagine yourself rocking back and forth in a hammock or lying on a beach listening to the surf; then focus on this image as you breathe deeply to help relax your muscles and regain control. Take several deep breaths, and allow your body to release the tension so you can resume reading and concentrate on your work. Try that right now.

As a long-term solution to tension, nothing works better than success. Just as failure fuels tension, success tends to weaken it. Each successful experience helps to diminish feelings of inadequacy. Early success in a course—passing the first

BRAIN BOOSTER

Are you curious?

Think about how babies learn they can make a toy squeak or that a kitten might bite. Is there a quiz or a flashcard involved? Human brains are wired to explore and learn from the results. As you pursue this adventure called a college education, remember that curiosity about new ideas can be one of your best assets. In every class, find something that you want to know more about, and go for it! The spark that ignites your interest might lie waiting in the textbook, in a lecture, or in an assignment. Fan that spark by going to the Internet, asking your professor, reading a book, doing an experiment, or talking to other students. Your natural curiosity might lead to a college major, a career, a lifelong hobby, or an A in the class.

—Adapted from Brain Rules: 12 Principles for Surviving and Thriving at Work, Home, and School, *by John Medina*

exam, for instance—can make a big psychological difference and replace anxiety with confidence.

Spark an Interest.   Make a conscious effort to stimulate your curiosity before reading, even if it feels contrived. First, look over the assigned reading for words or phrases that attract your attention, glance at the pictures, check the number of pages, and then ask yourself the following questions: "What do I already know about this topic?" and "What do I want to learn about it?"

With practice, this method of thinking before reading can create a spark of enthusiasm that will make the actual reading more purposeful and make concentration more direct and intense.

Set a Time Goal.   An additional trick to spark your enthusiasm is to set a time goal. Study time is not infinite; and short-term goals create a self-imposed pressure to pay attention, speed up, and get the job done. After looking over the material, predict the amount of time you will need to finish it. Estimate a reasonable completion time, and then push yourself to meet the goal. The purpose of a time goal is not to "speed read"

Reader's **TIP**   **Improving Concentration**

- Create an environment that says, "Study."
- Use a calendar, assignment book, or smartphone calendar for short- and long-term planning.
- Keep a daily to do list.
- Take short breaks.
- Visualize yourself as a successful college graduate.
- Reduce anxiety by passing the first test.
- Spark an interest.
- Set time goals for completing daily assignments.

the assignment but to be realistic about the amount of time to spend on a task and to learn how to estimate future study time. The Reader's Tip summarizes how you can raise your level of concentration while studying.

SUCCESSFUL ACADEMIC BEHAVIORS

Learning Objective 4

Adopt successful college behaviors

Good concentration geared toward college success involves more than the ability to comprehend reading assignments. College success demands concentrated study, self-discipline, and the demonstration of learning. If the "focused athlete" can be successful, so can the "focused student." Begin to evaluate and eliminate behaviors that waste your time and divert you from your goals. Direct your energy toward activities that will enhance your chances for success. Adopt the following behaviors of successful students.

Attend Class.   At the beginning of the course, college professors distribute an outline of what they plan to cover during each class period. Although they may not always check class attendance, the organization of the daily course work assumes perfect attendance. College professors *expect* students to attend class; and they usually do not repeat lecture notes or give makeup lessons for those who are absent, although some post lecture notes on a course Web site. Be responsible and set yourself up for success by coming to class. You paid for it!

Be on Time.   Professors usually present an overview of the day's work at the beginning of each class, as well as answer questions and clarify assignments. Arriving late puts you at an immediate disadvantage. You are likely to miss important "class business" information. In addition, tardy students distract both the professor and other students. Put on a watch and get yourself moving.

Recognize Essential Class Sessions.   Every class session is important, but the last class before a major test is the most critical of all. Usually, students will ask questions about the exam that will stimulate your thinking. In reviewing, answering questions, and rushing to finish uncovered material, the professor will often drop important clues to exam items. Unless you are critically ill, take tests on time because makeups are usually more difficult and may carry a grade penalty. In addition, be in class when the exams are returned to hear the professor's description of an excellent answer.

Preview Your Textbooks.   Give yourself a head start on understanding the organization and contents of your college textbooks with just a few quick steps: (1) Notice the cover and title. (2) Glance at the title page. What can you learn about the author from the information on this page? (3) Do the flip. Quickly rifle the pages from the back to the front. What pops out? Are there pictures, exercises to complete, repeated features? (4) Examine the table of contents. What are the major topics? Is there a pattern to their order or content? Notice the features at the end. Is there an index, a glossary of terms, an answer key?

EXERCISE 2

Preview This Text for the Big Picture

Preview to get an overview of the scope of this text and its sequence of topics. Think about how the chapter topics fit the goals of college reading. Glance at the chapter to get a sense of the organization and then answer the following questions:

1. Who are the authors? Are they professors? _____

   _____

   _____

2. What seems to be the purpose of the Reader's Tip boxes throughout the text?

   _____

   _____

3. What is MyReadingLab? _____

Read Assignments Before Class. Activate your knowledge on the subject before class by reading homework assignments. Look at the illustrations and read the captions. Jot down several questions that you would like to ask the professor about the reading. Then the lecture and class discussion can enhance your newly created knowledge network.

Review Lecture Notes Before Class. Always, always, always review your lecture notes before the next class period, preferably within twenty-four hours after the class. Review them with a classmate during a break or on the phone. Fill in gaps and make notations to ask questions to resolve confusion.

Consider Making an Audio Recording. If you are having difficulty concentrating or are a strong audio or linguistic learner, with the professor's permission, record the lecture. Take notes as you record, and you can later review your notes while listening to the recording. Electronic pens that record sound as you write are available.

Predict the Exam Questions. Never go to an exam without first predicting test items. Turn chapter titles, subheadings, and boldface print into questions, and then brainstorm the answers. Outline possible answers on paper. Preparation boosts self-confidence.

Pass the First Test. Do yourself a favor and overstudy for the first exam. Passing the first exam will help you avoid a lot of tension while studying for the second one.

Network with Other Students. You are not in this alone; you have lots of potential buddies who can offer support. Collect the names, phone numbers, and e-mail addresses of two classmates who are willing to help you if you do not understand the homework, miss a day of class, or need help on an assignment. Be prepared to help your classmates in return for their support.

Classmate _____ Phone _____ E-mail _____

Classmate _____ Phone _____ E-mail _____

Form a Study Group. Research involving college students has shown that study groups can be very effective. Studying with others is not cheating; it is making a wise use of available resources. A junior on the dean's list explained, "I e-mail my study buddy when I have a problem. One time I asked about an English paper because I couldn't think of my thesis. She asked what it was about. I told her and she wrote back, 'That's your thesis.' I just couldn't see it as clearly as she did." Use the Internet to create an academic support group to lighten your workload and boost your grades. Manage e-mail efficiently, as indicated in the following Reader's Tip.

Learn from Other Students' Papers. Talking about an excellent paper is one thing, but actually reading one is another. In each discipline, we need models of excellence. Find an A paper to read. Don't be shy. Ask the A students (who should be proud and flattered to share their brilliance) or ask the professor. Don't miss this important step in becoming a successful student.

Collaborate. When participating in group learning activities, set expectations for group study so that each member contributes, and try to keep the studying on target. As a group activity, ask several classmates to join you in discovering some campus resources by answering the questions in Exercise 3. First, brainstorm with the group to record answers that are known to be true. Next, divide responsibilities among group members to seek information to answer unknown items. Finally, reconvene the group in person or on the Internet to share responses.

Maintain Academic Honesty All colleges place a high premium on academic honesty. Working with classmates to help each other understand the material is an excellent strategy for learning, but the work you turn in must be entirely your own.

Reader's Tip — Managing School and Work E-Mail

Communication at colleges and businesses is typically done by e-mail. Colleges usually provide e-mail accounts for students and use them to send important information. Professors expect students to check their student e-mail often and to correspond with them in this way. Follow these guidelines to get your message across appropriately.

- Use correct grammar, spelling, and punctuation. Use standard English. Your message represents you.
- Always use an appropriate subject header to guide your reader. Write a new one for each new topic.
- Keep your message short and to the point. People are busy.
- Use consecutive uppercase letters sparingly. They YELL, which is called "flaming."
- Avoid **emoticons**—combinations of keyboard characters that represent emotions, such as smileys :-).
- Use an autoreply if you are away for a week or longer.
- Don't feel you have to reply to everything.
- If pressed for time, save your message as "new" and reply later.
- Delete unwanted advertisements without reading them (but first report them as spam).
- Do not reply to an entire group when an individual reply is more appropriate.
- Avoid sending joke e-mail.
- If you are unsure, seek permission before forwarding a message.
- When sending a single message to many people, mail the message to yourself and list other recipients as blind copies (bcc) to keep their e-mail addresses private.
- Monitor how much time you spend on e-mail.

Brainstorm together, but write your own papers. Never copy someone else's work or allow anyone to copy yours. This is a serious breach of academic honesty policies that can result in a zero on the assignment, an F in the class, or even dismissal from the college. Remember your goal is to learn not receive a meaningless grade.

EXERCISE 3 Campus Facts

Form a collaborative study group to answer the following questions:

1. What does a student need to obtain a college library card? Is there a fee? Can you access the library online? _____

_____

_____

2. If your instructor is an adjunct faculty member, how can you reach him or her? Is there a part-time faculty office? Where is it located, and what are the hours? _____

_____

3. Does your school have an academic support center? Where is it located? What must you do to schedule an appointment? _____

_____

_____

4. Are there convenient places on campus where you can purchase pens, pencils, or paper? Where are they located? _____

_____

5. Suppose you begin to feel unwell during class. Is there a nurse or health aide available? Where is the health services office? What are the staff able to provide students? Do they offer evening and weekend hours? _____

_____

_____

6. After the term begins, you realize that money is tight. Is there a career services office that helps students find jobs? Where must you go to find out about student employment? _____

_____

7. You were able to afford your tuition, but the cost of books is another story. Does your financial aid office provide textbook scholarships? What must you do to apply? What other types of scholarships or grants are available through this department? _____

_____

8. In a rush to get to class, you inadvertently lock your keys in your car. Where can you go to get help? _____

_____

9. You realize that you left some of your books underneath the seat in a previous class. However, when you return to collect them, the books are not there. Where would you go to locate missing items or to report them as missing?

_____

_____

10. Your car is on its last legs. You need to find another way to get to campus while the mechanic takes a look at it. Is there public transportation to campus? Where are the stops? Where can you go to find out about a possible ride share?

_____

_____

Use the Syllabus. A syllabus is a general outline of the goals, objectives, and assignments for the entire course. Typically, a syllabus includes examination dates, course requirements, and an explanation of the grading system. Most professors distribute and explain the syllabus on the first day of class.

Ask questions to help you understand the "rules and regulations" in the syllabus. Keep it handy as a ready reference, and use it as a plan for learning. Three-hole-punch it for your binder or staple it to your lecture notes; tape a second copy to your wall or door. Devise your own daily calendar for completing weekly reading and writing assignments.

The following is a syllabus for Introduction to Psychology. Study the course syllabus and answer the questions that follow.

INTRODUCTION TO PSYCHOLOGY

Class: 9:00–10:00 A.M. daily   Dr. Julie Wakefield
10-week quarter   Office: 718 Park Place
Office hours: 10:00–12:00 daily   Telephone: 555–651–3361
                                                       E-mail: JuWakeABC.edu

Required Texts

Psychology: An Introduction, by Josh R. Gerow
Paperback: Select one book from the attached list for a report.

Course Content

The purpose of Introduction to Psychology is to overview the general areas of study in the field of psychology. An understanding of psychology gives valuable insights into your choices and behaviors and those of others. The course will also give you a foundation for later psychology courses.

Methods of Teaching

Thematic lectures will follow the topics listed in the textbook assignments. You are expected to read and master the factual material in the text as well as take careful notes in class. Tests will cover both class lectures and textbook readings.

Research Participation

All students are required to participate in one psychological experiment. Details and dates are listed on a separate handout.

Grading

Grades will be determined in the following manner:

Tests (4 tests at 15% each)	60%
Final exam	25%
Written report	10%
Research participation	5%

Tests

Tests will consist of both multiple-choice and identification items as well as two essay questions.

Important Dates

Test 1: 1/13

Test 2: 1/29

Test 3: 2/10

Test 4: 2/24

Written report: 3/5

Final exam: 3/16

Written Report

Your written report should answer one of three designated questions and reflect your reading of a book from the list. Each book is approximately 200 pages long. Your report should be at least eight typed pages. More information to follow.

Assignments

Week 1: Ch. 1 (pp. 1–37), Ch. 2 (pp. 41–75)

Week 2: Ch. 3 (pp. 79–116)

  TEST 1: Chapters 1–3

Week 3: Ch. 4 (pp. 121–162), Ch. 5 (pp. 165–181)

Week 4: Ch. 5 (pp. 184–207), Ch. 6 (pp. 211–246)

  TEST 2: Chapters 4–6

Week 5: Ch. 7 (pp. 253–288), Ch. 8 (pp. 293–339)

Week 6: Ch. 9 (pp. 345–393)

  TEST 3: Chapters 7–9

Week 7: Ch. 10 (pp. 339–441), Ch. 11 (pp. 447–471)

Week 8: Ch. 11 (pp. 476–491), Ch. 12 (pp. 497–533)

  TEST 4: Chapters 10–12

Week 9: Ch. 13 (pp. 539–577), Ch. 14 (pp. 581–598)

  WRITTEN REPORT

Week 10: Ch. 14 (pp. 602–618), Ch. 15 (pp. 621–658)

  FINAL EXAM: Chapters 1–15

EXERCISE 4

Review the Syllabus

Refer to the syllabus to answer the following items with *T* (true), *F* (false), or *CT* (can't tell):

_____ 1. This professor is available for student conferences in the afternoon.

_____ 2. Tests will be based on both classroom lectures and assigned readings.

_____ 3. The written report counts for the same percent of a student's final grade as one test.

_____ 4. One of the four tests occurs at midterm.

_____ 5. The syllabus does not provide a due date for research participation.

EXERCISE 5

Review Your Own Course Syllabus

Examine your syllabus for this college reading course, and answer the following questions:

1. Will you have weekly or daily quizzes or tests in this course? _____

_____

2. Does the instructor penalize students for poor attendance? _____

_____

3. What is your instructor's policy regarding late work? _____

_____

4. Does your instructor allow makeup tests, quizzes, or assignments? _____

_____

5. Are tardies penalized? _____

_____

6. Will you be taking both a midterm and a final exam in this class? _____

_____

7. Does your instructor require any special projects or reports? Are due dates given for these? _____

_____

8. Are any other materials required for this class, aside from reading the textbook? _____

_____

9. Does your instructor require any outside reading, such as a novel, during the term? _____

    _____

10. Do you have any questions that do not appear to be addressed within the syllabus? Write them on the following lines. _____

    _____

    _____

SUMMARY POINTS

1. How can I be an active learner?
- Manage attention, effort, learning strategies, and resources effectively.
- Develop an understanding of how the brain pays attention and work on the automatic aspects of reading.
- Identify my learning style preferences and use study strategies that take advantage of them.
- Improve concentration.
- Adopt behaviors that lead to academic success.

2. What are my learning style preferences and how can I use them to my advantage?
- Identify my cognitive style preferences: extroverted-introverted; sensing-intuitive; thinking-feeling; judging-perceiving.
- Determine if I prefer learning globally ("the big picture") first or analytically (details, step-by-step).
- Determine my sensory learning strength: visual, auditory, tactile/kinesthetic.
- Recognize which multiple intelligences are my strengths: word smart, picture smart, logical smart, body smart, people smart, self smart, music smart, or nature smart.

3. How can I improve my ability to concentrate?
- Identify common distractions: external and internal.
- Take control of distractions by creating a place to study, organizing time, taking study breaks, making a to do list, increasing self-confidence, improving self-concept, reducing anxiety, sparking an interest in the subject, and setting a time goal.

4. What behaviors should I adopt for college success?
Attend class, be on time, be present for essential class sessions, preview my textbooks, read before class, review lecture notes before class, make audio recordings of lectures, predict exam questions, build confidence by passing the first test, network with other students, form a study group, learn from other students' A papers, collaborate with other students on assignments, maintain academic honesty, and use the syllabus

MyReadingLab™   For more help with Active Learning, go to your learning path in MyReadingLab at
www.myreadinglab.com

SELECTION 1 Psychology

BEFORE reading the following selection, take a few minutes to analyze your active learning potential and answer the following questions:

1. **Physical Environment** Where are you and what time is it? _____

_____

What are your external distractions? _____

_____

2. **Internal Distractions** What is popping into your mind and interfering with your concentration? _____

_____

3. **Spark Interest** Glance at the selection and predict what it will cover. What do you already know about this topic? What about the selection will be of interest to you? _____

_____

4. **Set Time Goals** How long will it take you to read the selection? _____ minutes. To answer the questions? _____ minutes.

Increase Word Knowledge

What do you know about these words?

| assumptions | biases | converge | divergent | hypotheses |
| belittle | contradicts | jibe | illumination | unobstrusively |

Your instructor may give a true-false vocabulary review before or after reading.

Time Goal

Record your starting time for reading. _____ : _____

CREATIVITY

Watch a video on creativity via your ebook at www.myreadinglab.com and then answer the related questions in the VIDEO LINK section or via MyReadingLab.

Scan this QR code to hear this reading

BECOMING MORE CREATIVE

What makes one person more creative than another? Asking questions, thinking of explanations other than just the most obvious ones, and examining assumptions and biases are key characteristics of active learners. These characteristics also involve creativity as much as they do reasoning.

5   Take a few moments to answer these items based on the Remote Associates Test—a test of the mental flexibility necessary for creativity. Your task is to come up with a fourth word that is associated with each item in a set of three words. For example, an appropriate answer for the set *news—clip—wall* is *paper*. Got the idea? Now try these. (The

10 answers are given at the end of this selection, but don't look until you've really tried!)

1. piggy—green—lash
2. surprise—political—favor
3. mark—shelf—telephone
15 4. stick—maker—tennis
5. cream—cottage—cloth

Creative thinking requires you to associate elements of a problem in new ways by finding unexpected connections among them. People who are uncreative rely on *convergent thinking*, following a particular set of steps that they think will converge on

20 one correct solution. Then, once they have solved a problem, they tend to develop a mental set and approach future problems the same way. Creative people, in contrast, exercise *divergent thinking*; instead of stubbornly sticking to one tried-and-true path, they explore side alleys and generate several possible solutions. They come up with new hypotheses, imagine other interpretations, and look for connections that are not

25 immediately obvious. For artists and novelists, of course, creativity is a job requirement, but it also takes creativity to invent a tool, put together a recipe from leftovers, find ways to distribute unsold food to the needy, decorate your room . . . .

CREATIVE PERSONALITY TRAITS

Creative people do not necessarily have high IQs. Personality characteristics seem more important, especially these three.

30 *Nonconformity.* Creative individuals are not overly concerned about what others think of them. They are willing to risk ridicule by proposing ideas that may initially appear foolish or off the mark. Geneticist Barbara McClintock's research was ignored or belittled by many for nearly 30 years. But she was sure she could show how genes move around and produce sudden changes in heredity. In 1983, when

35 McClintock won the Nobel Prize, the judges called her work the second greatest genetic discovery of our time, after the discovery of the structure of DNA.

Curiosity. Creative people are open to new experiences; they notice when reality contradicts expectations, and they are curious about the reason. For example, Wilhelm Roentgen, a German physicist, was studying cathode rays when he noticed

40 a strange glow on one of his screens. Other people had seen the glow, but they ignored it because it didn't jibe with their understanding of cathode rays. Roentgen studied the glow, found it to be a new kind of radiation, and thus discovered X-rays.

Persistence. After that imaginary light bulb goes on over your head, you still have to work hard to make the illumination last. Or, as Thomas Edition, who invented the

45 real light bulb, reportedly put it, "Genius is one percent inspiration and ninety-nine

One way to develop creativity is to be curious about the world around you. Visit an art museum, for example. As you review the artwork, consider what the artist had in mind when creating the piece.

Image Source/Alamy

percent perspiration." No invention or work of art springs forth full-blown from a person's head. There are many false starts and painful revisions along the way.

ENCOURAGING CREATIVITY

If you are thinking critically (and creatively!), you may wonder whether these personal qualities are enough. Some individuals may be more creative than others, but
50 there are also *circumstances* that foster creative accomplishment.

Creativity flourishes when schools and employers encourage intrinsic motivation and not just extrinsic rewards such as gold stars and money. Intrinsic motives include a sense of accomplishment, intellectual fulfillment, the satisfaction of curiosity, and the sheer love of the activity.

55 Creativity also increases when people have control over how to perform a task or solve a problem, are evaluated unobtrusively instead of being constantly observed and judged, and work independently. Organizations encourage creativity when they let people take risks, give them plenty of time to think about problems, and welcome innovation.

60 In sum, if you hope to become more creative, there are two things you can do. One is to cultivate qualities in yourself: your skills, curiosity, intrinsic motivation, and self-discipline. The other is to seek out the kinds of situations that will permit you to express your abilities and experiment with new ideas.

Answers to the mental flexibility quiz: back, party, book, match, cheese

(767 words)

—From Carole Wade and Carol Tavris,
Psychology, 10th ed.

Time Goals

Record your finishing time._____ : _____

Calculate your total reading time. _____

Rate your concentration as high ———— medium ———— or low _____.

Recall what you have read, and review what you have learned.

Your instructor may choose to give a true-false comprehension review.

WRITE ABOUT THE SELECTION   MyReadingLab™

Complete this **Exercise** on **myreadinglab.com**

Did this reading selection change your definition of creativity?

Response Suggestion: Describe someone you consider to be a creative person. Be sure to give specific details to support your view. Next, analyze this person's traits in light of the information in this reading. Explain any similarities and differences between the characteristics of the person you described and those discussed in the reading.

▶ VIDEO LINK   MyReadingLab™

Complete this **Exercise** on **myreadinglab.com**

Now that you have read the selection and viewed the video on Creativity, check your understanding by answering with *T* (true) or *F* (false):

_____ 1. Author Daniel Pink says that creativity is a characteristic of every human being.

_____ 2. According to the video, the "secret sauce" of creativity is getting people with different knowledge and talents together.

_____ 3. The reading selection and the video credit persistence as an important ingredient in following through with a creative idea.

_____ 4. According to the video, one of the reasons for an abundance of creative output in the U.S. is that American culture tends not to punish failure.

_____ 5. E-books, car navigation systems and video games are all mentioned as ideas originating in the Media Lab at MIT (Massachusetts Institute of Technology).

CHECK YOUR COMPREHENSION MyReadingLab™

Complete this **Exercise** on **myreadinglab.com**

After reading the selection, answer the following questions with *a, b, c,* or *d*. To help you analyze your strengths and weaknesses, the question types are indicated.

Main Idea _____ 1. What is the best statement of the entire selection's main point?
   a. Everyone is creative in some way.
   b. Persistence is an important characteristic of creative people.
   c. Creativity increases when people have control over how to perform a task.
   d. Specific personal characteristics as well as environmental conditions influence creativity.

Inference _____ 2. According to this article, which is true of creativity?
   a. Creativity can be developed under the right circumstances.
   b. The ability to be creative is inborn and cannot be changed.
   c. A scientist could not be thought of as creative.
   d. Creativity does not involve reasoning.

Inference _____ 3. Why did the authors include the mental flexibility exercise?
   a. To test reading skill
   b. To personally involve the reader in the topic
   c. To convince readers to become more creative
   d. To show that most readers lack creativity

Detail _____ 4. According to the article, which of the following are characteristics shared by creative people?
   a. Nonconformity, curiosity, and persistence
   b. Convergent thinking—approaching all tasks in the same way
   c. Divergent thinking—focusing on obvious answers to problems
   d. A tendency to look at ideas separately rather than focusing on connections

Main Idea _____ 5. The main point of the section titled "Creative Personality Traits" is that
   a. creative people are not too concerned about what others think of them.
   b. creative people are all the same.
   c. creative people seem to share certain personality traits.
   d. creative people are interested in new ideas.

Inference _____ 6. Which of the following would most likely describe a creative thinker?
   a. Learning reading strategies in a reading course and sticking with old methods to read a psychology textbook
   b. Connecting ideas learned in a history class to something learned in a geography class
   c. Seeing the skills learned in a writing class as unrelated to those learned in a reading course
   d. Determination to keep long-held views on a subject without examining alternate ideas

Inference _____ 7. Based on the explanation in the article, which would be an example of an *extrinsic* reward?

a. Pride in completing a good essay
b. Pleasure in reading a novel
c. A sense of accomplishment after finishing a difficult project
d. Receiving money for earning good grades

Main Idea _____ 8. Which sentence best states the main idea of the section "Encouraging Creativity"?

a. Certain conditions encourage and nourish creativity.
b. Intrinsic rewards are better than extrinsic rewards.
c. Creativity increases when people are paid more.
d. People are more creative when given specific guidelines and rules.

Inference _____ 9. Based on the examples in the selection, *intrinsic* rewards for good work would include

a. receiving a salary bonus.
b. being treated to a special meal.
c. pride.
d. earning a prize.

Detail _____ 10. Which two things do the authors advise you to do if you want to become more creative?

a. Look for a new job and don't worry about what others think.
b. Be persistent and stay with what you already know well.
c. Develop certain personal qualities and seek situations that allow you to try new things.
d. Do not question ideas that conflict with your own and do not take risks.

Answer the following with *T* (true) or *F* (false).

Inference _____ 11. According to this article creativity is a quality of artistic people only.

Inference _____ 12. Creative thinking would most likely flourish when students have a choice of ways to demonstrate their understanding of the course concepts.

Detail _____ 13. According to this selection, thinking of a way to feed hungry people is an example of creativity.

Detail _____ 14. People tend to be more creative when closely supervised.

Detail _____ 15. The article uses Thomas Edison's invention of the light bulb as an example of persistence.

1 SELECTION

BUILD YOUR VOCABULARY MyReadingLab™

Complete this **Exercise** on myreadinglab.com

According to the way the italicized word was used in the selection, indicate *a, b, c,* or *d* for the word or phrase that gives the best definition. The number in parentheses indicates the line of the passage in which the word is located.

_____ 1. "examining *assumptions*" (3)
　　a. facts
　　b. statistical evidence
　　c. beliefs
　　d. truths

_____ 2. "assumptions and *biases*" (3)
　　a. numbers
　　b. examples
　　c. facts
　　d. prejudices

_____ 3. "*converge* on one" (19)
　　a. come together
　　b. depart
　　c. disappear
　　d. split

_____ 4. "*divergent* thinking" (22)
　　a. unified
　　b. diverse
　　c. truthful
　　d. ethical

_____ 5. "new *hypotheses*" (24)
　　a. writings
　　b. works of art
　　c. certainties
　　d. educated guesses

_____ 6. "*belittled* by many (33)
　　a. put down
　　b. accepted
　　c. liked
　　d. praised

_____ 7. "*contradicts* expectations" (38)
　　a. disagrees with
　　b. verifies
　　c. confirms
　　d. demonstrates

_____ 8. "it didn't *jibe*" (41)
　　a. differ
　　b. conflict
　　c. fit
　　d. disagree

_____ 9. "make the *illumination* last" (44)
　　a. confusion
　　b. clear understanding
　　c. mystery
　　d. darkness

_____ 10. "evaluated *unobtrusively*" (56)
　　a. not noticeably
　　b. boldly
　　c. obviously
　　d. openly

Time Goals

Record your time for answering the questions: _____ : _____

Calculate your total time for reading and answering the questions: _____

What changes would you make to enhance your concentration on the next selection?

Concept Prep for Psychology

A Sampling of Careers in Psychology

Most careers in psychology require at least a Bachelor's degree. Many require a Master's degree or doctorate.

- Therapist
- Psychiatrist
- Professor
- School counselor or diagnostician

- Sports psychologist
- Researcher
- Advisor to businesses and other professionals
- Community health worker

What does psychology cover?

Psychology is the scientific study of behavior and the mind. Behavior is observed, studied, and measured with the ultimate objective of explaining why people act and think as they do. Special areas of study in psychology focus on the following questions:

Biological psychology: How do your genes, brain, and hormones affect your behavior?

Behavioral psychology: What stimulus in the environment triggers your response?

Cognitive psychology: How do you think and remember?

Life span psychology: How do thoughts, desires, and actions differ in infancy, childhood, adolescence, adulthood, and old age?

Sigmund Freud theorized that mundane behavior has underlying psychological causes.
Mary Evans Picture Library/Alamy

Why is Freud so important?

Sigmund Freud was a physician in Vienna, Austria, who formulated a theory of personality and a form of psychotherapy called *psychoanalysis.* Freud emerged as a leader in modern psychology and wrote twenty-four books popularizing his theories. After Freud's death in 1939, psychologists questioned many of his ideas and criticized him because of his focus on sexual desires. Still, Freud has contributed many ideas to our culture and words to our vocabulary.

Freud's theories evolved from observing and treating patients who suffered ailments without any visible physical basis but who responded favorably to hypnosis. He believed in treating their problems by tracing difficulties back to childhood experiences. Freud also believed in *dream interpretation,* a process in which the unconscious mind provides clues to psychological problems.

Freud's basic theories suggest that people are driven from early childhood by three principal unconscious forces: the *id* (an animal instinct and desire for pleasure), the *ego* (the sense of self that fights the id for reasonable compromises), and the *superego* (the social feeling of right and wrong and community values). Other terms that Freud established include *pleasure principle,* which refers to an instinctive need to satisfy the id regardless of the consequences; *libido,* which refers to sexual drive; and *egotism,* which refers to a sense of self-importance and conceit.

Other words we use today emerge from Freud's five stages of personality development: *oral, anal, phallic, latency,* and *genital.* An *oral personality* is fixated in the first stage of sucking and is satisfied by the pleasures of the mouth—for example, talking, smoking, eating, and chewing gum excessively. An *anal personality* is associated with the childhood period that involves bowel control and toilet training and as an adult is excessively focused on details and orderliness. Another term Freud popularized is *Oedipus complex,* which suggests that a young boy has a sexual desire for his mother. Finally, Freud was the originator of the *Freudian slip,* which is a misspoken word—such as *sex* for *six*—that reveals unconscious thoughts.

Who was Carl Jung?

Carl Jung was a Swiss psychologist who classified people as *introverts* (shy) or *extroverts* (outgoing). Jung was one of the original followers of Freud but later broke with him. Adding to Freud's theory of repressed personal experiences, Jung believed that we also inherit the memories and symbols of ancestors in an *inherited collective unconscious.* He believed this was exhibited in an inborn fear of snakes or spiders. Jung also developed theories about concrete and abstract learning stages. Many of his theories are used as a basis for the Myers-Briggs Type Indicator.

REVIEW QUESTIONS

After studying the material, answer the following questions:

1. Using visual images on note cards to improve memory of vocabulary words suggests what area of psychology? _____

2. Desiring a rocky road ice cream cone after passing a Baskin-Robbins store suggests what area of psychology? _____

3. Mapping physical activity in different areas of the brain as people read or listen to music suggests what area of psychology? _____

4. Exploring stages of adolescence suggests what area of psychology? _____

5. What is psychoanalysis? _____
   _____

6. What are the goals of the id, ego, and superego? _____
   _____
   _____

7. How does Freud relate dreams to reality? _____
   _____

8. Why did some psychologists break with Freud? _____
   _____

9. How do the theories of Jung and Freud differ? _____
   _____

10. What is Jung's inherited collective unconscious? _____
    _____

Your instructor may choose to give a true-false review of these psychology concepts.

SELECTION 2 History

BEFORE reading the following selection, take a few minutes to analyze your active learning potential and answer the following questions.

1. **Physical Environment**   Where are you, and what time is it?

_____

What are your external distractions? _____

_____

2. **Internal Distractions**   What is popping into your mind and interfering

with your concentration? _____

3. **Spark Interest**   Glance at the selection, and predict what it will cover.

What do you already know about the topic? What about the selection will be

of interest to you? _____

4. **Set Time Goals**   How long will it take you to read the selection?

_____ minutes. To answer the questions? _____ minutes.

Increase Word Knowledge

What do you know about these words?

competence	unprecedented	scarcities	incentives	barred
drafted	enlisted	camaraderie	prosperity	topsy-turvy

Your instructor may give a true-false vocabulary review before or after reading.

Time Goal

Record your starting time for reading. _____:_____

((•— **Scan this QR Code to hear this reading**

HOME FRONT WORKERS, ROSIE THE RIVETER, AND VICTORY GIRLS

War affects more than the soldiers who fight it and the people whose homelands are the battle sites. For those left at home in the United States during World War II, life was very different—perhaps in unexpected ways—from before the war. In some ways it was better.

CHANGES ON THE HOME FRONT

World War II opened up new possibilities for jobs, income, and labor organizing, for women as well as for men, and for new groups of workers. Disabled workers entered jobs previously considered beyond their abilities, fulfilling their tasks with skill and competence. For example, deaf people streamed into Akron, Ohio, to work in the
5 tire factories that became defense plants, making more money than they ever made before.

Along with new employment opportunities, workers' earnings rose nearly 70 percent. Income doubled for farmers and then doubled again. Labor union membership grew 50 percent, reaching an all-time high by the end of the war. In spite of
10 no-strike pledges, strikes pressured the aircraft industry in Detroit and elsewhere. A major strike of the United Mine Workers Union erupted in 1943. Congress responded with the Smith-Connally Act of 1943, which gave the president power to seize plants or mines wherever strikes interrupted war production.

Women and people of color joined unions in unprecedented numbers. Some
15 organized unions of their own. Energetic labor organizers like Luisa Moreno and Dorothy Ray Healy organized Mexican and Russian Jewish workers at the California Sanitary Canning Company into a powerful CIO cannery union that achieved wage increases and union recognition. Unions with white male leadership, however, admitted women and people of color reluctantly and tolerated them only during the
20 war emergency. Some unions required women to quit their jobs after the war.

NEW OPPORTUNITIES FOR WOMEN

World War II ushered in dramatic changes for American women. Wartime scarcities led to increased domestic labor as homemakers made do with rationed goods, mended clothing, collected and saved scraps and metals, and planted "victory gardens" to help feed their families. Employment opportunities for women also increased. As a result
25 of the combined incentives of patriotism and good wages, women streamed into the paid labor force. Many women took "men's jobs" while the men went off to fight.

Rosie the Riveter became the heroic symbol of the women war worker. Pictures of attractive "Rosies" building planes or constructing ships graced magazine covers and posters. Future Hollywood star Marilyn Monroe first gained attention when her
30 photograph appeared in *Yank*, a magazine for soldiers. The magazine pictured her not as the sex goddess she later became; but as a typical Rosie the Riveter clad in overalls, working at her job in a defense plant.

Until 1943, black women were barred from work in defense industries. Poet Maya Angelou recalled that African Americans had to fight for the jobs they wanted.
35 She became the first black streetcar conductor in San Francisco during the war, but not without a struggle. She made herself a promise that "made my veins stand out, and my mouth tighten into a prune: I WOULD HAVE THE JOB. I WOULD BE A CONDUCTORETTE AND SLING A FULL MONEY CHANGER FROM MY BELT. I WOULD." And she did.

40 For the first time, married women joined the paid labor force in droves and public opinion supported them. During the Great Depression of the 1930s, 80 percent of Americans had objected to the idea of wives working outside the home; by 1942, only 13 percent still objected. However, mothers of young children found very little help. In 1943, the federal government finally responded to the needs of
45 working mothers by funding day care centers. More than 3,000 centers enrolled 130,000 children. Still, the program served only a small proportion of working

This famous poster of "Rosie the Riveter" represents American women who worked in factories during World War II.

Stocktrek Images, Inc./Alamy

mothers. Most women relied on family members to care for their children. A Women's Bureau survey in 1944 found that 16 percent of mothers working in war industries had no child care arrangements. Meager to begin with and conceived as an emer-
50 gency measure, government funding for child care would end after the war.

Before the war, most jobs for women were low-paying, nonunion positions that paid an average of $24.50 a week. Wartime manufacturing jobs paid almost twice that—$40.35 a week. During the conflict, 300,000 women worked in the aircraft industry alone. Almira Bondelid recalled that when her husband went overseas, "I decided
55 to stay in San Diego and went to work in a dime store. That was a terrible place to work, and as soon as I could I got a job at Convair [an aircraft manufacturer]. . . . I worked in the tool department as a draftsman, and by the time I left there two years later I was designing long drill jigs for parts of the wing and hull of B-24 bombers."

New opportunities for women also opened up in the armed services. All sectors of
60 the armed forces had dwindled in the years between the two wars and needed to gain size and strength. Along with the 10 million men age 21 to 35 drafted into the armed services and the 6 million who enlisted, 100,000 women volunteered for the Navy WAVES (Women Accepted for Voluntary Emergency Service) and 140,000 for the Women's Army Auxiliary Corps (WAAC). In 1943, the WAAC became the Women's
65 Army Corps (WAC), dropping "Auxiliary" from the name.

CHANGES IN MARRIAGE AND FAMILY LIFE

Most female enlistees and war workers enjoyed their work and wanted to continue after the war. The extra pay, independence, camaraderie, and satisfaction that their jobs provided had opened their eyes to new possibilities. Although most of the well-paying positions for women disappeared after the war as the returning veterans reclaimed
70 their jobs, women did not disappear from the paid labor force. The numbers of employed women continued to rise in the postwar years. Edith Speert, like many others, was never again content as a full-time housewife and mother. Edith's husband, Victor, was sent overseas in 1944. During the eighteen months of their separation, they penned 1,300 letters to each other, sometimes two or three times a day. The letters
75 revealed the love and affection they felt for one another, but Edith did not hesitate to tell Victor how she had changed. In a letter from Cleveland, dated November 9, 1945, she wrote:

> *Sweetie*, I want to make sure I make myself clear about how I've changed. I want you to know *now* that you are not married to a girl that's interested
> 80 solely in a home—I shall definitely have to work all my life—I get emotional satisfaction out of working; and I don't doubt that many a night you will cook the supper while I'm at a meeting. Also, dearest—I shall never wash and iron—there are laundries for that! Do you think you'll be able to bear living with me? . . . I love you, Edith

85 Despite the shifting priorities of women, the war reversed the declining marriage and fertility rates of the 1930s. Between 1941 and 1945, the birthrate climbed from 19.4 to 24.5 per 1,000 population. The reversal stemmed, in part, from economic prosperity as well as the possibility of draft deferments for married men in the early war years. However, the desire to solidify relationships and establish con-
90 nections to the future during a time of great uncertainty perhaps served as the more powerful motivation. Thus, a curious paradox marked the war years: a widespread disruption of domestic life accompanied by a rush into marriage and parenthood.

CHANGES IN SEXUAL CONDUCT

At the same time that the war prompted family formation, wartime upheaval sent the sexual order topsy-turvy. For many young woman, moving to a new city or tak-
95 ing a wartime job opened up new possibilities for independence, excitement, and sexual adventure. One young worker recalled:

> Chicago was just humming, no matter where I went. The bars were jammed . . . you could pick up anyone you wanted to. . . . There were servicemen of all varieties roaming the streets all the time. There was never,
> 100 never a shortage of young, healthy bucks. . . . We never thought of getting tired. Two three hours of sleep was normal. . . . I'd go down to the office every morning half dead, but with a smile on my face, and report for work.

Some young women, known as "victory girls," believed that it was an act of patriotism to have a fling with a man in uniform before he went overseas. The independence
105 of these women raised fears of female sexuality as a dangerous, ungoverned force. The worry extended beyond the traditional concern about prostitutes and "loose women" to include "good girls" whose sexual standards might relax during wartime. Public health

campaigns warned enlisted men that victory girls would have their fun with a soldier and then leave him with a venereal disease, incapable of fighting for his country.

110   Wartime also intensified concerns about homosexuality. Urban centers and the military provided new opportunities for gay men and lesbians to form relationships and build communities. Although the military officially banned homosexuals, many served by keeping their orientation secret. If discovered, gay men faced severe punishment, including confinement in cages called "queer stockades" or in psychiatric
115 wards. Lesbians faced similar sanctions, although the women's corps, in an effort to assure the civilian world of their recruits' femininity, often looked the other way.

(1558 words)

—From Jacqueline Jones et al.,
Created Equal, 3rd ed.

SELECTION 2

Time Goals

Record your finishing time._____ : _____

Calculate your total reading time._____

Rate your concentration as high _____ medium _____ or low _____.

Recall what you have read, and review what you have learned.

Your instructor may choose to give for a true-false comprehension review.

WRITE ABOUT THE SELECTION   MyReadingLab™

Complete
this **Exercise** on
myreadinglab.com

Was there something in this selection that surprised you? For example, had you thought about the effect of a global war such as World War II on those at home in the United States? If you had, perhaps you had not considered that any effects might be positive. Think about the effects on the women's roles and sexual standards described in this selection and how they compare to today's American society.

Response Suggestion: Make a two-column list. On the left side list the changes in women's roles and sexual standards during World War II. On the right side, list today's conditions. Use these notes to write a four-paragraph essay in which you compare the two lists. Begin with a brief introductory paragraph. The second and third paragraphs should discuss the comparisons in the two areas of women's roles and sexual standards. In the fourth paragraph, briefly summarize and speculate on whether experiences during the war might have eventually led to the standards we live with today.

CHECK YOUR COMPREHENSION   MyReadingLab™

SELECTION 2

After reading the selection, answer the following questions with *a, b, c,* or *d.* To help you analyze your strengths and weaknesses, the question types are indicated.

Main Idea _____ 1. Which phrase best describes the topic of this selection?
a. Changes in women's roles during World War II
b. Changes on the home front during World War II
c. The effects of war on marriage and family life
d. The effects of war

Main Idea _____ 2. Which is the best statement of the main point of the entire selection?
a. War is difficult for everyone.
b. Many women filled jobs once held by the men who went to fight.
c. World War II had significant effects on the roles of women and others at home that changed family life and sexual standards.
d. Sexual standards were relaxed for some during World War II.

Inference _____ 3. Based on the information in this selection, Rosie the Riveter was
a. a symbol that represented the new roles women were filling during World War II.
b. an actual person named Rosie who worked in an airplane manufacturing plant.
c. the first role Marilyn Monroe had in the movies.
d. also known as a Victory Girl.

Inference _____ 4. One can logically infer that the B-24s Amelia Bondelid worked on were
a. airplanes.
b. aircraft carriers.
c. submarines.
d. landing crafts.

Detail _____ 5. According to the article, Maya Angelou worked as a _____ during the war.
a. streetcar conductor
b. poet
c. draftsman in an aircraft manufacturing plant
d. riveter building airplanes

Main Idea _____ 6. The main point of the section titled "Changes on the Home Front" is that
a. many deaf people were hired in tire factories in Akron, Ohio.
b. life was easier for some people during World War II.
c. World War II opened jobs and other opportunities for several groups of people who would not have been considered qualified before the war.
d. women and people of color joined and organized labor unions in California during World War II but were denied membership when the war ended.

Inference _____ 7. What is the most likely reason that the author included examples and quotes from women who lived during World War II?

    a. To highlight famous historical individuals

    b. To emphasize the large number of people whose lives were affected by the war

    c. To show that women enjoyed their new roles

    d. To personalize the facts so that readers can better understand their significance.

Detail _____ 8. The portion of Americans who believed women should not work outside the home changed from _____ to _____.

    a. 80% in the 1930s; 13% in 1942

    b. 100,000; 140,000

    c. 140,000; 100,000

    d. 13% in the 1930s; 80% in 1942

Detail _____ 9. Which of the following were among the reasons cited for rising marriage and birth rates during World War II?

    a. A poor economy and a desire to solidify relationships

    b. Economic prosperity and possible draft deferments for married men

    c. Changing sexual standards and disruption of domestic life

    d. Greater acceptance of gay and lesbian lifestyles

Detail _____ 10. Childcare for women working outside their homes _____.

    a. was not provided by the government during World War II.

    b. was provided entirely by family members of working mothers during World War II.

    c. was reluctantly funded by the government but discontinued after the war.

    d. was immediately recognized and generously funded by the government during the war.

Answer the following questions with (*T*) true or (*F*) false

Inference _____ 11. Many women as well as men wanted to do military service during World War II.

Inference _____ 12. Many women experienced fulfillment and satisfaction from working outside their homes and wanted to continue to work after the war.

Detail _____ 13. Victory girls considered it patriotic to have a fling with a soldier before he went to war.

Detail _____ 14. Although good jobs were less available for women after the war, the number of women working outside their homes continued to rise.

Detail _____ 15. Gay men and Lesbians endured harsh treatment in the military if their sexual orientation was discovered.

BUILD YOUR VOCABULARY   MyReadingLab™

Complete
this **Exercise** on
myreadinglab.com

SELECTION 2

According to the way the italicized word was used in the selection, indicate *a, b, c,* or *d* for the word or phrase that gives the best definition. The number in parentheses indicates the line of the passage in which the word is located.

_____ 1. "skill and *competence*" (4)
a. pride
b. capability
c. disability
d. energy

_____ 2. "*unprecedented* numbers" (14)
a. unheard-of
b. established
c. unsurprising
d. familiar

_____ 3. "Wartime *scarcities*" (21)
a. changes
b. surpluses
c. fears
d. shortages

_____ 4. "combined *incentives*" (25)
a. burdens
b. encouragements
c. requirements
d. needs

_____ 5. "*barred* from work" (33)
a. punished
b. permitted
c. fired
d. forbidden

_____ 6. "*drafted* into the armed services" (61)
a. volunteered
b. accepted
c. forced
d. denied entrance

_____ 7. "6 million who *enlisted*" (62)
a. volunteered
b. refused
c. enrolled in college
d. worked on the home front

_____ 8. "*camaraderie*, and satisfaction" (67)
a. loneliness
b. hostility
c. friendship
d. nervousness

_____ 9. "from economic *prosperity*" (88)
a. poverty
b. wealth
c. bankruptcy
d. statistics

_____ 10. "sent the sexual order *topsy-turvy*" (94)
a. into confusion
b. into perfection
c. into perspective
d. into playfulness

Time Goals

Record your time for answering the questions: _____ : _____

Calculate your total time for reading and answering the questions: _____

What changes would you make to enhance your concentration on the next selection?

Concept Prep for History

A Sampling of Careers for History Majors

Many careers in history require a Bachelor's degree. Some may require advanced degrees or additional specialized training.

- Teacher/College professor
- Lawyer
- Publisher
- Journalist
- Broadcaster
- Information specialist
- Business person

What events led up to World War II?

After Germany was defeated in World War I, supposedly the "war to end all wars," the *Allies* (United States, Britain, France, and Russia) expected Germany to pay for the war they helped start. The Allies also changed the world map by taking away much of the German empire. The German people were stunned at their defeat, angry over the demands of the victors, and eventually unable to meet their debt payments. *Adolf Hitler,* a skillful and charismatic leader, seized this opportunity and tapped into the country's anger. He promised to restore national pride, and consequently many Germans were drawn to him. He became the leader of the *Nazi* Party, adopted the *swastika* as its symbol, and eventually became dictator of Germany.

Prime Minister Winston Churchill, President Franklin D. Roosevelt, and Soviet leader Joseph Stalin pose for pictures at the Yalta Conference in 1945.
Keystone/Hulton Archive/Getty Images

Hitler strengthened the military, forged an alliance with Japan and Italy, and attacked and conquered much of continental Europe. When Britain, under the leadership of Prime Minister *Winston Churchill,* refused to bargain with Germany, Hitler ordered the *Luftwaffe,* the German air force, to destroy Brittan from the air. The air raids, known as the *blitz,* failed in their purpose when the Royal Air Force (RAF) won the Battle of Britain. Hitler than attacked Russia.

What was the U.S. role in the war?

The United States, under *Franklin D. Roosevelt,* remained neutral. *Isolationists* opposed foreign involvement. That changed, however, on December 7, 1941, at 7:02 A.M., when the Japanese bombed *Pearl Harbor,* an American naval base in Hawaii. America declared war that same day. *General Douglas MacArthur* and *Admiral Chester Nimitz* were put in charge of forces in the Pacific, and *General Dwight D. Eisenhower* led the Allied soldiers in Europe.

What was D-Day?

Allied forces planned the liberation of Europe, and on June 6, 1944—on what came to be known as *D-Day*—thousands of brave soldiers secretly left England and stormed the beaches of Normandy, France. After two weeks of desperate fighting, the troops moved inland and liberated Paris by August. The Allied armies drove toward *Berlin,* the capital of Germany, and on April 30, Hitler committed suicide to avoid capture. The Germans surrendered one week later, and the European part of the war was over. Hitler, driven by his anti-Semitic hatred, had ordered the killing of more than 6 million innocent Jews. Many were taken by trains to concentration camps for extermination in gas chambers. This horrible carnage was called the *Holocaust*.

How did the war with Japan end?

The American forces in the Pacific were moving from island to island against fierce Japanese resistance.

Victories were won with great loss of life. Upon FDR's death, Harry Truman had become president and was told of the *Manhattan Project*, a top-secret plan to develop an atomic bomb. On August 6, 1945, the *Enola Gay* flew over *Hiroshima, Japan*, and dropped an atomic bomb that obliterated the city. Three days later, a second bomb was dropped over *Nagasaki*. Within a few days, the Japanese asked for peace, and a month later they officially surrendered to General MacArthur aboard the battleship U.S.S. *Missouri* in Tokyo Bay. World War II had come to an end.

REVIEW QUESTIONS

After studying the material, answer the following questions:

1. How did the end of World War I affect the beginning of World War II? _____
   _____

2. Why were the Germans drawn to Hitler's message? _____
   _____

3. Who were Germany's allies in World War II? _____
   _____

4. Why did the Luftwaffe strike England? _____
   _____

5. Who were the isolationists? _____
   _____

6. What prompted the United States to enter the war? _____
   _____

7. What was the Holocaust? _____
   _____

8. What was D-Day? _____
   _____

9. What ended the war in Europe? _____
   _____

10. What ended the war in Japan? _____
    _____

Your instructor may choose to give a true-false review of these history concepts.

SELECTION 3 | # Environmental Science

BEFORE reading the following selection, take a few minutes to analyze your active learning potential and answer the following questions:

1. **Physical Environment**   Where are you and what time is it? _____

_____

What are your external distractions? _____

_____

_____

2. **Internal Distractions**   What is popping into your mind and interfering

with your concentration? _____

3. **Spark Interest**   Glance at the selection and predict what it will cover.

What do you already know about this topic? What about the selection will be

of interest to you? _____

_____

4. **Set Time Goals**   How long will it take you to read the selection?

_____ minutes. To answer the questions? _____ minutes.

Increase Word Knowledge

What do you know about these words?

implications	grassroots	potable	alleviate	municipality
desertification	eco-tourism	coupled	marketable	spigot

Your instructor may give a true-false vocabulary review before or after reading.

Time Goal

Record your starting time for reading: _____ : _____

VOLUNTEERS HELP PROTECT THE ENVIRONMENT

((•── Scan this QR Code to hear this reading

SELECTION 3

In many developing countries, environmental problems are magnified by communities' direct dependence on their local environment for drinking water, fuel wood, or land for farming. Environmental damage can have enormous consequences on a community's livelihood; likewise, meeting a growing community's needs can have
5 important implications for the environment.

Peace Corps Volunteers are leaders in grassroots efforts to protect the environment, working on projects such as establishing forest conservation plans and developing alternatives to wood as a fuel source. They collaborate with various organizations to promote environmental education through projects like recycling, wildlife protection,
10 and park management. Volunteers also work to provide potable water to rural and urban communities and to alleviate waterborne diseases.

BULGARIA

Joseph "Joey" Bristol is an environmental management and training volunteer posted in a small town in the northern foothills of the Central Balkan Mountains in Bulgaria.

Joey has worked with the municipality for nearly two years on a variety of proj-
15 ects such as eco-tourism development, water testing education, and teaching English to the municipal administration. Together, Joey and the municipality have realized positive environmental change in the region.

In order to stimulate the local tourism market and to promote low-impact use of the mountains, Joey has also spent time working to gather, organize and profes-
20 sionally present local knowledge about hiking and biking trails in the region. Presently, the ecological department of the municipality is working to implement a separate

Peace Corps volunteers with Cambodian instructors at a language class in Cambodia.
Heng Sinith/AP Images

waste collection and recycling program. An uncommon endeavor in Eastern Europe, starting a recycling program has not been without difficulty and roadblocks. However, the community is proud to celebrate and begin using new recycling bins on Earth
25 Day this year.

MOROCCO

Aimee Petras, serving in the Anti Atlas Mountains—a site known for its unique Argane forests—is assisting her community in several environmental projects. First, Aimee's goal was to teach young students that keeping your environment healthy can be rewarding in several ways. At the local primary schools, Aimee focused on
30 how something as small as planting a tree can have a positive impact on a community. By planting trees, they would not only help to beautify their community, but they would also prevent soil erosion and desertification, a major challenge in Morocco. Second, after teaching the benefits of tree planting, Aimee actually practiced what she taught. She helped plant 3,500 olive trees that not only provide a positive environ-
35 ment, the tree groves also help to improve income generation and job creation abilities in the community.

Sarah Shaffer, serving in the Middle Atlas—a site with ecological and biological importance—is helping her community through the promotion of eco-tourism. Sarah is working with her community to design, construct and organize a small bed
40 and breakfast. The bed and breakfast will try to draw more people in to better understand and realize the important ecology of the area. This is a way to build a direct relationship to the people who provide food and housing, who share their knowledge of local flora and fauna, and who produce souvenirs and handicrafts. The revenue of the business would be distributed directly into the surrounding
45 community.

In addition, Sarah is working to create a "neddi," or women's and girls' club. In her village, many of the women marry young or stay in their household. This coupled with the heavy, unpaid work burden placed on them; girls have little opportunity to develop marketable skills or to make significant choices for themselves. By developing
50 a neddi, Sarah hopes to increase their handcraft skills. In the long term, she hopes to encourage the women to form their own business association. This would be one group helping to showcase the handcrafts, made from nature, and promoting eco-tourism in the area.

MADAGASCAR

Before Mark Fabian's help, the people in his community had a hard time maintaining
55 a good supply of clean, safe drinking water. Over the last year, Mark has been working with community members, local authorities, and others to supervise the design and construction of a gravity-fed water system.

But before they dealt with the water, Mark worked with the community to plant trees and vetiver grass, a special plant that helps conserve soil on the hillsides
60 of the watershed. They chose fruit trees because people would be reluctant to cut them down in the future for firewood. And, not only do they produce healthy fruit, the trees also help reduce soil erosion, and clean the rain and runoff as the water reaches the spring.

After several days of planting trees, people began seeing a method to his madness—
65 or riddle that is. This task has resulted in clean flowing water in the spring. In addition, the runoff from the new, clean water spigot now flows into a fishpond, which also

SELECTION 3

irrigates some nearby rice paddies. Mark Fabian's project represents a model not only of collaboration among the community, local authorities and non-governmental organizations, but also a model of integrated watershed management and the provision of

70 useable, safe drinking water.

(829 words)

—Courtesy of the Peace Corps

Time Goals

Record your finishing time. _____ : _____

Calculate your total reading time. _____

Rate your concentration as high _____ medium _____ or low _____ .

Recall what you have read, and review what you have learned.

Your instructor may choose to give you a true-false comprehension review.

WRITE ABOUT THE SELECTION   MyReadingLab™

Complete
this **Exercise** on
myreadinglab.com

What are Peace Corps volunteers doing to protect the environment in countries around the world?

Response Suggestion: Make an informal outline that lists each country mentioned and the environmental projects the volunteers are developing. Are there any similarities?

SELECTION 3

CHECK YOUR COMPREHENSION MyReadingLab™

After reading the selection, answer the following questions with *a, b, c,* or *d.* To help you analyze your strengths and weaknesses, the question types are indicated.

Complete this **Exercise** on **myreadinglab.com**

Main Idea —————— 1. The best statement of the main idea of the entire selection is

    a. volunteers are helping local communities to provide safe drinking water.

    b. Sarah Shaffer is working on several environmental projects in Morocco.

    c. Peace Corps volunteers are working on environmental protection projects in many countries.

    d. there are many opportunities for volunteers to improve living conditions around the world.

Detail —————— 2. Joey Bristol's work in Bulgaria includes

    a. developing hiking and biking trails.

    b. planting trees.

    c. teaching English to local children.

    d. helping local people to market their hand-made products.

Inference —————— 3. We can conclude from the passage that Eastern Europe

    a. is ahead of other countries in protecting the environment.

    b. is just beginning to address environmental protection issues such as recycling.

    c. has concentrated on economic development instead of environmental issues.

    d. is more concerned about education than the environment.

Main Idea —————— 4. Aimee Petras's work is focused on

    a. teaching children about trees.

    b. promoting the many ecological and economic benefits of trees.

    c. developing jobs in Morocco.

    d. improving life for the Moroccan people.

Detail —————— 5. In the section about Aimee Petras's work, which of the following is NOT mentioned as a benefit of planting trees?

    a. They prevent soil erosion.

    b. They provide a source of income from their fruit.

    c. They generate job opportunities.

    d. They contribute to better air quality.

Detail —————— 6. Which of the following is NOT listed as a goal for Sarah Shaffer's bed and breakfast project?

    a. To develop tourism in the area

    b. To provide jobs for people who are knowledgeable of the local flora and fauna

    c. To draw attention to the important ecological importance of the area

    d. To provide a place for the "neddi" to meet

Inference ———— 7. The author implies that women in Morocco

    a. have many opportunities to earn income.

    b. are largely restricted to responsibilities in their homes.

    c. have significant control over their own lives.

    d. have no marketable skills.

Main Idea ———— 8. The main idea of the section on Mark Fabian's work in Madagascar is that

    a. he helped develop a thriving fish pond.

    b. the water system he helped develop controls soil erosion.

    c. he helped develop a gravity-fed water system that has several positive effects.

    d. the clean water is used to irrigate rice paddies.

Inference ———— 9. From the passage we can conclude that Mark Fabian

    a. did not expect the far-reaching benefits of the water system.

    b. intended only to plant the trees.

    c. came to Madagascar with the water plan fully developed and ready to begin.

    d. planned and prepared extensively before beginning construction of the gravity-fed water system.

Inference ———— 10. From the passage, we can conclude that

    a. the Peace Corps encourages volunteers to include local people and government leaders in identifying, developing, and implementing projects.

    b. Peace Corps volunteers have little knowledge or training before arriving at their posts.

    c. Peace Corps volunteers are mostly in their 20s and 30s.

    d. the Peace Corps pays for these projects.

Answer the following with *T* (true) or *F* (false).

Inference ———— 11. Joey Bristol and Sarah Shaffer expect that tourists can be attracted to the areas in which they are working with the Peace Corps.

Detail ———— 12. Aimee Petras taught children about the benefits of trees but did not participate in actually planting trees.

Detail ———— 13. Aimee Petras and Sarah Shaffer work in different regions of Morocco.

Inference ———— 14. We can infer from the passage that Morocco struggles to prevent further growth of its desert areas.

Detail ———— 15. Mark Fabian worked alone in designing the water system in his town and only involved others in building it.

BUILD YOUR VOCABULARY   MyReadingLab™

Complete
this **Exercise** on
myreadinglab.com

According to the way the italicized word was used in the selection, indicate *a, b, c,* or *d* for the word or phrase that gives the best definition. The number in parentheses indicates the line of the passage in which the word is located.

_____ 1. *"implications* for the environment" (5)
    a. consequences
    b. benefits
    c. financial impacts
    d. schemes

_____ 2. *"grassroots* efforts" (6)
    a. farming
    b. overall
    c. involving ordinary people
    d. important

_____ 3. "provide *potable* water" (10)
    a. portable
    b. fit for drinking
    c. easily accessed
    d. recreational

_____ 4. *"alleviate* waterborne diseases"(11)
    a. encourage
    b. deliver
    c. lessen
    d. infect

_____ 5. "worked with the *municipality*" (16)
    a. elderly population
    b. hospital
    c. school
    d. town

_____ 6. "and *desertification*" (32)
    a. destruction of deserts
    b. enjoyment of deserts
    c. study of deserts
    d. process of becoming a desert

_____ 7. "promotion of *eco-tourism*" (38)
    a. environmentally friendly tourism
    b. less expensive tourism
    c. tourism that damages the environment
    d. environmental education

_____ 8. *"coupled* with the heavy" (47)
    a. promised
    b. married
    c. combined
    d. doubled

_____ 9. "develop *marketable* skills" (49)
    a. technological
    b. manual
    c. high cost
    d. can be sold

_____ 10. "clean water *spigot*" (66)
    a. stream
    b. faucet
    c. bucket
    d. pump

SELECTION 3

Time Goal

Record your time for answering the questions. _____ : _____

Calculate your total time for reading and answering the questions. _____

What changes would you make to enhance your concentration on the next selection?

CREDITS

Video screen captures reproduced with permission of BBC Motion Gallery Education: Creativity; TOMS Shoes: Changing the World; The Effects of Stress; The New Entrepreneur; DNA and the Criminal Justice System; Illiteracy in the United States; Global Warming; The Magic Number of Beauty; The American Diet.

Wade, Carole, Tavris, Carol, *Psychology*, 10th, © 2011. Printed and Electronically reproduced by permission of Pearson Education, Inc., Upper Saddle River, New Jersey.; Jones, Jacqueline A., Wood, Peter H., Borstelmann, Thomas, May, Elaine Tyler, Ruiz, Vicki L., *Created Equal:* A *History of the United States, Volume 2 (From 1865)*, 3rd, © 2009. Printed and Electronically reproduced by permission of Pearson Education, Inc., Upper Saddle River, New Jersey.; Courtesy of the Peace Corps.

Answer Key for two essays in **Chapter 1, Active Learning**, in *Bridge to College Reading*.

Selection 2, "Home Front Workers, Rosie the Riveter, and Victory Girls."

Comprehension   Vocabulary

1.	B	6. C	11. True
2.	C	7. D	12. True
3.	A	8. A	13. True
4.	A	9. B	14. True
5.	A	10. C	15. True
6.	C		

1.	B	6. C
2.	A	7. A
3.	D	8. C
4.	B	9. B
5.	D	10. A

Selection 3, "Volunteers Help Protect the Environment"

Comprehension   Vocabulary

1.	C	6. D	11. True
2.	A	7. B	12. False
3.	B	8. C	13. True
4.	B	9. D	14. True
5.	D	10. A	15. False

1.	A	6. D
2.	C	7. A
3.	B	8. C
4.	C	9. D
5.	D	10. B

Reading Strategies, Schema, and Metacognition

Adapted from: Bridging the Gap: College Reading by Brenda D. Smith and Leeann Morris

Being a strategic reader is one step in becoming a scholarly, academic reader. You will be learning strategies to help you read and study materials in order to learn. All study strategies involve a system, or steps to take **before**, **during**, and **after** reading.

Before You Read

You have probably noticed that when you already know something about a subject, it is easier to read about that subject. Somehow the ideas seem clearer, and the vocabulary is familiar. Conversely, when you read about something that is unfamiliar, it takes longer and seems harder. The reason for that phenomenon is your prior knowledge, also known as **"schema"** (plural form: **schemata**). When you are engaged in a reading task, you need to **"activate your schema:"** that is, you recall what you already know about a topic. You make connections with something you have already experienced or read. **Activating schema** (or recalling prior knowledge) is something you need to do before you actually start reading a text.

When you are given a reading assignment, do not just jump in and start reading. You need to **preview, or survey,** your chapter or essay before you begin. Worry not: This is not cheating! You should look over the material. Look at the title to determine the topic. Read the introduction and the summary to find the main idea. See how long the assignment is, and if there are any questions at the end of the reading. Look at them to see what you are supposed to get out of the reading. Notice any subtitles or bolded words, insets, charts, graphs, or pictures. Notice if the material is organized in any particular way, such as explaining a process or listing reasons. All of this should not take too long; perhaps five minutes. While you are previewing your assignment, **activate your schema**. Think about whether you already know something about the topic, or if you have a connection to it. By the time you actually read the assignment, you should have a sense of how much time you need to spend on it, if you already have a background on it on which to build new knowledge, and what your purpose is for reading.

While You Are Reading

During the course of the term, you will be learning annotation, Cornell Note-taking, and other ways of taking notes on a variety of texts. These techniques will help you to stay focused and avoid zoning out, which is a common problem. Whatever strategy you use, you should choose it deliberately. It is helpful to have a variety of strategies to choose from, and your choice should be based on your knowledge of yourself as a reader. Do you already know a lot about the reading? Then perhaps your notes do not need to be overly long, and your reading will be quick and easy. You can make predictions about what comes next. Is this a subject you know nothing about? Then your notes need to be more complete and your reading will probably take longer. When you reach a point in the reading that seems particularly difficult or confusing, what will you do? Maybe you need to reread a section. Perhaps you need to read ahead because the clarification of the idea is further along. Maybe you will need to look up words or get some background information to help you understand the subject at hand. **You need to know how you are doing while you are reading!** Knowing when to slow down or speed up, whether to look up words or not, understanding when you understand and when you don't understand involves some self-knowledge and self-awareness. This process is called "**metacognition,**" and it basically means "knowing about knowing." Your "metacognition" will tell you that something is difficult, that you must slow down, that you don't understand, or that your notes are inadequate. You need to not only monitor your comprehension, but you also need to know how to self-correct; that is, you need to know strategies to help yourself better understand what you are reading. Metacognition allows you to control and direct your own strategies as you read.

After You Read

After reading a selection in a textbook, you may be tested on it. You can use your textbook annotations and notes to anticipate questions for tests. You need to think about what you have read and try to incorporate it along with your prior knowledge. Make connections from the text to your prior knowledge, to yourself, to other texts you have read, and, if appropriate, to the world. Reflect and react to what you have read. Are these concepts you wish to accept, or reject? Should the ideas be incorporated into your knowledge base? There may be ways to help you remember facts and details, such as mnemonic devices, but one of the best ways to remember something is to connect it to something else, to see the relationships among the ideas, and the relationship between the new information and what is already part of your schema. Talking, writing, and thinking about what you have read are powerful ways to help you remember new information.

Comprehension Skills

Main Idea

Learning Objectives

From this chapter, readers will learn to:

1 Distinguish topics, main ideas, and supporting details
2 Apply a strategy for finding the main idea
3 Identify stated main ideas
4 Distinguish major and minor details
5 Identify unstated main ideas
6 Identify main ideas of longer selections
7 Write a summary

Sitting with Vincent van Gogh by Joann Wells Greenbaum

WHAT IS A TOPIC?

Learning Objective 1

Distinguish topics, main ideas, and supporting details

In this chapter we will discuss and practice what many experts believe is the most important reading skill and the key to comprehension: recognizing the main idea of a paragraph, passage, or selection. As you read—and regardless of what you are reading, whether it is a chapter from your history text or an article in the Sunday paper—it is important to answer the question "What's the point?" However, before attempting to discover the central point of a piece of writing, you must have a good sense of its topic.

A **topic** is like the title of a book or song. It is a word, name, or phrase that labels the subject but does not reveal the specific contents of the passage. What's more, boldface heads within a chapter reflect subordinate topics, or subtopics. Similarly, individual passages beneath those heads have their own topics.

Think of the topic of a passage as a big umbrella under which specific ideas or details can be grouped. For example, consider the words *carrots, lettuce, onions,* and *potatoes*. What general term would pull together and unify these items?

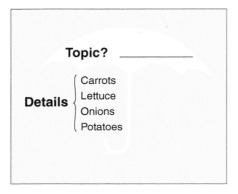

Topic? _____

Details {
Carrots
Lettuce
Onions
Potatoes
}

Topic: _____

EXERCISE 1

Identifying Topics

Each of the following lists includes three specific items or ideas that could relate to a single topic. At the top of each list, write a general topic under which the specific ideas can be grouped.

1. _____

french fried

au gratin

scalloped

2. _____

snow

rain

sleet

3. _____

triathlon

5K

marathon

WHAT IS A MAIN IDEA?

Using the topic as an initial indicator, the **main idea** of a passage becomes more focused and is the central message that the author is trying to convey about the material. It is a sentence that condenses thoughts and details into a general, all-inclusive statement of the author's point.

Reading specialists use various terms when referring to the main idea. In classroom discussions, a variety of words are used to help students understand its meaning. How many of these have you heard?

Main point	Gist	Central thought
Central focus	Controlling idea	Thesis

The last word on the list, *Thesis*, is a familiar word in English composition classes. You have probably had practice in stating a thesis sentence for English essays, but you may not have had as much practice in stating the main idea of a reading selection. Can you see the similarity between a thesis and a main idea statement?

How important is it to be able to find and comprehend the main idea? Experts say that it is *crucial to your comprehension of any text*. In fact, if all reading comprehension techniques were combined and reduced to one essential question, that question might be "What is the main idea the author is trying to get across to the reader?" Whether you read a single paragraph, a chapter, or an entire book, your most important single task is to understand the main idea of what you read.

WHAT ARE SUPPORTING DETAILS?

Details are statements that support, develop, and explain a main idea. Specific details can include reasons, incidents, facts, examples, steps, and definitions.

There are important differences between *major details*, which are critical to the support of the main idea and your understanding of a passage, and *minor details*, which amplify the major details. One way to distinguish the two is to pay attention to signal words, which link thoughts and help you anticipate the kind of detail that is coming next. Key signal words for major supporting details are *one, first, another, furthermore, also,* and *finally*. Key signal words for minor details are *for example, to be specific, that is,* and *this means*. We will deepen our discussion of major and minor details later in this chapter.

DISTINGUISHING TOPICS, MAIN IDEAS, AND DETAILS: A CLOSER LOOK

We have seen that a topic is a general category, and that a main idea is the author's central message about the topic. Let's explore the difference between them—and the importance of supporting details—a little more closely.

The diagram that follows depicts the relationship among topics, main ideas, and major and minor details.

- The topic is the broad subject.
  ↑
- The main idea makes a point about the topic.
  ↑

- Major details develop and explain the main idea.

- Minor details elaborate on the major ones.

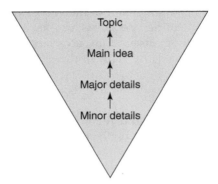

    Caffeine is a general term or topic that unifies the items *coffee, tea, cola,* and *chocolate*. If those items were used as details in a paragraph, the main idea could not be expressed by simply saying "caffeine." The word *caffeine* would answer the question "What is the passage about?" However, only your evaluation of the supporting details in the paragraph would answer the question "What is the author's main idea?"

    Think of some of the very different paragraphs about caffeine that a writer could devise using the same four details as support. If you were that writer, what would be the main idea or thesis—using the four items as details—of your paragraph?

Topic: Caffeine

Main idea or thesis: _____

_____

EXAMPLE   Read the following examples of different main ideas that could be developed in a paragraph about the topic of caffeine. Explanations appear in italicized type.

1. Consumption of caffeine is not good for your health. *(Details would enumerate health hazards associated with each item.)*
2. Americans annually consume astonishing amounts of caffeine. *(Details would describe amounts of each consumed annually.)*
3. Caffeine makes money as the Starbucks star rises. *(Details would show the profits and expansion of the coffee giant.)*
4. Reduce caffeine consumption with the decaffeinated version of popular caffeine-containing beverages. *(Details would promote the decaffeinated version of each item.)*

EXAMPLE   Following are examples of a topic, main idea, and supporting detail.

Topic   **EARLY COGNITIVE DEVELOPMENT**

Main Idea ⌐ Cognitive psychologists sometimes study young children to observe the very begin-
      ⌐ nings of cognitive activity. For example, when children first begin to utter words and

Detail ⌐ sentences, they overgeneralize what they know and make language more consistent
      ⌐ than it actually is.

—Christopher Peterson,
Introduction to Psychology

EXPLANATION   The topic pulls your attention to a general area, and the main idea provides the focus. The detail offers elaboration and support.

EXERCISE 2   **Differentiating Topic, Main Idea, and Supporting Details**

This exercise is designed to check your ability to differentiate statements of the main idea from the topic and supporting details. Compare the items within each group, and indicate whether each one is a statement of the main idea *(MI)*, a topic *(T)*, or a specific supporting detail *(SD)*.

Group 1

_____ a. For poor farm families, life on the plains meant a sod house or a dugout carved out of the hillside for protection from the winds.

_____ b. One door and usually no more than a single window provided light and air.

_____ c. Sod houses on the plains

—James W. Davidson et al.,
Nation of Nations

Group 2

_____ a. She was the daughter of English poet Lord Byron and of a mother who was a gifted mathematician.

_____ b. Babbage and the programming countess

_____ c. Ada, the Countess of Lovelace, helped develop the instructions for doing computer programming computations on Babbage's analytical engine.

_____ d. In addition, she published a series of notes that eventually led others to accomplish what Babbage himself had been unable to do.

—Adapted from H. L. Capron,
Computers: Tools for an Information Age, 6th ed.

Group 3

_____ a. Mexican American political gains

_____ b. During the 1960s, four Mexican Americans—Senator Joseph Montoya of New Mexico and Representatives Eligio de la Garza and Henry B. Gonzales of Texas and Edward R. Roybal of California—were elected to Congress.

_____ c. In 1974, two Chicanos were elected governors—Jerry Apodaca in New Mexico and Raul Castro in Arizona—becoming the first Mexican American governors since the early twentieth century.

_____ d. Since 1960, Mexican Americans have made important political gains.

—James Kirby Martin et al.,
America and Its Peoples, Vol. 2, 4th ed.

STRATEGIES FOR FINDING THE MAIN IDEA

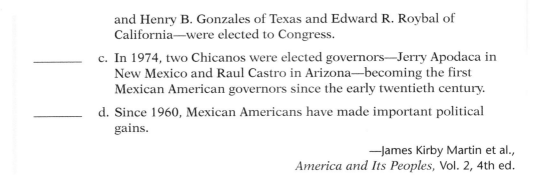

Learning Objective 2

Apply a strategy to find the main idea

Not surprisingly, reading is easier when we know something about the topic. This illustrates the importance of schemata and should remind us to be alert to opportunities to learn about a broad range of subjects. When we are open to new experiences and read widely, we build a base of background knowledge that makes future learning easier. The research described below shows that readers who are familiar with the topic of a selection, use a different strategy for finding the main idea than readers who are unfamiliar with the topic.

Prior Knowledge and Constructing the Main Idea

How exactly do you figure out the main idea of a paragraph or passage? Researchers have investigated the processes readers use to construct main ideas. One researcher, Peter Afflerbach, asked graduate students and university professors to "think aloud" as they read passages on both familiar and unfamiliar topics.[1] These expert readers spoke their thoughts to the researcher before, during, and after reading. From these investigations, Afflerbach concluded that expert readers use different strategies for familiar and unfamiliar materials.

Here is the important finding: This research showed that *already knowing something about the topic is the key* to easy reading. When readers are familiar with the subject, constructing the main idea is effortless and, in many cases, automatic. These readers quickly assimilate the unfolding text into already well-developed knowledge networks. They seem to organize text into chunks for comprehension and later retrieval. These "informed" readers do not have to struggle with information overload. Again, this shows that the rich get richer, and the initial struggle to build knowledge has many benefits.

By contrast, expert readers with little prior knowledge of the subject are absorbed in trying to make meaning out of unfamiliar words and confusing sentences. Because they are struggling to recognize ideas, few mental resources remain for constructing a main idea. These "uninformed" experts are reluctant to guess at a main idea and to predict a topic. Instead, they prefer to read all the

---

[1]P. Afflerbach, "How Are Main Idea Statements Constructed? Watch the Experts!," *Journal of Reading* 30 (1987): 512–18; and "The Influence of Prior Knowledge on Expert Readers' Main Idea Construction Strategies," *Reading Research Quarterly* 25 (1990): 31–46.

information before trying to make sense of it. Constructing the main idea is a difficult and deliberate task for these expert but uninformed readers. Even a proven expert reader in history, for example, might struggle to read chemistry books until enough knowledge is built for main idea construction to be automatic.

The following strategies for getting the main idea were reported by Afflerbach's expert readers. Can you see the differences in the thinking processes of the informed and uninformed experts?

"Informed" Expert Readers

Strategy 1. The informed expert readers previewed the passage before reading and took a guess at the main idea. Then they read for confirmation.

Strategy 2. The informed experts automatically paused while reading to summarize or condense information. They stopped at natural breaks in the material to let ideas fall into place.

"Uninformed" Expert Readers

Strategy 1. Expert readers who did not know about the subject were unwilling to take a guess at the main idea. Instead, they read the material, determined the topic, and then looked back to pull together a main idea statement.

Strategy 2. Other uninformed experts read the material and reviewed it to find key terms and concepts. They tried to bring the key terms and concepts together into a main idea statement.

Strategy 3. Still other uninformed experts read the material and then proposed a main idea statement. They double-checked the passage to clarify or revise the main idea statement.

What differences do you see between these approaches? Since introductory college textbooks address many topics that are new and unfamiliar, freshmen readers will frequently need to use the strategies of uninformed expert readers to comprehend the main ideas of their college texts. Until you build up your reserves of prior knowledge through the college courses you take, constructing main ideas for course textbooks is likely to be a *conscious effort* rather than an automatic phenomenon.

Identifying Main Ideas Among Sentences

Before identifying main ideas in paragraphs, practice with a simple list of sentences. Read the sentences in the following group. They are related to a single topic, with one sentence expressing a main idea and two other sentences expressing detailed support. Circle the number of the sentence that best expresses the main idea, and write the general topic for the group.

EXAMPLE

1. The 1960 debate between John Kennedy and Richard Nixon boosted Kennedy's campaign and elevated the role of television in national politics.

2. Televised presidential debates are a major feature of U.S. presidential elections.

3. Ronald Reagan's performance in 1980 and 1984 debates confirmed the public view of him as decent, warm, and dignified.

Topic: _____

—Adapted from James MacGregor Burns et al.,
Government by the People, 20th ed.

EXPLANATION The second sentence best expresses the main idea, declaring the importance of televised presidential debates. The other two sentences are details offering specific facts in support of the topic, which is the importance of televised presidential debates.

EXERCISE 3 ## Discovering Topics and Main Ideas in Sentence Groups

Circle the number of the sentence that best expresses the general main idea, and write the general topic.

Group 1

1. Dentists are trying virtual reality headsets for their patients to help reduce anxiety about dental care.

2. Gradual exposure to takeoff and landing in a virtual environment allows would-be travelers to face their phobias and prepare to take the next step, a real flight.

3. Overcoming fear is a fast-growing application of virtual reality.

4. Topic: _____

—Alan Evans et al.,
Technology in Action, 2nd ed.

Group 2

1. At present, the meaning of correlations between brain size and intelligence is not clear.

2. For example, females have about the same average intelligence as males, but generally have smaller brains.

3. The Neanderthals had larger brains than we do, but there is no evidence that they were smarter.

4. Topic: _____

—Adapted from Stephen M. Kosslyn
and Robin S. Rosenberg,
Psychology: The Brain, the Person, the World, 2nd ed.

Group 3

1. Relying on his extensive industry experience, JetBlue founder and CEO David Neeleman focused most of his energy on a few key factors that he felt would make or break his company.

2. JetBlue fills planes to capacity, gets more flying hours out of each aircraft, and saves on maintenance costs because its fleet is brand-new.

3. By hiring younger, more productive workers and giving them stock options in lieu of high wages, JetBlue keeps labor expenses down to 25 percent of revenues (compared to Southwest's 33 percent and Delta's 44 percent).

4. Topic: _____

_____

—Adapted from Ricky W. Griffin and Ronald J. Ebert,
Business, 8th ed.

To determine the main idea of a paragraph, article, or book, follow the basic steps shown in the box, and ask the questions posed in the Reader's Tip. The order of the steps may vary depending on your prior knowledge of the material. If you are familiar with the material, you might find that constructing the main idea is automatic and you can select significant supporting details afterward. If you are unfamiliar with the material, as may often be the case in textbook reading, you would need to identify the details through key terms and concepts first, and from them you would form a topic and a main idea statement.

Routes to the Main Idea

For Familiar Material

Preview ▶ ▶ ▶ Determine topic ▶ ▶ ▶ Read ▶ ▶ ▶ Identify key details ▶ ▶ ▶ Find main idea

For Unfamiliar Material

Preview ▶ ▶ ▶ Read ▶ ▶ ▶ Identify key details ▶ ▶ ▶ Determine topic ▶ ▶ ▶ Find main idea

---

Questioning for the Main Idea

Like paragraphs, visual images also suggest main ideas. Photographers and artists compose and select images to communicate a message. Look at the picture shown on next page and then answer the questions that follow.

What is the general topic of the photograph? _____

_____

What details seem important? _____

_____

_____

What is the main idea the photographer is trying to convey about the topic?

_____

_____

_____

Marion Curtis/StarPix/AP Images

In this photo, champion swimmer Dara Torres stands next to an advertisement that she did for the "got milk" campaign. The details of the ad show a slim and fit Torres, dressed in a bikini. From the white moustache on her upper lip and the "got milk?" tagline, the viewer assumes she has just had a sip of the beverage. Though the details are sparse, the viewer can see that Torres is muscular and attractive. Though partially covered in this photo, the words of the advertisement refer to the muscle-building protein and nutrients of milk and suggest that Torres drinks three glasses every day. The advertisers hope viewers also know Torres has won twelve Olympic medals, three of them at the age of 41, and was the first woman over 40 to swim in the Olympics. The details in the picture and text plus some viewers' background knowledge make the message persuasive: If we want to be fit, trim, and strong, we should drink milk.

Reader's TIP — Using Questions to Find the Main Idea

1. **Determine the topic.** *Who or what is this reading about?*
   Find a general word or phrase that names the subject. The topic should be broad enough to include all the ideas, yet restrictive enough to focus on the direction of the details. For example, the topic of an article might be correctly identified as politics, federal politics, or corruption in federal politics, but the last might be the most descriptive of the actual contents.
2. **Identify details.** *What are the major supporting details?*
   Look at the details and key terms that seem to be significant to see if they point in a particular direction. What aspect of the topic do they address? What seems to be the common message? Details such as kickbacks to senators, overspending on congressional junkets, and lying to the voters could support the idea of corruption in federal politics.
3. **Find the main idea.** *What is the message the author is trying to convey about the topic?*
   The statement of the main idea should be:

   * A complete sentence
   * Broad enough to include the important details
   * Focused enough to describe the author's slant

   The author's main idea about corruption in federal politics might be that voters need to ask for an investigation of seemingly corrupt practices by federal politicians.

STATED MAIN IDEAS

Learning Objective 3

Identify stated main ideas

The Topic Sentence

As in the photo, an author's main point can be directly stated in the material. When the main idea is stated in a sentence, the statement is called a **topic sentence** or **thesis statement.** Such a general statement is helpful to the reader because it provides an overview of the material.

Read the following examples and answer the questions for determining the main idea using the three-question technique.

EXAMPLE Managers can regain control over their time in several ways. One is by meeting whenever possible in someone else's office, so that they can leave as soon as their business is finished. Another is to start meetings on time without waiting for late-comers. The idea is to let late-comers adjust their schedules rather than everyone else adjusting theirs. A third is to set aside a block of time to work on an important project without interruption.

Main Idea

This may require ignoring the telephone, being protected by an aggressive secretary, or hiding out. Whatever it takes is worth it.

—Joseph Reitz and Linda Jewell,
Managing

1. Who or what is this passage about? ————————————————

   ——

2. What are the major details? ————————————————————

   ——

   ——

3. What is the main idea the authors are trying to convey about the topic? ————

   ——

   ——

   ——

EXPLANATION   The passage is about managers controlling their time. The major details are *meet in another office, start meetings on time,* and *block out time to work*. The main idea, stated in the beginning as a topic sentence, is that managers can do things to control their time.

EXAMPLE   New high-speed machines also brought danger to the workplace. If a worker succumbed to boredom, fatigue, or simple miscalculation, disaster could strike. Each year of the late nineteenth century some 35,000 wage earners were killed by industrial accidents. In Pittsburgh iron and steel mills alone, in one year 195 men died from hot metal explosions, asphyxiation, and falls, some into pits of molten metal. Men and women working in textile mills were poisoned by the thick dust and fibers in the air; similar toxic atmospheres injured those working in anything from twine-making plants to embroidery factories. Railways, with their heavy equipment and unaccustomed speed, were especially dangerous. In Philadelphia over half the railroad workers who died between 1886 and 1890 were killed by accidents. For injury or death, workers and their families could expect no payment from employers, since the idea of worker's compensation was unknown.

—James W. Davidson et al.,
Nation of Nations

1. Who or what is this passage about? ————————————————

   ——

2. What are the major details? ————————————————————

   ——

   ——

3. What is the main idea the author is trying to convey about the topic? _____

_____

_____

_____

EXPLANATION   The passage is about injuries from machines. The major details are *35,000 killed*, *195 died from explosions and other accidents in Pittsburgh iron and steel mills*, *poisoned dust killed workers in textile mills*, and *half of the rail workers who died were killed in accidents*. The main idea is that new high-speed machines brought danger to the workplace.

How Common Are Stated Main Ideas?

Research shows that students find passages easier to comprehend when the main idea is directly stated within the passage. How often do stated main ideas appear in college textbooks? Should the reader expect to find that most paragraphs have stated main ideas?

For psychology texts, the answer seems to be about half and half. One research study found that stated main ideas appeared in *only 58 percent* of the sampled paragraphs in introductory psychology textbooks.[2] In one of the books, the main idea was directly stated in 81 percent of the sampled paragraphs, and the researchers noted that the text was particularly easy to read.

Given these findings, we should recognize the importance of being skilled in locating and, especially, in constructing main ideas. In pulling ideas together to construct a main idea, you will be looking at the big picture and not left searching for a single suggestive sentence.

Where Are Stated Main Ideas Located?

Should college readers wish for all passages in all textbooks to begin with stated main ideas? Indeed, research indicates that when the main idea is stated at the beginning of the passage, the text tends to be comprehended more easily. In their research, however, Smith and Chase found only 33 percent of the stated main ideas to be positioned as the first sentence of the paragraph.

Main idea statements can be positioned at the beginning, in the middle, or at the end of a paragraph. Both the beginning and concluding sentences of a passage can be combined to form a main idea statement.

EXERCISE 4   **Locating Stated Main Ideas**

The following diagrams and examples demonstrate the different possible positions for stated main ideas within paragraphs. Annotate as you read the examples, and then insert the main ideas and supporting details into the blank spaces provided beside the geometric diagrams.

---

[2]B. Smith and N. Chase, "The Frequency and Placement of Main Idea Topic Sentences in College Psychology Textbooks," *Journal of College Reading and Learning* 24 (1991): 46–54.

1. An introductory statement of the main idea is given at the beginning of the paragraph.

EXAMPLE

Under hypnosis, people may recall things that they are unable to remember spontaneously. Some police departments employ hypnotists to probe for information that crime victims do not realize they have. In 1976, twenty-six young children were kidnapped from a school bus near Chowchilla, California. The driver of the bus caught a quick glimpse of the license plate of the van in which he and the children were driven away. However, he remembered only the first two digits. Under hypnosis, he recalled the other numbers and the van was traced to its owners.

—David Dempsey and Philip Zimbardo,
Psychology and You

2. A concluding statement of the main idea appears at the end of the paragraph.

EXAMPLE

Research is not a once-and-for-all-times job. Even sophisticated companies often waste the value of their research. One of the most common errors is not providing a basis for comparisons. A company may research its market, find a need for a new advertising campaign, conduct the campaign, and then neglect to research the results. Another may simply feel the need for a new campaign, conduct it, and research the results. Neither is getting the full benefit of the research. When you fail to research either the results or your position *prior* to the campaign, you cannot know the effects of the campaign. For good evaluation you must have both before and after data.

—Edward Fox and Edward Wheatley,
Modern Marketing

3. Details are placed at the beginning to arouse interest, followed by a statement of the main idea in the middle of the paragraph.

EXAMPLE

After losing $1 billion in Euro-Disney's first year of operation, the company realized that Paris was not Anaheim or Orlando. French employees were insulted by the Disney dress code, and European customers were not accustomed to standing in line for rides or eating fast food standing up. Disney had to adjust and customize its market mix after learning that international customers are not all alike. The company ditched its controversial dress code, authorized wine with meals, lowered admission prices, hired a French investor relations firm, and changed the name to Disneyland Paris to lure the French tourist.

—Adapted from Michael Mescon et al.,
Business Today, 8th ed.

Details: _____
1. _____
2. _____
Main Idea: _____
Details: 3. _____
4. _____

4. Both the introductory and concluding sentences state the main idea.

EXAMPLE

You cannot avoid conflict but you can learn to face it with a four-step conflict resolution plan. Before you bring up the issue that's upsetting you, know what you want to achieve. Have a positive outcome in mind. Then listen to what the other side says, but go beyond that to try to understand as well. Express empathy for their position. It may not be easy, but try to see the big picture. Place the conflict in context. Finally, if at all possible, end your discussion on a positive note. Set the stage for further discussion by

Main Idea: _____
Details: 1. _____
2. _____
3. _____
4. _____
Main Idea: _____

keeping those lines of communication open. Use these four strategies for handling tensions constructively and enjoy stronger social bonds.

—Adapted from Rebecca J. Donatelle,
Access to Health, 8th ed.

5. Details combine to make a point, but the main idea is not directly stated.

EXAMPLE

This creature's career could produce but one result, and it speedily followed. Boy after boy managed to get on the river. The minister's son became an engineer. The doctor's sons became "mud clerks"; the wholesale liquor dealer's son became a bar-keeper on a boat; four sons of the chief merchant, and two sons of the county judge, became pilots. Pilot was the grandest position of all. The pilot, even in those days of trivial wages, had a princely salary—from a hundred and fifty to two hundred and fifty dollars a month, and no board to pay. Two months of his wages would pay a preacher's salary for a year. Now some of us were left disconsolate. We could not get on the river—at least our parents would not let us.

—Mark Twain,
Life on the Mississippi

Unstated Main Idea:

Details:

1.

2.

3.

4.

EXPLANATION   Although not directly stated, the main idea is that young boys in the area have a strong desire to leave home and get a prestigious job on the Mississippi River.

EXERCISE 5

Using Questions to Find Stated Main Ideas

Read the following passages, and use the three-question system to determine the author's main idea. For each passage in this exercise, the answer to the third question will be stated somewhere within the paragraph.

PASSAGE A

The concept and practice of group harmony or *wa* is what most dramatically differentiates Japanese baseball from the American game. Contract holdouts for additional money, for example, are rare in Japan. A player usually takes what the club decides to give him, and that's that. Demanding more money is evidence that a player is putting his own interests before those of the team. Temper tantrums—along with practical joking, bickering, complaining, and other norms of American clubhouse life—are viewed in Japan as unwelcome intrusions into the team's collective peace of mind.

—Robert Whiting,
You Gotta Have Wa

1. Who or what is this about? _____

   _____

   _____

2. What are the major details? _____

   _____

   _____

   _____

3. What is the main idea the author is trying to convey about the topic? _____

   _____

   _____

   _____

4. Underline the main idea.

PASSAGE B

The participants were male college students. Each student, placed in a room by himself with an intercom, was led to believe that he was communicating with one or more students in an adjacent room. During the course of a discussion about personal problems, he heard what sounded like one of the other students having an epileptic seizure and gasping for help. During the "seizure," it was impossible for the participant to talk to the other students or to find out what, if anything, they were doing about the emergency. The dependent variable was the speed with which the participant reported the emergency to the experimenter. The likelihood of intervention depended on the number of bystanders the participant thought were present. The more people he thought were present, the slower he was in reporting the seizure, if he did so at all. Everyone in a two-person situation intervened within 160 seconds, but nearly 40 percent of those who believed they were part of a larger group never bothered to inform the experimenter that another student was seriously ill.

—Richard Gerrig and Philip Zimbardo,
Psychology and Life, 17th ed.

1. Who or what is this about? _____

   _____

   _____

2. What are the major details? _____

_____

_____

_____

3. What is the main idea the authors are trying to convey about the topic? _____

_____

_____

_____

4. Underline the main idea.

PASSAGE C

Research has shown that girls and boys learn to use language differently in their sex-separate peer groups. Typically, a girl has a best friend with whom she sits and talks, frequently telling secrets. It's the telling of secrets, the fact and the way that they talk to each other, that makes them best friends. For boys, activities are central: their best friends are the ones they do things with. Boys also tend to play in larger groups that are hierarchical. High-status boys give orders and push low-status boys around. So boys are expected to use language to seize center stage: by exhibiting their skill, displaying their knowledge, and challenging and resisting challenges.

—Adapted from Deborah Tannen,
"How Male and Female Students Use Language Differently,"
The Chronicle of Higher Education, June 19, 1991

1. Who or what is this about? _____

_____

_____

2. What are the major details? _____

_____

_____

_____

3. What is the main idea the author is trying to convey about the topic? _____

_____

_____

_____

4. Underline the main idea.

WHAT ARE MAJOR AND MINOR DETAILS?

Learning Objective 4

Distinguish major and minor details

Textbooks are packed full of details, but fortunately all details are not of equal importance. Major details tend to support, explain, and describe main ideas—they are essential. Minor details, by contrast, tend to support, explain, and describe the major details. Ask the following questions to determine which details are major in importance and which are not:

1. Which details logically develop the main idea?
2. Which details help you understand the main idea?
3. Which details make you think the main idea you have chosen is correct?

Key signal words, like those listed in the Reader's Tip, form transitional links among ideas and can sometimes help you distinguish between major and minor details.

Develop the habit of annotating by circling major details. Later, expand your annotating by underlining minor details.

EXAMPLE

Selena was the undisputed queen of Tejano, the music of the Texas-Mexico border. Her music epitomized the complexity of the border culture. Tejano music originated in the nineteenth century, when European immigrants introduced the accordion to the Texas-Mexico border. A fast-paced blend of Latin pop, German polka, and country rhythms, Tejano music combined the oompah music of Europeans with Mexican ballads known as *cumbias* and *rancheras*. Unlike many earlier Latina personalities, like Rita Hayworth and Raquel Welch, who gained their fame only after changing their names and projecting an exotic and sexy image, Selena never abandoned her Mexican American identity. Selena, who was 23 years old when she was slain, nevertheless achieved extraordinary popularity.

—Adapted from James Kirby Martin et al.,
America and Its Peoples, Vol. 2, 5th ed.

1. The topic of the passage is

   a. Slaying of Selena.
   b. Tejano music.
   c. Queen of Tejano music.
   d. Mexican ballads.

Reader's TIP   Signals for Significance

- Key words for major details:
  one   first   another   furthermore   also   finally
- Key words for minor details:
  for example   to be specific   that is   this means

2. Indicate whether each of the following details is major or minor in support of the author's topic:

   a. Selena was true to her Mexican American identity.
   b. Raquel Welch changed her name.
   c. Selena was popular when she was slain at 23.

3. Underline the sentence that best states the main idea of this passage.

EXPLANATION For the first response, the topic of the passage is *c*. Both *b* and *d* are too broad and *a* is an unfortunate detail. For the second item, *a* is a major detail because her music is Tejano, *b* is a minor detail not directly related to Selena, and *c* is a major detail because she is no longer living. The first sentence states the main idea.

EXERCISE 6

Identifying Topics, Stated Main Ideas, and Details in Passages

Read the following passages and apply the three-question system. Select the letter of the author's topic, circle major details, identify minor ones, and underline the main idea. For each passage in this exercise, the answer to the third question will be stated somewhere within the paragraph.

PASSAGE A

Building and equipping the pyramids focused and transformed Egypt's material and human resources. Artisans had to be trained, engineering and transportation problems solved, quarrying and stone-working techniques perfected, and laborers recruited. In the Old Kingdom, whose population has been estimated at perhaps 1.5 million, more than 70,000 workers at a time were employed in building the great temple-tombs. No smaller work force could have built such a massive structure as the Great Pyramid of Khufu.

—Mark Kishlansky et al.,
Civilization in the West, 4th ed.

_____ 1. The topic of the passage is

   a. Training Laborers for the Pyramids.
   b. Resources Needed for Building Pyramids.
   c. Pyramid Building Problems.
   d. The Pyramids.

2. Indicate whether each of the following details is major or minor in support of the author's topic:

   _____ a. The Old Kingdom had an estimated population of 1.5 million.

Main Idea

_____ b. More than 70,000 workers at a time were employed in building the great temple-tombs.

_____ c. Artisans had to be trained.

3. Underline the sentence that best states the main idea of this passage.

PASSAGE B

If you're upset or tired, you're at risk for an emotion-charged confrontation. If you ambush someone with an angry attack, don't expect her or him to be in a productive frame of mind. Instead, give yourself time to cool off before you try to resolve a conflict. In the case of the group project, you could call a meeting for later in the week. By that time, you could gain control of your feelings and think things through. Of course, sometimes issues need to be discussed on the spot; you may not have the luxury to wait. But whenever it's practical, make sure your conflict partner is ready to receive you and your message. Select a mutually acceptable time and place to discuss a conflict.

—Adapted from Steven A. Beebe, Susan J. Beebe, and Diana K. Ivy, *Communication*

_____ 1. The topic of the passage is

a. Planning for Conflict Resolution.
b. Confrontation.
c. Being Productive.
d. Solving Problems.

2. Indicate whether each of the following details is major or minor in support of the author's topic:

_____ a. Give yourself time to cool off before you try to resolve a conflict.

_____ b. If you're upset, you're at risk for a confrontation.

_____ c. Call a meeting a week later for a group project.

3. Underline the sentence that best states the main idea of this passage.

PASSAGE C

In a Utah case, the defendant fell asleep in his car on the shoulder of the highway. Police stopped, smelled alcohol on his breath, and arrested him for driving while intoxicated. His conviction was reversed by the Utah Supreme Court because the defendant was not in physical control of the vehicle at the time, as required by the law. In freeing the defendant, the Supreme Court judged that the legal definition of sufficiency was not established in this case because the act observed by the police was not sufficient to confirm the existence of a guilty mind. In other words, the case against him failed because he was not violating the law at the time of the arrest and because it was also possible that he drove while sober, then pulled over, drank, and fell asleep.

—Adapted from Jay S. Albanese,
Criminal Justice, Brief Edition

_____ 1. The topic of the passage is
     a. Driving Drunk.
     b. The Utah Supreme Court.
     c. Sleeping Behind the Wheel.
     d. Establishing Sufficiency for Drunken Driving.

     2. Indicate whether each of the following details is major or minor in support of the author's topic:

         _____ a. Police arrested the defendant for driving while intoxicated.
         _____ b. The defendant was not violating a law at the time of the arrest.
         _____ c. The case was tried in Utah.

     3. Underline the sentence that best states the main idea of this passage.

UNSTATED MAIN IDEAS

Learning Objective 5

Identify unstated main ideas

Unfortunately, even if details are obvious, you cannot always depend on the author to provide a direct statement of a main idea. To add drama and suspense to a description or narrative, the main idea may be hinted at or implied rather than directly stated. Main ideas are often unstated in other media as well, such as movies and photographs.

Look at the details in the photo to decide what message the photographer is trying to communicate. Determine the topic of the picture, propose a main idea using your prior knowledge, and then list some of the significant details that support this point.

What is the topic? _____

_____

_____

What are the significant supporting details? _____

_____

_____

What point is the photograph trying to convey about the topic? _____

_____

_____

Mike Gullett/AP Images

The topic of the photo is the devastation of homes and lives by what appears to have been a tornado. The details depict at least one home almost completely destroyed while another appears to be less damaged. Debris piled at the side of the street suggests that clean-up has begun. Viewers can infer that the people in the picture live in this neighborhood and that the man and child in the foreground have a close connection to one of these homes. Perhaps one of them is where they lived. He is comforting the child. The main idea is that people's lives have been tragically disrupted by the destruction of a neighborhood, but they comfort each other and move forward. The main idea is not directly stated but is suggested by the details in the picture.

Unstated Main Ideas in Sentences

Before identifying unstated main ideas in paragraphs, practice with a simple list of sentences. First, read the related sentences in the following group. Next, create a sentence that states a general main idea for the three related thoughts.

EXAMPLE

1. A landmark 1990 study found that 30 percent of Americans under 35 had read a newspaper the day before—a much lower percentage than their parents.
2. Attempts to win a younger audience have included *USA Today*'s color and glitz, originally aimed at younger readers.
3. By 2000, daily newspaper circulation was down to 52.8 million from a 62.8 million high in 1988.

—John Vivian,
The Media of Mass Communication

Main idea: ―――――――――――――――――――――――――――――――

―――――――――――――――――――――――――――――――――――――――

> **EXPLANATION**   The first sentence states that young readership is low. The second states an attempt to lure young readers, and the third states that circulation has declined by 10 million. The general main idea reflected in these sentences is that daily newspapers are not winning young readers and circulation is down.

EXERCISE 7

Determining Unstated Main Ideas

Read the following related sentences and state the main idea:

Group 1

1. The AIDS virus (HIV), which seemed to arise abruptly in the early 1980s, and the new varieties of flu virus that frequently appear, are not the only examples of newly dangerous viruses.
2. A deadly virus called the Ebola virus menaces central African nations periodically, and many biologists fear its emergence as a global threat.
3. In 2003, a deadly new disease called SARS (severe acute respiratory syndrome) appeared in China and soon spread throughout the world.

—Neil Campbell et al.,
Essential Biology

Main idea: ―――――――――――――――――――――――――――――

―――――――――――――――――――――――――――――――――――――――

Group 2

1. President George Washington converted the paper thoughts outlined in the Constitution into an enduring, practical governing process, setting precedents that balance self-government and leadership.
2. Thomas Jefferson, a skilled organizer and a resourceful party leader and chief executive, adapted the presidency to the new realities of his day with territorial expansions and sponsorship of the Lewis and Clark expedition westward.
3. President Lincoln is remembered for saving the Union and is revered as the nation's foremost symbol of democracy and tenacious leadership in the nation's ultimate crisis.

—James MacGregor Burns,
Government by the People, 20th ed.

Main idea: ―――――――――――――――――――――――――――――

―――――――――――――――――――――――――――――――――――――――

Group 3

1. Sales prospects are much more inclined to buy from people who make them feel good and with whom they have developed a personal bond, so begin by building a rapport.
2. Ask questions to find out the prospect's real needs, and describe the product or service accordingly to focus on the buyer's benefits.
3. Go for the final close and remember to ask for the order and stop talking so the customer can make the purchase.

—Michael Mescon et al.,
Business Today, 8th ed.

Main idea: _____

_____

Unstated Main Ideas in Paragraphs

Determining the main idea of a paragraph will be easier if you use the three-step questioning strategy. The questions used to find an unstated main idea have a subtle difference, though. As you approach a passage with an implied or unstated main idea, begin by asking, "What is this about?" Reading carefully to identify key terms and major supporting details, draw a conclusion about the topic. Once you have determined the general topic of the paragraph, then ask yourself, "What do all or most of the key terms or major details suggest?" It is now up to you to figure out the author's point. Think as you read. Create an umbrella statement that brings these concepts together into a main idea statement.

EXAMPLE

Michael Harner proposes an ecological interpretation of Aztec sacrifice and cannibalism. He holds that human sacrifice was a response to certain diet deficiencies in the population. In the Aztec environment, wild game was getting scarce, and the population was growing. Although the maize-beans combination of food that was the basis of the diet was usually adequate, these crops were subject to seasonal failure. Famine was frequent in the absence of edible domesticated animals. To meet essential protein requirements, cannibalism was the only solution. Although only the upper classes were allowed to consume human flesh, a commoner who distinguished himself in a war could also have the privilege of giving a cannibalistic feast. Thus, although it was the upper strata who benefited most from ritual cannibalism, members of the commoner class could also benefit. Furthermore, as Harner explains, the social mobility and cannibalistic privileges available to the commoners through warfare provided a strong motivation for the "aggressive war machine" that was such a prominent feature of the Aztec state.

—Serena Nanda,
Cultural Anthropology, 4th ed.

Main Idea

1. Who or what is this about? _____

_____

_____

2. What are the major details? _____

_____

_____

3. What is the main idea the author is trying to convey about the topic? _____

_____

_____

EXPLANATION   The passage is about Aztec sacrifice and cannibalism. The major details are: Diet deficiencies occurred, animals were not available, and members of the upper class and commoners who were war heroes could eat human flesh. The main idea is that Aztec sacrifice and cannibalism met protein needs of the diet and motivated warriors to achieve.

EXERCISE 8

Identifying Unstated Main Ideas

Read the following passages and apply the three-question system. Select the letter of the author's topic, identify major and minor details, circle major details, identify minor ones, and choose the letter of the sentence that best states the main idea.

PASSAGE A

Each year in the United States approximately 50,000 miscarriages are attributed to smoking during pregnancy. On average, babies born to mothers who smoke weigh less than those born to nonsmokers, and low birth weight is correlated with many developmental problems. Pregnant women who stop smoking in the first three or four months of their pregnancies give birth to higher-birth-weight babies than do women who smoke throughout their pregnancies. Infant mortality rates are also higher among babies born to smokers.

—Rebecca J. Donatelle,
Health: The Basics, 4th ed.

_____ 1. The topic of the passage is

a. Infant Mortality.
b. Smoking.
c. Smoking and Pregnancy.
d. Smoking and Miscarriages.

2. Indicate whether each of the following details is major or minor in support of the author's topic:

_____ a. Low birth weight is correlated with many developmental problems.

———— b. Infant mortality rates are also higher among babies born to smokers.

———— c. Babies born to mothers who smoke weigh less than those born to nonsmokers.

———— 3. Which sentence best states the main idea of this passage?

a. Smoking during pregnancy increases the chance of miscarriages, low-weight babies, and infant mortality.
b. Smoking during pregnancy causes many miscarriages.
c. Ceasing smoking during pregnancy can increase infant birth weight.
d. Smoking is a major contributor to infant mortality.

PASSAGE B

The young reporter with the slow Missouri drawl stamped the cold of the high Nevada desert out of his feet as he entered the offices of the Virginia City *Territorial Enterprise*. It was early in 1863. The newspaper's editor, Joseph T. Goodman, looked puzzled at seeing his Carson City correspondent in the home office, but Samuel Clemens came right to the point: "Joe, I want to sign my articles. I want to be identified to a wider audience." The editor, already impressed with his colleague of six months, readily agreed. Then came the question of a pen name, since few aspiring writers of the time used their legal names. Clemens had something in mind: "I want to sign them 'Mark Twain,'" he declared. "It is an old river term, a leadsman's call, signifying two fathoms—twelve feet. It has a richness about it; it was always a pleasant sound for a pilot to hear on a dark night; it meant safe water."

—Roderick Nash and Gregory Graves,
From These Beginnings, Vol. 2, 6th ed.

———— 1. The topic of the passage is

a. Becoming a Reporter.
b. How Mark Twain Got His Name.
c. Safe Water on the River.
d. Working for the Virginia City *Territorial Enterprise*.

2. Indicate whether each of the following details is major or minor in support of the author's topic:

———— a. Clemens had worked for the newspaper for six months.

———— b. The newspaper's editor was Joseph T. Goodman.

———— c. Clemens wanted to sign his articles to be known to a wider audience.

_____ 3. Which sentence best states the main idea of this passage?

    a. Samuel Clemens worked as a young reporter for the Virginia City _Territorial Enterprise._

    b. The newspaper's editor, Joseph T. Goodman, was impressed with the young reporter, Samuel Clemens.

    c. "Mark Twain" is a river term that means two fathoms—twelve feet.

    d. The young reporter, Samuel Clemens, decided to take the pen name "Mark Twain."

PASSAGE C

Credit card companies entice students to apply for cards and take on debt with free T-shirts, music CDs, and promises of an easy way to pay for spring break vacations. Many students, however, can't even keep up with the minimum payment. In fact, it is estimated that in one year 150,000 people younger than 25 will declare personal bankruptcy. That means for 150,000 young people, their first significant financial event as an adult will be to declare themselves a failure. And for each one who goes into bankruptcy, there are dozens just behind them, struggling with credit card bills. In one 4-month period, for instance, a Texas A&M freshman piled up $2,500 of charges on two Visa cards and four retail credit cards. The student couldn't afford to pay the $25 minimum a month on all the cards, so she accumulated $150 in late fees and over-credit-limit fees.

—Adapted from Michael Mescon et al.,
Business Today, 8th ed.

_____ 1. The topic of the passage is

    a. The Credit Card Industry.

    b. Paying Off Debt.

    c. Bankruptcy Options.

    d. Danger of Credit Cards for College Students.

2. Indicate whether each of the following details is major or minor in support of the author's topic:

    _____ a. Credit card companies give away music CDs.

    _____ b. Young people are declaring bankruptcy over credit card debt.

    _____ c. A Texas A&M freshman cannot pay her minimum payments.

_____ 3. Which sentence best states the main idea of this passage?

    a. Credit card companies engage in illegal activities to hook students on debt.

    b. It should be illegal for credit card companies to enroll college students who have no means of payment.

    c. Credit card companies entice college students into debt that can be financially disastrous.

    d. Bankruptcy is an easy option for college students with overwhelming credit card debt.

EXERCISE 9

Writing Unstated Main Ideas

Read the following passages and use the three-question system to determine the author's main idea. Remember to annotate by circling major details. Pull the ideas together to state the main ideas in your own words.

PASSAGE A

According to the U.S. Department of the Census, by 2050, Hispanics will make up 24.5 percent of the population, up from 10.2 percent in 1996. The annual growth rate of the Hispanic population is expected to be 2 percent through the year 2030. To put this growth in perspective, consider the fact that even at the height of the baby boom explosion in the late 1940s and early 1950s, the country's annual population increase never reached 2 percent. Demographers, it seems, are alerting us to the enormous importance of such change. Says Gregory Spencer, Director of the Census Bureau's Population Projections Branch, "The world is not going to be the same in thirty years as it is now."

—Ronald Ebert and Ricky Griffin,
Business Essentials, 2nd ed.

1. Who or what is this about? _____

_____

_____

2. What are the major details? _____

_____

_____

_____

3. What is the main idea the author is trying to convey about the topic? _____

_____

_____

_____

PASSAGE B

American executives like to get right down to business and engage in fast and tough face-to-face bargaining. However, Japanese and other Asian businesspeople often find this behavior offensive. They prefer to start with polite conversation, and they rarely say no in face-to-face conversations. As another example, South Americans like to sit or stand very close to each other when they talk business—in fact almost nose-to-nose. The American business executive tends to keep backing away as the South American moves closer.

— Gary Armstrong and Philip Kotler,
Marketing: An Introduction, 10th ed.

1. Who or what is this about? _____

2. What are the major details? _____

_____

3. What is the main idea the details are making about the topic? _____

_____

_____

PASSAGE C

In 1979 when University of Minnesota psychologist Thomas Bouchard read a newspaper account of the reuniting of 39-year-old twins who had been separated from infancy, he seized the opportunity and flew them to Minneapolis for extensive tests. Bouchard was looking for differences. What "the Jim twins," Jim Lewis and Jim Springer, presented were amazing similarities. Both had married women named Linda, divorced, and married women named Betty. One had a son James Alan, the other a son James Allan. Both had dogs named Toy, chain-smoked Salems, served as sheriff's deputies, drove Chevrolets, chewed their fingernails to the nub, enjoyed stock car racing, had basement workshops, and had built circular white benches around trees in their yards. They also had similar medical histories: Both gained 10 pounds at about the same time and then lost it; both suffered what they mistakenly believed were heart attacks, and both began having late-afternoon headaches at age 18.

Identical twins Oskar Stohr and Jack Yufe presented equally striking similarities. One was raised by his grandmother in Germany as a Catholic and a Nazi, while the other was raised by his father in the Caribbean as a Jew. Nevertheless, they share traits and habits galore. They like spicy foods and sweet liqueurs, have a habit of falling asleep in front of the television, flush the toilet before using it, store rubber bands on their wrists, and dip buttered toast in their coffee. Stohr is domineering toward women and yells at his wife, as did Yufe before he was separated.

—David G. Myers,
Psychology

1. Who or what is this about? _____

_____

_____

2. What are the major details? _____

_____

_____

_____

3. What is the main idea the author is trying to convey about the topic? _____

_____

_____

_____

INTERPRETING THE MAIN IDEA OF LONGER SELECTIONS

Learning Objective 6

Identify main ideas of longer selections

Understanding the main idea of longer selections requires a little more thinking than does finding the main idea of a single paragraph. Since longer selections, such as articles or chapters, contain more material, tying the ideas together can be a challenge. Each paragraph of a longer selection usually represents a new aspect of a supporting detail. In addition, several major ideas may contribute to developing the overall main idea. Your job is to group the many pieces under one central theme.

For longer selections, organize the paragraphs into related sections and think of a label that describes the common threads. Think of these labels as the major supporting details. Then ask, "What point do they make about the topic?"

Use the suggestions in the Reader's Tip to determine the main idea of longer selections. The techniques are similar to those used in previewing and skimming, two skills that also focus on the overall central theme.

EXERCISE 10

Getting the Main Idea of Longer Selections

Read each passage, and use the strategies in the Reader's Tip to determine the author's main idea. This time, write brief labels in the margin and underline the supporting details.

PASSAGE A: THE BENEFITS OF A GOOD NIGHT'S SLEEP

College students are well known for "all nighters," during which they stay up through the night to study for an exam or to finish—or even to start—a paper due in the morning. Lack of sleep is nothing to brag or laugh about. Sleep is vital to your life and can help you function at optimal levels both physically and mentally.

On the physical side, sleep helps regulate your metabolism and your body's state of equilibrium. On the mental side, it helps restore your ability to be optimistic and to have a high level of energy and self-confidence. To keep your body in balance, more sleep is needed when you are under stress, experiencing emotional fatigue, or undertaking an intense intellectual activity such as learning.

During sleep, most people experience periods of what is called rapid eye movement (REM). These movements can be observed beneath closed eyelids. In REM sleep, the

Getting the Main Idea of Longer Selections

- **Think about the title.** What does the title suggest about the topic?
- **Read the first paragraph or two to find a statement of the topic or thesis.** What does the selection seem to be about?
- **Read the subheadings** and, if necessary, glance at the first sentences of some of the paragraphs. Based on these clues, what does the article seem to be about?
- **Look for clues that indicate how the material is organized.** Is the purpose to define a term, to prove an opinion or explain a concept, to describe a situation, or to persuade the reader toward a particular point of view? Is the material organized into a list of examples, a time order or sequence, a comparison or contrast, or a cause-and-effect relationship?
- **As you read, organize the paragraphs into subsections.** Give each subsection a title and write it in the margin. Think of it as a significant supporting detail.
- **Determine how the overall organization and subsections relate to the whole.** What is the main idea the author is trying to convey in this selection?

body is quiet but the mind is active, even hyperactive. Some researchers believe that REM sleep helps you form permanent memories; others believe that this period of active brain waves serves to rid your brain of overstimulation and useless information acquired during the day. REM sleep is the time not only for dreams but also for acceleration of the heart rate and blood flow to the brain.

During non-REM sleep, in contrast, the body may be active—some people sleepwalk during this period—but the mind is not. In spite of this activity, non-REM sleep is the time when the body does its repair and maintenance work, including cell regeneration.

Although much still needs to be learned about sleep and its functions, few would disagree that sleep plays a role in the maintenance of good mental health.

—B. E. Pruitt and Jane J. Stein,
Decisions for Healthy Living

1. What does the title suggest about the topic? _____
   _____
   _____

2. What sentence in the first paragraph suggests the main idea? _____
   _____
   _____

BRAIN BOOSTER

Brains Need the Right Amount of Sleep

As you settle into a weekly schedule that allots specific times for studying, remember that sleep is very important to learning. Scientists cannot say how much sleep is right for you, but for most people it is between 7 and 8 hours. Research studies show that getting less or more sleep than your brain needs causes difficulty paying attention, thinking logically, and performing physical tasks. Schedule bedtime and wake-up time at about the same times each day to get the most from your brain.

—Adapted from Brain Rules: 12 Principles for Surviving and thriving at Home, Work and School *by John J. Medina*

3. What subtitles would you give the second, third, and fourth paragraphs? ____

_____

_____

4. What is the main idea of the selection? _____

_____

_____

PASSAGE B: SCIENTISTS DEBATE ANIMAL INTELLIGENCE

For years, any scientist who claimed that animals could think was likely to be ignored or laughed at. Today, however, the study of animal intelligence is booming, especially in the interdisciplinary field of cognitive ethology. (Ethology is the study of animal behavior, especially in natural environments.) Cognitive ethologists argue that some animals can anticipate future events, make plans, and coordinate their activities with those of their comrades.

In the 1920s, Wolfgang Kohler put chimpanzees in situations in which some tempting bananas were just out of reach and watched to see what the apes would do. Most did nothing, but a few turned out to be quite clever. If the bananas were outside the cage, the chimp might pull them in with a stick. If they were hanging overhead, and there were boxes in the cage, the chimp might pile up the boxes and climb on top of them to reach the fruit. Often the solution came after the chimp had been sitting quietly for a while. It appeared as though the animal had been thinking about the problem and was struck by a sudden insight.

When we think about animal cognition, we must be careful because even complex behavior that appears to be purposeful can be genetically prewired and automatic. The assassin bug of South America catches termites by gluing nest material on its back as camouflage, but it is hard to imagine how the bug's tiny dab of brain tissue could enable it to plan this strategy consciously. Yet explanations of animal behavior that leave out any sort of consciousness at all and that attribute animals' actions entirely to instinct do not seem to account for some of the amazing things that animals can do. Like the otter that uses a stone to crack mussel shells, many animals use objects in the natural environment as tools, and in some nonhuman primates the behavior is learned.

For example, chimpanzee mothers occasionally show their young how to use stones to open hard nuts. Orangutans in one particular Sumatran swamp have learned to use sticks as tools, held in the mouths, to pry insects from holes in tree trunks and to get seeds out of cracks in a bulblike fruit, whereas nearby groups of orangutans use only brute force to get to the delicacies. Even some nonprimates may have the capacity to learn to use tools, although the evidence remains controversial among ethologists. Female bottlenose dolphins off the coast of Australia attach sea sponges to their beaks while hunting for food, which protects them from sharp coral and stinging stonefish, and they seem to have acquired this unusual skill from their mothers.

—Carole Wade and Carol Tavris,
Psychology, 10th ed.

1. What does the title suggest about the topic? _____
   _____
   _____
   _____

2. Which sentence in the first paragraph suggests the main idea? _____
   _____

3. What subtitles would you give paragraphs one through four? (Answers may vary.) _____
   _____
   _____

4. What is the main idea of the selection? _____
   _____
   _____
   _____

PASSAGE C: IMMIGRATION IN THE 1800s

What had been a trickle in the 1820s—some 128,502 foreigners came to U.S. shores during that decade—became a torrent in the 1850s, with more than 2.8 million migrants to the United States. Although families and single women emigrated, the majority of the newcomers were young European men of working age.

This vast movement of people, which began in the 1840s and continued throughout the nineteenth century, resulted from Europe's population explosion and the new farming and industrial practices that undermined or ended traditional means of livelihood. Poverty and the lack of opportunity heightened the appeal of leaving home. As one Scottish woman wrote to an American friend in 1847, "We cannot make it better here. All that we can do is if you can give us any encouragement is to immigrate to your country."

Famine uprooted the largest group of immigrants: the Irish. In 1845, a terrible blight attacked and destroyed the potato crop, the staple of the Irish diet. Years of devastating hunger followed. One million Irish starved to death between 1841 and 1851; another million and a half emigrated. Although not all came to the United States, those who did arrived almost penniless in eastern port cities without the skills needed for good jobs. With only their raw labor to sell, employers, as one observer noted, "will engage Paddy as they would a dray horse." Yet, limited as their opportunities were, immigrants saved money to send home to help their families or to pay for their passage to the United States.

German immigrants, the second largest group of newcomers during this period (1,361,506 arrived between 1840 and 1859), were not facing such drastic conditions. But as Henry Brokmeyer observed, "Hunger brought me . . . here, and hunger is the cause of European immigration to this country."

—Gary B. Nash et al.,
The American People, 6th ed., Vol. 1

1. What does the title suggest about the topic? _____

   _____

   _____

2. What subtitles could you give paragraphs one through four? _____

   _____

   _____

   _____

3. Is there one sentence that sums up the main idea in the passage? _____

   _____

   _____

4. What is the main idea of the selection? _____

   _____

   _____

SUMMARY WRITING: A MAIN IDEA SKILL

Learning Objective 7

Write a summary

A **summary** is a series of brief, concise statements, in your own words, of the main idea and the significant supporting details. The first sentence should state the main idea or thesis; subsequent sentences should incorporate the significant details. Minor details and material irrelevant to the learner's purpose should be omitted. The summary should be written in paragraph form and should always be shorter than the material being summarized. It should not contain anything that is not in the original, and it must be written in your own words.

Why Summarize?

Summaries can be used for textbook study, especially when anticipating answers for essay exam questions and for condensing the plot, theme, and characters of novels and short stories. For writing research papers, summarizing is an essential skill. Using your own words to put the essence of an article into concise sentences requires a thorough understanding of the material. As one researcher noted, "Since so much summarizing is necessary for writing papers, students should have the skill before starting work on research papers. How much plagiarism is the result of inadequate summarizing skills?"[3]

Writing a research paper may mean that you will have to read as many as 30 articles and four books over a period of a month or two. After each reading, you want to take enough notes so you can write your paper without returning to the library for another look at the original reference. Since you will be using so many different references, do your note taking carefully. The complete sentences of a summary are more explicit than underscored text or the highlighted topic-phrase format of an outline. Your summary should demonstrate a synthesis of the information. The Reader's Tip outlines how to write an effective summary.

Read the following excerpt on political authority as if you were doing research for a term paper and writing a summary on a note card. Mark key terms that you would include. Before reading the example provided, anticipate what you would include in your own summary.

Reader's Tip · How to Summarize

- **Keep in mind the purpose of your summary.** Your task or assignment will determine which details are important and how many should be included.
- **Decide on the main idea the author is trying to convey.** Make this main idea the first sentence in your summary.
- **Decide on the major ideas and details that support the author's point.** Mark the key terms and phrases. Include in your summary the major ideas and as many of the significant supporting details as your purpose demands.
- **Do not include irrelevant or repeated information.** A summary stays very focused and concise.
- **Use appropriate transitional words and phrases.** They'll show the relationship between ideas.
- **Use paragraph form.** Don't use a list or write in incomplete sentences.
- **Do not add your personal opinion.** Stick to the content of the material you are summarizing.

---

[3]K. Taylor, "Can College Students Summarize?" *Journal of Reading* 26 (March 1983): 540–44.

Types of Authority

Where is the source of the state's authority? Weber described three possible sources of the right to command, which produced what he called traditional authority, charismatic authority, and legal authority.

Traditional Authority

In many societies, people have obeyed those in power because, in essence, "that is the way it has always been." Thus, kings, queens, feudal lords, and tribal chiefs did not need written rules in order to govern. Their authority was based on tradition, on long-standing customs, and it was handed down from parent to child, maintaining traditional authority from one generation to the next. Often, traditional authority has been justified by religious tradition. For example, medieval European kings were said to rule by divine right, and Japanese emperors were considered the embodiment of heaven.

Charismatic Authority

People may also submit to authority, not because of tradition, but because of the extraordinary attraction of an individual. Napoleon, Gandhi, Mao Tse-tung, and Ayatollah Khomeini all illustrate authority that derives its legitimacy from charisma—an exceptional personal quality popularly attributed to certain individuals. Their followers perceive charismatic leaders as persons of destiny endowed with remarkable vision, the power of a savior, or God's grace. Charismatic authority is inherently unstable. It cannot be transferred to another person.

Legal Authority

The political systems of industrial states are based largely on a third type of authority: legal authority, which Weber also called rational authority. These systems derive legitimacy from a set of explicit rules and procedures that spell out the ruler's rights and duties. Typically, the rules and procedures are put in writing. The people grant their obedience to "the law." It specifies procedures by which certain individuals hold offices of power, such as governor or president or prime minister. But the authority is vested in those offices, not in the individuals who temporarily hold the offices. Thus, a political system based on legal authority is often called a "government of laws, not of men." Individuals come and go, as American presidents have come and gone, but the office, "the presidency," remains. If individual officeholders overstep their authority, they may be forced out of office and replaced.

—Alex Thio,
Sociology, 3rd ed.

1. To begin your summary, what is the main point? _____

    _____

    _____

    _____

2. What are the major areas of support? _____

    _____

    _____

3. Should you include an example for each area? _____
_____

Begin your summary with the main point, which is that Weber describes the three sources of authority as traditional, charismatic, and legal. Then define each of the three sources, but do not include examples.

Read the following summary and notice how closely it fits your own ideas.

> *Political Authority*
> Weber describes the three command sources as traditional, charismatic, and legal authority. Traditional authority is not written but based on long-standing custom such as the power of queens or tribal chiefs. Charismatic authority is based on the charm and vision of a leader such as Gandhi. Legal authority, such as that of American presidents, comes from written laws and is vested in the office rather than the person.

EXERCISE 11

Summarizing Passages

Read the following passages, and mark the key terms and phrases. Begin your summary with a statement of the main point, and add the appropriate supporting details. Use your markings to help you write the summary. Be brief, but include the essential elements.

PASSAGE A: TECHNOLOGY ADDICTIONS

As technology becomes an ever larger part of our daily lives, the risk of overexposure to it grows for people of all ages. Some people, in fact, become addicted to new technologies, such as smart phones, video games, networking sites, and the Internet in general.

Many experts suggest that technology addiction is real and can present serious problems for those addicted. An estimated 5 to 10 percent of Internet users will likely experience Internet addiction. Younger people are also more likely to be addicted to the Internet than middle-aged users. Approximately 11 percent of college students report that Internet use and computer games have interfered with their academic performance.

Internet addicts have multiple signs and symptoms, such as general disregard for one's health, sleep deprivation, depression, neglecting family and friends, lack of physical activity, euphoria when online, lower grades in school, and poor job performance. Internet addicts may feel moody or uncomfortable when they are not online. Online addicts may be using their behavior to compensate for feelings of loneliness, marital or work problems, a poor social life, or financial problems.

—Rebecca J. Donatelle,
Access to Health, 8th ed.

Use your marked text to write a summary.

PASSAGE B: ALCOHOL ADVERTISING AND COLLEGE STUDENTS

The alcohol industry knows a receptive market when it sees it. Each year, college students spend a reported $5.5 billion ($446 per student) on alcohol, consuming some 4 billion cans' worth of alcohol and accounting for 10 percent of total beer sales. For brewers, student beer drinking spells not just current sales, but future profits as well, because most people develop loyalty to a specific beer between the ages of 18 and 24. To secure this lucrative market, brewers and other alcohol producers spend millions of dollars each year promoting their products to college students. One conservative estimate places annual expenditures for college marketing between $15 million and $20 million. According to one survey, alcohol advertising of local specials in many college newspapers has increased by more than half over the past decade, stymying college and community efforts to reduce binge drinking.

—Rebecca J. Donatelle,
Health: The Basics, 4th ed.

Use your marked text to write a summary.

PASSAGE C: ADVANTAGES OF COMMUNITY COLLEGES

Community colleges provide a number of specific benefits. First, their low tuition cost places college courses and degrees within the reach of millions of families that could not otherwise afford them. Today, it is at community colleges that we find many students who are the first generation of their families to pursue a postsecondary degree. Compared to students who attend four-year colleges, a larger share of community college students are also paying their own way. The low cost of community colleges is especially important during periods of economic recession. Typically, when the economy slumps (and people lose their jobs), college enrollments—especially at community colleges—soar.

Second, community colleges have special importance to minorities. Currently, one-half of all African American and Hispanic undergraduates in the United States attend community colleges.

Third, although it is true that community colleges serve local populations, many two-year colleges also attract students from around the world. Many community colleges recruit students from abroad, and more than one-third of all foreign students enrolled on a U.S. campus are studying at community colleges.

Finally, while the highest priority of faculty who work at large universities typically is research, the most important job for community college faculty is teaching. Thus, although teaching loads are high (typically four or five classes each semester), community colleges appeal to faculty who find their greatest pleasure in the classroom. Community college students often get more attention from faculty than their counterparts at large universities.

—John J. Macionis,
Sociology, 10th ed.

Use your marked text to write a summary.

Chronic Stress and the Brain

Stress is an aroused physical state in which adrenaline is released to help us react quickly when we're in danger. When the danger has passed, cortisol kicks in to calm us down. Stress is designed to keep us from being eaten by predators that stalked ancient plains. The problem is that today most of us no longer face such dangers, and our stress is likely to last for extended lengths of time. It is when adrenaline levels stay high for a long time, like when we worry about how to pay for tuition and books, that stress is harmful. Chronic stress scars our blood vessels, reduces our ability to fight illness, and inhibits learning. It can actually disconnect neural networks and prevent the growth of new ones. The worst damage is done when we feel powerless. What to do? Exercise and proper amounts of sleep can help. Some people find meditation and prayer effective. Just as important, however, is to establish a can-do attitude and a plan. Analyze the situation and take control! Decide on small steps that give you power over your situation: Visit the college financial aid office, look for a part-time job that works around your class and study schedule, or apply for a federal work study job on campus. Seek help when necessary. Make chronic stress history!

—*Adapted from* Brain Rules: 12 Principles for Surviving and Thriving at Home, Work, and School *by John Medina*

SUMMARY POINTS

1. **How do I distinguish topics, main ideas, and supporting details?**
   - Topics are broad. They describe who or what a selection is about. They are usually expressed in a word or a phrase.
   - Main ideas support and develop the topic. They express the point the author and details are making about the topic. They are expressed in a sentence, which may or may not be stated directly in the selection.
   - Major supporting details develop and explain the main idea. Minor details elaborate on the major details. Supporting details are often indicated by signal words. Certain signal words are typically used to mark major details and others typically mark minor details.

2. **What strategies can I use to find the main idea?**
   - The best strategy depends on whether you are familiar with the topic:
     If you have schemata on the topic, preview, determine topic, read, identify details, find main idea.
     If you do not have schemata on the topic, preview, read, identify key details, determine topic, find main idea.
   - Use questions:
     Who or what is this reading about? (topic)
     What are the major supporting details?
     What is the message the author is trying to convey about the topic? (main idea)

3. **How can I identify stated main ideas?**
   - Main ideas that are stated in a sentence within a selection are called topic sentences or thesis statements

- Use the same three questions and strategies listed above to determine the main idea.
- Look for a sentence that reflects the main idea. It can be located at the beginning, in the middle, or at the end of a paragraph.

4. How can I distinguish major and minor supporting details.
- Determine which details develop the main idea and which explain the major details.
- Recognize signal words that often indicate major or minor details.

5. How can I identify unstated main ideas?
- Use the same three questions and strategies that are used to find stated main ideas.

6. How can I identify the main ideas of longer selections?
- Determine the topic.
- Organize the paragraphs into related sections and ask what labels could be used to describe groups of these ideas.
- Ask what point these groups of ideas are making about the topic.

7. How can I write a summary?
- Determine the supporting details and main point. Use paragraph form. The first sentence should state the main idea. Organize the details into the remaining sentences in the order they occur in the selection. Do not include anything that is not in the original selection.

MyReadingLab™   For more help with Main Ideas go to your learning path in MyReadingLab at
www.myreadinglab.com

SELECTION 1   Psychology

P REVIEW the next selection to predict its purpose and organization and to formulate your learning plan.

Activate Schemata

Why do some people who experience tragedy cope with it better than others? What methods do you use to stay healthy and happy when life is difficult?

Establish a Purpose for Reading

Psychologists have found that certain ways of dealing with stress help people manage difficulty and maintain emotional well-being. Read to find out what you can do to cope with stressful situations.

Increase Word Knowledge

What do you know about these words?

optimistic	cope	physiological	tranquility	buffer
predicament	reappraising	adversity	longitudinal	bereaved

Your instructor may give a true-false vocabulary review before or after reading.

Integrate Knowledge While Reading

Questions have been inserted in the margins to stimulate your thinking while reading. Remember to

Predict	Picture	Relate	Monitor	Correct	Annotate

MyReadingLab™

THE EFFECTS OF STRESS

Watch a video on stress via your ebook at www .myreadinglab.com and then answer the related questions in the VIDEO LINK section or via MyReadingLab.

Good for everyday stress?

COPING WITH STRESS

We have noted that most people who are under stress, even those living in difficult situations, do not become ill. In addition to feeling optimistic and in control, and not wallowing around in negative emotions, how do they manage to cope?

5   The most immediate way to deal with the physiological tension of stress and negative emotions is to take time out and reduce the body's physical arousal. Many people, from infants to the old, respond beneficially to the soothing touch of massage. Another successful method is the ancient Buddhist practice of *mindfulness meditation,*

Scan this QR Code to hear this reading

What about serious stress situations?

10 which fosters emotional tranquility. The goal is to learn to accept feelings of anger, sadness, or anxiety without judging them or trying to get rid of them (a form of secondary control). A third effective buffer between stressors and illness is exercise. People who are physically fit have fewer health problems than people who are less fit even when they are under the same pressures. They also show lower physiological
15 arousal to stressors. These activities, along with my others that calm your body and focus your mind—prayer, music, dancing, baking bread—are all good for health. But if your house has burned down or you need a serious operation, other coping strategies will be necessary.

SOLVING THE PROBLEM

Years ago, at the age of 23, a friend of ours named Simi Linton was struck by tragedy.
20 Linton, her new husband, and her best friend were in a horrific car accident. When she awoke in a hospital room, with only a vague memory of the crash, she learned that her husband and friend had been killed and that she herself had permanent spinal injury and would never walk again.

How in the world does anyone recover from such a devastating event? Some
25 people advise survivors of disaster or tragedy to "get it out of your system" or to "get in touch with your feelings." But survivors know they feel miserable. What should they *do*? This question gets to the heart of the difference between *emotion-focused* and *problem-focused coping*. Emotion-focused coping concentrates on the emotions the problem has caused, whether anger, anxiety, or grief. For a period
30 of time after any tragedy or disaster, it is normal to give in to these emotions and feel overwhelmed by them. In this stage, people often need to talk endlessly about the event in order to come to terms with it, make sense of it, and decide what to do about it

Does everyone do this?

Eventually, most people become ready to concentrate on solving the problem
35 itself. The specific steps in problem-focused coping depend on the nature of the problem: whether it is a pressing but one-time decision; a continuing difficulty, such as living with a disability; or an anticipated event, such as having an operation. Once the problem is identified, the coper can learn as much as possible about it from professionals, friends, books, and others in the same predicament. Becoming
40 informed increases the feeling of control and can speed recovery.

As for Simi Linton, she learned how to do just about everything in her wheel-chair (including dancing!). and she went back to school. She got a Ph.D. in psychology, remarried, and became a highly respected teacher, counselor, writer, and activist committed to improving conditions and opportunities for people with disabilities.

RETHINKING THE PROBLEM

Cognitive refers to thinking?

45 Some problems cannot be solved; these are the unavoidable facts of life, such as an inability to have children, losing your job, or developing a chronic illness. Now what? Health psychologists have identified three effective cognitive coping methods:

1. **Reappraising the situation.** Although you may not be able to get rid of a stressor, you can choose to think about it differently, a process called *reap-*
50 *praisal*. Reappraisal can turn anger into sympathy, worry into determination, and feelings of loss into feelings of opportunity. Maybe that job you lost was dismal but you were too afraid to quit and look for another; now you can. Reappraisal improves well-being and reduces negative emotions.

© Randy Glasbergen.
www.glasbergen.com

GLASBERGEN

**"The key to stress management is knowing
how to vent your frustration."**

Randy Glasbergen/glasbergen.com

2. **Learning from the experience.** Some people emerge from adversity with new-found or newly acquired skills, having been forced to learn something they had not known before—say, how to cope with the medical system or how to manage a deceased parent's estate. Others discover sources of courage and strength they did not know they had. Those who draw lessons from the inescapable tragedies of life, and find meaning in them, thrive as a result of adversity instead of simply surviving it. The ability to find meaning in adversity may even slow the course of serious diseases. In a longitudinal study of men with HIV who had been recently bereaved, those who "tried not to think about it" showed sharper declines in immune function than men who found meaning and purpose in the loss. The latter said they had acquired greater appreciation of the loved one, a perception of life as being fragile and precious, or other benefits. "I would say that his death lit up my faith," said one man.

3. **Making social comparisons.** In a difficult situation, successful copers often compare themselves to others who they feel are less fortunate. Even if they have fatal diseases, they find someone who is worse off. One AIDS patient said in an interview, "I made a list of all the other diseases I would rather not have than AIDS. Lou Gehrig's disease; being in a wheelchair; rheumatoid arthritis, when you are in knots and in terrible pain." Sometimes successful copers also compare themselves to those who are doing better than they are. They might say, "Look at her—she's had such family troubles and survived that awful bout with cancer, and she's happier than ever with her life. How did she do it?" or "He and I have the same kinds of problems. How come he's doing so much better in school than I am? What does he know that I don't?" Such comparisons are beneficial when they provide a person with information about ways of coping, managing an illness, or improving a stressful situation.

(1,115 Words)

—From Carole Wade and Carol Tavris, *Psychology*, 10th ed.

Can I think of times I've used one of these three methods? →

Recall

Stop to talk, write, and think about the selection.

Your instructor may choose to give you a true-false comprehension review.

WRITE ABOUT THE SELECTION   MyReadingLab™

Complete
this **Exercise** on
myreadinglab.com

Imagine that your best friend has just broken up with his or her romantic partner. She is very upset and wants to drop out of college. She has come to you for support and advice. What will you suggest?

   Response Suggestion: List the coping methods in this selection along with a brief description. Based on your friend's situation and what you have read, write a "prescription" that will help her through this crisis.

Your instructor may choose to give you a true-false comprehension review.

 VIDEO LINK   MyReadingLab™

Complete
this **Exercise** on
myreadinglab.com

Now that you have read the selection and viewed the video on *The Effects of Stress*, check your understanding by answering with *T* (true) or *F* (false):

_____ 1. Brain chemicals such as adrenaline and cortisol released when people experience stress are sometimes helpful.

_____ 2. According to the video, chronic stress causes neurons in the brain to shrink.

_____ 3. The video cites technology as a time- and energy-saving factor in reducing stress.

_____ 4. Accelerated aging, aggression, and depression are mentioned as possible effects of chronic stress.

_____ 5. The video states that the damaging effects of chronic stress are permanent.

Summarize

Using this selection as a source, summarize the information that you might want to include in a research paper entitled "Coping with Stress: Getting from Stress to Contentment."

SKILL DEVELOPMENT: FIND THE MAIN IDEA

Answer the following with *T* (true) or *F* (false):

_____ 1. The main point of the second paragraph is that several methods help people deal effectively with the physical tension produced by stress.

_____ 2. In the section "Solving the Problem," the main point is that people should avoid focusing on their emotions and work on solving the problem instead.

_____ 3. The main point of the entire section "Rethinking the Problem" is that three cognitive methods are helpful in dealing with stressful situations.

_____ 4. The main point of "Reappraising the Situation" is that thinking about a situation in a different way can lead to more positive feelings about it.

CHECK YOUR COMPREHENSION   MyReadingLab™

After reading the selection, answer the first item in your own words and answer the subsequent questions with *a, b, c,* or *d.* To help you analyze your strengths and weaknesses, the question types are indicated.

Main Idea

Complete this **Exercise** on **myreadinglab.com**

1. Who or what is the topic? ————————————————————

————————————————————————————————————

What is the main idea the author is trying to convey about the topic? ————

————————————————————————————————————

————————————————————————————————————

————————————————————————————————————

Detail ———— 2. According to this article, which response to a major stressor is likely to come first?

   a. Emotional expressions
   b. Problem-focused coping
   c. Learning from the experience
   d. Making social comparisons

Inference ———— 3. The article implies that

   a. everyone responds to stress in the same way.
   b. working on solutions to the problem usually comes after dealing with emotions.
   c. people should avoid emotion-focused coping.
   d. it is not possible to recover from extreme stress situations.

Inference ———— 4. Which of the following is most likely to help a person calm the physical effects of stress?

   a. Recognizing that others have worse worries
   b. Reappraising the situation
   c. Talking about what happened
   d. A hug or soothing touch

Inference ———— 5. What is the most likely reason the author included the story about Simi Linton?

   a. Because she is a friend of the author
   b. To show that learning about your situation can relieve stress
   c. To inspire others that one person was able to live happily and productively despite a devastating situation
   d. To entertain the reader with a personal victory over tragedy

Detail ———— 6. The section on "Rethinking the Problem" expands on

   a. the physiological effects of stress.

    b. problem-focused coping.

    c. emotion-focused coping.

    d. the level of stress the person is experiencing.

Detail _____ 7. Which of the following is NOT mentioned as a way of reducing physiological symptoms of stress?

    a. mindfulness meditation

    b. exercise

    c. prayer

    d. a hot bath

Detail _____ 8. Finding a greater appreciation of life after the loss of a loved one would be an example of

    a. emotion-focused coping.

    b. mindfulness meditation.

    c. learning from the experience.

    d. physiological arousal.

Inference _____ 9. Based on the article, which of the following would be an ineffective and perhaps even harmful attempt to manage stress?

    a. Avoiding thinking about the situation

    b. Taking a walk

    c. Expressing feelings in a journal

    d. Recognizing that others have worse situations

Inference _____ 10. Interviewing Simi Linton or reading a book about her experience would be an example of which method of coping with stress?

    a. Addressing physiological tension

    b. Emotion-focused coping

    c. Reappraising the situation

    d. Making social comparisons

Answer the following with *T* (true) or *F* (false).

Inference _____ 11. Simi Linton probably never felt hopeless or helpless to deal with her situation.

Inference _____ 12. Information in this article explains why a person who suffers a life-changing disease or injury might decide to become a doctor or nurse.

Detail _____ 13. According to the article, finding some purpose in a difficult situation can slow the course of disease.

Detail _____ 14. According to this article, most people who are under stress do not become ill as a result.

Detail _____ 15. Seeking professional therapy is not mentioned as a way of coping with serious stressful situations.

BUILD YOUR VOCABULARY   MyReadingLab™

Complete
this **Exercise** on
myreadinglab.com

According to the way the italicized word was used in the selection, indicate *a*, *b*, *c*, or *d* for the word or phrase that gives the best definition. The number in parentheses indicates the line of the passage in which the word is located.

_____ 1. "feeling *optimistic*" (2)
  a. negative
  b. discouraged
  c. doubtful
  d. hopeful

_____ 2. "manage to *cope*" (4)
  a. carry on
  b. suffer
  c. collapse
  d. give up

_____ 3. "the *physiological* tension" (5)
  a. relating to the body
  b. relating to the mind
  c. relating to emotions
  d. relating to psychological health

_____ 4. "emotional *tranquility*" (10)
  a. stability
  b. upset
  c. unrest
  d. peacefulness

_____ 5. "effective *buffer*" (12)
  a. attack
  b. explanation
  c. protection
  d. definition

_____ 6. "in the same *predicament*" (39)
  a. flow
  b. situation
  c. class
  d. group

_____ 7. "*Reappraising* the situation" (48)
  a. refusing
  b. re-examining
  c. previewing
  d. pretesting

_____ 8. "emerge from *adversity*" (54)
  a. success
  b. opportunity
  c. difficulty
  d. hospital

_____ 9. "a *longitudinal* study" (61)
  a. short
  b. long-term
  c. scientific
  d. detailed

_____ 10. "recently *bereaved*" (62)
  a. suffered the death of a loved one
  b. fallen in love
  c. married
  d. in an argument

Concept Prep for Psychology

A Sampling of Careers in Psychology

Most careers in psychology require at least a bachelor's degree. Many require a master's degree or doctorate.
- Social worker
- Health psychologist
- Criminal psychologist
- Industrial–organizational psychologist
- Child psychologist

What is classical conditioning?

Classical conditioning is the learning that takes place when a subject is taught, or conditioned, to make a new response to a neutral stimulus. This is illustrated by the research of *Ivan Pavlov*, a Russian scientist in the late nineteenth century. Pavlov was studying the basic processes of digestion, focusing on salivation in dogs. Because salivation is a *reflex*, it is an unlearned, automatic response in dogs. When presented with food, dogs will automatically salivate. As his research progressed, Pavlov noticed that the dogs would salivate at the sight of the assistant who delivered the food. At this point, Pavlov decided to investigate learning.

Pavlov reasoned that no learning was involved in the dog's automatic salivation (the *unconditioned response*) when presented with food (the *unconditioned stimulus*). He wondered, however, if he could teach the dogs to salivate at the sound of a bell. To investigate this, Pavlov decided to pair the sound of a bell with the presentation of the food—sound first, food second. The bell alone was a *neutral stimulus* that had never before caused salivation. After a number of *trials* (presenting sound and food together), the dogs became conditioned to associate the sound of the bell with the food. The dogs soon would salivate at the sound, even when the food was withheld. Learning had taken place; Pavlov had taught the dogs to react to a neutral stimulus. Once learning or conditioning had taken place, the sound became a *conditioned stimulus* and the salivation became a *conditioned response*. To take this experiment a step further, if the sound is consistently presented without food, the salivation response will gradually weaken until the dogs completely stop salivating at the sound of the bell *(extinction)*. Pavlov's work on animals and learning laid the groundwork for the American behaviorists of the twentieth century.

What is behaviorism?

At the beginning of the twentieth century, many American psychologists disagreed with Freud's psychoanalytical approach. They wanted to measure behavior in the laboratory and explain personality in terms of learning theories and observable behaviors. *B. F. Skinner* was a leader in this new movement. He borrowed from Pavlov's work and conducted research on operant conditioning.

Skinner posed questions such as, What are your beliefs about rewards and punishments? Do consequences affect your behaviors? Are you a reflection of your positive and negative experiences? Skinner believed that consequences shape behavior and that your personality is merely a reflection of your many learned behaviors.

Two pigeons seek food in a box developed by psychologist B. F. Skinner as part of his operant conditioning research.
Bettmann/Corbis

Skinner demonstrated *operant conditioning* (behaviors used to operate something) "by putting a rat inside a small box that came to be known as a *"Skinner box."* The rat explored the box until eventually it found that it could make food appear by pressing a lever. The rat enjoyed the food and dramatically increased the lever pressings. The food was a *positive reinforcer* for the lever pressing. In other words, the food reinforced the behavior and increased it. To stop the lever-pressing behavior *(extinction)*, the rat was given a shock each time the lever was touched. The shock was a *negative reinforcer*. Rewards are positive reinforcers, and punishments are negative reinforcers.

Behavior modification, a type of *behavior therapy*, uses the principles of classical and operant conditioning to increase desired behaviors and decrease problem behaviors. You can use these principles to train a pet, stop a smoking habit, or overcome a fear of flying. Does the desire to make a good grade (reward) affect your studying behavior? Skinner would say yes.

REVIEW QUESTIONS

After studying the material, answer the following questions:

1. Who was Ivan Pavlov? _____

   _____

2. What is a reflex? _____

   _____

3. What is a neutral stimulus? _____

   _____

4. Why is the response to the food called unconditioned? _____

   _____

5. What is a conditioned stimulus? _____

   _____

6. What is extinction? _____

7. How did B. F. Skinner differ from Freud? _____

   _____

8. How does operant conditioning differ from classical conditioning? _____

   _____

9. What is the role of a positive reinforcer? _____

   _____

10. In behavior modification, what makes you want to change behaviors?

   _____

Your instructor may choose to give a true-false review of these psychology concepts.

PREVIEW the next selection to predict its purpose and organization and to formulate your learning plan.

Activate Schema

What is the proper ethical response to encountering a seriously injured person?
Why do teens join street gangs?
What kind of violence is prevalent among urban street gangs?

Establish a Purpose for Reading

Why is someone on the sidewalk, bleeding? In this story, read about the fatal consequences of an act of gang violence with the intention of discovering the author's unstated message about gang culture in our society. As you read, be aware of the author's use of symbolism, and note the way the rainy setting and the reactions of other characters contribute to the story's mood and the main character's realizations.

Increase Word Knowledge

What do you know about these words?

scripted	excruciating	clutching	rumble	lurched
soothing	relentless	foraging	loathing	hysterically

Your instructor may give a true-false vocabulary review before or after reading.

Integrate Knowledge While Reading

Questions have been inserted in the margins to stimulate your thinking while reading. Remember to

Predict	Picture	Relate	Monitor	Correct	Annotate

((•─ **Scan this QR Code to hear this reading**

ON THE SIDEWALK, BLEEDING

The boy lay on the sidewalk bleeding in the rain. He was sixteen years old, and he wore a bright purple silk jacket, and the lettering across the back of the jacket read THE ROYALS. The boy's name was Andy, and the name was delicately scripted in black thread on the front of the jacket, just over the heart. ANDY.

5   He had been stabbed ten minutes ago. The knife entered just below his rib cage and had been drawn across his body violently, tearing a wide gap in his flesh. He lay on the sidewalk with the March rain drilling his jacket and drilling his body and

washing away the blood that poured from his open wound. He had known excruciating pain when the knife had torn across his body, and then sudden comparative
10 relief when the blade was pulled away. He had heard the voice saying, "That's for
you, Royal!" and then the sound of footsteps hurrying into the rain, and then he had
fallen to the sidewalk, clutching his stomach, trying to stop the flow of blood.

Why would the author choose the name Royal?

   He tried to yell for help, but he had no voice. He did not know why his voice
had deserted him, or why the rain had become so steadily fierce, or why there was
15 an open hole in his body from which his life ran redly, steadily. It was 11:13 P.M., but
he did not know the time.

   There was another thing he did not know.

   He did not know he was dying. He lay on the sidewalk, bleeding, and he thought
only: *That was a fierce rumble. They got me good that time*, but he did not know

Why are these words in italics?

20 he was dying. He would have been frightened had he known. In his ignorance he lay
bleeding and wishing he could cry out for help, but there was no voice in his throat.
There was only the bubbling of blood from between his lips whenever he opened his
mouth to speak. He lay in his pain, waiting, waiting for someone to find him.

   He could hear the sound of automobile tires hushed on the rain-swept streets,
25 far away at the other end of the long alley. He lay with his face pressed to the sidewalk, and he could see the splash of neon far away at the other end of the alley,
tinting the pavement red and green, slickly brilliant in the rain.

   He wondered if Laura would be angry.

   He had left the jump to get a package of cigarettes. He had told her he would
30 be back in a few minutes, and then he had gone downstairs and found the candy
store closed. He knew that Alfredo's on the next block would be open until at least
two, and he had started through the alley, and that was when he had been ambushed.

   He could hear the faint sound of music now, coming from a long, long way off.
He wondered if Laura was dancing, wondered if she had missed him yet. Maybe she
35 thought he wasn't coming back. Maybe she thought he'd cut out for good. Maybe

Gang members flash hand signals.
Hector Mata/AFP/Getty Images

she had already left the jump and gone home. He thought of her face, the brown eyes and the jet-black hair, and thinking of her he forgot his pain a little, forgot that blood was rushing from his body.

40 Someday he would marry Laura. Someday he would marry her, and they would have a lot of kids, and then they would get out of the neighborhood. They would move to a clean project in the Bronx, or maybe they would move to Staten Island. When they were married, when they had kids . . .

He heard footsteps at the other end of the alley, and he lifted his cheek from the sidewalk and looked into the darkness and tried to cry out, but again there was only 45 a soft hissing bubble of blood on his mouth.

The man came down the alley. He had not seen Andy yet. He walked, and then stopped to lean against the brick of the building, and then walked again. He saw Andy then and came toward him, and he stood over him for a long time, the minutes ticking, ticking, watching him and not speaking.

50 Then he said, "What's a matter, buddy?"

Andy could not speak, and he could barely move. He lifted his face slightly and looked up at the man, and in the rain-swept alley he smelled the sickening odor of alcohol and realized the man was drunk. He did not know he was dying, and so he felt only mild disappointment that the man who found him was drunk.

55 The man was smiling.

"Did you fall down, buddy?" he asked. "You mus' be as drunk as I am." He grinned, seemed to remember why he had entered the alley in the first place, and said, "Don' go 'way. I'll be ri' back."

The man lurched away. Andy heard his footsteps, and then the sound of the man 60 colliding with a garbage can, and some mild swearing, and then the sound of the man urinating, lost in the steady wash of the rain. He waited for the man to come back.

It was 11:39.

When the man returned, he squatted alongside Andy. He studied him with drunken dignity.

65 "You gonna catch cold there," he said. "What's the matter? You like layin' in the wet?"

Andy could not answer. The man tried to focus his eyes on Andy's face. The rain spattered around them.

"You like a drink?"

70 Andy shook his head.

How was the drunk compassionate?

"I gotta bottle. Here," the man said. He pulled a pint bottle from his inside jacket pocket. He uncapped it and extended it to Andy. Andy tried to move, but pain wrenched him back flat against the sidewalk.

"Take it," the man said. He kept watching Andy. "Take it." When Andy did not 75 move, he said, "Nev' mind, I'll have one m'self." He tilted the bottle to his lips, and then wiped the back of his hand across his mouth. "You too young to be drinkin' anyway. Should be 'shamed of yourself, drunk and layin' in a alley, all wet. Shame on you. I gotta good mind to call a cop."

Andy nodded. Yes, he tried to say. Yes, call a cop. Please. Call one.

80 "Oh, you don' like that, huh?" the drunk said. "You don' wanna cop to fin' you all drunk an' wet in an alley, huh: Okay, buddy. This time you get off easy." He got to his feet. "This time you lucky," he said again. He waved broadly at Andy, and then almost lost his footing. "S'long, buddy," he said.

Wait, Andy thought. *Wait, please, I'm bleeding.*

85   "S'long," the drunk said again, "I see you aroun'," and then he staggered off up the alley.

     Andy lay and thought: *Laura, Laura. Are you dancing?*

     The couple came into the alley suddenly. They ran into the alley together, running from the rain, the boy holding the girl's elbow, the girl spreading a newspaper over her

90 head to protect her hair. Andy lay crumpled on the pavement and he watched them run into the alley laughing, and then duck into the doorway not ten feet from him.

     "Man, what rain!" the boy said. "You could drown out there."

     "I have to get home," the girl said. "It's late, Freddie. I have to get home."

     "We got time," Freddie said. "Your people won't raise a fuss if you're a little late.

95 Not with this kind of weather."

     "It's dark," the girl said, and she giggled.

     "Yeah," the boy answered, his voice very low.

     "Freddie? . . ."

     "Um?"

100   "You're . . . standing very close to me."

     "Um."

     There was a long silence. Then the girl said, "Oh," only that single word, and Andy knew she had been kissed, and he suddenly hungered for Laura's mouth. It was then that he wondered if he would ever kiss Laura again. It was then that he

105 wondered if he was dying.

     No, he thought, *I can't be dying, not from a little street rumble, not from just being cut. Guys get cut all the time in rumbles. I can't be dying. No, that's stupid. That don't make any sense at all.*

     "You shouldn't," the girl said.

110   "Why not?"

     "I don't know."

     "Do you like it?"

     "Yes."

     "So?"

115   "I don't know."

     "I love you, Angela," the boy said.

     "I love you, too, Freddie," the girl said, and Andy listened and thought: *I love you, Laura. Laura, I think maybe I'm dying. Laura, this is stupid but I think maybe I'm dying. Laura, I think I'm dying.*

120   He tried to speak. He tried to move. He tried to crawl toward the doorway where he could see two figures embrace. He tried to make a noise, a sound, and a grunt came from his lips, and then he tried again, and another grunt came, a low animal grunt of pain.

     "What was that?" the girl said, suddenly alarmed, breaking away from the boy.

     "I don't know," he answered.

125   "Go look, Freddie."

     "No. Wait."

     Andy moved his lips again. Again the sound came from him.

     "Freddie!"

     "What?"

130   "I'm scared."

     "I'll go see," the boy said.

     He stepped into the alley. He walked over to where Andy lay on the ground. He stood over him, watching him.

"You all right?" he asked.

135 "What is it?" Angela said from the doorway.

"Somebody's hurt," Freddie said.

"Let's get out of here," Angela said.

"No. Wait a minute." He knelt down beside Andy. "You cut?" he asked.

Andy nodded. The boy kept looking at him. He saw the lettering on the jacket
140 then. THE ROYALS. He turned to Angela.

"He's a Royal," he said.

"Let's . . . what . . . what . . . do you want to do, Freddie?"

"I don't know. I don't know. I don't want to get mixed up in this. He's a Royal.
We help him, and the Guardians'll be down on our necks. I don't want to get mixed
145 up in this, Angela."

"Is he . . . is he hurt bad?"

"Yeah, it looks that way."

"What shall we do?"

"I don't know."

150 "We can't leave him here in the rain," Angela hesitated. "Can we?"

"If we get a cop, the Guardians'll find out who," Freddie said. "I don't know,
Angela. I don't know."

Angela hesitated a long time before answering. Then she said, "I want to go
home, Freddie. My people will begin to worry."

155 "Yeah," Freddie said. He looked at Andy again. "You all right?" he asked. Andy
lifted his face from the sidewalk, and his eyes said: *Please, please help me*, and
maybe Freddie read what his eyes were saying, and maybe he didn't.

Behind him, Angela said, "Freddie, let's get out of here! Please!" There was urgency in her voice, urgency bordering on the edge of panic. Freddie stood up. He
160 looked at Andy again, and then mumbled, "I'm sorry." He took Angela's arm and
together they ran towards the neon splash at the other end of the alley.

Why, they're afraid of the Guardians, Andy thought in amazement. *But why
should they be? I wasn't afraid of the Guardians. I never turkeyed out of a rumble
with the Guardians. I got heart. But I'm bleeding.*

165 The rain was soothing somehow. It was a cold rain, but his body was hot all over,
and the rain helped cool him. He had always liked rain. He could remember sitting
in Laura's house one time, the rain running down the windows, and just looking out
over the street, watching the people running from the rain. That was when he'd first
joined the Royals.

170 He could remember how happy he was when the Royals had taken him. The
Royals and the Guardians, two of the biggest. He was a Royal. There had been meaning to the title.

Now, in the alley, with the cold rain washing his hot body, he wondered about
the meaning. If he died, he was Andy. He was not a Royal. He was simply Andy, and
175 he was dead. And he wondered suddenly if the Guardians who had ambushed him
and knifed him had ever once realized he was Andy. Had they known that he was
Andy or had they simply known that he was a Royal wearing a purple silk jacket?
Had they stabbed *him*, Andy, or had they only stabbed the jacket and the title and
what good was the title if you were dying?

180 *I'm Andy*, he screamed wordlessly, *For Christ's sake, I'm Andy.*

An old lady stopped at the other end of the alley. The garbage cans were stacked
there, beating noisily in the rain. The old lady carried an umbrella with broken ribs,
carried it with all the dignity of a queen. She stepped into the mouth of the alley,

What would you have done at this point? What is ethical?

SELECTION 2

shopping bag over one arm. She lifted the lids of the garbage cans delicately, and she
185 did not hear Andy grunt because she was a little deaf and because the rain was beating a steady relentless tattoo on the cans. She had been searching and foraging for the
better part of the night. She collected her string and her newspapers, and an old hat
with a feather on it from one of the garbage cans, and a broken footstool from another of the cans. And then delicately she replaced the lids and lifted her umbrella
190 high and walked out of the alley mouth with a queenly dignity. She had worked
quickly and soundlessly, and now she was gone.

The alley looked very long now. He could see people passing at the other end of
it, and he wondered who the people were, and he wondered if he would ever get to
know them, wondered who it was of the Guardians who had stabbed him, who had
195 plunged the knife into his body.

"That's for you, Royal!" the voice had said, and then the footsteps, his arms being released by the others, the fall to the pavement. "That's for you, Royal!" Even in
his pain, even as he collapsed, there had been some sort of pride in knowing he was
a Royal. Now there was no pride at all. With the rain beginning to chill him, with the
200 blood pouring steadily between his fingers, he knew only a sort of dizziness. He
could only think: *I want to be Andy.*

It was not very much to ask of the world.

He watched the world passing at the other end of the alley. The world didn't
know he was Andy. The world didn't know he was alive. He wanted to say, "Hey, I'm
205 alive! Hey, look at me! I'm alive! Don't you know I'm alive? Don't you know I exist?"

He felt weak and very tired. He felt alone, and wet and feverish and chilled, and
he knew he was going to die now, and the knowledge made him suddenly sad. He
was not frightened. For some reason, he was not frightened. He was filled with an
overwhelming sadness that his life would be over at sixteen. He felt all at once as if
210 he had never done anything, never seen anything, never been anywhere. There were
so many things to do, and he wondered why he'd never thought of them before,
wondered why the rumbles and the jumps and the purple jackets had always seemed
so important to him before, and now they seemed like such small things in a world
he was missing, a world that was rushing past at the other end of the alley.

215 *I don't want to die*, he thought. *I haven't lived yet.*

It seemed very important to him that he take off the purple jacket. He was very
close to dying, and when they found him, he did not want them to say, "Oh, it's a
Royal." With great effort, he rolled over onto his back. He felt the pain tearing at his
stomach when he moved, a pain he did not think was possible. But he wanted to
220 take off the jacket. If he never did another thing, he wanted to take off the jacket.
The jacket had only one meaning now, and that was a very simple meaning.

If he had not been wearing the jacket, he wouldn't have been stabbed. The knife
had not been plunged in hatred of Andy. The knife hated only the purple jacket. The
jacket was a stupid meaningless thing that was robbing him of his life. He wanted the
225 jacket off his back. With an enormous loathing, he wanted the jacket off his back.

He lay struggling with the shiny wet material. His arms were heavy; pain ripped
fire across his body whenever he moved. But he squirmed and fought and twisted
until one arm was free and then the other, and then he rolled away from the jacket
and lay quite still, breathing heavily, listening to the sound of his breathing and the
230 sounds of the rain and thinking: *Rain is sweet, I'm Andy.*

She found him in the doorway a minute past midnight. She left the dance to
look for him, and when she found him, she knelt beside him and said, "Andy, it's me,
Laura."

Does Andy deserve to die? How is his life wasted?

What is the author's view of gang culture?

He did not answer her. She backed away from him, tears springing into her eyes,
235 and then she ran from the alley hysterically and did not stop running until she found
a cop.

And now, standing with the cop, she looked down at him, and the cop rose and
said, "He's dead," and all the crying was out of her now. She stood in the rain and said
nothing, dead boy on the pavement, looking at the purple jacket that rested a foot
240 away from his body.

The cop picked up the jacket and turned it over in his hands.

"A Royal, huh?" he said.

The rain seemed to beat more steadily now, more fiercely.

She looked at the cop and, very quietly, she said, "His name is Andy."
245 The cop slung the jacket over his arm. He took out his black pad, and he flipped
it open to a blank page.

What happens next?

"A Royal," he said.

Then he began writing.

(3,040 words)

—Evan Hunter
Happy New Year, Herbie, and Other Stories

Recall

Stop to self-test, relate, and react.

Your instructor may choose to give you a true-false comprehension review.

WRITE ABOUT THE SELECTION   MyReadingLab™

Complete
this **Exercise** on
myreadinglab.com

How do Andy's thoughts of his own life evolve from the beginning to the end of the
story?

Response Suggestion: Use the italicized thoughts to trace Andy's emotional journey.

SKILL DEVELOPMENT: FIND THE MAIN IDEA

Answer the following with *T* (true) or *F* (false):

_____ 1. One of the central themes of this story is that Andy initially thought
the jacket gave him identity, but he learned instead that it robbed
him of his identity.

_____ 2. The main point of the story is that Andy could have lived if others
had helped him.

_____ 3. The fact that the murder happened in March is a major detail.

CHECK YOUR COMPREHENSION   MyReadingLab™

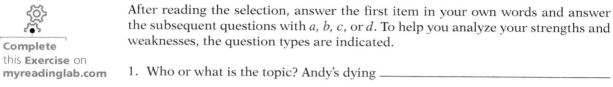

Complete
this **Exercise** on
myreadinglab.com

After reading the selection, answer the first item in your own words and answer the subsequent questions with *a, b, c,* or *d.* To help you analyze your strengths and weaknesses, the question types are indicated.

Main Idea

1. Who or what is the topic? Andy's dying _____

   What is the main idea the author is trying to convey about the topic?_____

   _____

Detail _____ 2. All of the following are true about Andy's jacket *except*

   a. it was purple.
   b. *The Royals* was written on the back.
   c. *Andy* was written on the left side of the front.
   d. it was torn in the back from the stab wounds.

Inference _____ 3. The reader can assume that the primary reason Andy was stabbed was because

   a. he was threatening a member of the Guardian gang.
   b. he was wearing a jacket that said *The Royals*.
   c. he witnessed Guardians engaged in illegal activity in the alley.
   d. he was dating a girlfriend of the Guardians.

Inference _____ 4. The reader can conclude that the drunk

   a. thought he was helping Andy.
   b. was afraid and did not want to help Andy.
   c. understood that Andy was dying.
   d. saw the blood and left.

Inference _____ 5. The reader can conclude that Angela and Freddie

   a. would not have called the police if Andy did not have the jacket.
   b. recognized Andy from the dance.
   c. feared retribution from the Guardians.
   d. contacted Laura so that she could find Andy.

Inference _____ 6. The reader can conclude all the following about the old lady *except*

   a. she never heard Andy.
   b. she was salvaging items from trash, as if poor or homeless.
   c. the author felt she carried herself with dignity despite her actions.
   d. she saw trouble and wanted no involvement.

Inference _____ 7. The author suggests that the person who could most accurately be called a coward in the story is

   a. the drunk.
   b. the old lady.
   c. Freddie.
   d. Laura.

SELECTION 2

Inference _____ 8. The author suggests that Andy took off the jacket because

    a. he did not want Laura to find him wearing the jacket.
    b. he wanted other members of the Royals to be proud of him.
    c. he wanted to reclaim his personal identity.
    d. as a sign of honor, he wanted to avoid implicating gang members in his death.

Inference _____ 9. The author suggests all the following about the cop *except*

    a. he recognized Andy as a person.
    b. he recorded the death as a meaningless gang killing.
    c. he was familiar with the activities of the gangs.
    d. he was not surprised to find a dead boy in the alley.

Inference _____ 10. The author suggests that Andy's anger at his death was directed primarily toward

    a. the Guardians.
    b. the Royals.
    c. himself.
    d. Angela and Freddie.

Answer the following with *T* (true) or *F* (false):

Inference _____ 11. The jacket was first a symbol of inclusion for Andy and then it became a symbol of meaningless death.

Inference _____ 12. According to the story, the time that elapsed from the stabbing until Andy was found by Laura was 58 minutes.

Detail _____ 13. Andy cut through the alley because it was the shortest way to the candy store, which was open until 2:00.

Inference _____ 14. The author suggests that there are other gangs in the area besides the Guardians and the Royals.

Inference _____ 15. As Andy got closer to death, he thought more about his wasted life and less about Laura.

BUILD YOUR VOCABULARY   MyReadingLab™

Complete this **Exercise** on **myreadinglab.com**

According to the way the italicized word was used in the selection, select *a, b, c,* or *d* for the word or phrase that gives the best definition. The number in parentheses indicates the line of the passage in which the word is located.

_____ 1. "*scripted* in black thread" (3)
   a. painted
   b. carved
   c. blocked
   d. handwritten

_____ 2. "known *excruciating* pain" (8–9)
   a. immediate
   b. humiliating
   c. agonizing
   d. tantalizing

_____ 3. "*clutching* his stomach" (12)
   a. tightly holding
   b. scratching
   c. tearing
   d. skinning

_____ 4. "fierce *rumble*" (19)
   a. knife
   b. gang member
   c. gang fight
   d. gang order

_____ 5. "man *lurched* away" (59)
   a. sneaked
   b. staggered
   c. ran
   d. excused himself

_____ 6. "rain was *soothing*"(165)
   a. cold
   b. endless
   c. calming
   d. irritating

_____ 7. "steady *relentless* tattoo" (186)
   a. noisy
   b. ugly
   c. rhythmical
   d. persistent

_____ 8. "*foraging* for the better part" (186)
   a. singing
   b. searching for food
   c. speaking aloud
   d. hiding

_____ 9. "enormous *loathing*" (226)
   a. hatred
   b. eagerness
   c. strain
   d. energy

_____ 10. "ran from the alley *hysterically*" (235)
   a. quickly
   b. fearfully
   c. sadly
   d. frantically

SELECTION 2

119

Concept Prep for Literature

A Sampling of Careers for English Majors

A bachelor's degree in English serves as a strong base for many careers in which a command of oral and written language is necessary. Some careers may also require post-graduate degrees.

- Announcer
- Editor
- Attorney
- Broadcaster
- Journalist
- Librarian

What is literature?

Literature, the art form of language, is invented from the author's imagination. The purpose is to entertain an audience, to explore the human condition, and to reveal universal truths through shared experiences. As a reader, you are allowed inside the minds of characters, and you learn about life as the characters live it. After reading, you are enriched. Literature includes four categories, or *genres*: essays, fiction, poetry, and drama. Although the four genres differ in intent, they share many of the same elements.

What are literary elements?

Plot. The *plot* describes the action in a story, play, or epic poem. It is a sequence of incidents or events.

Events in the story build progressively to reveal conflict to the reader. The *conflict* is a struggle or a clash of ideas, desires, or actions. Conflicts can exist between the main character and another character, external forces, or within the character.

As the plot moves forward, the *suspense* builds. The conflict intensifies to a peak, or *climax*, which comes near the end of the story and is the turning point. The *denouement* is the outcome of conflicts. Then the action falls and leads to a *resolution*, which answers any remaining questions.

Characters. In literature you are told what characters think and feel. Thus, by the experience of "living through" significant events with the character, you are better able to understand the complexities of human nature.

Point of View. The *point of view* in literature is not defined as bias or opinion. Rather, it describes who tells the story. It can be in *first person*, as the *I* in a diary; *second person*, using the word *you*; or most commonly, *third person*, in which the author is the all-knowing observer.

Tone. The *tone* is the writer's attitude toward the subject or the audience. Word clues may suggest that the author is being humorous. Cutting remarks, on the other hand, may suggest *sarcasm*. The author's emotional and intellectual attitude toward the subject also describes the *mood*, or overall feeling of the work.

Setting. All stories exist in a time and place. Details must be consistent with the setting or else they distract your attention. The *setting* is the backdrop for the story and the playground for the characters.

Figures of Speech and Symbolism. Literary writing appeals to the five senses and, unlike scientific or academic writing, uses images to convey a figurative or symbolic meaning rather than an exact literal

Awarded the Nobel Prize for Literature in 1993, author Toni Morrison also won a Pulitzer Prize for her novel *Beloved*.
Evan Agostini/Getty Images

meaning. *Metaphors* and *similes* are the most common, and they both suggest a comparison of unlike things.

The imagery or *symbolism* in a story can be an object, action, person, place, or idea that carries a condensed and recognizable meaning. For example, an opened window might represent an opportunity for a new life.

Theme. The *theme* is the main idea or the heart and soul of the work. The theme is a central insight into life or universal truth. This message is never preached but is revealed to your emotions, senses, and imagination through powerful, shared experiences. The theme should not be reduced to a one-sentence moral such as "Honesty is the best policy" or "Crime does not pay." Instead, ask yourself, "What has the main character learned during the story?" or "What insight into life does the story reveal?"

REVIEW QUESTIONS

After studying the material, answer the following questions:

1. What is literature? _____

   _____

2. What is plot? _____

3. What is the climax of "On the Sidewalk, Bleeding"? _____

4. What is the resolution? _____

   _____

5. How do you learn about the characters in "On the Sidewalk, Bleeding"? _____

   _____

   _____

6. What is the most common point of view in a story? _____

7. How does the definition of *point of view* differ in literature and in the question "What is your point of view on cloning?" _____

   _____

8. What do you feel is the author's attitude toward the subject in "On the Sidewalk, Bleeding"? _____

   _____

9. What is the overriding symbol in "On the Sidewalk, Bleeding"? _____

   _____

10. What is the theme of a story? _____

    _____

Your instructor may choose to give a true-false review of these literary concepts.

SELECTION 3   Criminal Justice

PREVIEW the next selection to predict its purpose and organization and to formulate your learning plan.

Activate Schemata

Have you seen television programs or read novels that feature crimes solved with mathematical models? The idea is spreading and is the subject of research that bridges criminal justice, mathematics, sociology, and even anthropology.

Establish a Purpose for Reading

The research described in this selection holds promise for determining who is likely to have committed a crime. Read to find out how it works and why police departments and even advertisers would be interested in it.

Increase Word Knowledge

What do you know about these words?

algorithm	simulated	mimicked	perpetrator	rivalries
exploits	implications	nodes	hackers	anthropology

Your instructor may give a true-false vocabulary review before or after reading.

Integrate Knowledge While Reading

Questions have been inserted in the margins to stimulate your thinking while reading. Remember to

Predict	Picture	Relate	Monitor	Correct	Annotate

((•─ **Scan this QR Code to hear this reading**

FIGHTING VIOLENT GANG CRIME WITH MATH

University of California at Los Angeles (UCLA) mathematicians working with the Los Angeles Police Department to analyze crime patterns have designed a mathematical algorithm to identify street gangs involved in unsolved violent crimes. Their research is based on patterns of known criminal activity between gangs, and repre-
5   sents the first scholarly study of gang violence of its kind.

CREATION AND TESTING

What is an algorithm?

In developing their algorithm, the mathematicians analyzed more than 1,000 gang crimes and suspected gang crimes, about half of them unsolved, that occurred over a 10-year period in an East Los Angeles police district known as Hollenbeck, a small

That's a lot!

area in which there are some 30 gangs and nearly 70 gang rivalries.

10   To test the algorithm, the researchers created a set of simulated data that closely mimicked the crime patterns of the Hollenbeck gang network. They then dropped some of the key information out—the victim, the perpetrator or both—and tested how well the algorithm could calculate the missing information.

"If police believe a crime might have been committed by one of seven or eight
15   rival gangs, our method would look at recent historical events in the area and compute probabilities as to which of these gangs are most likely to have committed

Applied mathematics?

crime," said the study's senior author, Andrea Bertozzi, a professor of mathematics and director of applied mathematics at UCLA.

SELECTION 3

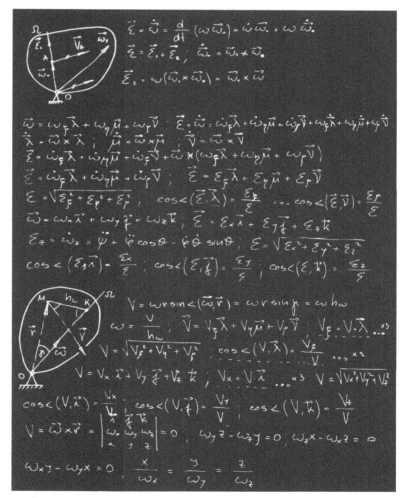

Mathematical algorithms are helping to address unsolved violent gang crime.
Eric Milos/Shutterstock

RESULTS

About 80 percent of the time, the mathematicians could narrow it down to three
20 gang rivalries that were most likely involved in a crime.

"Our algorithm placed the correct gang rivalry within the top three most likely
rivalries 80 percent of the time, which is significantly better than chance," said Martin
Short, a UCLA adjunct assistant professor of mathematics and co-author of the
study. "That narrows it down quite a bit, and that is when we don't know anything
25 about the crime victim or perpetrator."

A big improvement

The mathematicians also found that the correct gang was ranked No. 1—rather
than just among the top three—50 percent of the time, compared with just 17 percent by chance.

"We can do even better," Bertozzi said. "This is the first paper that takes this new
30 approach. We can improve on that 80 percent by developing more sophisticated
methods."

APPLICATIONS

"Our algorithm exploits gang activity patterns to produce the best probability of
which gang, or which three gangs, may have been responsible for the crimes," she
said. Police can investigates further when the gangs are narrowed down.

35 Bertozzi and her colleagues have been working with the LAPD on a variety of
classes of crime. The implications of the research go beyond fighting gangs and
beyond fighting crime.

"The algorithm we devised could apply to a much broader class of problems
that involve activity on social networks," Bertozzi said. "You have events—they could
40 be crimes or something else—that occur in a time series and a known network.
There is activity between nodes, in this case a gang attacking another gang. With
some of these activities, you know exactly who was involved and with others, you do
not. The challenge is how to make the best educated judgment as to who was
involved in the unknown activities. We believe there are a number of social net-
45 works that have this same kind of pattern."

Identifying hackers would be an example; helping businesses target advertising
to consumers who would be most interested in their products and services in a way
that would protect privacy would be another.

Can I think of other uses?

"An advertiser may not care who individual people are but just how they
50 behave," Bertozzi said. "Advertisers could target consumers by knowing their shopping behavior without knowing their identities."

The lead author of the study is Alexey Stomakhin, a UCLA doctoral student in
applied mathematics who worked for a year to design the algorithm that can fill in
the missing information.

THE BEST JOB IN THE WORLD

55 Bertozzi describes her work as "the best job in the world—working with great young
mathematicians and having an impact on society." She noted that UCLA is ranked
No. 2 in the U.S. in applied mathematics. Bertozzi is interested in applying mathematics to address practical problems that affect peoples' lives.

"Nowhere else are they doing research like this—only at UCLA," Short said.
60 Last year Bertozzi, Short and colleagues, including Jeffrey Brantingham in anthropology, reported a new mathematical model that allows them to analyze different
types of criminal "hotspots"—areas where many crimes occur, at least for a time.

SELECTION 3

Main Idea

The new research is federally funded by the National Science Foundation, the U.S. Army Research Office's mathematics divisions, the U.S. Office of Naval
65 Research, and the U.S. Air Force Office of Scientific Research.

(774 words)
—Stuart Wolpert,
UCLA Newsroom

Recall

Stop to talk, write, and think about the selection.

Your instructor may choose to give you a true-false comprehension review.

WRITE ABOUT THE SELECTION   MyReadingLab™

Complete
this **Exercise** on
myreadinglab.com

Bertozzi said that she has the best job in the world. Would you enjoy work like this? Or would you like to be on the receiving end of her work, using it to identify criminals or advertising targets? What does she love about her job? What makes a job appealing to you?

Response Suggestion: In one paragraph, use the reasons Bertozzi cites and expand on them to explain why someone might love that job. In a second paragraph, describe the kind of work you aim to do and the characteristics that you believe will make it "the best job in the world."

Summarize

Write a one-paragraph summary of this selection to serve as notes that would prepare you for a class discussion or a test.

SKILL DEVELOPMENT: FIND THE MAIN IDEA

Answer the following with *T* (true) or *F* (false):

_____ 1. The main point of the section "Creation and Testing" is that about half of the crimes used to develop this model were unsolved.

_____ 2. The main point of the "Results" section is that the algorithm worked well enough to be helpful in identifying gangs responsible for crimes.

_____ 3. The main point of "Applications" is that the algorithm can be useful not only in solving crimes but in other areas as well.

_____ 4. The main point of the entire selection is that mathematician Andrea Bertozzi loves her job.

CHECK YOUR COMPREHENSION MyReadingLab™

After reading the selection, answer the following questions with *a, b, c,* or *d.* To help you analyze your strengths and weaknesses, the question types are indicated.

Main Idea

⚙
Complete
this **Exercise** on
myreadinglab.com

SELECTION 3

1. Who or what is the topic? _____

_____

_____

What is the main idea the author is trying to convey about the topic? _____

_____

_____

_____

Detail _____ 2. What was the original purpose of this research?
 a. To identify the Los Angeles gangs responsible for crimes
 b. To help police identify computer hackers
 c. To arrest the leaders of violent gangs
 d. To make social comparisons

Inference _____ 3. It is reasonable to conclude from this article that
 a. the results of this research cannot be used in any other way than mentioned in the article.
 b. the results of research are sometimes useful for purposes other than originally intended.
 c. Bertozzi and her team will not do further research like this.
 d. research always achieves the intended purpose.

Inference _____ 4. Given information in the article, why would the researchers focus on the Hollenbeck area of East Los Angeles?
 a. It was chosen at random for research purposes.
 b. It was the only area approved by the LAPD.
 c. UCLA is located in that area.
 d. It appears to have a very heavy incidence of gang-related crime.

Inference _____ 5. The algorithm apparently could predict which gang committed a crime and
 a. the location of the crime.
 b. the time and place of the crime.
 c. the victim, or both the perpetrator and victim.
 d. the victim.

Detail _____ 6. The algorithm was based on what information?
 a. knowledge of the Hollenbeck streets
 b. police theories and recent events in the Hollenbeck area

c. known facts about gang members

d. information provided by gang members

Detail _____ 7. How often was the algorithm able to correctly identify the perpetrator?

a. 100 percent of the time

b. 80 percent of the time

c. 75 percent of the time

d. 50 percent of the time

Detail _____ 8. How often was the algorithm able to correctly narrow the gangs involved to three?

a. 100 percent of the time

b. 80 percent of the time

c. 75 percent of the time

d. 50 percent of the time

Inference _____ 9. Uses for the results of this research mentioned in this article include all of the following *except*

a. naming individuals who might like to buy certain products.

b. finding groups of consumers likely to be interested in certain products.

c. identifying hackers who manipulate computer information illegally.

d. identifying gangs likely to have committed a certain crime.

Detail _____ 10. Who funded this research?

a. the Los Angeles Police Department

b. the University of California at Los Angeles

c. various divisions of the federal government

d. Andrea Bertozzi, Martin Short, and Alexey Stomakhin

Answer the following with *T* (true) or *F* (false).

Inference _____ 11. The article implies that gang members assisted with this research.

Detail _____ 12. The algorithm did a better job of identifying the perpetrator than would happen by chance.

Inference _____ 13. If police use this algorithm, they do not have to do further investigation.

Detail _____ 14. A doctoral student designed the algorithm for this project.

Detail _____ 15. One reason Bertozzi enjoys her work is that it benefits society.

SELECTION 3

BUILD YOUR VOCABULARY MyReadingLab™

Complete
this **Exercise** on
myreadinglab.com

According to the way the italicized word was used in the selection, indicate *a, b, c,* or *d* for the word or phrase that gives the best definition. The number in parentheses indicates the line of the passage in which the word is located.

_____ 1. "a mathematical
algorithm" (3)
   a. a subject for study
   b. a college degree
   c. an answer to a
      problem
   d. procedure for solving
      a problem

_____ 2. "*simulated* data" (10)
   a. artificial
   b. authentic
   c. real
   d. genuine

_____ 3. "*mimicked* the crime
patterns" (11)
   a. changed
   b. released
   c. imitated
   d. viewed

_____ 4. "the *perpetrator*" (12)
   a. the police
   b. one who investigates a
      crime
   c. the victim of a crime
   d. one who commits a
      crime

_____ 5. "gang *rivalries*" (20)
   a. partnerships
   b. friendships
   c. competitions
   d. networks

_____ 6. "*exploits* gang activity
patterns" (32)
   a. misuses
   b. takes advantage of
   c. ignores
   d. benefits

_____ 7. "*implications* of the
research" (36)
   a. dangers
   b. significance
   c. errors
   d. details

_____ 8. "activity between
nodes" (41)
   a. swellings on a plant
   b. departments
   c. events, points of
      activity
   d. enlarged part of the
      body

_____ 9. "Identifying *hackers*" (46)
   a. manufacturers
   b. people who illegally
      access computer
      systems
   c. experts who provide
      computer help
   d. a beginner

_____ 10. "in *anthropology*" (60–61)
   a. the study of human
      beings
   b. the study of women
   c. the study of
      criminology
   d. the study of medicine

VOCABULARY BOOSTER

Who's Who in Medicine?

| **Suffixes** | *-ist, -ician:* "one who" | *-ologist:* "one who studies" |

- *dermatologist:* skin doctor (*derma*: skin)

  Dermatologists remove skin cancers.

- *internist:* medical doctor for internal organs (*internus*: inside)

  The *internist* will administer a series of tests to determine the cause of Ben's mysterious pain.

- *intern:* a medical school graduate serving an apprenticeship at a hospital

  The *interns* work under the close supervision of doctors on the staff.

- *gynecologist:* doctor for reproductive systems of women (*gyne*: women)

  The *gynecologist* recommended a Pap smear to check for cervical cancer.

- *obstetrician:* doctor who delivers babies (*obstetrix*: midwife)

  Many *obstetricians* are also gynecologists.

- *pediatrician:* doctor for children (*paidos*: children)

  Pediatricians sometimes use antibiotics to treat infections.

- *ophthalmologist* or *oculist:* doctor who performs eye surgery

  The *ophthalmologist* performed cataract surgery on the woman.

- *optometrist:* specialist for measuring vision

  An *optometrist* tests eyesight and fits glasses and contact lenses.

- *optician:* specialist who makes visual correction lenses for eyeglasses and contact lenses

  Opticians usually work behind the scene, often at an optometrist's office.

- *orthopedist:* doctor who corrects abnormalities in bones and joints (*orthos*: straight or correct)

  The *orthopedist* set up his practice near a ski area.

- *orthodontist:* dentist for straightening teeth

  Her braces had to be adjusted every six weeks by the *orthodontist*.

- *cardiologist:* heart doctor (*cardio*: heart)

  Cardiologists treat patients who have had heart attacks.

- *psychiatrist:* doctor for treating mental disorders (*psycho*: mind)

  The *psychiatrist* prescribed drugs for the treatment of depression.

- *psychologist:* counselor for treating mental disorders

The *psychologist* administered tests to determine the cause of the child's behavior.

- *neurologist:* doctor for disorders of the brain, spinal cord, and nervous system (*neuron:* nerve)

  Neurologists are searching for new treatments for patients who have suffered spinal cord injuries.

- *oncologist:* doctor for treating cancer and tumors (*onkos:* mass)

  The *oncologist* recommended various methods for dealing with the cancerous tumor.

- *urologist:* doctor specializing in the urinary tract (*ouro:* urine)

  The urologist was treating several patients for impotence.

- *podiatrist:* specialist in the care and treatment of the foot (*pod:* foot)

  The *podiatrist* knew the best way to deal with blisters, corns, and bunions.

- *anesthesiologist:* doctor who administers anesthesia to patients undergoing surgery (*anesthesia:* insensibility)

  Usually, a patient will meet the *anesthesiologist* just before surgery.

- *hematologist:* doctor who studies the blood and blood-forming organs (*hemat:* blood)

  A hematoma is treated by a *hematologist*.

- *radiologist:* doctor using radiant energy for diagnostic and therapeutic purposes (*radio:* radiant waves)

  After the removal of a cancerous tumor, further treatment by a *radiologist* is usually recommended.

Review

Part I

Indicate whether the following sentences are true (*T*) or false (*F*):

_____ 1. *Radiologists* are physicians who evaluate x-rays.

_____ 2. A *psychologist* is unable to prescribe medications for patients.

_____ 3. If a mental illness is suspected, a patient may be referred to a *psychiatrist*.

_____ 4. An *internist* is a medical school graduate serving an apprenticeship at a hospital.

_____ 5. *Dermatologists* recommend the daily use of sunscreen.

_____ 6. A *neurologist* specializes in the treatment of heart attacks.

_____ 7. Medical school is required in order to become an *optician*.

Main Idea

———— 8. *Pediatricians* examine babies.

———— 9. *Oncologists* specialize in eye treatment.

———— 10. A *hematologist* might help a patient whose blood fails to clot properly.

Part II

Choose the doctor from the boxed list that best fits the job description.

anesthesiologist	podiatrist	urologist	cardiologist	orthodontist
orthopedist	optometrist	obstetrician	intern	ophthalmologist

11. Performs eye surgery ————————————

12. Treats diseases of the foot ————————————

13. Delivers babies ————————————

14. Works with bones and joints ————————————

15. Treats disorders of the urinary tract ————————————

16. Administers anesthesia ————————————

17. Dispenses contact lenses ————————————

18. Treats heart problems ————————————

19. Corrects problems with teeth ————————————

20. Apprentice to physician or surgeon ————————————

Your instructor may choose to give a multiple-choice review.

CREDITS

Video screen captures reproduced with permission of BBC Motion Gallery Education: Creativity; TOMS Shoes: Changing the World; The Effects of Stress; The New Entrepreneur; DNA and the Criminal Justice System; Illiteracy in the United States; Global Warming; The Magic Number of Beauty; The American Diet.

Griffin, Ricky W., and Ronald J. Ebert. *Business*, 8th ed., © 2006, pp. 229, 89–90, 57, 572. Reproduced in print and electronic formats by permission of Pearson Education, Inc., Upper Saddle River, New Jersey.; Donatelle, Rebecca J. *Access to Health*, 8th ed. Copyright © 2004 by Pearson Education, Inc., publishing as Benjamin Cummings. Reprinted by permission of Pearson Education, Inc., Glenview, IL.; Pruitt, B. E. and Jane J. Stein. *Decisions for Healthy Living*. San Francisco: Pearson Benjamin Cummings, 2004. Reprinted by permission of the authors.; Wade, Carole, Tavris, Carol, *Psychology*, 10th, © 2011. Printed and Electronically reproduced by permission of Pearson Education, Inc., Upper Saddle River, New Jersey.; Donatelle, Rebecca J. *Access to Health*, 8th ed. Copyright © 2004 by Pearson Education, Inc., publishing as Benjamin Cummings. Reprinted by permission of Pearson Education, Inc., Glenview, IL.; Wade, Carole, Tavris, Carol, *Psychology*, 10th, © 2011. Printed and Electronically reproduced by permission of Pearson Education, Inc., Upper Saddle River, New Jersey.; Hunter, Evan. "On the Sidewalk, Bleeding" from *Happy New Year, Herbie, and Other Stories* by Evan Hunter. New York: Simon & Schuster, 1963. Reprinted by permission of Gelfman Schneider Literary Agents, Inc., as agent for Hui Corp.; By Stuart Wolpert / UCLA Newsroom.

Answer Key for Chapter 2, Main Idea, in *Bridge to College Reading*

What is a Topic?
Topic: Vegetables

Exercise 1: Identifying Topics
1. potatoes
2. precipitation
5. races

Exercise 2: Differentiating Topic, Main idea, and Supporting Details

Group 1:	a. Main Idea (MI)	b. Supporting Detail (SD)	c. Topic (T)	
Group 2:	a. SD	b. T	c. MI	d. SD
Group 3:	a. T	b. SD	c. SD	d. MI

Exercise 3: Discovering Topics and Main Ideas in Sentence Groups

Group 1: Sentence 3. Topic: Virtual Reality in Conquering Fear
Group 2: Sentence 1. Topic: Relationship between Brain Size and Intelligence
Group 3: Sentence 1. Topic: Factors in JetBlue's Success

Exercise 4: Locating Stated Main Ideas
1. Main Idea: People can recall information under hypnosis.
Details: 1. Police Use it to probe
       2. Children kidnapped from bus
       3. Driver saw license plate
       4. Recalled other numbers

2. Main Idea: Good evaluation is needed before and after data.
Details: 1. Not one shot on research
       2. Errors without comparisons
       3. Research results after campaign
       4. Research position prior to campaign

3. Details: 1. French against uniforms
       2. French against standing to eat
Main Idea: Disney adjusted to fit international tastes
       3. ditched dress code
       4. added wine and lowered fees

4. Main Idea: Use conflict resolution strategies
       Details: 1. Envision outcome
             2. Listen to other side
             3. Place in context
             4. Leave lines open for talk
     Main Idea: Use these four strategies

5. Unstated Main Idea: Boys wanted jobs on the river.
　　　　Details: 1. Became engineer
　　　　　　　　2. became mud clerks
　　　　　　　　3. became barkeeper
　　　　　　　　4. most wanted to be pilots for salary

Exercise 5:   Using Questions to Find Stated Main Ideas

Passage A:
1. Baseball in Japan vs. baseball in the U.S.A.
2. Holdouts are rare in Japan; players put team interests before their own; actions that take away from team peace are unwelcome.
3. The practice of group harmony makes Japanese baseball quite different from American baseball
4. Underline: first sentence

Passage B:
1. Factors influencing whether or not people help others.
2. Experiment with college males; students I other room faked seizure; speed with which participant reported emergency measured; 2- person group quickest to intervene.
3. The likelihood of intervention depended on the number of bystanders the participant thought were present.
4. Underline: "The likelihood of intervention depended…."

Passage C:
1. Language use of boys and girls
2. Talking is central to female friendships; activities are central to male friendship; boys play in larger, hierarchical groups; boys use language to achieve center state and establish rank.
3. Girls and boys use language differently in their sex-separate peer groups.
4. Underline: first sentence.

Exercise 6: Identifying Topics, Stated Main Ideas, and Details in Passages

Passage A
1. D   2. a. Minor   b. Major   c. Major   3. Underline: first sentence
Passage B
1. D   2. a. Major   b. Major   c. Minor   3. Underline: Last sentence.
Passage C.
1. D   2. a. Major   b. Major   c. Minor
3. Underline: "In freeing the defendant, the Supreme Court judged that the legal definition…."

Exercise 7: Determining Unstated Main Ideas

Group 1: Main Idea: Dangerous, newly emerging viruses present a global threat
Group 2:   Main Idea: Early presidents made major contributions that strengthened the presidency and the country.
Group 3: Main Idea: Use these 3 steps in making an effective sales presentation.

Exercise 8: Identifying Unstated Main ideas
Passage A:
1. C   2. a. Minor   b. Major   c. Major   3. A
Passage B:
1. B   2. a. Minor   b. Minor   c. Major   3. D
Passage C:
1. D   2. a. Minor   b. Major   c. Minor   3. C

Exercise 9: Writing Unstated Main Ideas

Passage A
1. Hispanic population growth
2. Hispanics 24.5% of population by 2050; annual growth rate of 2% until 2030 but never reached that level during baby boom
3. Demographers feel the rapid growth in the Hispanic population in the early 2000s is of enormous importance.

Passage B:
1. Cultural differences in business practices
2. American practices; Japanese and other Asian practices; South American practices
3. Business practices vary among cultures.

Passage C:
1. Similarities between twins.
2. "Jim twins" married, divorced, remarried women of same name; both had same habits, cars, hobbies, and medical histories; Stohr and Yufe had same traits and habits.
3. Studies show that identical twins, even those separated at birth, have amazing similarities.

Exercise 10: Getting the Main Idea of Longer Selections
Passage A:
1. It's about the benefits of sleep.
2. the last sentence.
3. Possible: Physical and Mental Benefits; REM sleep; non-REM sleep.
4. Sleep is vital for physical and mental health.

Passage B:
1. It suggests that there is some disagreement among scientists about animal intelligence.
2. Last sentence
3. 1- Cognitive ethology; 2 – Chimps think? 3 – Instinct or Thinking? 4 – Use of Tools

Passage C:
1. It's about immigration in the 1800s.
2. Possible: 1: Immigration Increase; 2: Immigration Causes; 3: Irish Famine; 4: German Hunger.
3. No, not completely.
4. A number of factors contributed to the large increase in European immigrants in the mid-1800s.
Exercise 11: Summarizing Passages (to be discussed in class.) Summarize Passage C in approximately 100 words or so.

Patterns of Organization

Learning Objectives

From this chapter, readers will learn to:

1 Recognize transitional words
2 Recognize patterns of organization
3 Recognize mixed patterns of organization

Heroes on Wheels (1985), Jane Wooster Scott. Oil on canvas. SuperStock.

TEXTBOOK ORGANIZATION: THE BIG PICTURE

The **pattern of organization** in a textbook is the presentation plan, format, or structure for the message. Why is it important to identify organizational patterns in textbooks and other pieces of writing? Basically, such patterns serve as the book's blueprint, showing the reader how the book was built. They signal how facts and ideas are presented. The number of details in a textbook can be over-whelming. Identifying the pattern of organization of a section or chapter can help you master the complexities of the material. If you know the pattern of organization, you can predict the format of upcoming information.

Although key transitional words can signal a particular pattern, the most important clue to the pattern is the main idea itself because it usually dictates the organizational pattern. Your aim as a reader is to identify the main idea. To accomplish that, be alert to the signal words, anticipate the overall pattern of organization, and place the major supporting details into the outline or pattern used by the author.

WHAT DO TRANSITIONAL WORDS DO?

Learning Objective 1

Recognize transitional words

Small words can carry a big load. A single word can signal the level of importance, a connection, or a direction of thought. For example, if a friend begins a sentence by saying "I owe you $100," would you prefer that the next word be *and* or that it be *but*? The word *and* signals addition and would give you high hopes for the return of your money. However, the word *but* signals a change of thought which, in this case, would be in a negative direction. If the next word were *first*, you would anticipate a sequence of events before repayment. If it were *consequently*, you would hope the positive result would be your $100.

Such words are **transitional words**—sometimes called *signal words*—that connect parts of sentences or whole sentences and lead you to anticipate either a continuation of or a change in thought. Transitions show the relationships of ideas within sentences, between sentences, and between paragraphs. Writers use transitions to keep their readers' comprehension on track and to guide them through the logic of the message. To avoid repetition, authors choose from a variety of signal words to indicate the transition of thought. These signal words or transitions can be categorized as shown in the following examples and in the Reader's .

Words That Signal Addition

in addition	moreover	furthermore	and	also	another

EXAMPLE

José was given a raise after six months at his job. *In addition*, he became eligible for health insurance benefits.

After causing a disturbance in the movie theater, Brian and his friends were asked to leave. *Furthermore*, they were barred from attending that theater ever again.

Words That Signal Examples or Illustrations

for example	for instance	to illustrate	such as	including

EXAMPLE

Traffic seems to be getting heavier. *For instance,* last year it took only twenty minutes to get to school, and now it takes thirty.

Some experts believe that a fetus in the womb can be affected by sounds *such as* classical music or the mother's voice.

Words That Signal Time or Sequence

first	second	finally	last	afterward	after	during
while	before	then	previously	until	now	next

EXAMPLE

Apply sunscreen while walking on the beach and *before* swimming in the surf. *Afterward,* reapply the sunscreen even if it is waterproof.

To build a good financial foundation, *first* pay yourself in the form of savings, and *then* pay your bills.

Words That Signal Comparison

similarly	likewise	in the same manner	like	as	just as	as well

EXAMPLE

If you treat someone with kindness, he or she will probably treat you in kind. *Likewise,* if you treat someone with disrespect, you will probably be disrespected.

Portland is a port city in Oregon; *similarly,* it is a seaport in Maine.

Words That Signal Contrast

however	but	nevertheless	whereas
on the contrary	conversely	yet	in contrast
even though	on the other hand	although	instead

EXAMPLE

Using a knife to cut a bagel can be dangerous to the fingers. *On the other hand,* using a bagel holder keeps fingers safe from the falling blade.

Today many families eat dinner separately and on the run, *whereas* in the past the family dinner hour was a time for bonding and an opportunity to instill values or share dreams.

Reader's TIP Signal Words for Transition

- **Addition:** in addition • furthermore • moreover
- **Examples:** for example • for instance • to illustrate • such as
- **Time:** first • second • finally • last • afterward
- **Comparison:** similarly • likewise • in the same manner
- **Contrast:** however • but • nevertheless • whereas • on the contrary
  • conversely • in contrast
- **Cause and Effect:** thus • consequently • therefore • as a result

Words That Signal Cause and Effect

thus	consequently	therefore	as a result
accordingly	because	so	hence

EXAMPLE

Because of his work to end apartheid in South Africa, Nelson Mandela spent twenty-seven years in prison. Upon his release, Mandela treated his oppressors with respect and worked to unite the country. *Consequently*, he shared a Nobel Peace Prize with then-president de Klerk.

There has been a severe shortage of rainfall this year. *Therefore*, we have instituted a ban on outdoor watering.

EXERCISE 1

Signal Words

Choose a signal word from the boxed lists to complete the sentences that follow.

however	for example	in addition	consequently	in the meantime

1. Forget the boring tourist narrative and turn walking around a city into a hip audio tour experience with Soundwalk podcasts. In New York, _____, you can pop in a fifty-minute podcast to explore Chinatown, the meat-packing district, or Wall Street.

2. The United States has an ever-increasing demand for oil. _____, we are researching alternative sources of energy, such as solar energy, to reduce our dependence on oil.

3. _____ to alternative energy research, we may begin drilling for oil on a small portion of our public lands to lessen our dependence on foreign sources of oil.

4. Drilling on public lands, _____, is not popular with environmentalists who believe the drilling cannot be done without spoiling the land.

5. _____, we can strive to be more fuel-efficient to help reduce our demand for energy.

| furthermore | for example | nevertheless | finally in contrast |

6. African American music in twentieth-century America evolved from ragtime, to jazz, to rhythm and blues, to soul, and _____, to rap.

7. The concert tickets were outrageously priced. _____, this was a once-in-a-lifetime opportunity, and other luxuries would have to be sacrificed to compensate for the expense.

8. Mardi Gras as celebrated in New Orleans is similar to Carnaval as celebrated throughout Latin America. Carnaval lasts for five days; _____, Mardi Gras lasts only one day.

9. Internet car sales, rather than hurting auto dealerships, have actually helped them. _____, most customers conduct research on the Web but still visit a dealer to actually buy automobiles. A well-informed consumer who is ready to purchase makes the salesperson's job easier.

10. Since Melissa failed to notify her parents that she had backed into another vehicle in the college parking lot, they were outraged to learn of the accident through a third party. _____, due to her lack of honesty, Melissa's parents decided that she would no longer be covered under their auto insurance policy.

PATTERNS OF ORGANIZATION IN TEXTBOOKS

Learning Objective 2

Recognize patterns of organization in textbooks

As transitional words signal connections and relationships of ideas within and among sentences, they also help signal the overall organizational pattern of the message. When you write, you choose a pattern for organizing your thoughts. That organizational pattern is probably dictated by the main idea of your message. Before beginning to write, you must ask, "If this is what I want to say, what is the best logical pattern to organize my message?"

The next exercise contains examples of the patterns of organization you will encounter in textbooks. Some are used much more frequently than others, and some are typical of particular disciplines. For example, history textbooks often use the patterns of time order and cause and effect. Management textbooks frequently use the simple listing pattern, whereas psychology textbooks make heavy use of the definition-and-example pattern. The Reader's Tip following the exercise lists each type of pattern of organization along with some related signal words.

BRAIN BOOSTER

Brains Like Patterns

Human brains are designed to notice patterns because patterns are how we make sense of the world. We learn through repeated experience that a toy pushed off the table falls to the floor, so we expect that to happen every time. When we see an incomplete circle, our brains attempt to complete it. If we miss a word in a spoken sentence, we fill in the blank with something that makes sense. Each time the pattern repeats, our neuronal network grows larger and stronger. Use this natural feature of your brain to your advantage when reading! Look for the pattern the author used to organize the information. When you see the pattern, you can make better sense of the author's message.

—*Adapted from* 12 Brain/Mind Learning Principles in Action: Developing Executive Functions of the Human Brain, *by Caine, Caine, McClintic, and Klimek*

EXERCISE 2

Patterns of Organization

Notice the graphic organizer that accompanies each pattern of organization described in the following sections. After reading each example, enter the key points into the blank graphic organizer to show that you understand the pattern.

Simple Listing

With **simple listing,** items are randomly listed in a series of supporting facts or details. These supporting elements are of equal value, and the order in which they are presented is of no importance. Changing the order of the items does not change the meaning of the paragraph.

Signal words, often used as transitional words to link ideas in a paragraph with a pattern of simple listing, include *in addition, also, another, several, for example, a number of.*

EXAMPLE

THE BIG FIVE

Although many theories of personality have been proposed, the most widely accepted theory today is the five-factor theory or "the Big Five," as it is sometimes called. This theory claims that characteristics of personality can be described by how an individual rates on dimensions of extraversion, neuroticism, conscientiousness, agreeableness, and openness to experience. Research has confirmed that these five factors are present regardless of cultural background.

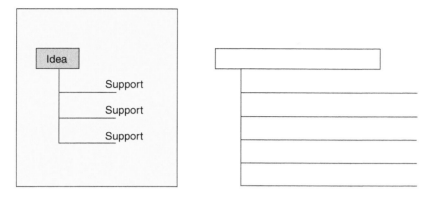

Definition

Frequently in a textbook, an entire paragraph is devoted to defining a complex term or idea. With **definition,** the concept is defined initially and then expanded with examples and restatements. In a textbook, a defined term is usually signaled by *italic* or **bold** type.

EXAMPLE   ULTRASOUND

Ultrasound is a technique that uses sound waves to produce an image that enables a physician to detect structural abnormalities. Useful pictures can be obtained as early as five or six weeks into pregnancy. Ultrasound is frequently used in conjunction with other techniques such as amniocentesis and fetoscopy.

—John Dacey and John Travers,
Human Development, 2nd ed.

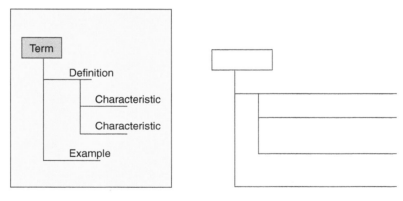

Description

Description is like listing; the characteristics that make up a description are no more than a simple list of details.

EXAMPLE   CARIBBEAN

Caribbean America today is a land crowded with so many people that, as a region (encompassing the Greater and Lesser Antilles), it is the most densely populated part of the Americas. It is also a place of grinding poverty and, in all too many localities, unrelenting misery with little chance for escape.

—H. J. De Blij and Peter O. Muller,
Geography: Realms, Regions, and Concepts, 7th ed.

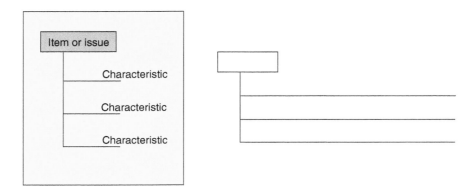

Time Order, Sequence, or Narration

Items are listed in the order in which they occurred or in a specifically planned order in which they must develop. In this case, the **chronological** or **time order** is important, and changing it would change the meaning. Narrative writing, which tells a story, is an example of writing in which time order is important.

Signal words that are often used for time order, sequence, or narration include *first, second, third, after, before, when, until, at last, next, later.* Actual time periods, such as days or years, also signal sequence and time.

EXAMPLE

THE MORMON MOVEMENT

The idea of the Mormon Church began when a young Joseph Smith, Jr., went into the New York woods in 1820 and was told by God that the true church of God would be reestablished. In 1823, another revelation led him to find buried golden plates and translate the *Book of Mormon.* Smith attracted thousands of followers and in the 1830s moved from Ohio to Missouri to Illinois to seek religious freedom for his group. In 1844 Smith was shot by an angry mob. After his death, a new leader, Brigham Young, led the Mormons to the Great Salt Lake.

Topic:		Topic:	
When did it happen?	What happened?	When did it happen?	What happened?

Comparison

With **comparison**, items are presented according to similarities between or among them. Signal words that are often used for comparison include *similar, in the same way, likewise, just like*.

EXAMPLE   JAZZ GREATS

Jazz greats Louis Armstrong and Billie Holiday overcame similar obstacles in their struggling early years. Both were raised in the slums by working mothers, and both learned the discipline needed for success through hard work. As a teen, Armstrong hauled coal from 7 A.M. to 5 P.M. for 75 cents a day and then practiced on his trumpet after work. Similarly, after school, Holiday scrubbed the white stone steps of neighbors' houses to earn an average of 90 cents a day, and then she came home to practice her singing.

Contrast

With **contrast,** items are presented according to differences between or among them. Signal words that are often used for contrast include *different, in contrast, on the other hand, but, however, bigger than.*

EXAMPLE   ORANGES

An orange grown in Florida usually has a thin and tightly fitting skin, and it is also heavy with juice. Californians say that if you want to eat a Florida orange you have to get into a bathtub first. On the other hand, California oranges are light in weight and have thick skins that break easily and come off in hunks.

—John McPhee,
Oranges

Comparison and Contrast

Some passages combine comparison and contrast into a single paragraph. This combination is called a **comparison-and-contrast** pattern and is demonstrated in the following example.

EXAMPLE   **HISPANIC AMERICANS**

The primary groups in the rising new minority are Mexican Americans and Cuban Americans. Mexican Americans are heavily concentrated in the Southwest, whereas Cuban Americans are concentrated in Florida, particularly in the Miami area. Together the groups are called Hispanic Americans or Latinos. Although their histories are different, they share several similarities. They both speak the Spanish language and most of them, at least 85 percent, are Roman Catholic.

The graphic below is helpful for organizing the details of all three variations of the comparison-and-contrast patterns.

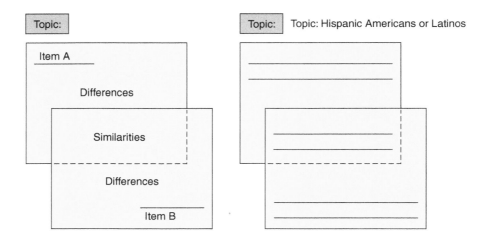

Cause and Effect

With **cause and effect,** an element is shown as producing another element. One is the *cause* or the "happening" that stimulated the particular result or *effect*. A paragraph may describe one cause or many causes, as well as one or many results. Signal words that are often used for cause and effect include *for this reason, consequently, on that account, hence, because*.

EXAMPLE   **WINTER CAMP AT VALLEY FORGE**

General George Washington's Continental army set up camp on the frozen grounds of Valley Forge in December 1777 and experienced dire consequences. The winter was particularly cold that year, and the soldiers lacked straw and blankets. Many froze in their beds. Food was scarce, and soldiers died of malnutrition. Because of the misery and disease in the camp, many soldiers deserted the army and went home.

Topic:	
Cause Why did it happen?	Effect What happened?

Topic:	
Cause Why did it happen?	Effect What happened?

Classification

To simplify a complex topic, authors frequently begin introductory paragraphs by stating that the information that follows is divided into a certain number of groups or categories. The divisions are then named and the parts are explained. Signal words often used for **classification** include *two divisions, three groups, four elements, five classes, six levels, seven categories,* and so on.

EXAMPLE   **PREDATION**

Predation, the interaction in which one species kills and eats another, involves two groups. The predator, or consumer, must be alert and skillful to locate and capture the prey. The consumable group, or prey, constantly must adapt its behavior to defend against being eaten.

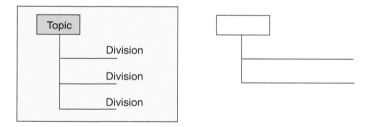

Addition

The **addition** pattern is used to provide more information related to something that has already been explained. Signal words are *furthermore, again, also, further, moreover, besides, likewise.*

EXAMPLE   **ENTREPRENEUR QUINCY JONES**

Not only is Quincy Jones the talented producer who helped drive Michael Jackson's "Beat It" to a number one hit and "Thriller" to the best-selling album of all time, he is also the founder of *VIBE* magazine and the co-owner of *SPIN* magazine. Furthermore, Jones, who has been awarded twenty-six Grammys and a Grammy Legend, is chairman and CEO of the Quincy Jones Media Group.

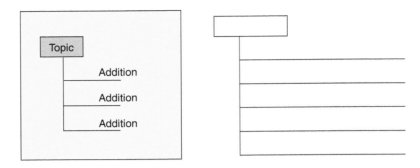

Summary

A **summary,** which usually comes at the end of an article or chapter, condenses the main idea or thesis into a short and simple concluding statement with a few major supporting details. Signal words are *in conclusion, briefly, to sum up, in short, in a nutshell.*

EXAMPLE   **WWII TOTAL WAR**

In conclusion, World War II was more of a total war than any previous war in history. Some 70 nations took part in the war, and fighting took place on the continents of Europe, Asia, and Africa. Entire societies participated, either as soldiers, war workers, or victims of occupation and mass murder.

—Adapted from James Kirby Martin et al.,
America and Its People

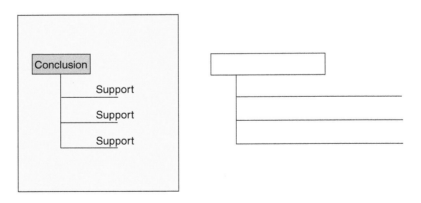

Location or Spatial Order

Location or **spatial order** identifies the whereabouts of a place or object. Signal words are *north, east, south, west, next to, near, below, above, close by, within, without, adjacent to, beside, around, to the right or left side, opposite.*

EXAMPLE   **EGYPT**

The Republic of Egypt is located in the northeastern corner of Africa. The northern border of Egypt is the Mediterranean Sea. Libya is the country to the west, and the Sudan lies to the south. Across the Suez Canal and to the east lies Israel.

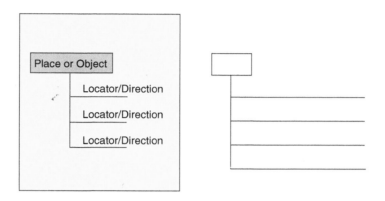

Generalization and Example

In the **generalization-and-example** pattern, a general statement or conclusion is supported with specific examples. Signal words include *to restate that, that is, for example, to illustrate, for instance.*

EXAMPLE   **SMOKING**

To restate it in simple terms, smoking kills. The American Cancer Society estimates that tobacco smoking is the cause of 30 percent of all deaths from cancer. Lung cancer is the leading cause of death from cancer in the United States, with 85 percent to 90 percent of these cases linked to smoking. Save your life by not smoking.

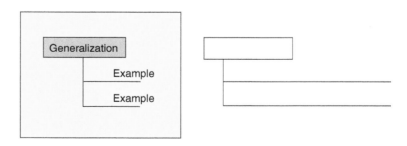

> **Reader's TIP** — **Patterns of Organization and Signal Words**
>
> - **Addition:** furthermore • again • also • further • moreover • besides • likewise
>   (provides more information)
> - **Cause and Effect:** because • for this reason • consequently • hence • as a result • thus • due to • therefore
>   (shows one element as producing or causing a result or effect)
> - **Classification:** groups • categories • elements • classes • parts
>   (divides items into groups or categories)
> - **Comparison:** in a similar way • similar • parallel to • likewise • in a like manner
>   (lists similarities among items)
> - **Contrast:** on the other hand • bigger than • but • however • conversely • on the contrary • although • nevertheless
>   (lists differences among items)
> - **Definition:** can be defined • means • for example • like
>   (initially defines a concept and expands with examples and restatements)
> - **Description:** is • as • is made up of • could be described as
>   (lists characteristics or details)
> - **Generalization and Example:** to restate • that is • for example • to illustrate • for instance
>   (explains with examples to illustrate)
> - **Location or Spatial Order:** next to • near • below • above • close by • within • without • adjacent to • beside • around • to the right or left side • opposite
>   (identifies the whereabouts of objects)
> - **Simple Listing:** also • another • several • for example
>   (randomly lists items in a series)
> - **Summary:** in conclusion • briefly • to sum up • in short • in a nutshell
>   (condenses major points)
> - **Time Order, Sequence, or Narration:** first • second • finally • after • before • next • later • now • at last • until • thereupon • while • during
>   (lists events in order of occurrence)

CLUES TO THE ORGANIZATIONAL PATTERN

Active readers use several clues to determine the organizational pattern of the material. The most experienced readers predict the pattern from a brief preview and confirm their predictions as they read. No one clue is enough, though. It takes all of the following elements to be sure:

1. **Transitional words:** Use the lists in this chapter to help you recognize the function of the transitional words and phrases. Remember, though, that some words may be used in more than one pattern.
2. **Graphic organizers:** If the details fit in the graphic organizer, this is additional evidence that the predicted pattern is correct.
3. **Relationship among the details and the main idea:** This is the most reliable evidence a reader has to identify the pattern. Good readers are always most concerned about recognizing the main idea and the details that support it.

EXERCISE 3

Identifying Paragraph Patterns

Each of the following items presents the first two sentences of a paragraph stating the main idea and a major supporting detail. Select the letter that indicates the pattern of organization that you would predict for each.

_____ 1. Jim Vicary coined the term *subliminal advertising,* claiming that inserting messages like "Eat popcorn" and "Drink Coca-Cola" into movies would increase consumption. According to Vicary, the messages, flashed too fast for the human eye to recognize but registered in the brain, would prompt a rush to the snack bar.

   a. summary
   b. classification
   c. definition
   d. comparison and contrast

_____ 2. Now an integral part of the recruiting strategy, companies of all sizes are finding that e-cruiting, job recruiting over the Internet, has many benefits. To begin, the Internet is a fast, convenient, and inexpensive way to find prospective job candidates.

   a. description
   b. simple listing
   c. time order
   d. classification

_____ 3. As a result of the Great Depression, Hollywood flourished. Cheap tickets, free time, and the lure of fantasy brought 60 million to 80 million Americans to the movies each week.

   a. comparison and contrast
   b. simple listing
   c. cause and effect
   d. description

_____ 4. Queens ruled England in the second half of the sixteenth century. In 1553, Mary I took the throne. She was followed in 1558 by Elizabeth I, who ruled for the next 45 years.

   a. summary
   b. contrast

      c. classification

      d. time order

_____ 5. Although both artists lived in Spain, Pablo Picasso and Salvador Dali had styles that differed dramatically. Picasso depicted his subjects in abstract terms, whereas Dali painted the stark reality of the image.

      a. description

      b. comparison and contrast

      c. time order

      d. simple listing

_____ 6. Michelangelo depicted the creation of Eve on a panel that is almost in the center of the Sistine Chapel ceiling. *The Creation of Adam,* a larger and more famous panel, is located adjacent to it and toward the back of the chapel.

      a. simple listing

      b. time order

      c. location or spatial order

      d. definition

_____ 7. In short, the Internet can be a source of dangerous misinformation. Anyone can develop a Web site and fill it with distortions of the truth and inflammatory accusations.

      a. classification

      b. summary

      c. definition

      d. time order

_____ 8. In case of a sprained ankle, you should first apply ice to constrict the blood vessels and stop internal bleeding. Next, elevate your foot above the level of your heart to further control bleeding by making the blood flow away from the injured area.

      a. summary

      b. classification

      c. generalization and example

      d. sequence

EXERCISE 4

Patterns of Organization and Main Idea

Read the following passages, and use the three-question system to determine the author's main idea. In addition, indicate the dominant pattern of organization used by the author. Select from the following list:

classification   definition   cause and effect   comparison and contrast

Passage A

Also called ice pellets, sleet is formed when raindrops or melted snowflakes freeze as they pass through a subfreezing layer of air near Earth's surface. Sleet does not stick to trees and wires, and it usually bounces when it hits the ground. An accumulation of sleet sometimes has the consistency of dry sand.

—Frederick K. Lutgens and Edward J. Tarbuck,
The Atmosphere, 9th ed.

1. Who or what is this about? _____

2. What are the major details? _____

_____

_____

_____

_____

3. What is the overall pattern of organization? _____

4. What is the main idea the authors are trying to convey about the topic? _____

_____

_____

Passage B

There are so many types of water available to drink in the United States, how can we group them and distinguish among them? If we prefer to drink water with bubbles—carbonation—we can choose carbonated water. This type of water contains carbon dioxide gas that either occurs naturally or is added to the water. Mineral water is another beverage option. Mineral waters contain 250 to 500 parts per million of minerals. While many people prefer the unique taste of mineral water, a number of brands contain high amounts of sodium so they should be avoided by people who are trying to reduce their sodium intake. Distilled water is processed in such a way that all dissolved minerals are removed. This type of water is often used in steam irons, as it will not clog the iron with mineral buildup. Purified water has been treated so that all dissolved minerals and contaminants are removed, making this type of water useful in research and medical procedures. Of course, we can also drink the tap water found in our homes and in public places.

—Adapted from Janice Thompson and Melinda Manore,
Nutrition: An Applied Approach

1. Who or what is this about? _____

_____

2. What are the major details? _____

_____

_____

_____

3. What is the overall pattern of organization? _____

4. What is the main idea the authors are trying to convey about the topic?

_____

_____

_____

Passage C

The law of demand states that the quantity demanded will increase as the price is lowered as long as other factors that affect demand do not change. The makers of M&M candy conducted an experiment in the law of demand, holding the necessary demand-affecting conditions constant. Over a 12-month test period, the price of M&Ms was held constant in 150 stores while the content weight of the candy was increased. By holding the price constant and increasing the weight, the price (per ounce) was lowered. In the stores where the price was dropped, sales rose by 20 to 30 percent almost overnight. As a result of the law of demand, a reduction in prices caused the quantity demanded to rise.

—Adapted from Paul R. Gregory,
Essentials of Economics, 6th ed.

1. Who or what is this about? _____

_____

2. What are the major details? _____

_____

_____

3. What is the overall pattern of organization? _____

4. What is the main idea the author is trying to convey about the topic? _____

_____

_____

_____

Passage D

I immediately noted differences in the early [basketball] practices. Girls' attention to directions was far superior to the boys', most of whom found it physically impossible not to be distracted by any movement anywhere in the gym. Whereas the

> ### BRAIN BOOSTER
>
> **Watering the Brain**
>
> Our brains are made up of about 80 percent water, and brain function depends on maintaining adequate hydration. Only water will do! The sugars in coffee, tea, and soft drinks bind to the water in them, the body processes them as foods, and the benefits of the water are lost. In fact, these drinks actually act as diuretics and dehydrate the body rather than hydrate it. If you feel listless, sleepy, or cannot concentrate, you might just need a drink of water.
>
> —*Adapted from* Brain-Based Learning: The New Paradigm of Teaching, *2nd ed., by Eric Jensen (p. 66) Corwin Press, 2008*

boys generally either went deadpan or shot me the evil "how dare you" death stare when I corrected their play, the girls often sincerely apologized for any mistake. My stereotypically gawky center, when told not to leave her feet on defense, said, "I know. I'm sorry. I'm terrible." Strangest of all, they actually wanted to talk to me and the other coach, something teenage boys found equivalent to having their nose hairs individually plucked out in front of an audience.

—Brendan O'Shaughnessy,
"It's a Whole New Ballgame for Veteran Coach"

1. Who or what is this about? _____

_____

_____

_____

2. What are the major details? _____

_____

_____

3. What is the overall pattern of organization? _____

4. What is the main idea the author is trying to convey about the topic? _____

_____

_____

_____

MIXED ORGANIZATIONAL PATTERNS

Learning Objective 3

Recognize mixed patterns of organization

Suppose you were writing an orientation article describing support services available at your own college. You could present the resources in a **simple listing** pattern, or you could discuss them in the **sequence** or **time order** in which a freshman is likely to need them or in terms of the most convenient geographic locations to students. Within your article, you might use a **description** or **definition** pattern to identify a relatively unknown service on campus, with examples of how it has helped others. You could demonstrate **cause and effect** with facts and statistics on how using services has helped students. You might also choose to **compare and contrast** a special service with that at another college.

You could supply **additional** information by presenting the qualifications of professional staff providing the services. To wrap things up, you could create an overall **summary** about the support services. Thus, one long article might have an overall **simple listing** pattern of organization yet contain individual paragraphs that follow other patterns.

EXERCISE 5

Identifying Combined Organizational Patterns

Read the following textbook excerpts and answer the questions that follow. Note how combined organizational patterns may help you understand the main idea of a longer piece of writing. Signal words are set in bold type to help you identify a particular pattern.

Passage 1

Does the title suggest a pattern?

What Are Dust Devils?

A common phenomenon in arid regions of the world is the whirling vortex called the dust devil. Although they resemble tornadoes, dust devils are generally much smaller and less intense than their destructive cousins. Most dust devils are only a few meters in diameter and reach heights no greater than about 100 meters (300 feet). **By definition,** these whirlwinds are usually short-lived microscale phenomena. Most form and die out within minutes. In rare instances dust devils have lasted for hours.

Unlike tornadoes, which are associated with convective clouds, dust devils form on days when clear skies dominate. **In contrast,** these whirlwinds form from the ground upward, exactly opposite of tornadoes. Because surface heating is critical to their formation, dust devils occur most frequently in the afternoon when surface temperatures are highest.

Which pattern is suggested by the boldface words?

When the air near the surface is considerably warmer than the air a few dozen meters overhead, the layer of air near Earth's surface becomes unstable. In this situation warm surface air begins to rise, **causing** air near the ground to be drawn into the developing whirlwind. **As a result,** the rotating winds that are associated with dust devils are produced by the same phenomenon that causes ice skaters to spin faster as they pull their arms closer to their bodies. As the inwardly spiraling air rises, it carries sand, dust, and other loose debris dozens of meters into the air. It is this material that makes a dust devil visible. Occasionally, dust devils form above vegetated surfaces. Under these conditions, the vortices may go undetected unless they interact with objects at the surface.

—Adapted from Frederick K. Lutgens and Edward J. Tarbuck,
The Atmosphere, 9th ed.

1. Who or what is this about? _____

_____

2. What overall pattern is suggested by the title? _____

_____

3. What is the pattern of organization in the first paragraph? _____

_____

4. What is the pattern of organization in the second paragraph? _____

_____

5. What is the pattern of organization in the third paragraph? _____

_____

6. What is the main idea the authors are trying to convey about the topic? _____

_____

_____

Passage 2

The Success of eBay

eBay is one of the most successful e-commerce businesses. **Unlike** Amazon.com, it does not need expensive warehouses and storage facilities. eBay earns its revenues by charging a small fee to sellers who list their products on eBay for sale. **While other** dot-com companies have suffered losses in recent years, eBay, **on the other hand,** has been consistently profitable, earning almost $150 million in annual profits.

eBay exists in all major countries (eBay Germany, eBay Austria, eBay Canada, and so on). It operates a worldwide virtual auction market in which registered sellers can list products and registered buyers can enter bids for them. Participants in this virtual market can follow the progress of bids online as each auction progresses. (Usually an ending time of each auction is listed.)

Products auctioned on eBay range from the ordinary to the unique or exotic. On a given day, wooden crates of rough jade ($15.95), a Tibetan bronze Buddha ($88), a 1913 Catholic dictionary ($204), a 1725 bible ($348), and an 1895 U.S. Navy steam launch engine ($2,025) can be found on auction.

eBay deals with problems of dishonesty. **That is,** eBay maintains bulletin boards of comments submitted by eBay subscribers, organized by the identification number of eBay buyers and sellers. These ratings provide information on records of past honesty and reliability. A "cheating" buyer or seller would not be able to buy or sell on eBay after disclosure of negative comments.

eBay **offers several** enormous **advantages** to buyers and sellers. **First,** the seller can gain access to a large number of potential buyers of unusual products by paying a small fee to eBay. **Second,** buyers have the opportunity to bid on thousands of products and services without leaving the comfort of their homes. Historically, exotic products such as Rembrandt paintings and Kennedy presidential memorabilia were auctioned by prestigious auction houses such as Sotheby's, which typically collected fees of 15 percent or more. It appears to be only a matter of time until rare and expensive items will be auctioned on eBay.

—Adapted from Paul R. Gregory,
Essentials of Economics, 6th ed.

1. Who or what is this about? _____

_____

2. What overall pattern is suggested by the title? _____

_____

3. What is the pattern of organization in the first paragraph? _____

_____

4. What is the pattern of organization in the second paragraph? _____

_____

5. What is the pattern of organization in the third paragraph? _____

_____

6. What is the pattern of organization in the fourth paragraph? _____

_____

7. What is the pattern of organization in the final paragraph? _____

_____

SUMMARY POINTS

1. How can I recognize transitional words?
- Become familiar with the function of common transitional words. *For example*, logically introduces an example that elaborates on a previous point. *However*, indicates a contrast to an idea that was just discussed.
- Train yourself to notice these markers. They are like road signs that guide you through the author's thinking. They can suggest the organization pattern and ultimately help you understand the material.

2. How can I recognize the pattern of organization?
- Recognizing the pattern in which the author organized the details is an important key to understanding the material. Train yourself to look for the pattern.
- Use these clues to the pattern:
  Transitional words
  Graphic organizers
  The relationship among the details and the main idea

3. How can I recognize mixed patterns of organization?
- Keep in mind that authors frequently use several patterns in a single chapter, section, or even a paragraph. Be alert to the transitional words and changes in thought.
- Determine the dominant pattern, the one that best represents the author's main point. Be aware of the patterns that help to present supporting ideas, and see how they contribute to the primary pattern and main idea.

MyReadingLab™   For more help with Patterns of Organization go to your learning path in MyReadingLab at www.myreadinglab.com

Narrative

Pᴿᴇᴠɪᴇᴡ the next selection to predict its purpose and organization and to formulate your learning plan.

Activate Schema

What is your definition of a nerd?
Have you ever felt tongue-tied when talking to someone you're attracted to?
Is an online relationship the same as a face-to-face one?

Establish a Purpose for Reading

Read the personal narrative to be entertained and to discover what the author learned from his experiences.

Increase Word Knowledge

What do you know about these words?

allusions	mutate	scuttle	lair	trivially
fluke	simultaneously	charade	feigned	pregnant

Your instructor may give a true-false vocabulary review before or after reading.

Integrate Knowledge While Reading

Questions have been inserted in the margin to stimulate your thinking while reading. Remember to

Predict	Picture	Relate	Monitor	Correct	Annotate

((•— Scan this QR
Code to hear
this reading

Why is this a problem?

Iɴsᴛᴀɴᴛ Mᴇssᴀɢᴇ, Iɴsᴛᴀɴᴛ Gɪʀʟꜰʀɪᴇɴᴅ

For several years I had a problem unusual among Internet geeks: I had too much success with women. I used the Internet as a means of communication with women I had already met offline in order to overcome my social awkwardness and forge romantic relationships. Sounds healthy? It wasn't.

5   It started in my sophomore year in high school. I went to one of those big Eastern public schools that pumps out students in a way that would make 19th-century industrialists throw their top hats into the air and shout "Huzzah!" Even we students thought of ourselves as a faceless mob of subproletarians waiting for the next episode of *American Idol* to take away the pain of our meaningless existence.

10   I was at the bottom of the barrel: a plump, silent, painfully awkward dweeb who clung to his Latin textbook as if it held the secrets to existence. The only good thing that happened to me that year was meeting Chelsea.

I'm creating a mental picture! →

We talked for maybe 5 minutes about video games between classes, and of that time I spent 4 minutes and 59 seconds dripping in nervous sweat and trying to swal-
15   low my stutter. Whenever I tried to say something charming, my sentence dropped off with an invisible ellipsis. My words of wit fell flat, and my skillful cultural allusions deteriorated into a stream of loosely associated quotations from *Star Trek*.

I was the quintessential nerd with the quintessential nerd problem: I was uncharismatic and I knew it. By the time the bell rang for the beginning of class, I had
20   seen her favorable grin mutate horribly into a thousand-yard stare. I knew that look well. I had seen it before in the eyes of every person confused by my appearance or put off by my manner.

I had to scuttle the conversation and find a way to salvage my bruised ego, so I asked for her screen name on instant messenger. After an agonizing moment in
25   which I prayed to every god in the Dungeons & Dragons pantheon, she gave it to me on the back of a candy wrapper. As she walked away, I had the 16-year-old equivalent of a major heart attack.

Back home, I gazed forlornly at the crumpled candy wrapper, wondering if I should contact her. Descending the stairs into my basement computer lair, I decided
30   that it was worth a shot. What's the worst that could happen? I could make myself look like an idiot and never have a chance with her again.

This possibility being trivially different from the situation I was already in, I signed on and said "hello" with one of those ever-youthful emoticons. I gulped hard and buckled down for another tempestuous voyage into total failure.

35   Then something magical happened. I don't know what it was exactly. Somewhere in the dark reaches of the Internet I went through a transformation sequence worthy of a Japanese children's cartoon. I suddenly shifted from an overweight, overdressed frog to a charming, handsome, technology-savvy prince.

Many romances begin through email and instant messaging.
Ken Seet/Corbis

Online I could shuffle off the nervous coil that had previously bound me to failure. As soon as my fingers touched the keys, I was not just another face in an endless crowd. With words on a screen, I would never stutter. I could take as long as I wanted to think of the perfect answer to every question, and the perfect response to every flirtation.

As we talked this way, I could feel her warm to me, her words changing to favor me like a sly smile. Before we had finished our second night of online conversation, she was my girlfriend. My heart trembled when I saw her message with those smiley-face words: "Would you like to go out with me?"

Is this healthy or even ethical?

I was hooked. It was as if the Internet had allowed me to turn flirtation and seduction into a video game. But I didn't know if my Internet charms were just a fluke or if they were real. I wanted, no, needed to know that the cool person I became when my fingers caressed the keys was actually me. Therefore, with a scientific resolve possessed only by physicists and 80th-level paladins, I set out to repeat my success. I didn't want another girlfriend per se, but rather I wanted the affirmation that would come with being able to get another girlfriend.

A few days later I met Rachel during lunch and after a short conversation got her instant-messenger screen name. After two days, she, too, wanted to date me. I was beginning to see a pattern. The more women I seduced, the more often I could escape my loser identity and become the super-cool cyber Casanova I thought I deserved to be.

I did it again and again. In five minutes I could persuade a girl to give me her screen name and a week after that I could persuade her to go out with me. By the end of the year, I had six girlfriends simultaneously, all maintained through a complicated system of instant messenger, e-mail messages and heavily orchestrated dates.

Some of these girlfriends were as nerdy as I was, while others were cheerleaders and prep-scholars, but the particulars mattered less than the rush of simply being able to charm a girl into liking me, over and over, and then maintaining it.

Often I would be chatting online with five girls at once, each conversation a distinct flirtation (one about puns, another about philosophy); it was like spinning plates. Many of these girls I rarely met in person, but we had deep and steady online relationships.

I also went out on actual dates with a select few: movies and museums, dinner and dancing, and everything else I thought teenage couples should do. Each date was carefully planned so no other girl would catch me.

Nothing was too challenging. I first seduced my best friend's girlfriend and, when they broke up, I seduced his new girlfriend. I had a girlfriend in New York and one in Philadelphia. I had a girl I met on a train and a girl I met in a nightclub. I had a Republican and a Democrat, an artist and an engineer, a Christian and an atheist.

Something is going to go wrong.

Each thought I was theirs, yet I was so caught up in the thrill of it all that I felt not a pang of guilt. My love life was a technology that I had practiced and mastered; all I had to do was press the same buttons in the right order every time, and the secrets of human love would come pouring out. The Internet was more than just a direct wire to the world. It had become a vehicle for my desire to be loved.

I kept up the charade for three years as my sense of challenge waned and my cynicism grew. It was a Sunday night in senior year and I had just returned from watching a movie with one of my girlfriends when my phone buzzed with a new text message. It was from Amber, the girl who had been with me longest: "I love you."

I love you. Those three words shocked me into repentance. I didn't love her back; in fact, love hadn't even been part of the equation for me. With the help of my
90 computer I could seduce girls I couldn't even speak to in person, but no amount of smiley faces, words, or LOLs could make me love someone I didn't. My charm was real, but my affection was feigned.

I realized I had to undo what I had done before I lost track of what really mattered to me and to the people I had duped. I dealt with it the hard way. I sat down
95 at my computer and started ending relationships, typing again and again those dreaded four words: "We need to talk." I felt relief as the lie came clear.

Over the next few months my life became a series of break-ups, one after another, as I emptied my contact-list harem of 19 phony relationships. Sometimes I broke up with them, sometimes they broke up with me. The result was the same:
100 freedom. But if the Internet had accelerated my entry into these relationships, it made getting out of them agonizingly time-consuming.

When two nerds break up in person, the threat of eye contact typically ends the conversation in minutes. It's painful, but at least it's quick. When two nerds break up
105 over the phone, it can take about an hour. With e-mail or instant messages, the fight can last longer than a special edition *Lord of the Rings* movie. Eternities dropped off the clock as I waited through the pregnant silences between every line. I endured this over and over.

Don't mistake my story for a technophobe's cautionary tale, however. I was blinded by the common belief that somehow a relationship forged on the Internet
110 isn't real. When I saw that fated text message—"I love you"—I realized the truth. The Internet is not a separate place a person can go to from the real world. The Internet is the real world. Only faster.

When I flew out to college that autumn, I felt as if I was stepping into sunshine after four years in the dark. I could start fresh alongside hundreds of others who
115 were ripe to shed their high school selves. If I could step away from the lies I had put on the computer screen, I could find a way both to be charming and true to the person I really am.

What is the message of this story? →

Months later I met Lara at a midnight showing of *The Rocky Horror Picture Show.* She sat with me long after the movie was over, enduring exhaustion and a
120 sticky seat just to be with me. "Here," she said, shifting forward in that subtle way girls do when they're interested but don't want to make it obvious. In her hand was a piece of paper. "Here's my screen name." I smiled at her. "Thanks," I said. "You'll be the only person on my contact list."

(1,680 words)

Roger Hobbs,
"Instant Message, Instant Girlfriend." From
The New York Times, May 25, 2008. © 2008 *The New York Times*.

Recall

Stop to self-test, relate, and react.
Your instructor may choose to give you a true-false comprehension review.

WRITE ABOUT THE SELECTION   MyReadingLab™

Complete
this **Exercise** on
myreadinglab.com

Hobbs describes himself as the "quintessential (the most perfect embodiment of) nerd," but his persona changed completely online.

Response Suggestion: List the characteristics that made him a nerd. Explain why you think these characteristics disappeared in his online relationships. Conclude with your prediction about his future, face-to-face relationships. Do you think his online experiences changed his ability to interact with a woman in person?

SKILL DEVELOPMENT: IDENTIFY ORGANIZATIONAL PATTERNS

Answer the following questions with *T* (true) or *F* (false):

_____ 1. The organizational pattern is narrative or time order.

_____ 2. The author flashes back in time to tell the story.

CHECK YOUR COMPREHENSION   MyReadingLab™

After reading the selection, answer the following questions with *a, b, c,* or *d.* To help you analyze your strengths and weaknesses, the question types are indicated.

Complete
this **Exercise** on
myreadinglab.com

Main Idea ———— 1. The best statement of the main idea of this selection is
    a. the author was awkward in personal relationships with women.
    b. the author became addicted to online conquests and relationships.
    c. although he was uncomfortable talking to women in person, the author felt comfortable interacting with them online.
    d. through a series of Internet relationships, the author learned that online relationships must be treated with the same respect and care as face-to-face ones.

Detail ———— 2. The story spans which years of Hobbs's life?
    a. Most of high school
    b. One year of high school
    c. The first two years of college
    d. All of his college career

Detail ———— 3. Hobbs mentions all of the following personal interests *except*
    a. watching *American Idol.*
    b. watching *Star Trek.*
    c. listening to music.
    d. playing video games.

Inference ———— 4. The details in the article suggest that
    a. Hobbs eventually felt guilty for the way he treated his online girlfriends.
    b. Hobbs lost friends because of his online relationships.
    c. Hobbs did not enjoy his online relationships.
    d. Hobbs continued to use the Internet to meet women during college.

Main Idea ———— 5. The main point of the first few paragraphs is
    a. Hobbs learned he could talk easily with women online.
    b. Hobbs was very awkward and uncomfortable talking with women in person.
    c. Hobbs enjoyed talking to women about *Star Trek.*
    d. Hobbs was not concerned about his social awkwardness.

Detail ———— 6. One characteristic Hobbs mentions to illustrate his lack of social attractiveness is
    a. out-of-style clothes.
    b. poor athletic skills.
    c. acne.
    d. stuttering.

Inference _____ 7. We can infer from Hobbs's comment "I had the 16-year-old equivalent of a major heart attack" that

    a. he had a chronic heart ailment.
    b. he was shocked Chelsea actually gave him her screen name.
    c. he felt ill.
    d. he intended to contact her online immediately.

Inference _____ 8. We can infer from the selection that

    a. the author was unaware of his face-to-face affect on women.
    b. the author was accustomed to being rejected by the women he approached.
    c. the author's first attempt at connecting with a woman online was unsuccessful.
    d. the author had many failures before he was able to establish an online relationship.

Detail _____ 9. Which of the following is true about the author's first online communication with Chelsea?

    a. He was immediately confident of his ability to charm her.
    b. He expected to be rejected.
    c. He talked to her about *Star Trek*.
    d. He failed at connecting with her but kept trying until he succeeded.

Detail _____ 10. What event caused Hobbs to realize he had to end his online addiction?

    a. Rachel broke up with him.
    b. Amber wrote that she loved him.
    c. Despite his successes, he realized he was still socially awkward.
    d. Two of the women found out that he was courting many women online.

Answer the following with *T* (true) or *F* (false).

Inference _____ 11. The author was more satisfied by the thrill of success than he was with the actual relationships.

Detail _____ 12. Hobbs never actually met his online girlfriends.

Inference _____ 13. Hobbs never realized that he could have a meaningful, face-to-face relationship.

Detail _____ 14. Hobbs found breaking up online easy.

Inference _____ 15. Although it got out of control, Hobbs's Internet addiction helped him overcome his social awkwardness.

BUILD YOUR VOCABULARY MyReadingLab™

Complete this **Exercise** on **myreadinglab.com**

According to the way the italicized word is used in the selection, indicate *a, b, c,* or *d* for the word or phrase that gives the best definition. The number in parentheses indicates the line of the passage in which the word is located.

_____ 1. "skillful cultural *allusions*" (16–17)
   a. dreams
   b. references
   c. methods
   d. qualities

_____ 2. "grin *mutate* horribly" (20)
   a. transform
   b. freeze
   c. emerge
   d. disappear

_____ 3. "to *scuttle* the conversation" (23)
   a. continue
   b. enliven
   c. abandon
   d. begin

_____ 4. "basement computer *lair*" (29)
   a. desk
   b. setup
   c. keyboard
   d. den

_____ 5. "being *trivially* different" (32)
   a. significantly
   b. dramatically
   c. emotionally
   d. unimportantly

_____ 6. "just a *fluke*" (49)
   a. a bit of luck
   b. fact
   c. compliment
   d. mistake

_____ 7. "six girlfriends *simultaneously*" (62)
   a. happily
   b. at the same time
   c. in a complicated way
   d. quickly

_____ 8. "kept up the *charade*" (83)
   a. fun
   b. pretense, make-believe
   c. conversation
   d. drama

_____ 9. "affection was *feigned*" (92)
   a. sincere
   b. satisfying
   c. artificial
   d. skillful

_____ 10. "the *pregnant* silences" (107)
   a. with child
   b. sweet
   c. contented
   d. full of meaning

SELECTION 2 History

PREVIEW the next selection to predict its purpose and organization and to formulate your learning plan.

Activate Schema

Who was Sojourner Truth?
Why did the Civil War throw women into many leadership roles?

Establish a Purpose for Reading

Although history books tend to be mostly about the accomplishments of men, over time, women also have made contributions and pursued political and other professions. Who were some of the early women leaders? After recalling what you already know about women in history, read the selection to explain the contributions of individuals and groups toward changing the image of women.

Increase Word Knowledge

What do you know about these words?

restrictive	detriment	defiant	communal	hecklers
pursue	hygiene	incessant	convalescent	naive

Your instructor may give a true-false vocabulary review before or after reading.

Integrate Knowledge While Reading

Questions have been inserted in the margin to stimulate your thinking while reading. Remember to

Predict	Picture	Relate	Monitor	Correct	Annotate

WOMEN IN HISTORY

(((•─ **Scan this QR Code to hear this reading**

THREE RADICAL WOMEN

Amelia Bloomer (1818–1894) published the first newspaper issued expressly for women. She called it *The Lily.* Her fame, however, rests chiefly in dress reform. For six or eight years she wore an outfit composed of a knee-length skirt over full pants gathered at the ankle, which were soon known everywhere as "bloomers." Wherever
5 she went, this style created great excitement and brought her enormous audiences—including hecklers. She was trying to make the serious point that women's fashions, often designed by men to suit their own tastes, were too restrictive, often to the

Why would Bloomer have hurt the movement?

detriment of the health of those who wore them. Still, some of her contemporaries
thought she did the feminist movement as much harm as good.

10 Very few feminists hoped to destroy marriage as such. Most of them had husbands and lived conventional, if hectic, lives. And many of the husbands supported
their cause. Yet the feminists did challenge certain marital customs. When Lucy
Stone married Henry Blackwell, she insisted on being called "Mrs. Stone," a defiant
gesture that brought her a lifetime of ridicule. Both she and her husband signed a
15 marriage contract, vowing "to recognize the wife as an independent, rational being."
They agreed to break any law which brought the husband "an injurious and unnatural superiority." But few of the radical feminists indulged in "free love" or joined
communal marriage experiments. The movement was intended mainly to help
women gain control over their own property and earnings and gain better legal
20 guardianship over their children. Voting also interested them, but women's suffrage
did not become a central issue until later in the century.

Why was voting a later issue?

Many black women were part of the movement, including the legendary
Sojourner Truth (1797–1883). Born a slave in New York and forced to marry a man
approved by her owner, Sojourner Truth was freed when the state abolished slavery.
25 After participating in religious revivals, she became an active abolitionist and

Former slave Isabella Van Wagener became the abolitionist
Sojourner Truth.
MPI/Getty Images

feminist. In 1851 she saved the day at a women's rights convention in Ohio, silencing hecklers and replying to a man who had belittled the weakness of women:

> The man over there says women need to be helped into carriages and lifted over ditches, and to have the best place everywhere. Nobody ever helps me
> 30 into carriages or over puddles, or gives me the best place—and ain't I a woman? . . . look at my arm! I have ploughed and planted and gathered into barns, and no man could head me—and ain't I a woman? I could work as much and eat as much as a man—when I could get it—and bear the lash as well! And ain't I a woman? I have borne thirteen children, and seen most of
> 35 'em sold into slavery, and when I cried out my mother's grief, none but Jesus heard me—and ain't I a woman?

What makes this speech powerful? Read it aloud.

CHANGING THE IMAGE AND THE REALITY

The accomplishments of a few women who dared pursue professional careers had somewhat altered the image of the submissive and brainless child-woman. Maria Mitchell of Nantucket, whose father was an astronomer, discovered a comet at the
40 age of twenty-eight. She became the first woman professor of astronomy in the U.S. (at Vassar in 1865). Mitchell was also the first woman elected to the American Academy of Arts and Sciences and a founder of the Association for the Advancement of Women. Elizabeth Blackwell applied to twenty-nine medical schools before she was accepted. She attended all classes, even anatomy class despite the sneers of some
45 male students. As a physician, she went on to make important contributions in sanitation and hygiene.

Why would there be sneers in anatomy?

By about 1860 women had effected notable improvements in their status. Organized feminists had eliminated some of the worst legal disadvantages in fifteen states. The Civil War altered the role—and the image—of women even more drasti
50 cally than the feminist movement did. As men went off to fight, women flocked into government clerical jobs. And they were accepted in teaching jobs as never before. Tens of thousands of women ran farms and businesses while the men were gone. Anna Howard Shaw, whose mother ran a pioneer farm, recalled:

How did the Civil War force an image change?

> It was an incessant struggle to keep our land, to pay our taxes, and to live.
> 55 Calico was selling at fifty cents a yard. Coffee was one dollar a pound. There were no men left to grind our corn, to get in our crops, or to care for our livestock; and all around us we saw our struggle reflected in the lives of our neighbors.

Women took part in crucial relief efforts. The Sanitary Commission, the Union's
60 volunteer nursing program and a forerunner of the Red Cross, owed much of its success to women. They raised millions of dollars for medicine, bandages, food, hospitals, relief camps, and convalescent homes.

North and South, black and white, many women served as nurses, some as spies and even as soldiers. Dorothea Dix, already famous as a reformer of prisons and in-
65 sane asylums, became head of the Union army nurse corps. Clara Barton and "Mother" Bickerdyke saved thousands of lives by working close behind the front lines at Antietam, Chancellorsville, and Fredericksburg. Harriet Tubman led a party up the Combahee River to rescue 756 slaves. Late in life she was recognized for her heroic act by being granted a government pension of twenty dollars per month.

70   Southern white women suffered more from the disruptions of the Civil War than did their northern sisters. The proportion of men who went to war or were killed in battle was greater in the South. This made many women self-sufficient during the war. Still, there was hardly a whisper of feminism in the South.

The Civil War also brought women into the political limelight. Anna Dickson 75 skyrocketed to fame as a Republican speaker, climaxing her career with an address to the House of Representatives on abolition. Stanton and Anthony formed the National Woman's Loyal League to press for a constitutional amendment banning slavery. With Anthony's genius for organization, the League in one year collected 400,000 signatures in favor of the Thirteenth Amendment.

80   Once abolition was finally assured in 1865, most feminists felt certain that suffrage would follow quickly. They believed that women had earned the vote by their patriotic wartime efforts. Besides, it appeared certain that black men would soon be allowed to vote. And once black men had the ballot in hand, how could anyone justify keeping it from white women—or black women? Any feminist who had pre-85 dicted in 1865 that women would have to wait another fifty-five years for suffrage would have been called politically naive.

Why was suffrage slow to come?

(1,102 words)

—From Leonard Pitt,
We Americans

Recall

Stop to self-test, relate, and react.
Your instructor may choose to give you a true-false comprehension review.

WRITE ABOUT THE SELECTION   MyReadingLab™

Complete this **Exercise** on **myreadinglab.com**

Have we been taught to believe that dynamic women are the exception rather than the rule in history? Is this idea confirmed when we see stories of women only in box inserts and footnotes in history textbooks? How did the actions of many early women "somewhat alter the image of the submissive and brainless child-woman"? Is that image still being altered?

Response Suggestion: List some dynamic women, and discuss how each has changed stereotypical thinking.

SKILL DEVELOPMENT: IDENTIFY ORGANIZATIONAL PATTERNS

Fill in the organizational diagrams to reflect the simple-listing pattern of the first part of the selection and the cause-and-effect pattern of the second part.

Patterns of Organization

[   ]

Topic: [   ]

Cause Why did it happen?	Effect What happened?

CHECK YOUR COMPREHENSION   MyReadingLab™ ·

After reading the selection, answer the following questions with *a, b, c,* or *d.* To help you analyze your strengths and weaknesses, the question types are indicated.

Complete
this **Exercise** on
myreadinglab.com

SELECTION 2

Main Idea _____ 1. What is the best statement of the main point of this selection?

   a. Women made impressive gains because of their work during the Civil War.
   b. Many women made early contributions to changing the stereotypical image of the female role.
   c. Bloomer, Stone, and Truth changed a radical image into a reality.
   d. Women were slow to get the right to vote despite their efforts.

Detail _____ 2. In originating "bloomers," Amelia Bloomer's greatest concern was

   a. fashion.
   b. principle.
   c. expense.
   d. good taste.

Inference _____ 3. The major purpose of Sojourner Truth's quoted speech was to

   a. prove that women are stronger than men.
   b. reprimand men for social courtesy.
   c. dramatize the strengths of women.
   d. praise childbearing as a womanly virtue.

Detail _____ 4. Lucy Stone's major motive in retaining the name "Mrs. Stone" after marriage was to

   a. condone "free love" without marriage.
   b. de-emphasize the responsibilities of marriage.
   c. purchase property in her own name.
   d. be recognized as an independent person equal to her husband.

Detail _____ 5. The article explicitly states that women worked during the Civil War in all the following *except*

   a. farms and businesses.
   b. the military.
   c. government clerical jobs.
   d. the Red Cross.

Inference _____ 6. The author implies that the eventual assumption of responsible roles by large numbers of women was primarily due to

   a. the feminist movement.
   b. the determination and accomplishments of female professionals.
   c. a desire to give women a chance.
   d. economic necessity.

Inference _____ 7. The author believes that the Civil War showed Southern women to be

    a. as capable as but less vocal than Northern women.
    b. more capable than their Northern sisters.
    c. capable workers and eager feminists.
    d. less able to assume responsible roles than Northern women.

Inference _____ 8. The author's main purpose in mentioning the accomplishments of Maria Mitchell is to point out that

    a. she discovered a comet.
    b. her professional achievements in astronomy were exceptional and thus somewhat improved the image of women.
    c. she was the first woman professor of astronomy in the United States.
    d. she was a founder of the Association for the Advancement of Women.

Detail _____ 9. The article states or implies that all the following women worked to abolish slavery *except*

    a. Anna Howard Shaw.
    b. Harriet Tubman.
    c. Anna Dickson.
    d. Stanton and Anthony.

Inference _____ 10. In the author's opinion, the long wait by women after the Civil War for suffrage

    a. was predictable in 1865.
    b. would not have been expected in 1865.
    c. was due to the vote of black men.
    d. was justified.

Answer the following with *T* (true) or *F* (false):

Detail _____ 11. Women were granted the right to vote in 1920.

Detail _____ 12. Sojourner Truth had been a Southern slave.

Inference _____ 13. The author implies that feminist leaders were more concerned with their own right to vote than with the abolition of slavery.

Detail _____ 14. From the very beginning, the right to vote was the focal point of the women's movement.

Detail _____ 15. Sojourner Truth had thirteen children.

BUILD YOUR VOCABULARY   MyReadingLab™

Complete
this **Exercise** on
myreadinglab.com

According to the way the italicized word was used in the selection, indicate *a, b, c,* or *d* for the word or phrase that gives the best definition. The number in parentheses indicates the line of the passage in which the word is located.

SELECTION 2

_____ 1. "were too *restrictive*" (7)
a. showy
b. expensive
c. complicated
d. confining

_____ 2. "to the *detriment* of" (8)
a. harm
b. anger
c. apology
d. objection

_____ 3. "a *defiant* gesture" (13)
a. unlucky
b. resistant
c. admirable
d. ignorant

_____ 4. "*communal* marriage experiments" (18)
a. permanent
b. living together in groups
c. illegal
d. uncommon

_____ 5. "silencing *hecklers*" (27)
a. soldiers
b. rioters
c. disciples
d. verbal harassers

_____ 6. "*pursue* professional careers" (37)
a. strive for
b. abandon
c. acknowledge
d. indicate

_____ 7. "sanitation and *hygiene*" (46)
a. garbage disposal
b. biology
c. preservation of health
d. mental disorders

_____ 8. "an *incessant* struggle" (54)
a. earlier
b. final
c. novel
d. unceasing

_____ 9. "*convalescent* homes" (62)
a. sanitary
b. government
c. reclaimed
d. recuperating

_____ 10. "called politically *naive*" (86)
a. unsophisticated
b. well informed
c. dishonest
d. unfortunate

Concept Prep for Art History

A Sampling of Careers in Art History

- Museum curator
- Antiques dealer
- Educator

- Researcher for museums, galleries, auction houses, or organizations that maintain historic sites

Why study art history?

Just as written history is a verbal record of the events and people of the past, fine art is a visual interpretation of reality and a reflection of past taste and values. Art tells us about people and their culture, as illustrated in the earliest primitive cave drawings depicting animals and hunters or in the elaborate tombs in the Egyptian pyramids, built for the pharaohs. Through art, we can glimpse a likeness of Elizabeth I, feel the power of a ship battle at sea, or view the majesty of the American frontier. Artists link us to the past through beauty, creativity, and emotion.

When we say "the arts," what do we mean? The *arts* and the *fine arts* refer to creative works in painting, sculpture, literature, architecture, drama, music, opera, dance, and film. A work that is especially well crafted is said to be fine art.

The Starry Night (1889), Vincent van Gogh. Oil on canvas, 29 × 36 1/4" (73.7 × 92.1 cm). The Museum of Modern Art, New York, NY/SuperStock.

Museums, a word derived from Greek to mean places presided over by the Muses, display fine arts in paintings and sculpture. Some of the greatest museums in the world are the *Louvre* in Paris, the *Prado* in Madrid, and the *Metropolitan Museum of Art* in New York City.

Who are some of the great artists?

- One of the most extraordinary artists was *Leonardo da Vinci* (1452–1519). He was considered a *Renaissance man* because of his genius, insatiable curiosity, and wide interests in art, engineering, anatomy, and aeronautics. He painted the *Mona Lisa*, the world's most famous painting. This woman with the mysterious smile whose eyes seem to follow you is displayed in the Louvre behind several layers of bulletproof glass.
- *Michelangelo* (1475–1564) was a sculptor, painter, architect, and poet. Before he was 30 years old, he created the famous marble statue of *David*, which portrays the biblical king in his youth. Michelangelo was commissioned by the pope to paint the ceiling of the *Sistine Chapel* in the Vatican in Rome. For four years, the artist worked on his back in the chapel to complete *The Creation of Adam*, which contains more than 400 individual figures.
- The founder and leading artist of the *Impressionists* was *Claude Monet* (1840–1926). Critics said the feathery brushstrokes and play of light in his works conveyed the "impression" of a particular moment. Monet advocated getting out of the studio and painting outdoors, facing the subject. He painted many scenes of the gardens and water lily ponds surrounding his home in *Giverny* near Paris.

- *Vincent van Gogh* (1853–1890) borrowed from the Impressionists but achieved another dimension in the swirling brushstrokes of his work to convey his unique vision. His sunflower paintings and *Starry Night* are among his most famous works, but in his lifetime van Gogh sold only one painting. He suffered from depression and spent his last years in a mental institution. In an argument with another artist, he cut off his own ear.
- *Pablo Picasso* (1881–1973) is one of the most influential of all modern artists. Because traditional skills in painting were so easy for him, he looked for new modes of expression. He was the originator of cubism, an abstract style of painting that displays several perspectives of an object simultaneously. One of his most acclaimed paintings is *Guernica,* a haunting visual protest against the savagery of war.
- By the twentieth century, female artists were becoming more prominent. *Mary Cassatt* (1861–1914), an Impressionist, holds a unique place in American art. She was one of the first women artists to succeed professionally. Cassatt began her work in Pennsylvania but later settled in Paris. Domestic scenes became her theme, and she portrayed women and children in intimate settings.
- *Frida Kahlo* (1907–1954), a Mexican artist, is sometimes called the "portrait genie." She dramatized her life story in self-portraits, interweaving them with symbolism, myth, and surrealistic elements. Kahlo was studying to be a physician when a serious car accident hospitalized her. She took up painting and did not return to medicine. Her colorful creations reflect the endurance of life and the traditions of Mexico.
- *Georgia O'Keeffe* (1887–1986) was one of the first American artists to experiment with abstract form. She interpreted nature in beautiful geometric shapes. O'Keeffe combined the appearance of sculpture and photography in her paintings of flowers, sun-bleached animal bones, clouds, and surreal desert scenes. Her clear, bright colors reflect her love of the Southwest and American independence.

REVIEW QUESTIONS

After studying the material, answer the following questions:

1. What do works included in "the arts" have in common? _____
   _____

2. Where is the Louvre? _____

3. What is a Renaissance man? _____

4. What is unusually engaging about Mona Lisa's face? _____
   _____

5. What story is painted on the ceiling of the Sistine Chapel? _____
   _____

6. How did the Impressionists get their name? _____
   _____

7. What scenes did Monet paint at Giverny? _____

8. Which painter advocated painting outdoors? _____

9. How did van Gogh disfigure himself? _____

10. Why did Picasso turn to cubism? _____

Your instructor may choose to give a true-false review of these art history concepts.

SELECTION 3   Business

PREVIEW the next selection to predict its purpose and organization and to formulate your learning plan.

Activate Schema

Do you prefer pizzas from Domino's, Pizza Hut, or Papa John's?
If your dream could become a reality, what small business would you start?

Establish a Purpose for Reading

Downsizing, outsourcing, women's increasing presence in the workforce, and Internet technology are now shaping the American entrepreneurial spirit. The advantages and rewards of small business ownership are great, but so are the risks. What do you expect to learn from this selection about Papa John's and small businesses? After recalling what you already know about start-up businesses, read the selection to learn what defines a small business, why people open them, and why Papa John's is successful.

Increase Word Knowledge

What do you know about these words?

void	successive	droves	dominant	titans
novice	debut	vaulted	stagnant	heritage

Your instructor may give a true-false vocabulary review before or after reading.

Integrate Knowledge While Reading

Questions have been inserted in the margin to stimulate your thinking while reading. Remember to

Predict	Picture	Relate	Monitor	Correct	Annotate

THE NEW ENTREPRENEUR
Watch a video on young entrepreneurs via your ebook at www.myreadinglab.com and then answer the related questions in the VIDEO LINK section or via MyReadingLab.

Scan this QR Code to hear this reading

Why are bubbles bad?

What companies succeeded?

Why Is Papa John's Rolling in the Dough?

SELECTION 3

As a high school student working at a local pizza pub, John Schnatter liked everything about the pizza business. "I liked making the dough; I liked kneading the dough; I liked putting the sauce on; I liked putting the toppings on; I liked running the oven," recalls Schnatter. Obsessed
5 with perfect pizza topping and bubble-free melted cheese, Schnatter knew that something was missing from national pizza chains: superior-quality traditional pizza delivered to the customer's door. And his dream was to one day open a pizza restaurant that would fill that void.

Schnatter worked his way through college making pizzas, honing
10 the techniques and tastes that would someday become Papa John's trademark. Shortly after graduating from Ball State University with a business degree, he faced his first business challenge. His father's tavern was $64,000 in debt and failing. So Schnatter sold his car, used the money to purchase $1,600 of used restaurant equipment, knocked out a broom closet in the back of his father's
15 tavern, and began selling pizzas to the tavern's customers. Soon the pizza became the tavern's main attraction and helped turn the failing business around. In 1985 Schnatter officially opened the first Papa John's restaurant. Then he set about opening as many stores as the market would bear.

But Schnatter needed a recipe for success. With Little Caesar's promoting deep
20 discounts and Domino's emphasizing fast delivery, Papa John's needed a fresh approach to compete successfully with the big chains. If you were John Schnatter, how would you grow a small pizza operation into one that could compete with national players? Would you franchise your concept? Would you remain a private enterprise or go public? Would you expand overseas? Where would you focus your efforts?

UNDERSTANDING THE WORLD OF SMALL BUSINESS

25 Many small businesses start out like Papa John's: with an entrepreneur, an idea, and a drive to succeed. In fact, the United States was originally founded by people involved in small business—the family farmer, the shopkeeper, the craftsperson. Successive waves of immigrants carried on the tradition, launching restaurants and laundries, providing repair and delivery services, and opening newsstands and bakeries.

30 The 1990s were a golden decade of entrepreneurship in the United States. Entrepreneurs launched small companies in droves to fill new consumer needs. Many took advantage of Internet technologies to gain a competitive edge. Some succeeded; others failed. But the resurgence of small businesses helped turn the U.S. economy into the growth engine for the world.

35 Today, over 5.8 million small companies exist in the United States. But defining what constitutes a small business is surprisingly tricky, because *small* is a relative term.

One reliable source of information for small businesses is the Small Business Administration (SBA). This government agency serves as a resource and advocate for small firms, providing them with financial assistance, training, and a variety of
40 helpful programs. The SBA defines a small business as a firm that (a) is independently owned and operated, (b) is not dominant in its field, (c) is relatively small in terms of annual sales, and (d) has fewer than 500 employees. The SBA reports that

80 percent of all U.S. companies have annual sales of less than $1 million and that about 60 percent of the nation's employers have fewer than five workers.

FACTORS CONTRIBUTING TO THE INCREASE IN THE NUMBER OF SMALL BUSINESSES

45 Three factors are contributing to the increase in the number of small businesses today: technological advances, an increase in the number of women and minority business owners, and corporate downsizing and outsourcing.

TECHNOLOGY AND THE INTERNET

The Internet, together with e-commerce, has spawned thousands of new business ventures. ShippingSupply.com is one such firm. Karen Young, a collector of knick-
50 knacks, founded this small business when she was looking for affordable packing and shipping materials for her mail-order items. On a whim, Young decided to market bubble wrap, plastic foam, and shipping tubes she purchased directly from manufac-turers to eBay sellers. Today, ShippingSupply.com has eight full-time employees, occupies 7,000 feet of warehouse space, and has over 35,500 customers in its
55 database.

RISE IN NUMBER OF WOMEN AND MINORITY SMALL-BUSINESS OWNERS

The number of women-owned small businesses has also increased sharply over the past three decades—from 5 percent to over 39 percent of all small businesses. these businesses now employ more than 18.5 million people and ring up more than $3.1 trillion in annual sales. Women are starting small businesses for a number of reasons.
60 Some choose to run their own companies so they can enjoy a more flexible work arrangement; others start their own businesses because of barriers to corporate ad-vancement, known as the glass ceiling. Josie Natori is a perfect example of such a scenario. By her late twenties, Natori was earning six figures as the first female vice president of investment banking at Merrill Lynch. But Natori knew that her chances
65 of further advancement were slim in the male-dominated financial world. So she started her own lingerie line. Today, Natori is the owner of a multi-million-dollar fashion empire that sells elegant lingerie and evening wear.

DOWNSIZING AND OUTSOURCING

Contrary to popular wisdom, business start-ups soar when the economy sours. Dur-ing hard times, many companies downsize or lay off talented employees, who then
70 have little to lose by pursuing self-employment. In fact, several well-known compa-nies were started during recessions. Tech titans William Hewlitt and David Packard joined forces in Silicon Valley in 1938 during the Great Depression. Bill Gates start-ed Microsoft during the 1975 recession. And the founders of Sun Microsystems, Compaq Computer, Adobe Systems, Silicon Graphics, and Lotus Development
75 started their companies in 1982–in the midst of a recession and high unemployment.

To make up for layoffs of permanent staff, some companies **outsource** or sub-contract special projects and secondary business functions to experts outside the organization. Others turn to outsourcing as a way to permanently eliminate entire company departments. Regardless of the reason, the increased use of outsourcing
80 provides opportunities for smaller businesses to serve the needs of larger enterprises.

Do Internet companies have low start-up costs?

Is this a cause-and-effect relationship?

SELECTION 3

John Schnatter, founder and president of the
Papa John's Pizza chain.
Mark Von Holden.WireImage/Getty Images

BEHIND THE SCENES: PAPA JOHN'S PIPING HOT PERFORMANCE

John Schnatter did a remarkable job of expanding from a single pizza store he started
in his father's tavern. Three years after Schnatter opened his first Papa John's, he
expanded outside of the Louisville, Kentucky, area. He was no novice. He knew the
grass roots of the pizza business, he had an intuitive grasp of what customers wanted,
85 and he knew how to make pizzas taste a little bit better than the competition. Moreover, he had the qualities of an entrepreneur: driven, intense, willing to make things
happen, visionary, and very competitive.

John Schnatter used franchising to grow the business. Today about 75 percent
of Papa John's are franchised; the rest are company-owned. He was encouraged by
90 Kentucky Fried Chicken, Long John Silver's, Chi Chi's, and other Kentucky-born
restaurants that had successfully taken their franchised restaurants national.
Schnatter thought, "What the heck, maybe I could do it too." But to keep growth
under control, Papa John's didn't just move into an area and open up 200 stores.
95 Schnatter grew the stores one at a time—spending up to six months to a year assessing an area's potential.

It wasn't long before Papa John's began grabbing business from such giants as Pizza Hut, Little Caesar's, and delivery king Domino's. Then in 1999 Papa John's made its European debut by acquiring Perfect Pizza Holdings, a 205-unit delivery and carryout pizza chain in the United Kingdom. The acquisition gave Papa John's 100 instant access to proven sites that would have been difficult to obtain. Besides the real estate, Perfect Pizza had a good management team that Schnatter could fold into his organization.

Today, Papa John's has vaulted past Little Caesar's to become the nation's third-largest pizza chain. The company now boasts over 2,700 stores in 47 states and 9 105 international markets. Annual sales have mushroomed to about $1.7 billion. In spite of its tremendous growth, Schnatter insists on maintaining the highest quality standards. He does so by keeping things simple. About 95 percent of the restaurants are takeout only. The menu is simple—just two types of pizza, thin crust or regular—no exotic toppings, no salads, no sandwiches, and no buffalo wings. Owners are trained 110 to remake pies that rate less than 8 on the company's 10-point scale. If the cheese shows a single air bubble or the crust is not golden brown, out the offender goes. Schnatter's attention to product quality has earned the company awards. Papa John's was twice voted number one in customer satisfaction among all fast-food restaurants in the American Consumer Satisfaction Index.

115 To keep things in order, Schnatter visits four to five stores a week, often unannounced. He also trains managers how to forecast product demand. Stores project demand one to two weeks in advance. They factor in anything from forthcoming promotions to community events to the next big high school football game. If a big game is on TV, Schnatter wants to make sure the store owners are ready for the surge 120 in deliveries.

Still, like many companies today, Papa John's faces new challenges. It's becoming increasingly difficult to grow the company's share of the pie. Although Americans consume pizza at a rate of 350 slices a second, the pizza industry is stagnant and highly competitive. Growth usually comes at the expense of a competitor's existing 125 business. Moreover, to keep profitability in line, Schnatter has scaled back company expansion plans and even closed some unprofitable outlets. But Schnatter is determined to succeed. And if one strength rises above the others in Schnatter's path to success, it's his ability to recruit and retain the right people. "There's nothing special about John Schnatter except the people around me," Schnatter says. "They make me 130 look better" and they make Papa John's what it is—committed to its heritage of making superior-quality, traditional pizza.

(1,640 words)

—Courtland L. Bovée, John V. Thrill, and Barbara E. Schatzman,
Business in Action, 2nd ed. © 2004, pp. 91, 109–110.
Reprinted by permission of Pearson Education, Inc.,
Upper Saddle River, NJ

Recall

Stop to self-test, relate, and react.

Your instructor may choose to give you a true-false comprehension review.

WRITE ABOUT THE SELECTION   MyReadingLab™

Complete
this **Exercise** on
myreadinglab.com

What factors contribute to the opening of small businesses? Why did John Schnatter open his pizza business?

Response Suggestion: Discuss and explain the cause-and-effect relationship of at least five factors that prompt people to take risks and start something new.

 VIDEO LINK   MyReadingLab™

Complete
this **Exercise** on
myreadinglab.com

Now that you have read the selection and viewed the video on The New Entrepreneur, check your understanding by answering with *T* (true) or *F* (false):

_____ 1. According to the video, only one in four college seniors will have a job when they graduate.

_____ 2. Like John Schnatter of Papa John's Pizza, John Campbell started a pizza business while in college.

_____ 3. The video also features a college student who started a photography business.

_____ 4. The video states that the majority of new businesses are successful.

_____ 5. The "new entrepreneur" is likely to be a student who starts a business as an alternative to beginning a career in the traditional job market.

SKILL DEVELOPMENT: IDENTIFY ORGANIZATIONAL PATTERNS

Answer the following with *T* (true) or *F* (false):

_____ 1. The first and last sections are examples with anecdotal information about a real business.

_____ 2. The section "Understanding the World of Small Business" defines a small business.

_____ 3. The organizational pattern of the section "Factors Contributing to the Increase in the Number of Small Businesses" is cause and effect.

_____ 4. The organizational pattern of the section "Downsizing and Outsourcing" is comparison and contrast.

CHECK YOUR COMPREHENSION   MyReadingLab™

After reading the selection, answer the following questions with *a, b, c,* or *d.* To help you analyze your strengths and weaknesses, the question types are indicated.

Complete
this **Exercise** on
myreadinglab.com

SELECTION 3

Main Idea _____ 1. Which is the best statement of the main idea of this selection?

a. Through hard work, Papa John's has expanded globally and become the third largest pizza company in the world.
b. The golden decade for entrepreneurship has peaked but is not over, as proved by Papa John's Pizza.
c. Current factors are contributing to a rise in the number of small businesses, and Papa John's Pizza is a glowing example of one such entrepreneurial success.
d. The highly competitive pizza business requires more than good tomato sauce to turn dough into dollars.

Detail _____ 2. When John Schnatter started his pizza business, he had all the following *except*

a. years of experience making pizza dough.
b. a college degree in business.
c. training in running the pizza ovens.
d. restaurant equipment from his father's business.

Inference _____ 3. The author implies that John Schnatter

a. pulled his father's business out of a $64,000 debt.
b. closed his father's tavern to open his pizza parlor.
c. was financed in the pizza business by his father.
d. continued to use the formula of liquor sales with pizza.

Detail _____ 4. As defined by the Small Business Administration, a small business is all of the following *except*

a. it has fewer than 500 employees.
b. it is independently operated.
c. it is owned by stock holders.
d. it is not dominant in its field.

Inference _____ 5. The author suggests that Karen Young's ShippingSupply.com business is

a. primarily a retail store that customers enter to buy supplies.
b. a prime candidate for franchising.
c. a mail-order knickknack venture.
d. a firm that conducts business over the Internet, with supplies shipped from a warehouse.

Inference _____ 6. The author implies that a glass ceiling is

a. a barrier to high-level corporate advancement.
b. a more flexible work arrangement.

c. an entry into investment banking.

d. a barrier to male-dominated entry-level positions.

Detail _____ 7. Downsizing in a company means to

a. fire incompetent workers.

b. lay off valued employees.

c. freeze hiring until profits improve.

d. subcontract for special projects.

Inference _____ 8. An example of outsourcing done by an American company would be

a. selling products in India.

b. hiring experienced European workers for an American company.

c. contracting for payroll accounting to be done by a company in Ireland.

d. buying coffee beans from Latin America and processing them in the United States.

Inference _____ 9. The author suggests that Schnatter's success can be attributed to all the following *except*

a. hiring good people.

b. adding a variety of items to the menu.

c. insisting on high-quality standards for pizzas.

d. personally visiting stores to keep things in order.

Inference _____ 10. The reader can conclude that of the company's 2,700 stores,

a. most are owned by Schnatter.

b. all but 340 stores are now franchised.

c. the company owns about 675 of them.

d. Perfect Pizza Holdings franchised 2,400 stores.

Answer the following with *T* (true), *F* (false), or *CT* (can't tell):

Detail _____ 11. During a recession and times of high unemployment, few new businesses are started.

Detail _____ 12. According to the Small Business Administration, over half of the small American businesses hire fewer than five workers.

Inference _____ 13. Schnatter bought Perfect Pizza in the United Kingdom because it was poorly managed.

Inference _____ 14. The author suggests that Papa John's plans to expand into salads and sandwiches.

Inference _____ 15. The author suggests that the pizza industry is rapidly increasing its customer base and adding new patrons who have never tried pizza.

SELECTION 3

BUILD YOUR VOCABULARY   MyReadingLab™

Complete
this **Exercise** on
myreadinglab.com

According to the way the italicized word was used in the selection, select *a, b, c,* or *d* for the word or phrase that gives the best definition. The number in parentheses indicates the line of the passage in which the word is located.

_____ 1. "would fill that *void*" (8)
   a. goal
   b. empty space
   c. union
   d. demand

_____ 2. "*Successive* waves of immigrants" (27)
   a. one after another
   b. eager
   c. unsteady
   d. overwhelming

_____ 3. "launched small companies in *droves*" (31)
   a. efforts
   b. desperation
   c. reactions
   d. large numbers

_____ 4. "not *dominant* in its field" (41)
   a. growing
   b. foremost
   c. secure
   d. competitive

_____ 5. "Tech *titans*" (71)
   a. enthusiasts
   b. explorers
   c. giants
   d. hobbyists

_____ 6. "was no *novice*" (83)
   a. beginner
   b. pushover
   c. coward
   d. follower

_____ 7. "its European *debut*" (98)
   a. achievement
   b. marketing ploy
   c. market entry
   d. diversity

_____ 8. "has *vaulted* past Little Caesar's" (103)
   a. sneaked
   b. crawled
   c. leaped
   d. slowly moved

_____ 9. "pizza industry is *stagnant*" (123)
   a. nervous
   b. cutthroat
   c. small
   d. not growing

_____ 10. "committed to its *heritage*" (130)
   a. logo
   b. brand
   c. management
   d. tradition

VOCABULARY BOOSTER

What's In, What's Out? What's Hot, What's Not?

Prefixes	**Root**
en-, em-: "in"	*e-, ec-, ef-, ex-:* "out"
non-: "not"	*calor-:* "heat"

Words with *en-, em-:* "in"

Jackson was able to *employ* several of his friends as tech reps for his Internet software company.

- *encapsulate:* to place in a capsule; to condense or summarize

  Drug manufacturers *encapsulate* some medications so that they are easier to swallow.

- *enclave:* any small, distinct area or group within a larger one

  Before the Berlin Wall came down, West Berlin was a democratic *enclave* surrounded by Communist East Germany.

- *enmesh:* to catch in a net; entangle

  Animal rights groups are against the use of nets in tuna fishing because dolphins can become *enmeshed* in the nets and die.

- *ensemble:* all parts of a thing considered only as the whole, not separately, such as an entire costume or a group of musicians, singers, dancers, or actors.

  The cast of ABC's drama *Grey's Anatomy* is an *ensemble* of many actors.

- *embed:* to fix or place firmly in a surrounding mass; to insert, as a clause in a sentence

  The senator knew that to get her controversial proposal passed by Congress, she had to *embed* it in a more popular bill.

- *embroiled:* to be involved in conflict or confusion

  The twins were *embroiled* in a wrestling match when their father finally had to separate them.

- *embellish:* to beautify with ornamental or elaborate details

  The speechwriter's goal was to enhance but not overly *embellish* the governor's speeches.

- *enroll:* to register or become a member of a group

  Jenny needed to *enroll* in the Psychology 101 class before it became filled.

Words with *e-, ec-, ef-, ex-:* "out"

Renew your driver's license before it *expires*, so you can avoid taking the driving test again.

- *eclipse:* any obscuring of light (darkening) especially of planets; to surpass by comparison

  To protect your eyes during a solar *eclipse*, wear sunglasses and look at the sun only through a pinhole in a piece of paper.

- *emaciated:* abnormally thin, as if wasting away

  Tanica had lost so much weight on a fad diet that she looked *emaciated*.

- *eccentric:* peculiar or odd; not having the same center

  The neighbor on the corner is an *eccentric* man who wears pajamas to the grocery store.

- *effervescent:* bubbling; lively or enthusiastic

  The *effervescent* spring water foamed and sparkled as Juan poured it.

- *exalt:* raise or elevate in rank or character; praise highly

  In his opening remarks, the club president *exalted* the literary talent and accomplishments of the guest speaker.

- *exaggerate:* to stretch the limits of the truth or overstate

  John always *exaggerates* the size of the fish he claims he almost caught.

Words with *non-:* "not"

Military personnel such as surgeons or chaplains who are not fighters are considered *noncombatants*.

- *nonchalant:* coolly indifferent, unconcerned, unexcited

  Tonia's *nonchalant* way of accepting dates makes it seem that she just has nothing better to do.

- *nondescript:* undistinguished or dull, a person or thing of no specific type or kind; not easy to describe

  Students decorated the *nondescript* dorm rooms to reflect their own tastes and personalities.

- *nonpartisan:* objective; not controlled by an established political party

  It is necessary to forge *nonpartisan* politics when the government is split evenly between two parties.

- *nonplussed:* completely puzzled, totally perplexed so as to become unable to continue

  The stand-up comedian was inexperienced and became totally *nonplussed* by the hecklers in the audience.

- *nonconformist:* someone who refuses to act in accordance with established customs

  A *nonconformist* would not be a good candidate for a private school where uniforms are worn.

Words with *calor*-: "heat"

When capitalized, the word *Calorie* refers to a kilocalorie (1,000 small calories) and is used to measure the amount of energy produced by food when oxidized in the body.

- *calorie:* a specific unit of heat (cal.) in physics; a unit expressing the energy value of food (Cal.) in nutrition

   Judy tries to eat low-*calorie* meals, including salads, fish, lots of vegetables, and few desserts, to maintain a healthy weight.

- *caloric:* of or pertaining to calories or heat; high in calories

   People who eat highly *caloric* meals must exercise more to maintain a healthy weight.

- *scald:* to burn with hot liquid or steam; to bring to a temperature just short of the boiling point

   Some recipes require the cook to *scald* milk before adding it to the other ingredients.

- *caldera:* a basinlike depression or collapsed area caused by the explosion of the center of a volcano

   The scientists were injured by hot lava when they got too close to the edge of the *caldera* of a still-active volcano.

- *cauldron*: a large kettle for boiling

   Shakespeare's *Macbeth* includes a scene with witches stirring a boiling mixture in a *cauldron*.

REVIEW QUESTIONS

Part I

Indicate whether the following sentences are true (*T*) or false (*F*):

_____ 1. A person known to *embellish* is not a plain speaker.

_____ 1. We tend to *exalt* those whom we hold in low regard.

_____ 3. A *nonchalant* attitude could also be described as deeply caring.

_____ 4. A chef can *scald* milk without boiling it.

_____ 5. The brass instruments are a part of the band's *ensemble*.

_____ 6. An *eccentric* relative likely has some unusual behaviors.

_____ 7. Someone who dresses in a *nondescript* manner would stand out in a crowd.

_____ 8. *Nonconformists* are likely to care a good deal about what others think of them.

_____ 9. A dormitory room could be considered an *enclave* within the dorm itself.

_____ 10. Jewelers have a talent for *embedding* precious stones in gorgeous settings.

Part II

Choose the best *antonym* from the boxed list for the words below.

criticize	compliant	chill	dislodge	fatten
interested	minimized	undecorated	untangled	usual

11. eccentric _____

12. embellished _____

13. exalt _____

14. exaggerated _____

15. emaciate _____

16. enmeshed _____

17. embed _____

18. nonchalant _____

19. scald _____

20. nonconformist _____

Your instructor may choose to give a multiple-choice review.

CREDITS

Video screen captures reproduced with permission of BBC Motion Gallery Education: Creativity; TOMS Shoes: Changing the World; The Effects of Stress; The New Entrepreneur; DNA and the Criminal Justice System; Illiteracy in the United States; Global Warming; The Magic Number of Beauty; The American Diet.

Lutgens, Frederick K. and Edward J. Tarbuck, illustrated by Dennis Tasa. *The Atmosphere: An Introduction to Meteorology*, 9th ed., © 2004, pp. 378, 444, 147, 195. Reproduced in print and electronic formats by permission of Pearson Education, Inc., Upper Saddle River, New Jersey.; Thompson, Janice and Melinda Manore. *Nutrition: An Applied Approach*, pp. 244–245, 60. Copyright © 2005 Pearson Education, Inc., publishing as Benjamin Cummings. Reprinted by permission of Pearson Education, Inc., Glenview, IL.; Gregory, Paul R. *Essentials of Economics*, 6th ed., © 2005, p. 41. Reproduced in print and electronic formats by permission of Pearson Education, Inc., Upper Saddle River, New Jersey.; Lutgens, Frederick K. and Edward J. Tarbuck, illustrated by Dennis Tasa. *The Atmosphere: An Introduction to Meteorology*, 9th ed., © 2004, pp. 378, 444, 147, 195. Reproduced in print and electronic formats by permission of Pearson Education, Inc., Upper Saddle River, New Jersey.; Gregory, Paul R. *Essentials of Economics*, 6th ed., © 2005, pp. 41, 66, 68. Reproduced in print and electronic formats by permission of Pearson Education, Inc., Upper Saddle River, New Jersey.; Pitt, Leonard. from *We Americans*. Copyright © 1987 Kendall/Hunt Publishing Company. Reprinted with permission.

-Answer Key for Chapter 3 in Bridge to College Reading "Patterns of Organization." P. 131-180.

Page Numbers May be Inaccurate!

p. 134-135, EXERCISE 1, "Signal words"

1. for example   2. Consequently   3. in addition   4. However   5. in the meantime
6. Finally   7. Nevertheless   8. in contrast   9. for example   10. furthermore

P.136-143 EXERCISE 2 "Patterns of Organization"   Patterns are shown with their examples

Simple Listing: The Big Five

Five-factor theory of personality
  Extraversion
  Neuroticism
  Agreeableness
  Openness to experience

Definition: Ultrasound

Ultrasound
  Sound waves to produce image
    Detect abnormalities
    Pictures at 5-6 weeks of pregnancy
  Ex: Used in pregnancy with amniocentesis & fetoscopy

Description: Caribbean

  Caribbean

    Most densely populated region in Americas
    Region of Greater & Lesser Antilles
    Grinding poverty & misery

Time Order, Sequence, or Narration: The Mormon Movement

Topic: Mormon Movement

When did it happen?	What Happened?
1820	Smith's revelation of Church
1823	Found plates and translated *Book of Mormon*
1830s	Moved West
1844	Smith shot
After Smith's death	Young got to Salt Lake

Comparison and Contrast: Hispanic Americans

Topic: Hispanic Americans or Latinos

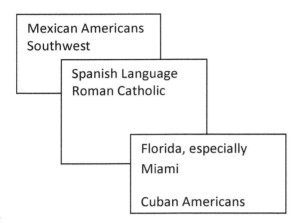

Mexican Americans
Southwest

Spanish Language
Roman Catholic

Florida, especially
Miami

Cuban Americans

Cause and Effect: Winter Camp at Valley Forge

Topic: Winter Camp at Valley Forge

Cause: Why did it happen?	Effect: What happened?
Cold weather	Soldiers froze
No straw or blanket	
Scarce Food	Died of malnutrition
Disease and misery	Soldiers deserted army

Classification: Predation

Predation

Predator: Consumer
Prey: food

Addition: Entrepreneur Quincy Jones

Quincy Jones

Producer of Jackson Hits
Founder of *Vibe*
Co-owner of *Spin*
Awarded 26 Grammys and Legend
Chair and CEO of Media Group

Summary: WWII Total War

WWII Total War

70 nations participated
Fought on 3 continents
Entire societies participated

Location or Spatial Order: Egypt

Egypt
Mediterranean on North
Libya to West
Sudan to South
Israel to East

Generalization and Example: Smoking

Smoking kills
30% of all cancer deaths
Lung cancer leading death cause

P. 145-146 Exercise 3, **Identifying Paragraph Patterns**

1. C   2. B   3. C   4. D   5. B   6. C   7. B   8. D

P. 146-149 Exercise 4, Patterns of Organization and Main Idea

PASSAGE A:
1. Sleet
2. Sleet is also called ice pellets; sleet is formed when raindrops or melted snow pass through cold air; sleet does not stick to trees and wires; sleet bounces on impact; accumulated sleet is like dry sand.
3. Definition
4. Sleet is formed when liquid precipitation freezes near the earth's surface.

Passage B:

1. Types of drinking water
2. Carbonated, mineral, distilled, purified, and tap
3. Classification
4. There are several distinct categories of drinking water.

PASSAGE C:
1. M&Ms and the law of demand
2. Quantity demanded increases with lowered per ounce price; the M&M study supported the law of demand.

3. Cause and effect

4. The M&M experiment supports the law of demand-the quantity demanded will increase as the price is lowered, with all other factors remaining constant.

PASSAGE D:

1. Basketball practice differences between boys and girls

2. Girls had better attention to directions; girls often apologized for mistakes; girls enjoyed talking with the coaches.

3. Comparison and Contrast

4. Coaching girls is a different experience than coaching boys.

p. 150-152, Exercise 5, Identifying Combined Organizational Patterns

Passage 1:

1. dust devils   2. Definition   3. Definition   4. Contrast   5. cause and effect

6. While dust devils may be considered relatives of tornadoes, several differences distinguish the two phenomena.

Passage 2:

1. How eBay has become successful   2. cause and effect   3. Contrast   4. description
5. simple listing   6. generalization and example   7. simple listing

P. 154-157, SELECTION 1, NARRATIVE: "INSTANT MESSAGE, INSTANT GIRLFRIEND"
P. 158: SKILL DEVELOPMENT: IDENTIFY ORGANIZATIONAL PATTERNS

1. True   True

p. 159. Check Your Comprehension

1. D   2. A   3. C   4. A   5. B   6. D   7. B   8. B   9. B   10. B
11, True   12. False   13. False   14. False   15. True

p, 161 Build Your Vocabulary

1. B   2. A   3. C   4. B or D   5. D   6. A   7. B   8. B   9. C   10. D

P. 162-166, Selection #2: History: "Women in History"
P. 126. CHECK YOUR COMPREHENSION

1. B   2. B   3. C   4. D   5. D   6. D   7. A   8. B   9. A   10. B
11. TRUE   12. FALSE   13. FALSE   14. FALSE   15. TRUE

P. 128 BUILD YOUR VOCABULARY

1. D   2. A   3. B   4. B   5. D   6. A   7. C   8. D   9. D   10. A

Inference

Learning Objectives

From this chapter, readers will learn to:

1 Define inference
2 Make reasonable inferences while reading
3 Recognize connotative language
4 Identify euphemisms and politically correct language
5 Interpret figurative language
6 Draw logical conclusions

Facsimile of *March: Peasants at Work on a Feudal Estate*, from the 'Tres Riches Heures du Duc de Berry' (1413–1416), Limbourg Brothers (fl.1400–1416). Victoria & Albert Museum, London, UK/ The Bridgeman Art Library/SuperStock.

WHAT IS AN INFERENCE?

Learning Objective 1

Define Inference

At the first and most basic level of reading, the *literal level*—the level that presents the facts—you can actually point to the words on the page to answer a literal question. However, at the second and more sophisticated level of reading—the *inferential level*—you no longer can point to such an answer but instead must form it from clues and suggestions within the text.

EXAMPLE

In the following passage from Michael Ondaatje's novel *The English Patient*, the author implies an activity, and the reader infers what is happening. Mark the point at which you understand the activity.

> She moves backwards a few feet and with a piece of white chalk draws more rectangles, so there is a pyramid of them, single then double then single, her left hand braced flat on the floor, her head down, serious. . . .
>
> She drops the chalk into the pocket of her dress. She stands and pulls up the looseness of her skirt and ties it around her dress. She pulls from another pocket a piece of metal and flings it out in front of her so it falls just beyond the farthest square.
>
> She leaps forward, her legs smashing down, her shadow behind her curling into the depth of the hall. She is very quick, her tennis shoes skidding on the numbers she has drawn into each rectangle, one foot landing, then two feet, then one again until she reaches the last square.[1]

EXPLANATION How many sentences did it take for you to infer that she is playing the game of hopscotch? You may have visualized the activity as early as the author's description of drawing "single then double then single"; or perhaps you caught on a bit later, when she jumps. In any case, you were able to make the inference when the clues from the text merged with your own prior knowledge.

Two different terms are used in discussing inferential thinking: the writer or speaker *implies* and the reader or listener *infers*. This merging of suggested thought is also figuratively called **reading between the lines.** Throughout this text, many of the thought questions, or think-alouds, appearing in the margins alongside the longer reading selections ask you to read between the lines.

At the inferential level, authors not only entertain readers but also subtly manipulate them. When you read, always consider what is left unsaid. This is true for the spoken word. For example, when asked, "How do you like your new boss?" you might answer, "She is always well dressed" rather than "I don't like her." By not volunteering information that directly answers the question, you convey your lack of approval or, certainly, your lack of enthusiasm. In some cases, this lack of information might send a damaging message. For example, when you graduate and look for that perfect position, you will need to ask professors and previous employers for job recommendations. Take care that the person you ask to recommend you is 100 percent on your team. The following exercise illustrates the power of what is left unsaid.

---

[1] As quoted in Stephanie Harvey and Anne Goudvis. *Strategies That Work* (Portland, ME: Stenhouse Publishers, 2000), p. 37.

EXERCISE 1

Reading Between the Lines

Read the two recommendations and decide whom you would hire.

Carlos has been working as an assistant for one year and has been a valuable member of our team. He aggressively tackles new accounts, making calls after hours to track down customers and ship needed products. He excels in sales and follows through with the details in keeping customers satisfied. We want to keep Carlos but have no openings for advanced positions. I highly recommend him for the position at your company.

Roger has worked for our company for one year as an assistant. Our company sells chicken by-products, mostly thighs and legs that are not used in America, to Russia and third world countries. Because of the international nature of our business, communication is extremely important. During his year with us, Roger has faithfully attended all meetings and has been friendly with our staff. We certainly wish him well.

Which one would you hire? Why? _____

_____

_____

_____

_____

_____

_____

_____

Any employer is wise enough to infer the meaning of a vaguely worded reference. Similarly, inferential skills are important in interpreting persuasive reports and arguments because facts that are detrimental to the supported position might be omitted to manipulate a reader's opinion. Such omissions send a "Reader Beware" signal. One of the most effective tools that selectively uses words and photos to send persuasive messages is advertising.

Cigarette advertisements, for example, entice the public through suggestion, not facts, to spend millions of dollars on a product that is known to be unhealthy. They use words and photos in a sophisticated way to lure consumers. Depending on the brand, smoking offers the refreshment of a mountain stream or the sophisticated elegance of the rich and famous. Never do the ads directly praise smoking or promise pleasure; instead, the ads *imply* smoking's positive aspects. The cigarette advertisers avoid lawsuits for false advertising by never putting anything tangible into print. The emotionalism of a full-page advertisement is so overwhelming that the consumer hardly notices the cautionary note in small print at the bottom of the page: "Warning: The Surgeon General Has Determined That Cigarette Smoking Is Dangerous to Your Health."

WHAT IS REQUIRED TO MAKE A REASONABLE INFERENCE?

Learning Objective 2

Make reasonable inferences while reading

Some experts describe the process of reading as a conversation between the author and the reader. Certainly, the conversation begins with the words on the printed page, but every reader brings a different set of background knowledge and experiences, or schemata, to them. Just as we use our accumulated wisdom to understand a friend's spoken story, we also interpret an author's message through the lens of our personal experience.

To make reasonable inferences, effective readers use logic to put together the author's clues—informational details, word choice—and their own knowledge and experience. Giving too much weight to any part of the equation can cause us to misinterpret the message. The diagram below helps to visualize the elements of a valid inference.

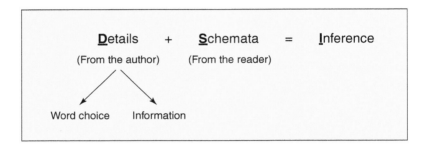

EXERCISE 2

Implied Meaning in Advertisements

Advertisers can directly state that a detergent cleans, but the task of advertising other products can be more complicated. Look through magazines and newspapers to locate three advertisements: one each for cigarettes, alcoholic beverages, and fragrances. Answer the following questions about each:

1. What is directly stated about the product?

2. What does the advertisement suggest about the product?

3. Who seems to be the suggested audience or customer for the product? Why?

Authors and advertisers have not invented a new comprehension skill; they are merely capitalizing on a highly developed skill of daily life. Think, for example, of the inferences you make every day by noticing what people say or don't say, by examining what they do or don't do, and by interpreting what others say or don't say about them. In fact, if you lacked these skills, you would miss out on a lot of the humor in jokes, cartoons, and sitcoms.

Implied Meaning in Humor

Jokes and cartoons require you to read between the lines and make connections. They are funny not so much because of what is said but because of what has been left unsaid. When you "catch on" to a joke, it simply means that you make the connection and recognize the **inference, the implied meaning.** To enjoy the joke, you link prior knowledge to what is being said. If you are telling a joke and your listener lacks the background knowledge to which the joke refers, your attempt will fall flat because the listener cannot understand the implied meaning. Listeners cannot connect with something they don't know, so be sure to choose the right joke for the right audience.

Biting humor has two levels of implied meaning. On the surface the joke makes us laugh. At a deeper level, however, the humor ridicules our beliefs, practices, or way of life.

EXAMPLE   What inference makes this joke funny?

> A toddler was used to going with his busy "stay-at-home" mom to meetings and errands for her many activities, which included the PTA, soccer car pool, and most often the League of Women Voters, of which the mom was president. One afternoon, as they arrived home from yet another meeting, the little boy greeted the family with, "Hi, everybody! We've been at the League of Running Motors!"

EXPLANATION   The inference is that the toddler was in the car so often that he misunderstood the words *League of Women Voters* and turned them into something that sounded similar and made more sense to him.

EXERCISE 3   **Implied Humor in Jokes**

Explain the inferences that make the following jokes funny.

JOKE 1

> "I wish I knew why I don't have any friends," Yvonne said to her roommate Beth. "I've been on the Dean's List every semester, I'm graduating with honors, I've been president of every club I've joined, and I have five great job offers to choose from. Why don't people like me?
>
> Beth looks over at Yvonne and says, "Well, it can be lonely at the top."

Inference: _____

_____

JOKE 2

> Dressed in Halloween costumes, the children eagerly waited at the bottom of the stairs for their Mom to put on her costume and join them for an evening of trick-or-treating. As their Mom walked down the stairs without her costume, her daughter said, "Mom, where's your costume?"
>
> The Mom answered, "I am wearing my costume. I am an overworked, overtired, Mom of three!"

Inference: _____

_____

JOKE 3

On the occasion of their 65th wedding anniversary, an elderly couple talked with family and friends about their many years together.

"What is the secret to having such a long, successful marriage," asked one of the friends. The man looked at his wife, and then back at the friend and said:

"'Yes dear,' 'Whatever you say dear,' 'I'll do that right away, dear.'"

Inference: _____

_____

JOKE 4

What prior knowledge must the reader have to understand the humor?

Question: What do you get when you cross Stephen King with a light bulb?
Answer: *The Shining*

Inference: _____

_____

BRAIN BOOSTER

The Brain's Pleasure Center and Learning

One of the oldest and most important survival mechanisms we and most creatures have is pleasure. We are motivated by the reward of pleasant sensations. When we feel happy, satisfied, or fulfilled, we want to repeat the actions that made us feel that way. The pleasure centers of human brains are located deep below the frontal cortex. The frontal cortex is associated with the brain chemical, dopamine, which is thought to create the feeling of well-being. How does this fact of brain function relate to learning? When we associate learning with pleasure—satisfaction in a job well done, the joy of learning something new, having fun with a learning game or sharing humor during class, for instance—negative emotions take a back seat, and we are relaxed enough to learn some more. Take advantage of this wonderful aspect of the human brain. Have fun!

Adapted from The Art of Changing the Brain *by James E. Zull*

EXERCISE 4

Implied Meaning in Cartoons

Explain the inferences that make the following cartoons funny.

"Oh no, we're being spammed!"

Arnie Levin/The New Yorker Collection/www.cartoonbank.com

Inference: _____

_____

_____

"I drove to the garden centre for a tree to offset my carbon footprint...
so now I've got to go back for another one..."

www.CartoonStock.com

Inference: _____

_____

_____

_____

_____

In cartoons, subtle expressions in the drawings, along with the words, imply meaning. In speech or writing, carefully chosen words imply attitude and manipulate the emotions of the reader.

CONNOTATIVE LANGUAGE

Learning Objective 3

Recognize connotative language

Notice the power of suggested meaning as you respond to the following questions:

1. If you read an author's description of classmates, which student would you assume is smartest?
   a. A student annotating items on a computer printout
   b. A student with earphones listening to a CD
   c. A student talking with classmates about the newest TV show.
2. Which would you find discussed in a vintage small town of the 1940s?
   a. Movies
   b. Cinema
   c. Picture shows
3. Who probably earns the most money?
   a. A businessperson in a dark suit, white shirt, and tie
   b. A businessperson in slacks and a sport shirt
   c. A businessperson in a pale-blue uniform

Can you prove your answers? It's not the same as proving when the Declaration of Independence was signed, yet you still have a feeling for the way each question should be answered. Even though a right or wrong answer is difficult to explain in this type of question, certain answers can still be defended as most accurate; in the preceding questions, the answers are *a, c,* and *a.* The answers are based on feelings, attitudes, and knowledge commonly shared by members of society.

A seemingly innocent tool, word choice is the first key to implied meaning. For example, compare the following sentences:

Esmeralda is skinny.

Esmeralda is slender.

If she is skinny, she is unattractive; but if she is slender she must be attractive. Both adjectives might refer to the same underweight person, but *skinny* communicates a negative feeling, whereas *slender* communicates a positive one. This feeling or emotionalism surrounding a word is called **connotation. Denotation,** on the other hand, is the specific meaning of a word. The connotative meaning goes beyond the denotative meaning to reflect certain attitudes and prejudices of society. Even though it may not seem premeditated, writers select words, just as advertisers select symbols and models, to manipulate the reader's opinions.

EXERCISE 5

Recognizing Connotation in Familiar Words

In each of the following word pairs, write the letter of the word with the more positive connotation:

_____	1. (a) issue	(b) problem
_____	2. (a) loneliness	(b) independence
_____	3. (a) tolerant	(b) pushover
_____	4. (a) difficult	(b) challenging
_____	5. (a) pale	(b) fair
_____	6. (a) direct	(b) rude
_____	7. (a) cop	(b) officer
_____	8. (a) take	(b) steal
_____	9. (a) lazy	(b) easygoing
_____	10. (a) unanswered	(b) ignored
_____	11. (a) abandon	(b) leave
_____	12. (a) know-it-all	(b) wise
_____	13. (a) lead	(b) dominate
_____	14. (a) mutt	(b) puppy
_____	15. (a) late	(b) delinquent
_____	16. (a) reasonable	(b) cheap
_____	17. (a) call	(b) yell
_____	18. (a) request	(b) beg
_____	19. (a) tell	(b) command
_____	20. (a) question	(b) interrogate

EXERCISE 6

Choosing Connotative Words

For each word listed, write a word with a similar denotative meaning that has a positive (or neutral) connotation and one that has a negative connotation. Answers will vary.

Inference

	Positive	**Negative**
eat	dine	devour
1. child	_____	_____
2. ruler	_____	_____
3. innocent	_____	_____
4. supportive	_____	_____
5. quiet	_____	_____

EXAMPLE

EXERCISE 7

Connotation in Textbooks

For each of the underlined words in the following sentences, indicate the meaning of the word and reasons why the connotation is positive or negative.

EXAMPLE

While the unions fought mainly for better wages and hours, they also championed various social reforms.

—Leonard Pitt,
We Americans

Championed: Means "supported"; suggests heroes and thus a positive cause

1. The ad was part of the oil companies' program to sell their image rather than their product to the public. In the ad they boasted that they were reseeding all the disrupted areas with a newly developed grass that grows five times faster than the grass that normally occurs there.

—Robert Wallace,
Biology: The World of Life

boasted: _____

_____

2. At noon, a group of prominent bankers met. To stop the hemorrhaging of stock prices, the bankers' pool agreed to buy stocks well above the market.

—James Kirby Martin et al.,
America and Its People

hemorrhaging: _____

_____

3. The nation's capital is <u>crawling</u> with lawyers, lobbyists, registered foreign agents, public relations consultants, and others—more than 14,000 individuals representing nearly 12,000 organizations at last count—all seeking to influence Congress.

—Robert Lineberry et al.,
Government in America, Brief Version, 2nd ed.

crawling: _____

_____

EUPHEMISMS AND POLITICALLY CORRECT LANGUAGE

Learning Objective 4

Identify euphemisms and politically correct language

A **euphemism** is a substitution of a mild, indirect, or vague term for one that is considered harsh, blunt, or offensive. It is a polite way of saying something that is embarrassing or indelicate. In the funeral business, for example, euphemisms abound. In fact, one Web site lists 213 terms for *death* or *dying* such as *pass to the great beyond* or *big sleep*. Remember that the word part *"eu-"* means "good."

When used to hide unpleasant ideas in politics or social interaction, euphemisms are sometimes called doublespeak or **politically correct language.** For example, *collateral damage* refers to civilian casualties. Other examples are the janitor being called the *sanitation engineer,* a handicapped person being called *differently abled,* or someone with a missing tooth being called *dentally disadvantaged.*

EXAMPLE

Euphemism: My stomach feels unsettled.

Politically correct: The troops were hit by friendly fire.

FIGURATIVE LANGUAGE

Learning Objective 5

Interpret figurative language

What does it mean to say, "She worked like a dog"?

To most readers, it means that she worked hard, but since few dogs work, the comparison is not literally true or particularly logical. **Figurative language** is, in a sense, another language because it is a different way of using "regular" words so that they take on new meaning. For example, "It was raining buckets" and "raining cats and dogs" are lively, figurative ways of describing a heavy rain. New speakers of English, however, who comprehend on a literal level, might look up in the sky for the descending pails or animals. The two expressions create an exaggerated, humorous effect, but on a literal level, they do not make sense.

Consider an example from a Shakespearean play. When Hamlet prepares to confront his mother, he says, "I will speak daggers to her, but use none." With an economy of expression, he vividly suggests his feelings. Much more is implied than merely saying, "I will speak sternly to her." No one expects he will use a knife on his mother, but the connotation is that the words will be sharp, piercing, and wounding. Words can be hurtful or enriching; and an author uses figurative language, sometimes called **imagery,** to stimulate readers' minds to imagine beyond the printed page by adding color, attitude, or wit.

Idioms

When first used, the phrases "works like a dog" and "raining cats and dogs" were probably very clever. Now they have lost their freshness but still convey meaning for those who are "in the know." Such phrases are called **idioms,** or expressions that do not make literal sense but have taken on a new, generally accepted meaning over many years of use.

EXAMPLE

She tried to keep a stiff upper lip during the ordeal.

His eyes were bigger than his stomach.

EXPLANATION   The first means to maintain emotional control and the second means to ask for more food than you are able to eat.

EXERCISE 8

Understanding Idioms

What do the following idioms mean?

1. burning the candle at both ends _____

   _____

2. to have the Midas touch _____

   _____

3. walking on air _____

   _____

4. to beef up _____

   _____

5. costs an arm and a leg _____

   _____

Similes

A **simile** is a comparison of two unlike things, using the word *like* or *as*.

EXAMPLE

And every soul, it passed me by,
Like the whizz of my crossbow!

—Samuel Taylor Coleridge,
The Rime of the Ancient Mariner

Metaphors

A **metaphor** is a direct comparison of two unlike things (without using *like* or *as*).

EXAMPLE

The corporate accountant is a computer from nine to five.

Miss Rosie was a wet brown bag of a woman who used to be the best looking gal in Georgia.

—Lucille Clifton,
Good Times

Literary Analogies

A **literary analogy** is a comparison of two unlike things that can be a simile or a metaphor.

EXAMPLE

Workers are the clockwork in assembly line production. (metaphor)

Time is like a river. (simile)

Hyperbole

Hyperbole, sometimes called **overstatement,** is an exaggeration to describe something as being more than it actually is. For example, *the lights of the village were brighter than a thousand stars*. An **understatement,** on the other hand, minimizes a point, such as saying, *"I covered expenses"* after winning $3 million in Las Vegas.

EXAMPLE

Hyperbole: I could sleep for twenty days and nights and still be tired.

Understatement: His clothes have seen better days.

Personification

Personification is the process of attributing human characteristics to nonhuman things.

EXAMPLE

The birds speak from the forest.

Time marches on.

Verbal Irony

Verbal irony is the use of words to express a meaning that is the opposite of what is literally said.[2] If the intent is to hurt, the irony is called **sarcasm.**

EXAMPLE

"What a great looking corporate outfit!" (Said to someone wearing torn jeans)

"There is nothing like a sunny day for a picnic." (Said during a thunderstorm)

---

[2]The general term *irony* refers to a twist in meaning or a surprise ending; it may involve a humorous or tragic undertone.

In *situational irony*, events occur contrary to what is expected, as if in a cruel twist of fate. For example, Juliet awakens and finds that Romeo has killed himself because he thought she was dead.

In *dramatic irony* the reader or audience is aware of certain details in a situation of which the characters are not.

EXERCISE 9   **Discovering Figurative Language in Essays**

Read the following essay titled "The Barrio" and enjoy the figurative language. Indicate *a* or *b* for the type of figurative language used, and write a response to each question.

> The train, its metal wheels squealing as they spin along the silvery tracks, rolls slower now. Through the gaps between the cars blinks a streetlamp and this pulsing light on a barrio streetlamp beats slower, like a weary heartbeat, until the train shudders to a halt, the light goes out, and the barrio is deep asleep.
>
> Members of the barrio describe the entire area as their home. It is a home, but it is more than this. The barrio is a refuge from the harshness and the coldness of the Anglo world. It is a forced refuge. There is no want to escape, for the feeling of the barrio is known only to its inhabitants, and the material needs of life can also be found here.
>
> The *tortilleria* [tortilla factory] fires up its machinery three times a day, producing steaming, round, flat slices of barrio bread. In the winter, the warmth of the tortilla factory is a wool *sarape* [blanket] in the chilly morning hours, but in the summer, it unbearably toasts every noontime customer.
>
> The *panaderia* [bakery] sends its sweet messenger aroma down the dimly lit street, announcing the arrival of fresh, hot sugary *pan dulce* [sweet rolls].
>
> The pool hall is a junior level country club where *chucos* [young men], strangers in their own land, get together to shoot pool and rap, while veterans, unaware of the cracking, popping balls on the green felt, complacently play dominoes beneath rudely hung *Playboy* foldouts.
>
> —Robert Ramirez,
> in *Models for Writers*, 8th ed.,
> by Alfred Rosa and Paul Escholz

_____   1. blinks a streetlamp: a. personification b. simile

_____   2. like a weary heartbeat: a. metaphor b. simile

_____   3. the barrio is deep asleep: a. personification b. simile

_____   4. tortilla factory is a wool *sarape*: a. metaphor b. simile

_____   5. toasts every noontime customer: a. personification b. simile

_____   6. [the aroma] announcing the arrival: a. personification b. simile

_____   7. pool hall is a junior level country club: a. personification b. metaphor

8. How does the figurative language add to the pleasure of the essay? _____

_____

_____

9. Why does the author use Spanish vocabulary words? _____

_____

_____

10. What is the connotation of words like *home* and *refuge* in describing the barrio?

_____

_____

Inference

EXERCISE 10

Figurative Language in Textbooks

The figurative expressions in the following sentences are underlined. Identify the type, define each expression, and if possible, suggest the reason for its use.

EXAMPLE

As a trained nurse working in the immigrant slums of New York, she knew that table-top abortions were common among poor women, and she had seen some of the tragic results.

—Leonard Pitt,
We Americans

EXPLANATION   table-top abortions: It is a metaphor, which may now be an idiom, and means "illegal." The connotation suggests the reality of where the operations probably occurred.

1. The Confederate States of America adopted a constitution and elected Jefferson Davis, a Mississippi senator and cotton planter, its provisional president. The divided house had fallen, as Lincoln had predicted.

—Adapted from Gary B. Nash et al.,
The American People: Creating a Nation and a Society,
6th ed., Vol. 1: To 1877

divided house: _____

_____

2. Henry VIII lived large. He was a bear of a man, famed for his ability to hunt all day while wearing out a pack of trained horses, for his prowess in wrestling bouts, including one with King Francis I of France, and of course, for having six wives.

—Mark Kishlansky et al.,
Civilization in the West, 6th ed.

lived large: _____

_____

a bear of a man: _____

_____

3. For some reason, I knew they were going to stop me. My heart clenched like a fist; the muscles in my back knotted up.

—Benjamin Alire Sáenz
Exile, El Paso, Texas

like a fist: _____

_____

FIGURATIVE LANGUAGE IN POETRY

Poets use connotations and imagery to appeal to the senses and convey striking pictures to us with great economy of words. Because much of the meaning in poetry is implied, this literary form can seem challenging. The highly condensed language of poetry makes every word valuable.

Some poems consist of short rhymes or descriptions of love or emotion, whereas others have a plot and characters. To understand a poem, read it several times and at least once out loud. Know the meanings of words, and pay attention to sentence structure and line breaks. Visualize what you read, and use each part of the poem to help you understand the other parts.

EXAMPLE The haiku poetic form, adapted from Japanese tradition, expresses an insight or impression in about 17 syllables and is usually arranged in three lines. What are the image and impression in the following prize-winning haiku by poet Raymond Roseliep?

> campfire extinguished,
> the woman washing dishes
> in a pan of stars

EXPLANATION When all light is extinguished outside, the stars are so bright that they illuminate the pan for washing.

EXERCISE 11 ## Understanding Poetry

Read the following two poems, and answer the questions. Remember to read the poems aloud at least once to appreciate the sound of the words. Look for figurative language and interpret its meaning.

Poem 1

THE NEGRO SPEAKS OF RIVERS (1921)

I've known rivers:
I've known rivers ancient as the world and older than the flow of human blood in human veins.
My soul has grown deep like the rivers.
I bathed in the Euphrates* when dawns were young.
I built my hut near the Congo** and it lulled me to sleep.
I looked upon the Nile and raised the pyramids above it.
I heard the singing of the Mississippi when Abe Lincoln went down to New Orleans, and I've seen its muddy bosom turn all golden in the sunset.
I've known rivers:
Ancient, dusky rivers.
My soul has grown deep like the rivers.

—Langston Hughes

*Euphrates: river flowing from Turkey to unite with the Tigris to make the Shatt-al-Arab
**Congo: Zaire river flowing from central Africa into the Atlantic.

Inference

1. What is the meaning of dusky. _____
   _____

2. List the similes the poet uses. _____
   _____
   _____
   _____
   _____
   _____
   _____

3. Write the examples of personification and their meanings? _____
   _____
   _____
   _____
   _____

4. Why does the poet refer to rivers in the Middle East, Africa, and the southern
   United States city of New Orleans? _____
   _____
   _____
   _____

5. What is the meaning the poet is trying to convey? _____
   _____
   _____
   _____

Poem 2

UNTITLED (BEFORE 1891)

The nearest dream recedes, unrealized.
The heaven we chase
Like the June bee
Before the school-boy
Invites the race;
Stoops to an easy clover—
Dips—evades—teases—deploys;
Then to the royal clouds

(continued)

Lifts his light pinnace*
Heedless of the boy
Staring, bewildered, at the mocking sky.

Homesick for the steadfast honey,
Ah! the bee flies not
That brews that rare variety.

—Emily Dickinson

_____

*pinnace: A ship's small boat

1. The entire poem is built upon a simile that likens dreams to what?

   _____

2. What figure of speech is "The heaven we chase" and what does it mean?

   _____

3. This poem presents a clear visual image. Describe the image in your own words.

   _____

   _____

4. Why is the boy "staring, bewildered, at the mocking sky. Homesick for the
   steadfast honey"? _____

   _____

5. In your own words, explain the meaning the poet is trying to convey about
   dreams. _____

   _____

MORE TYPES OF INFERENCES

Many types of text—not just advertising, humor, and poetry—demand that you read
between the lines in order to understand the author's goals or meaning. You can
make inferences based on facts, the voice of a narrator, descriptions, and actions.

Inferences from Facts

The way in which facts are juxtaposed can imply a certain message. For example,
an author selected the following facts from issues of *Time* magazine and presented
them consecutively to suggest an inference. No direct connection is stated, so the
reader must thoughtfully reflect on the suggested message. This pause for thought
adds power to the message.

EXAMPLE

28% Proportion of public libraries in the United States that offered Internet
access in 1996

95% Proportion of libraries that offered Internet access in 2002

Inference

17% Increase in library attendance between 1996 and 2002

Inference: _____

EXPLANATION   The inference is that library attendance has improved because many more libraries have Internet access. Before libraries buy more computers, however, specific data on daily use should be collected.

EXERCISE 12   **Drawing Inferences from Facts**

1 billion   Number of birds killed by flying into glass windows in the United States each year.

121 million Number of birds killed annually by U.S. hunters

1. Inference: _____

   _____

   _____

   _____

408   Species that could be extinct by 2050 if global warming trends continue.

6.6 tons Average amount of greenhouse gases emitted annually by each American, an increase of 3.4% since 1990.

2. Inference: _____

   _____

   _____

   _____

1   Rank of Super Bowl Sunday, among all the days of the year, in pizza sales at the major U.S. pizza chains

20%   Increase in frozen-pizza sales on Super Bowl Sunday

3. Inference: _____

   _____

   _____

Time Magazine, March 1, 2004;
January 19, 2004; February 2, 2004.

INFERENCES ABOUT A SPEAKER OR NARRATOR

Read the following excerpt about children and see if you can guess who is complaining:

> Children now love luxury. They have bad manners, contempt for authority. They show disrespect for elders. They contradict their parents, chatter before company, cross their legs and tyrannize their teachers.[4]

Did you assume that this is a contemporary description of modern youth? Although it may sound that way, actually the Greek philosopher Plato attributed the quotation to his student and fellow philosopher Socrates, who lived more than 2,300 years ago. Perhaps the only phrase in the excerpt that does not fit a modern speaker is the "cross their legs." The rest of the clues sound deceptively modern, leading readers to make an inappropriate assumption.

How can you tell whether an inference is valid or invalid? If an inference is appropriate or valid, it can be *supported by the clues within the passage.* The clues "add up," and the logic allows you to feel confidence in making certain assumptions. On the other hand, an inappropriate or invalid inference goes beyond the evidence and may be an "off the wall" stab at meaning that was never suggested or intended.

Readers and listeners alike are constantly making inferences; and as more information is revealed, self-corrections are sometimes necessary. For example, as we listen to strangers talk, we make assumptions about their backgrounds, motives, and actions. Thus, dialogue is an especially fertile ground for observing how the active mind looks for hidden meaning.

EXERCISE 13

Inferences from Dialogue

Considering the facts presented in the passage, mark the inferences as *V* (valid) or *I* (invalid).

PASSAGE 1

I'm eight years old. But I have the mind of a nineteen-year-old. Mom says it's making up for all the wrong Dad did. Today there's going to be a whole camera crew here. They're going to film different angles of me beating myself at chess. Then they want me to walk around the neighborhood in my Eagle Scout uniform. Dad doesn't want to talk to them. So I guess they'll do an exterior of the penitentiary.

—Matt Marinovich,
The Quarterly

_____ 1. A film is being shot about the child because he is so smart for his age.

_____ 2. The child is a boy.

_____ 3. The father was abusive to the mother and child.

---

[4]Suzy Platt, *Respectfully Quoted* (Washington, DC: Library of Congress, 1989), p. 42.

———— 4. The child has been raised by his mother.

———— 5. The father is in jail.

"Now how are we going to get across this monster?" Lisa asked.

"Easy," said John. "We take the rope over, get it around that big tree and use the winch to pull the Jeep across."

"But who swims the flood with the rope?"

"Well, I can't swim," he said, "but you're supposed to be so good at it."

—Anne Bernays and Pamela Painter,
What If?

———— 1. John wants Lisa to swim the rope across the water to attach it to the tree.

———— 2. Water has flooded the path of the Jeep.

———— 3. Lisa and John anticipated that they would be crossing water with the Jeep.

———— 4. Lisa and John are driving on a mountain trail after a storm.

———— 5. Lisa and John work together on a film crew.

INFERENCES BASED ON ACTION AND DESCRIPTION

Reading would be rather dull if authors stated every idea, never giving you a chance to figure things out for yourself. For example, in a mystery novel, you carefully weigh each word, each action, each conversation, each description, and each fact in an effort to identify the villain and solve the crime before it is revealed at the end. Although textbook material may not have the Sherlock Holmes spirit of high adventure, authors use the same techniques to imply meaning.

Note the inferences in the following example.

EXAMPLE   **JOHNSON IN ACTION**

Lyndon Johnson suffered from the inevitable comparison with his young and stylish predecessor. LBJ was acutely aware of his own lack of polish; he sought to surround himself with Kennedy advisers and insiders, hoping that their learning and sophistication would rub off on him. Johnson's assets were very real—an intimate knowledge of congress, an incredible energy and determination to succeed, and a fierce ego. When a young marine officer tried to direct him to the proper helicopter, saying, "This one is yours," Johnson replied, "son, they are all my helicopters."

LBJ's height and intensity gave him a powerful presence; he dominated any room he entered, and he delighted in using his physical power of persuasion. One Texas politician explained why he had given in to Johnson: "Lyndon got me by the lapels and put his face on top of mine and he talked and talked and talked. I figured it was either getting drowned or joining."

—Robert A. Divine et al.,
America Past and Present

Answer the following with *T* (true) or *F* (false):

_____ 1. Johnson was haunted by the style and sophistication of John F. Kennedy.

_____ 2. Johnson could be both egotistical and arrogant about his presidential power.

_____ 3. Even if he did not mentally persuade people, Johnson could physically overwhelm them into agreement.

EXPLANATION The answer to question 1 is *True*. He "suffered from the inevitable comparison" and he went so far as to retain the Kennedy advisers. Question 2 is *True*. The anecdote about the helicopters proves that. Question 3 is *True*. His delight in "using his physical powers of persuasion" and the anecdote about the Texas politician support that.

In the following exercises, you can see how authors use suggestions. From the clues given, you can deduce the facts.

EXERCISE 14

Inferences Based on Description of a Person

Looking back on the Revolutionary War, one cannot say enough about Washington's leadership. While his military skills proved less than brilliant and he and his generals lost many battles, George Washington was the single most important figure of the colonial war effort. His original appointment was partly political, for the rebellion that had started in Massachusetts needed a commander from the South to give geographic balance to the cause. The choice fell to Washington, a wealthy and respectable Virginia planter with military experience dating back to the French and Indian War. He had been denied a commission in the English army and had never forgiven the English for the insult. During the war he shared the physical suffering of his men, rarely wavered on important questions, and always used his officers to good advantage. His correspondence with Congress to ask for sorely needed supplies was tireless and forceful. He recruited several new armies in a row, as short-term enlistments gave out.

—Leonard Pitt,
We Americans

Answer the following with *T* (true) or *F* (false):

_____ 1. The author regards George Washington as the most brilliant military genius in American history.

_____ 2. Washington resented the British for a past injustice.

_____ 3. The author believes that Washington's leadership was courageous and persistent even though not infallible.

EXERCISE 15

Inferences Based on Action

When he came to the surface he was conscious of little but the noisy water. Afterward he saw his companions in the sea. The oiler was ahead in the race. He was swimming strongly and rapidly. Off to the correspondent's left, the cook's great white and corked back bulged out of the water, and in the rear the captain was hanging with his one good hand to the keel of the overturned dinghy.

There is a certain immovable quality to a shore, and the correspondent wondered at it amid the confusion of the sea.

—Stephen Crane,
The Open Boat

Answer the following with *a, b, c,* or *d*. Draw a map indicating the shore and the positions of the four people in the water to help you visualize the scene.

_____ 1. The reason that the people are in the water is because of

      a. a swimming race.
      b. an airplane crash.
      c. a capsized boat.
      d. a group decision.

_____ 2. In relation to his companions, the correspondent is

      a. closest to the shore.
      b. the second or third closest to the shore.
      c. farthest from the shore.
      d. in a position that is impossible to determine.

_____ 3. The member of the group that had probably suffered a previous injury is the

      a. oiler.
      b. correspondent.
      c. cook.
      d. captain.

EXERCISE 16

Inferences Based on Description of a Place

Mexico, by many indicators, should be among the most prosperous nations on earth. It is a large country, occupying some 72 percent of the land of Middle America and containing 57 percent of the population of that area. It has benefited throughout its history from some of the richest mineral deposits on earth—first its silver in the colonial period and now its petroleum and natural gas. Mexico's proximity to the technologically advanced and wealthy United States is also a potential economic advantage of significance as are its varied agricultural landscapes, which range from irrigated deserts in the north to tropical rain forests in parts of the gulf coastal lowlands. To understand Mexico's limited economic achievement, we must evaluate the treatment of its people.

—David Clawson and Merrill Johnson,
World Regional Geography, 8th ed.

Answer the following with *T* (true) or *F* (false):

_____ 1. The author implies that Mexico has fallen short of its economic potential.

_____ 2. The author implies that Mexico's lag in economic achievement is due to the treatment of its people.

_____ 3. The author implies that profits from Mexico's silver, oil, and gas were exploited or stolen by other countries.

USING PRIOR KNOWLEDGE TO MAKE INFERENCES

Just as a joke is funny only if you have the right background knowledge, college reading is easier if you have **prior knowledge** needed to grasp the details that are frequently implied rather than directly spelled out. For example, if a sentence began, "Previously wealthy investors were leaping from buildings in the financial district," you would know that the author was referring to the stock market crash of 1929 on Wall Street in New York City. The details fall into an already existing schema. Although the specifics are not directly stated, you have used prior knowledge and have "added up" the details to infer time and place.

EXERCISE 17

Inferring Time and Place

Read the following passages and indicate *a*, *b*, or *c* for the suggested time and place. Use your prior knowledge of "anchor dates" in history to logically think about the possible responses. Underline the clues that helped you arrive at your answers.

PASSAGE A

For disgruntled or abused women, divorce was sometimes available. Wives with grievances could sue for divorce in some colonies. For instance, although Puritan colonists preferred to keep couples together and often fined troublesome spouses or ordered them to "live happily together," they believed that some marriages could not be

---

BRAIN BOOSTER

Boost Brain Power Through Collaboration

Instead of growing vicious claws or sharp teeth for survival, humans grew large brains. The problems associated with giving birth to babies with adult-size heads, however, necessitate long childhoods during which brains and heads can grow. Long childhoods require the protection of adults from predators and other dangers that might kill a child. Long ago, humans learned to band together for the safety of everyone. Relationships with other humans were (and are) vital to survival and learning. Living in a group resulted in the development of emotions and the ability to read the emotions of others. What does this have to do with succeeding in college? Working cooperatively with other students and your professors is advantageous to you and everyone in your class. Embrace it!

As you do exercises that require making inferences, you are likely to see the importance of background knowledge. If you find your schemata lacking, work with a partner or two to pool your knowledge for the benefit of all.

Adapted from Brain Rules: 12 Principles
for Surviving and Thriving at Work, Home, and School
by John Medina

saved. Because Puritans viewed marriage as a legal contract rather than a religious sacrament, if one party violated the terms of a marital contract the marriage could be dissolved.

—Glenda Riley,
Inventing the American Woman: An Inclusive History,
3rd ed., Vol. 1: To 1877

_____ 1. The time period that this passage refers to is probably

    a. the 1600s–1700s.
    b. the 1800s–1900s.
    c. the 1900s–2000s.

_____ 2. The part of colonial America discussed here is likely

    a. uncolonized territory in the west.
    b. the northeast.
    c. the southern colonies.

    3. Underline the clues to your answers.

PASSAGE B

Families at dinner were startled by the sudden gleam of bayonets in the doorway and rose up to be driven with blows and oaths along the weary miles to the stockade. Men were seized in their fields or going along the road, women were taken from their wheels and children from their play. In many cases, on turning for one last look as they crossed the ridge, they saw their homes in flames, fired by the lawless rabble that followed on the heels of the soldiers to loot and pillage. So keen were these outlaws on the scent that in some instances they were driving off the cattle and other stock of the Indians almost before the soldiers had fairly started their owners in the other direction. Systematic hunts were made by the same men for Indian graves, to rob them of the silver pendants and other valuables deposited with the dead. A volunteer, afterward a colonel in the Confederate service, said: "I fought through the Civil War and have seen men shot to pieces and slaughtered by thousands, but the Cherokee removal was the cruelest work I ever knew."

—James Mooney,
Myths of the Cherokee, 19th Annual Report,
Bureau of American Ethnology

_____ 4. The time period discussed is probably

    a. the 1600s.
    b. the 1700s.
    c. the 1800s.

_____ 5. The place is most likely

    a. the Great Lakes region of the United States.
    b. the southeastern United States.
    c. the Texas-Mexican border.

    6. Underline the clues to your answers.

Passage C

As unskilled workers, most found employment in the low-status, manual-labor jobs in the factories, mines, needle trades, and construction. At that time, workers had no voice in working conditions, for labor unions had not yet become effective. The 84-hour workweek (14 hours per day, 6 days per week) for low wages was common. Jobs offered no paid vacations, sick pay, or pension plans. Child labor was commonplace, and entire families often worked to provide a subsistence-level family income. Lighting, ventilation, and heating were poor. In the factories, moving parts of machinery were dangerously exposed, leading to numerous horrific accidents. There was no workers' compensation, although many laborers were injured on the job. A worker who objected was likely to be fired and blacklisted. Exploited by the captains of industry, the immigrants became deeply involved in the labor-union movement, so much so that to tell the story of one without the other is virtually impossible.

—Vincent N. Parrillo,
Strangers to These Shores: Race and Ethnic Relations in the United States with Research Navigator, 8th ed. ©2006. Printed and electronically reproduced by permission of Pearson Education, Inc., Upper Saddle River, NJ.

_____ 7. The time period discussed is probably

      a. the late 1600s.
      b. the late 1700s.
      c. the late 1800s.

_____ 8. The place is probably

      a. California.
      b. New York.
      c. Mississippi.

      9. Underline the clues to your answers.

Expanding Prior Knowledge

Your response on the previous passages depends on your previous knowledge of history and your general knowledge. If you did not understand many of the inferences, you might ask, "How can I expand my prior knowledge?" The answer is not an easy formula or a quick fix. The answer is part of the reason that you are in college; it is a combination of broadening your horizons, reading more widely, and being an active participant in your own life. Expanding prior knowledge is a slow and steady daily process.

> ### Reader's Tip — Making Inferences
>
> - Consider the attitude implied in the author's choice of words.
> - Think about what might have been left out.
> - Unravel actions.
> - Interpret motives.
> - Use suggested meaning and facts to make assumptions.
> - Draw on prior knowledge to make connections.
> - Base conclusions on stated ideas and unstated assumptions.

DRAWING CONCLUSIONS

Learning
Objective 6

Draw logical
conclusions while
reading

To arrive at a conclusion, you must make a logical deduction from both stated ideas and from unstated assumptions. Drawing conclusions is much like making inferences, but it extends thinking a step further. Using hints as well as facts, you rely on prior knowledge and experience to interpret motives, actions, and outcomes. You draw conclusions on the basis of perceived evidence, but because perceptions differ, conclusions can vary from reader to reader. Generally, however, authors attempt to direct readers to preconceived conclusions. Read the following example and look for a basis for the stated conclusion.

EXAMPLE   **UNDERGROUND CONDUCTOR**

Harriet Tubman was on a northbound train when she overheard her name spoken by a white passenger. He was reading aloud an ad which accused her of stealing $50,000 worth of property in slaves, and which offered a $5000 reward for her capture. She lowered her head so that the sunbonnet she was wearing hid her face. At the next station she slipped off the train and boarded another that was headed south, reasoning that no one would pay attention to a black woman traveling in that direction. She deserted the second train near her hometown in Maryland and bought two chickens as part of her disguise. With her back hunched over in imitation of an old woman, she drove the chickens down the dusty road, calling angrily and chasing them with her stick whenever she sensed danger. In this manner Harriet Tubman was passed by her former owner who did not even notice her. The reward continued to mount until it reached $40,000.

—Leonard Pitt,
We Americans

Conclusion: Harriet Tubman was a clever woman who became a severe irritant to white slave owners.

What is the basis for this conclusion?

_____

_____

EXPLANATION   Her disguise and subsequent escape from the train station provide evidence of her intelligence and resourcefulness. The escalating amount of the reward, finally $40,000, proves the severity of the sentiment against her.

EXERCISE 18   **Drawing Conclusions**

Read the following passages. For the first passage, indicate evidence for the conclusion that has been drawn. For the latter passages, write your own conclusion as well as indicate evidence. Use the suggestions in the Reader's Tip on previous page.

Inference

Albert Einstein did not begin to talk until he was three years old, and he wasn't entirely fluent even by the time he was nine. His language skills were so poor that his parents seriously worried that he might be mentally retarded! Nevertheless, he eventually learned to speak not only his native German, but also French and English. However, he mixed German with his French, and he had a strong accent. His English, learned later in life, never became fluent—as countless satirists have noted, he made grammatical mistakes and had a heavy German accent.

—Stephen M. Kosslyn and Robin S. Rosenberg,
Psychology: The Brain, the Person, the World, 2nd ed.

Conclusion: Einstein's language skills were not an accurate reflection of his true intelligence.

What is the basis for this conclusion? _____

_____

_____

_____

PASSAGE B

In Massachusetts, Nicola Sacco and Bartolomeo Vanzetti—an immigrant shoe-factory worker and a poor fish peddler—were charged with and convicted of robbery and murder in 1920. The prosecutor insulted immigrant Italian defense witnesses and appealed to the prejudices of a bigoted judge and jury. Despite someone else's later confession and other potentially exonerating evidence, their seven-year appeals fight failed to win them retrial or acquittal. They were executed in 1927. At his sentencing in 1927, Vanzetti addressed presiding judge Webster Thayer. At one point in his moving speech, he said,

"I would not wish to a dog or a snake, to the most low and misfortunate creature of the earth—I would not wish to any of them what I have had to suffer for the things that I am not guilty of. . . . I have suffered because I was an Italian, and indeed I am an Italian."

—Vincent N. Parrillo,
*Strangers to These Shores: Race and Ethnic Relations in the United States with
Research Navigator,* 8th ed. ©2006. Printed and electronically reproduced
by permission of Pearson Education, Inc., Upper Saddle River, NJ.

Conclusion: _____

_____

_____

What is the basis for this conclusion? _____

_____

_____

_____

_____

_____

PASSAGE C

Many Irish were single women taking jobs as domestics or nannies for the native-born urban elite. In 1800, there was 1 domestic servant for every 20 families, but by 1840, the ratio had dropped to 1 servant for every 10 families. Unmarried Irish (and Scandinavian) young women often came first and worked in U.S. homes. Their daily typical workload was 16 hours of cooking, cleaning, tending to the children, and nursing the sick, six days a week. With little time to themselves, these women saved their earnings for passage money for other family members. Records from the Boston Society for the Prevention of Pauperism offer one illustration of the difficulties women had seeking jobs in a household compared to men finding work in labor gangs. Between 1845 and 1850, it received employment applications from 14,000 female foreigners in contrast to 5,034 male applications.

—Vincent N. Parrillo,
Strangers to These Shores: Race and Ethnic Relations in the United States with Research Navigator, 8th ed. ©2006. Printed and electronically reproduced by permission of Pearson Education, Inc., Upper Saddle River, NJ.

Conclusion: _____

_____

_____

What is the basis for this conclusion? _____

_____

_____

_____

EXERCISE 19

Building a Story Based on Inferences

This well-known story unfolds as the reader uses the clues to predict the final outcome and make inferences about the relationships among the characters. The author never directly tells the reader how Mrs. Mallard feels about her marriage but instead leaves many hints. Like a mystery, the story is fun to read because you are actively involved. Use your inferential skills to figure it out.

The Story of an Hour

Knowing that Mrs. Mallard was afflicted with a heart trouble, great care was taken to break to her as gently as possible the news of her husband's death.

It was her sister Josephine who told her, in broken sentences, veiled hints that revealed in half concealing. Her husband's friend Richards was there, too, near her. It was he who had been in the newspaper office when intelligence of the railroad disaster was received, with Brently Mallard's name leading the list of "killed." He had only taken the time to assure himself of its truth by a second telegram, and had hastened to forestall any less careful, less tender friend in bearing the sad message.

She did not hear the story as many women have heard the same, with a paralyzed inability to accept its significance. She wept at once, with sudden, wild abandonment, in her sister's arms. When the storm of grief had spent itself she went away to her room alone. She would have no one follow her.

There stood, facing the open window, a comfortable, roomy armchair. Into this she sank, pressed down by a physical exhaustion that haunted her body and seemed to reach into her soul.

She could see in the open square before her house the tops of trees that were all aquiver with the new spring life. The delicious breath of rain was in the air. In the street below a peddler was crying his wares. The notes of a distant song which some one was singing reached her faintly, and countless sparrows were twittering in the eaves.

There were patches of blue sky showing here and there through the clouds that had met and piled one above the other in the west facing her window.

She sat with her head thrown back upon the cushion of the chair, quite motionless, except when a sob came up into her throat and shook her, as a child who has cried itself to sleep continues to sob in its dreams.

She was young, with a fair, calm face, whose lines bespoke repression and even a certain strength. But now there was a dull stare in her eyes, whose gaze was fixed away off yonder on one of those patches of blue sky. It was not a glance of reflection, but rather indicated a suspension of intelligent thought.

There was something coming to her and she was waiting for it, fearfully. What was it? She did not know; it was too subtle and elusive to name. But she felt it, creeping out of the sky, reaching toward her through the sounds, the scents, the color that filled the air.

Now her bosom rose and fell tumultuously. She was beginning to recognize this thing that was approaching to posses her, and she was striving to beat it back with her will–as powerless as her two white slender hands would have been.

When she abandoned herself a little whispered word escaped her slightly parted lips. She said it over and over her breath: "Free, free, free!" The vacant stare and the look of terror that had followed it went from her eyes. They stayed keen and bright. Her pulses beat fast, and the coursing blood warmed and relaxed every inch of her body.

She did not stop to ask if it were not a monstrous joy that held her. A clear and exalted perception enabled her to dismiss the suggestion as trivial.

She knew that she would weep again when she saw the kind, tender hands folded in death; the face that had never looked save with love upon her, fixed and gray and dead. But she saw beyond that bitter moment a long procession of years to come that would belong to her absolutely. And she opened and spread her arms out to them in welcome.

There would be no one to live for during those coming years; she would live for herself. There would be no powerful will bending her in that blind persistence with which men and women believe they have a right to impose a private will upon a fellow creature. A kind intention or a cruel intention made the act seem no less a crime as she looked upon it in that brief moment of illumination.

And yet she had loved him–sometimes. Often she had not. What did it matter! What could love, the unsolved mystery, count for in face of this possession of self-assertion which she suddenly recognized as the strongest impulse of her being.

"Free! Body and soul free!" she kept whispering.

Josephine was kneeling before the closed door with her lips to the keyhole, imploring for admission. "Louise, open the door! I beg; open the door-you will make yourself ill. What are you doing, Louise? For heaven's sake open the door."

"Go away. I am not making myself ill." No; she was drinking in a very elixir of life through that open window.

Her fancy was running riot along those days ahead of her. Spring days, and summer days, and all sorts of days that would be her own. She breathed a quick prayer that life might be long. It was only yesterday she had thought with a shudder that life might be long.

She arose at length and opened the door to her sister's importunities. There was a feverish triumph in her eyes, and she carried herself unwittingly like a goddess of Victory. She clasped her sister's waist, and together they descended the stairs. Richards stood waiting for them at the bottom.

Some one was opening the front door with a latchkey. It was Brently Mallard who entered, a little travel-stained, composedly carrying his gripsack and umbrella. He had been far from the scene of the accident, and did not even know there had been one. He stood amazed at Josephine's piercing cry; at Richards' quick motion to screen him from the view of his wife.

But Richards was too late.

When the doctors came they said she had died of heart disease–of joy that kills.

—Kate Chopin

1. How did Mrs. Mallard's response to the news of her husband's death change during the story? _____

_____

_____

_____

_____

2. What does the author suggest about Richards' feelings for Mrs. Mallard? Underline the clues? _____

_____

_____

_____

3. Did you predict the real fate of Brently Mallard? What hints did the author provide?

_____

_____

_____

4. What was the real cause of Mrs. Mallard's death? _____

_____

5. What is the irony in the use of the phrases "heart trouble" at the beginning of the story, and "heart disease" as the cause of her death at the end? _____

_____

_____

_____

SUMMARY POINTS

1. What is the definition of *Inference*?
- In reading, an inference is an interpretation or understanding based on known facts or evidence. Making an inference is sometimes referred to as "reading between the lines" because inferences are not directly stated but must be deduced from details provided by the author.

2. How can I make reasonable inferences?
- Notice the clues the author provides in details such as word choice and information. Combine the details with your own schemata to understand the author's meaning.

3. How can I recognize connotative language?
- Connotative language communicates an attitude or emotional overtone that can be positive or negative without actually stating it directly. Watch for emotional language. To see the contrast, think of other words that would have communicated a different point of view or that convey no opinions.

4. How can I recognize euphemisms and politically correct language?
- Be alert to words or phrases that substitute a softer, more polite, or indirect term for a harsh, unpleasant, or uncomfortable one.
- When reading about controversial ideas, people, or events, notice wording that hides unpleasantness or that seeks to avoid offending any person or group.

5. How can I interpret figurative language?
- Become familiar with the common forms of figurative language: idioms, similes, metaphors, literary analogies, hyperbole, personification, and verbal irony.
- Remember that figurative language is not meant to be understood literally. Instead, it provides a more interesting or subtle way of expressing an idea than a direct statement can do.

6. How can I draw logical conclusions while reading?

- Drawing logical conclusions depends on using details provided by the author, one's own schemata, and recognizing assumptions made by the author. A conclusion goes a step further than an inference in that readers might arrive at different conclusions depending on their own opinions and backgrounds. Like inferences, though, a logical conclusion must still be based on a reasonable interpretation of the author's message.

MyReadingLab™ For more help with Inferences go to your learning path in MyReadingLab at www.myreadinglab.com

SELECTION
1

SELECTION 1 ## Short Story

PREVIEW the next selection to predict its purpose and organization and to formulate your learning plan.

Activate Schema

What do you expect from a short story?
What kind of security do hotels usually have?

Establish a Purpose for Reading

Short stories entertain, so read to enjoy and predict the outcome.

Increase Word Knowledge

What do you know about these words?

genteel	indigo	retreated	diffused	purity
cascading	insinuating	sanatorium	scurrying	swag

Your instructor may give a true-false vocabulary review before or after reading.

Integrate Knowledge While Reading

Inference questions have been inserted in the margin to stimulate your thinking and help you read between the lines. Remember to

Predict	Picture	Relate	Monitor	Correct	Annotate

A DIP IN THE POOLE

Scan this QR code to hear this reading

Why was the narrator watching Mr. Stuyvesant?

I was sitting in a heavy baroque chair in the Hotel Poole's genteel lobby, leafing through one of the plastic-encased magazines provided by the management, when the girl in the dark tweed suit picked Andrew J. Stuyvesant's pockets.

5   She worked it very nicely. Stuyvesant—a silver-haired old gentleman who carried a malacca walking stick and had fifteen or twenty million dollars in Texas oil—had just stepped out of one of the chrome-and-walnut elevators directly in front of me. The girl appeared from the direction of the curving marble staircase, walking rapidly and with elaborate preoccupation, and collided with him. She excused herself. Bowing in a gallant way, Stuyvesant allowed as how it was perfectly all right, my 10 dear. She got his wallet and the diamond stickpin from his tie, and he neither felt nor suspected a thing.

    The girl apologized again and then hurried off across the padded indigo carpeting toward the main entrance at the lobby's opposite end, slipping the items into a

tan suede bag she carried over one arm. Almost immediately, I was out of my chair
15 and moving after her. She managed to thread her way through the potted plants and
the dark furnishings to within a few steps of the double-glass doors before I caught
up with her.

I let my hand fall on her arm. "Excuse me just a moment," I said, smiling.

She stiffened. Then she turned and regarded me as if I had crawled out from one
20 of the potted plants. "I beg your pardon?" she said in frosty voice.

"You and I had best have a little chat."

"I am not in the habit of chatting with strange men."

"I think you'll make an exception in my case."

Her brown eyes flashed angrily as she said, "I suggest you let go of my arm. If
25 you don't, I shall call the manager."

I shrugged. "There's no need for that."

"I certainly hope not."

"Simply because he would only call me."

"What?"

30 "I'm chief of security at the Hotel Poole, you see," I told her. "What was once
referred to as the house detective."

She grew pale, and the light dimmed in her eyes. "Oh," she said.

I steered her toward the arched entrance to the hotel's lounge, a short distance
on our left. She offered no resistance. Once inside, I sat her down in one of the
35 leather booths and then seated myself opposite. A blue-uniformed waiter approached, but I shook my head and he retreated.

I examined the girl across the polished surface of the table. The diffused orange
glow from the small lantern in its center gave her classic features the impression of
purity and innocence, and turned her seal-brown hair into a cascading black wave.

Trinity Mirror/Mirrorpix/Alamy

227

40 I judged her age at about twenty-five. I said, "Without a doubt, you're the most beautiful dip I've ever encountered."

"I . . . don't know what you're talking about."

"Don't you?"

"Certainly not."

45 "A dip is underworld slang for a pickpocket."

She tried to affect indignation. "Are you insinuating that *I* . . .?"

"Oh come on," I said. "I saw you lift Mr. Stuyvesant's wallet and his diamond stickpin. I was sitting directly opposite the elevator, not fifteen feet away."

She didn't say anything. Her fingers toyed with the catch on the tan suede bag.

50 After a moment, her eyes lifted to mine, briefly, and then dropped again to the bag. She sighed in a tortured way. "You're right, of course. I stole those things."

I reached out, took the bag from her and snapped it open. Stuyvesant's wallet, with the needle-point of the stickpin now imbedded in the leather, lay on top of the various feminine articles inside. I removed them, glanced at her identification long

55 enough to memorize her name and address, reclosed the bag and returned it to her.

She said softly, "I'm . . . not a thief, I want you to know that. Not really, I mean." She took her lower lip between her teeth. "I have this . . . *compulsion* to steal. I'm powerless to stop myself."

"Kleptomania?"

60 "Yes. I've been to three different psychiatrists during the past year, but they've been unable to cure me."

I shook my head sympathetically. "It must be terrible for you."

"Terrible," she agreed. "When . . . when my father learns of this episode, he'll have me put into a sanatorium." Her voice quavered. "He threatened to do just that

65 if I ever stole anything again, and he doesn't make idle threats."

I studied her. Presently, I said, "Your father doesn't have to know what happened here today."

"He . . . he doesn't?"

"No," I said slowly. "There was no real harm done, actually. Mr. Stuyvesant will

70 get his wallet and stickpin back. And I see no reason for causing the hotel undue embarrassment through the attendant publicity if I report the incident."

Her face brightened. "Then . . . you're going to let me go?"

I drew a long breath. "I suppose I'm too soft-hearted for the type of position that I have. Yes, I'm going to let you go. But you have to promise me that you'll

75 never set foot inside the Hotel Poole again."

"Oh, I promise!"

"If I see you here in the future, I'll have to report you to the police."

"You won't!" she assured me eagerly. "I . . . have an appointment with another psychiatrist tomorrow morning. I feel sure he can help me."

80 I nodded. "Very well, then." I turned to stare through the arched lounge entrance at the guests and uniformed bellboys scurrying back and forth in the lobby. When I turned back again, the street door to the lounge was just closing and the girl was gone.

I sat there for a short time, thinking about her. If she was a kleptomaniac, I re-flected, then I was Mary, Queen of Scots. What she was, of course, was an accom-

85 plished professional pickpocket—her technique was much too polished, her hands much too skilled—and an extremely adept liar.

I smiled to myself, and stood and went out into the lobby again. But instead of resuming my position in the baroque chair before the elevator bank, or approaching the horseshoe-shaped desk, I veered left to walk casually through the entrance doors

90 and out to Powell Street.

Why did he memorize this information?

What is the significance of the story's title?

228

As I made my way through the thickening late-afternoon crowds—my right hand resting on the fat leather wallet and the diamond stickpin in my coat pocket—I found myself feeling a little sorry for the girl. But only just a little.

After all, Andrew J. Stuyvesant had been *my* mark from the moment I first no-
95 ticed him entering the Hotel Poole that morning—and after a three-hour vigil I had been within fifteen seconds of dipping him myself when she appeared virtually out of nowhere.

Wouldn't you say I was entitled to the swag?

(1,155 words)

—Bill Pronzini

How is this ending ironic?

Recall

Stop to self-test, relate, and react.

Your instructor may choose to give you a true-false comprehension review.

WRITE ABOUT THE SELECTION   MyReadingLab™

Complete this **Exercise** on **myreadinglab.com**

When did you figure out the ending? Was the ending predictable? How did the author manipulate and entertain you?

Response Suggestion: Evaluate the craft of this short story. How is the author a master of the format? What structural factors contributed to your enjoyment?

SKILL DEVELOPMENT: IMPLIED MEANING

According to the implied meaning in the selection, answer the following items with *T* (true) or *F* (false):

_____ 1. The reader can logically conclude that *swag* is most likely loot acquired by unlawful means.

_____ 2. When the man says, "Excuse me just a moment" to the female pickpocket, she looks at him with admiration.

_____ 3. The woman admits her guilt to the thief because she wants help for her kleptomania.

_____ 4. The man lets the woman pickpocket go because he is too soft-hearted.

_____ 5. The man implies that Mary, Queen of Scots, was also a kleptomaniac.

CHECK YOUR COMPREHENSION   MyReadingLab™

SELECTION 1

Answer the following items with *a*, *b*, *c*, or *d*. To help you analyze your strengths and weaknesses, the question types are indicated.

Main Idea _____ 1. Which is the best statement of the main idea of this selection?

Complete
this **Exercise** on
myreadinglab.com

    a. A life of crime has many risks.
    b. Lying can get you both into and out of jams.
    c. Criminals deceive by presenting themselves as law enforcement agents.
    d. A thief is cheated by another clever thief.

Inference _____ 2. The reader can conclude that the man sitting in the hotel lobby chair thinks that the woman pickpocket is

    a. somewhat inexperienced.
    b. unattractive.
    c. extremely skilled.
    d. quite polite.

Inference _____ 3. When the man catches up with the woman pickpocket at the hotel doors, he speaks to her in

    a. an evil way.
    b. an official manner.
    c. a joking voice.
    d. an icy fashion.

Inference _____ 4. The narrator does not want the woman to ever return to the hotel because

    a. he wants the territory for himself.
    b. he wants to protect the hotel.
    c. he does not want her to get caught.
    d. she is a kleptomaniac and needs treatment.

Inference _____ 5. The reader can conclude that the "light dimmed in her eyes" when the woman pickpocket realizes that

    a. the man wants the wallet she stole.
    b. the man is extremely angry with her.
    c. her father will be angry that she has stolen again.
    d. she has been caught in the act.

Inference _____ 6. The narrator would describe the actual concern experienced by the woman's father as

    a. sympathetic.
    b. nonexistent.
    c. therapeutic.
    d. threatening.

Inference _____ 7. The ending to this story indicates that when the man says earlier in the story, "It must be terrible for you," he was

    a. insincere.
    b. concerned.
    c. annoyed.
    d. troubled.

Inference _____ 8. By saying she has "an appointment with another psychiatrist tomorrow morning," the reader can conclude that the woman is

    a. finally ready to get help.
    b. following her father's orders.
    c. making up a story.
    d. planning another crime.

Inference _____ 9. The reader can infer from the phrase "the thickening late-afternoon crowds" that people are

    a. walking too slowly.
    b. just getting off work.
    c. out enjoying the weather.
    d. arriving at the hotel.

Inference _____ 10. The narrator's description of his sitting in the hotel lobby reveals that he is very

    a. patient.
    b. brave.
    c. sincere.
    d. talkative.

Answer the following with *T* (true) or *F* (false):

Detail _____ 11. The narrator suggests that he will use physical force if the woman pickpocket will not confess to her crime.

Inference _____ 12. The woman finally realizes that the narrator is a thief.

Inference _____ 13. When the woman pickpocket describes what will happen if her father learns of the episode, the narrator thinks her fear is reasonable.

Inference _____ 14. The reader can conclude that the narrator memorized the woman's name and address so that he can later report her to the hotel.

Inference _____ 15. The story title is a humorous play on words.

SELECTION 1

BUILD YOUR VOCABULARY   MyReadingLab™

Complete this **Exercise** on **myreadinglab.com**

According to the way the italicized word was used in the selection, select *a, b, c,* or *d* for the word or phrase that gives the best definition. The number in parentheses indicates the line of the passage in which the word is located.

_____ 1. "*genteel* lobby" (1)
   a. formal
   b. run-down
   c. tacky
   d. gentle

_____ 2. "*indigo* carpeting" (12)
   a. thick
   b. blue
   c. antique
   d. new

_____ 3. "he *retreated*" (36)
   a. withdrew
   b. hid
   c. sat in another booth
   d. returned to the kitchen

_____ 4. "*diffused* orange glow" (37)
   a. pretty
   b. bright
   c. small
   d. scattered

_____ 5. "impression of *purity*" (39)
   a. harshness
   b. blandness
   c. innocence
   d. dimness

_____ 6. "*cascading* black wave" (39)
   a. increasing
   b. swimming
   c. falling
   d. wet

_____ 7. "*insinuating* that" (46)
   a. lying
   b. flirting
   c. hoping
   d. suggesting

_____ 8. "into a *sanatorium*" (64)
   a. health spa
   b. hospital
   c. condo
   d. convent

_____ 9. "*scurrying* back" (81)
   a. rushing
   b. walking
   c. skating
   d. looking

_____ 10. "the *swag*" (99)
   a. a depression in the earth
   b. profits
   c. satisfaction
   d. sway

Concept Prep for Philosophy and Literature

A Sampling of Careers for Philosophy and Literature Majors

A degree in philosophy develops analytical and critical thinking skills useful in many careers.

- Business
- Journalism
- Law
- Education
- Public relations
- Religion

Likewise, a degree in literature serves as the foundation needed for a variety of careers.

The ancient Greeks laid the foundations for Western traditions in science, philosophy, literature, and the arts. They set the standards for proportion and beauty in art and architecture, and we continue to ponder their questions about the good life, the duties of a citizen, and the nature of the universe.

Who were the most notable Greek philosophers?

- One of the most notable philosophers was *Socrates,* the teacher of Plato. Socrates sought an understanding of the world while other teachers of the time taught students how to get along in the world. Socrates proclaimed himself to be the wisest of all the thinkers because he knew how little he knew. He used a method of teaching that explored a subject from all sides with questions and answers, as opposed to the lecture method. Today this teaching technique is known as the *Socratic method.* Socrates took no pay for his teachings. As an old man, he was condemned to death by the citizens of Athens who claimed he denied the gods and corrupted the youth. More likely, however, Socrates was a natural target for enemies and was made the scapegoat for the city's military defeat. As ordered, Socrates drank the poison hemlock and died. He left behind no written works, but his pupil Plato later immortalized Socrates's lively discussions in his own works.

- *Plato* is often considered the most important figure in Western philosophy. Without him, the thoughts of Socrates and previous philosophers might not be recorded. Plato used a dialogue format to explore many subjects such as ethics and politics. He founded a school in Athens called the Academy and became the teacher of Aristotle.

In Raphael's painting *School of Athens*, Plato and Aristotle converse.

School of Athens (Detail) (1511), Raphael. Stanza della Segnatura, Vatican Palace/Erich Lessing/Art Resource, New York.

- *Aristotle* was a disciple of Plato and then broke away to develop his own philosophy and school, called the Lyceum. He wrote on virtually every subject and laid the foundation for analytical reasoning and logic. He was the tutor of Alexander the Great. In the political unrest following Alexander's death, Aristotle remembered the fate of Socrates and fled Athens to escape prosecution.

What are literary genres?

Over hundreds of years, certain stories, essays, and poems have remained timeless in their appeal and relevance to human life. These works are considered *literature,* the art form of language. As you read a piece of literature, you are allowed inside the minds of characters, and you feel what they feel. You learn about life as the characters live it or as the poet entices you to feel it. After reading, you are enriched, as well as entertained. As defined in most college courses, literature includes four categories, or *genres:* poetry, drama, fiction, and essays.

Poetry

Poetry has its roots in the pleasure of rhythm, repetition, and sound. Before the written word, rhythm and repetition were used to help people organize and recall episodes in history. Poetry was danced, chanted, and performed with the whole body in tribal cultures as a way of keeping cultural truths alive. In the *Odyssey,* an ancient Greek epic by *Homer* that recounts the adventures of Odysseus during his return from the war in Troy to his home on a Greek island, the rhyme format made the epic easier to remember. Thus, the poem became a vehicle for preserving the lore of the sea, warfare, and Greek mythology.

Poetry appeals to the senses, offering strong visual images and suggestive symbolism to enhance pleasure. *Lyric* poems are brief and emotional, *narrative* poems tell a story with plot and characters, *dramatic* poems use dialogue to express emotional conflict, and *epic* poems tell a long narrative with a central hero of historical significance.

Drama

The origins of *drama* lie in religious ceremonies in ancient Greece, where masters of Greek drama competed for prizes. Without movies or television, the ancient Greeks created plays for religious instruction and for entertainment. These dramatic performances eventually evolved into the categories of comedy, tragedy, and romantic tragedy.

Plays are narratives and thus contain all the literary elements of short stories and novels. As in works of fiction, the main character in a play is sometimes called a *protagonist,* from the Greek word for "first actor." The character who is trying to move against or harm the main character is called the *antagonist* (from the prefix *anti-*).

Plays are written to be performed rather than read. The actors interpret the actions for the audience, and a single play can seem vastly different depending on which production company performs it. After hundreds of years, the plays of *William Shakespeare* are still relevant to the human condition; they entertained audiences in England in the late 1500s, on the American frontier in the mid-1800s, and both on stages and in movie theaters in the 2000s.

Fiction

Fiction creates an illusion of reality to share an experience and communicate universal truths about the human condition. Each work of fiction is subject to interpretation on many different levels. Short stories and novels are written to entertain by engaging you in the life of another human being.

- A *short story* is a brief work of fiction ranging from 500 to 15,000 words. It is a narrative with a beginning, middle, and end that tells a sequence of events. The *plot* of the story involves *characters* in one or more *conflicts.* As the conflict intensifies, the *suspense* rises to a *climax,* or turning point, which is followed by the *denouement,* or unraveling. Then the action falls for a *resolution.* Because the short story is brief and carefully crafted, some literary experts recommend reading a short story three times: first to enjoy the plot, second to recognize the elements, and third to appreciate how the elements work together to support the theme. Setting, point of view, tone, and symbolism all contribute to this appreciation.

- The *novel* is an extended fictional work that has all the elements of a short story. Because of its length, a novel usually has more characters and more conflicts than a short story.

The essay

An *essay* is a short work of nonfiction that discusses a specific topic. Much of your own college writing will follow an essay format. The *title* of an essay suggests the contents, the *thesis* is usually stated in the *introduction,* the *body* provides evidence to prove the thesis, and the *conclusion* summarizes in a manner to provoke further thought.

REVIEW QUESTIONS

After studying the material, answer the following questions:

1. What is the Socratic method of teaching? _____
   _____

2. For what underlying reason was Socrates forced to drink poison? _____
   _____
   _____

3. Why was Plato particularly important to the teachings of Socrates? _____
   _____

4. What acronym might you devise to remind you of the chronological order of
   the lives of the three famous philosophers? _____
   _____

5. What was a significant contribution of Aristotle? _____
   _____

6. What is a literary genre? _____
   _____

7. What was the original purpose of drama? _____
   _____

8. What was the purpose of the *Odyssey?* _____
   _____

9. Which genre is most frequently written by college students in the classroom
   setting? _____
   _____

10. What is the typical relationship between the protagonist and the antagonist?
    _____

Your instructor may choose to give a true-false review of these philosophy and literature concepts.

SELECTION 2   Short Story

Pʀᴇᴠɪᴇᴡ the next selection to predict its purpose and organization and to formulate your learning plan.

Activate Schemata

Do you see aspects of your parents in yourself? Are there other people in your life that you admire and imitate?

Establish a Purpose for Reading

Of course, parents and others who closely interact with children are important influences in their lives. They are the models for the adults children strive to become. Sometimes, children choose the least positive characteristics to imitate, perhaps in a misguided effort to please their role models. Read this fictional narrative to find out how one boy and his father demonstrate this fact of human nature.

Increase Word Knowledge

What do you know about these words?

postmistress	pigeonhole	fugitives	scopes	agent
siblings	poach	authorities	silkscreening	millstone

Your instructor may give a true-false vocabulary review before or after reading.

Integrate Knowledge While Reading

Questions have been inserted in the margins to stimulate your thinking while reading. Remember to

Predict	Picture	Relate	Monitor	Correct	Annotate

((•─ **Scan this QR
code to hear
this reading**

*Is this like your
post office?*

Tʜᴇ Mᴏᴜɴᴛᴀɪɴ Mᴀɴ

I walked to the post office to pick up my family's mail. When I opened the swinging doors, I saw that the dusty room was empty. Presently, the postmistress came out of her living area and stepped behind the counter.

5 While she checked a pigeonhole for mail, I looked at the "wanted" posters on the wall. They showed fugitives' faces and described their crimes. Some of the men were "armed and dangerous"; others were "extremely dangerous." I tried to memorize what they looked like, in case I saw one of them. If I did see one there wasn't much I could do, because I had no weapon. I would just have to run as fast as I could in the opposite direction. The postmistress handed me a roll of mail, and I went out

10 through the heavy wooden doors.

Why does he think this?

On my way home, I saw a couple of hunters outside the hotel bar. They were wearing plaid wool coats and fleece-lined boots. As I walked past, I saw a dead deer in the back of their pickup truck. The deer had no antlers—it looked like an illegal kill.

15 In the truck cab, a gun rack held two rifles. Both of the guns had scopes and shoulder straps. I could imagine the hunters marching through the woods like soldiers, guns slung over their shoulders, barrels pointing into the air. One of the men noticed me and asked, "Doing any hunting this season?" I shook my head no and walked on.

At the dinner table, my father spoke while my brother and sister and I listened. "There's a mountain man on the loose in Shade Gap," he said. "He kidnapped a teen-
20 ager. The F.B.I. went after him with a dog. First, he shot the dog; then he shot an agent. That man has courage."

"All these guns," my mother said from her post by the stove.

"He was lonely, so he took her," my father said. "They'll never catch him. He knows the mountains and the hollows, just like I know the land around here."

25 "Why do you need to know it?" my brother asked.

"If they come for me," my father said. "I'll know where to go."

"What will you do for food?" my sister asked.

"I'll be armed. I'll hunt for food."

Does everyone in the family feel the same about the Mountain Man?

"I saw a deer without antlers on a truck," I said.

30 "Enough!" my father shouted. "I've had enough of you kids for a while."

My siblings and I finished our meal in silence.

After dinner, my father left the house. While he was gone, my siblings and I watched television and did our homework. At a late hour, my mother picked up the phone and made a call. I could tell she was talking to the bartender down the street.
35 She said my name and handed me the phone.

"Come down here," my father said. "There are a couple of guys who want to talk to you."

I had to get partly dressed in order to go out—sweat pants, shoes but no socks, a coat but no shirt. When I walked into the hotel bar, I saw the same two hunters I'd seen earlier.

40 My father introduced me by saying, "This is my son. Soon to be my drunken son."

"You know," one of the hunters said, "we didn't poach that deer."

"No," said the other. "The deer jumped in front of the truck."

"If you want poachers," the first said, "go up the road. Those guys cut wood in
45 the day and poach at night."

Nickolay Khoroshkov/Shutterstock

SELECTION
2

Why did the father call his son to the bar?

"Have a drink," my father said.

I was too young to drink, so I had a soda. When I was finished, my father showed no sign of leaving the bar. I left by myself.

50 During the night, I woke to the sound of my father's voice. I couldn't make out most of what he was saying. Among the sharp sounds, I heard, "I can't make art with kids around. I go into my workroom, and soon enough I get interrupted. I have to stop what I'm doing and entertain children."

"They learn from you," my mother said.

55 "My oldest kid's a candy-ass. He'll never amount to anything. I'd give him a dollar to be good, but he'll be good for nothing."

When he started talking about me, I tried to stop listening.

A couple of days later, my family and I watched a news report on television. The Mountain Man had been on the run. Wherever he went, he took the teenage girl with him. The two of them had climbed stony ridges and hiked through valleys. They
60 stayed a step ahead of the authorities. Finally, they were spotted as they passed a farmhouse. An F.B.I. agent was stationed there. A boy who lived on the farm and the agent both shot at the kidnapper. One of the bullets killed him—it turned out to be from the agent's gun. The teenage girl had a chain around her neck, but she was unharmed.

After the report, my father said, "The F.B.I. goes after a lot of people, but why
65 did they have to shoot the Mountain Man?"

What is the purpose of this part of the story?

The next day, my father took me and my siblings with him to a beer distributor. He pulled his car into the loading area, under a large sign that read "Discount," and opened the car trunk. An attendant lifted two cases and put them down, and my father paid.

70 "I'm set now," he said as he drove home. "I don't need your company. I can drink on my own."

I went to my room to write some letters. The problem was, I didn't know who to write to. I had some relatives on the other side of the world—my mother's family—but I didn't have their addresses. Worse, I didn't know their language. I
75 looked around and saw a coupon on a cereal box. I could write away for a prize, a plastic ring with a hidden compartment, but I had no money to pay for it. So I went to the post office empty-handed.

As the postmistress checked for my family's mail, I looked around the room at the other offerings. There was penny candy for sale at the counter, two loaves of
80 bread next to the candy, and cigarettes on a shelf out of reach. Next to the mail window, there was the sheaf of "wanted" posters. Some of the criminals were murderers, others were kidnappers. The Mountain Man hadn't been on the loose long enough to make it onto a poster. The faces meant nothing to me.

At dinner, my mother served a new food. It was the reddest meat I'd ever seen.
85 It was so red, it didn't look cooked.

"Your father brought it home," my mother explained.

Did you suspect this?

"It's from that deer that was hit by the truck," my father said. "The hunters gave it to me. That deer is going to get two families through the winter."

He left the room. When he returned, he was carrying a couple of bottles of beer.

90 "I'm going into my workroom later," he said, "I'm silk-screening a book about politics. But right now, I'm going to drink to the Mountain Main."

I walked up a dirt lane that led away from town. Shortly, I came to an abandoned house. Its walls were still standing, but its door and windows were missing. The remains of a chimney stood at one corner, and an old millstone lay on the ground.

95   I thought I could live in the house. I wouldn't have heat, but I could build a fire at the bottom of the chimney. I could survive on the food I'd find in the fields and woods. I'd get lonely, but there was a girl in my class at school who might come with me. If she didn't, I would have to fasten her to the millstone, which looked quite heavy. I would become the Mountain Boy.

Why is the boy thinking about doing this?

(1,335 words)

By Thaddeus Rutkowski
From *The New York Times*, 3/11/12 © 2012 *The New York Times*. All rights reserved. Used by permission and protected by the Copyright Laws of the United States. The printing, copying, redistribution, or retransmission of this Content without express written permission is prohibited.

SELECTION 2

Thaddeus Rutkowski is the author of the novels Haywire, Tetched, and Roughhouse. He works as a copy editor, adjunct lecturer, and fiction-writing instructor. He lives in Manhattan with his wife and daughter.

Recall

Stop to talk, write, and think about the selection.

Your instructor may choose to give you a true-false comprehension review.

WRITE ABOUT THE SELECTION   MyReadingLab™

Complete this **Exercise** on **myreadinglab.com**

This short story raises many questions about parenting, about right and wrong, and about what shapes children as they grow to adulthood. What questions arose in your mind as you read? Which questions lingered there after you finished?

Response Suggestion: Select one or two important issues raised by the elements of this story. Write at least two paragraphs in which you discuss your thoughts about the actions of the characters regarding that issue. Refer directly to elements of the story as you explain your personal opinions and interpretations.

Your instructor may choose to give you a true-false comprehension review.

SKILL DEVELOPMENT: INFERENCE

Answer the following with *T* (true) or *F* (false):
Use the inferences implied in the selection to answer the following with *T* (true) or *F* (false).

_____   1. The narrator is a good, respectful boy.

_____   2. The kidnapped girl willingly continued to stay with the Mountain Man.

_____   3. The narrator had eaten deer meat many times.

_____   4. The narrator's father admires the Mountain Man.

_____   5. The narrator's father wants his oldest son to be more studious.

Inference

CHECK YOUR COMPREHENSION   MyReadingLab™

After reading the selection, answer the following questions with *a*, *b*, *c*, or *d*. To help you analyze your strengths and weaknesses, the question types are indicated.

Main Idea _____ 1. Which is the best statement of the main idea of this selection?

a. Parents have an important influence on their children.
b. A boy imagines becoming a kidnapper and "Mountain Man" to win his father's approval.
c. A boy is intrigued by "Wanted" posters in the post office.
d. Guns and alcohol are repeated elements of this story.

Detail _____ 2. Why does the narrator examine the "Wanted" posters?

a. So he could recognize the men and get away if he saw them
b. Because he is fascinated with criminals
c. Because he wanted to catch one
d. So he could retrieve a reward for identifying one

Inference _____ 3. From details in the first paragraph and throughout the story, we can logically infer that

a. the narrator lives in a large city.
b. the narrator lives in a small town.
c. the narrator lives in an apartment by himself.
d. the narrator lives on a farm far away from town.

Inference _____ 4. Which statement best describes the boy's feelings about the hunters?

a. He is impressed by the deer and the fact it will provide food.
b. He looks down on them because he disapproves of all hunting.
c. He admires them for killing the deer.
d. He is suspicious of them because their kill might be illegal.

Inference _____ 5. The setting of this story is most likely which time period?

a. The middle of the summer
b. The middle of the winter
c. A cool season, probably late fall.
d. It could be any time of year.

Inference _____ 6. Details throughout the story indicate that

a. the mother is unaware of the father's drinking.
b. the father abuses alcohol.
c. the narrator drinks alcohol to be like his father.
d. the other children in the family are unaware of any alcohol abuse.

Complete this **Exercise** on myreadinglab.com

240

Inference _____ 7. Which statement about the mother is best supported by the details in the story?

    a. She disapproves of her oldest son.
    b. She does not know where her husband goes in the evening.
    c. She is not interested in the father's influence on the children.
    d. She is concerned about guns.

Inference _____ 8. What is the father's occupation?

    a. He is a hunter who sells meat from wild game.
    b. He is a beer distributor.
    c. He is an artist who illustrates books.
    d. He is unemployed.

Inference _____ 9. Which statement about the narrator is best supported by the details in the story?

    a. He is a gifted student.
    b. He is a poor student.
    c. He is junior high or high school age.
    d. He is a college student.

Inference _____ 10. Which statement is best supported by the details in this story?

    a. The narrator has a close relationship with his siblings.
    b. The narrator's mother is very proud of him.
    c. The narrator wants his father to be proud of him.
    d. The narrator and his siblings are physically abused by their father.

Answer the following with *T* (true) or *F* (false).

Detail _____ 11. The mother's family is from a foreign country.

Inference _____ 12. The narrator is the youngest son in the family.

Detail _____ 13. The hunters gave meat from the deer to the family.

Inference _____ 14. The narrator's father is not proud of him.

Detail _____ 15. The narrator is one of three children in the family.

SELECTION 2

BUILD YOUR VOCABULARY   MyReadingLab™

Complete this **Exercise** on **myreadinglab.com**

SELECTION 2

According to the way the italicized word was used in the selection, indicate *a, b, c,* or *d* for the word or phrase that gives the best definition. The number in parentheses indicates the line of the passage in which the word is located.

_____ 1. "the *postmistress* came out" (2–3)
    a. mail carrier
    b. letter writer
    c. store manager
    d. post office manager

_____ 2. "checked a *pigeonhole*" (4)
    a. small, open box for storage
    b. bird's nest
    c. file drawer
    d. stack of papers

_____ 3. "showed *fugitives'* faces" (5)
    a. people running from the law
    b. police looking for criminals
    c. mountain men
    d. convicted criminals

_____ 4. "*scopes* and shoulder straps" (14)
    a. microscope
    b. gun cases
    c. horoscopes
    d. telescopes mounted on a gun

_____ 5. "shot an *agent*" (21)
    a. spy for the CIA
    b. business representative
    c. representative of the FBI
    d. diplomat

_____ 6. "My *siblings* and I" (31)
    a. cousins
    b. brothers and sisters
    c. parents
    d. friends

_____ 7. "didn't *poach* that" (42)
    a. kill
    b. take illegally
    c. cook
    d. run over

_____ 8. "of the *authorities*" (60)
    a. reporters
    b. police dogs
    c. law enforcement officials
    d. city governments

_____ 9. "*silk-screening* a book" (90)
    a. writing with a computer program
    b. illustrating with stencils and paint
    c. publishing
    d. reading using a special viewing device

_____ 10. "an old *millstone*" (94)
    a. stone used for grinding grain
    b. rock mined from a quarry
    c. stone used for paving
    d. valuable gem

This space was left intentionally blank for the preliminary edition in order to comply with copyright law. Text permission has not yet been obtained.

This space was left intentionally blank for the preliminary edition in order to comply with copyright law. Text permission has not yet been obtained.

SELECTION 3

This space was left intentionally blank for the preliminary edition in order to comply with copyright law. Text permission has not yet been obtained.

SELECTION 3

This space was left intentionally blank for the preliminary edition in order to comply with copyright law. Text permission has not yet been obtained.

SELECTION

3

This space was left intentionally blank for the preliminary edition in order to comply with copyright law. Text permission has not yet been obtained.

Concept Prep for Political Science

A Sampling of Careers in Political Science

A bachelor's degree in political science provides an excellent foundation for various careers, some of which might also require specialized training or an advanced degree.

- Intelligence officer
- Attorney
- Campaign manager
- City planner
- Non-profit organization manager
- Government official
- Teacher
- Diplomat

Did you take a literacy test to prove you could read when you registered to vote? Instead, you probably completed a simple postcard or registered seamlessly when you applied for a driver's license, but it was not always that easy. In the United States' past, the ability to read was commonly used as a ploy to discriminate against certain groups of people. In Southern and some Western states, literacy tests were commonly required for voter registration. This practice eliminated many African Americans from voting because they had little or no access to education. Similarly, literacy tests were also used to turn away "undesirable" immigrants in the early 1900s. Although literacy tests were ruled illegal by the Voting Rights Act of 1965 and a series of Supreme Court decisions, still today many citizens do not exercise their rights because of their inability to read. This change did not come easily. It was the result of pressure applied by people who knew the rights endowed by the United States Constitution and who were prepared to fight for them.

What is the U.S. Constitution?

The *Constitution* is a document that defines the structure of our government and the roles, powers, and responsibilities of public officials. It was signed in Philadelphia in 1787. Before the Constitution, the *Declaration of Independence* in 1776 affirmed our independence from England. The *Articles of Confederation* were written to govern the resulting new union of states that joined to fight for freedom and forge a new democracy. The articles created a loose union and left most of the authority with individual states. After the Revolution, as economic conflicts arose and more central control was needed, the Constitution was written to give more power to the federal government, replacing the Articles of Confederation. Our country is still governed by this same Constitution of 1787, which also guarantees our civil liberties and civil rights, including freedom of expression, due process, and equal protection.

Because no document is perfect, the writers of the Constitution allowed for amendments, and the Constitution has been amended 27 times.

What are the three branches of government?

The Constitution divides the federal government into the executive, legislative, and judicial branches.

- The *executive branch* consists of the president, whose powers include approving or vetoing (refusing to sign) laws passed by Congress, and the *president's cabinet,* an advisory group of 13 government department heads appointed by the president. For example, Hillary Clinton was a member of President Barack Obama's cabinet.

- The *legislative branch* of the government consists of the two houses of Congress: the Senate and the House of Representatives. The *Senate* with 100 members (two from each state) and the *House of Representatives* with 435 members (apportioned to each state according to population) pass federal laws and serve on committees that investigate problems and oversee the executive branch.

- The *judicial branch* consists of a system of federal courts, the highest of which is the *Supreme Court*. It consists of a chief justice and eight associate justices who are appointed by sitting presidents. The Supreme Court ensures uniformity in the interpretation of national laws.

Each of the three branches has checks and balances over the other branches so that power is shared.

What are political parties?

- Our president, senators, and representatives are nominated for office by a political party, an organization formed to support and elect candidates who uphold the views and beliefs of the group. Over the years, political parties have changed and some have disappeared. Today the two major parties are Republican and Democrat.

- The *Republican Party,* also called the GOP, for "Grand Old Party," began in 1854. Its symbol is the elephant, and Abraham Lincoln was the first Republican president. The party tends to be against expanding the size and responsibilities of the federal government and to support private enterprise. The party image is *conservative,* an ideology or set of beliefs that prefers the existing order and opposes change.

- The *Democratic Party* was organized by Thomas Jefferson in the late eighteenth century, and its first elected president was Andrew Jackson. The party tends to support the expansion of federal programs and a tax system with a greater burden on the rich and corporations. Its symbol is the donkey. The party image is *liberal,* an ideology that supports the strong role of government in economic and social issues.

Before elections, both parties pay organizations such as *Gallup* to conduct *polls,* questioning voters about the most important issues and sampling public opinion on voting preferences.

What are capitalism, Communism, and socialism?

- *Capitalism* is an economic system based on a free market for goods and services. Production centers such as factories seek profits and are owned by individuals as well as corporations and their stockholders, not the government.

As Secretary of State, Hillary Clinton served as a member of President Obama's cabinet during his first term in office. Several members of Obama's cabinet changed during his second term.

Pete Souza/MAI/Landov

The United States has a capitalist economy, although it is not purely capitalistic since government does impose regulations on business.

- *Communism* is almost the opposite of capitalism. It is an economic, political, and social system in which there is no individual ownership. The government controls businesses, and goods and property are owned in common by all citizens. Goods are available to all people as they are needed. The Communist system was envisioned by Karl Marx and is associated with the former Soviet Union and China.

- *Socialism* is an economic system advocating government or collective ownership of goods, rather than private ownership. In Karl Marx's theory, it represents the transition between capitalism and Communism in which people are paid according to work done. Communists are socialists, but not all socialists are Communists.

REVIEW QUESTIONS

After studying the material, answer the following questions:

1. Why were the Articles of Confederation replaced? _____

_____

2. How does the Declaration of Independence differ from the Constitution? ____

_____

_____

3. How many justices sit on the Supreme Court? _____

_____

4. In which branch of the government do members of the cabinet serve? _____

5. Which branch of the government passes laws? _____

6. In which house of Congress does each state have the same number of representatives? _____

_____

7. How do Republican and Democratic views on federal government expansion differ? _____

8. Would a push to reduce corporate taxes most likely be a liberal or conservative cause? _____

_____

9. Would a dynamic business owner prefer capitalism or socialism? _____

_____

10. In theory, under which system—capitalism or Communism—does a worker share equally in goods regardless of the work he or she does? _____

Your instructor may choose to give a true-false review of these political science concepts.

VOCABULARY BOOSTER

Can I Get That in Writing?

| **Roots** | *graph:* "write" | *scrib, scrip:* "write" |

Words with *graph:* "write"

Tests that use computer-readable answer sheets require that a no. 2 *graphite* pencil be used for marking the answers.

- **graph:** something written; a diagram or chart; a network of lines connecting points

  The calculus homework required a written solution and a corresponding *graph* for each problem.

- **graphic:** described in realistic detail; vivid; pertaining to any of the graphic arts such as painting, drawing, and engraving

  The movie's *graphic* violence guaranteed that it would not get anything other than an R rating.

- **phonograph:** a machine for reproducing sound from records in the form of cylinders or spiral-grooved rotating disks

  The early *phonograph* had a tuba-like device that transmitted sound.

- **cinematography:** the art or technique of motion-picture photography

  The movie that was named Best Picture at the Academy Awards also won the award for *cinematography*.

- **polygraph:** a lie detector

  A *polygraph* records changes in pulse rate or respiration to determine if a person is telling the truth.

- **geography:** the science dealing with differences between areas of the earth's surface, such as climate, population, elevation, vegetation, or land use

  Interactions between populations may be explained by *geography*—such as whether mountains or rivers separate them or whether they are in close proximity.

- **telegraph:** a system for sending distant messages or signals between two electronic devices connected by wire

  The telephone and e-mail have all but replaced the *telegraph* as a means of communicating.

Words with *scrib, scrip:* "write"

The bride and groom had an inscription engraved inside their wedding rings.

- **scribble:** to write hastily or carelessly; to cover with meaningless marks

  Before running to catch my bus, I quickly *scribbled* a note to my roommate that I would not be home for dinner.

- *transcribe:* to make a written or typed copy of spoken material; to translate into another language

  Saundra loved her job at the UN, where she *transcribed* multilingual meetings into English.

- *transcript:* a written, typewritten, or printed copy of something

  An official *transcript* of your college records is required when you transfer to another school.

- *ascribe:* to assign or attribute to a particular cause or source

  Stephen *ascribes* his good looks to his father's genes.

- *subscription:* a sum of money pledged as a contribution; the right to receive a magazine or other service for a sum; the act of appending one's signature to a document

  Public television relies on *subscriptions* pledged during its annual fund-raising drives.

- *prescription:* a written direction from a doctor for the preparation and use of a medicine

  Pharmacists read and fill *prescriptions* and usually warn about possible side effects of the prescribed drugs.

- *circumscribe:* to draw a circle around; to enclose within bounds or confine

  Since Emilio had just started to drive, he had a *circumscribed* area beyond which he was not allowed to take the family car.

- *script:* handwriting; written text of a play, movie, or television program

  The *script* of the play was revised when the screenwriters started work on the movie version of the story.

- *postscript:* an addition to a concluded and signed letter; a supplement appended to a book

  I forgot to tell my mom about my promotion until after I had signed the letter, so I added a *postscript* telling her about my new position.

- *description*: a representation of something in words or pictures; a sort or variety of thing

  The witness to the robbery gave the police sketch artist a good *description* of the suspect.

Review

Part I

Choose the best synonym from the boxed list for the words and phrases below.

graphic	scribble	transcript	subscription	prescription
script	postscript	transcribe	inscription	circumscribe

Inference

1. document showing dialogue _____   6. a copy _____

2. addendum _____   7. vivid _____

3. scrawl _____   8. translate _____

4. direction _____   9. written or carved words _____

5. purchase _____   10. limit _____

Part II

From the list, choose the word that best completes each sentence below.

| transcript | telegraph | geography | polygraph | cinematography |
| phonograph | ascribe | graphic | graph | prescription |

11. You must supply the most recent copy of your college _____ when transferring to another university.

12. Cult members tend to _____ only the best qualities to their leader.

13. _____ violence in a film results in a restricted rating.

14. Findings obtained from _____ tests are not ordinarily admitted as legal evidence in court.

15. If you are a visual learner, you prefer gaining information through pictures or a _____ rather than a lecture.

16. In the 1960s, people used the _____ to listen to music, since CD players were not yet available.

17. Studies of the _____ of the Appalachian Mountains found them to be among the oldest land masses in the United States.

18. Prior to the invention of the telephone, the _____ allowed traveling news reporters to promptly transmit their breaking stories back to city newspapers.

19. The older woman's _____ for a long, healthy life included proper nutrition, adequate exercise and rest, and lots of laughter.

20. Exceptional _____ can make the viewer feel transported to another place.

CREDITS

Answer Key to Chapter 4, "Inferences," in _Bridge to College Reading. Note: Page numbers are inaccurate._

P. 187 exercise 1. "Reading Between the Lines"

Carlos. He is aggressive, makes calls, excels in sales, and tends to details. His current employer wants to keep him and explicitly recommends him. Roger, on the other hand, is described only in terms of his personality and attendance. Nothing is said about performance. Roger is not directly recommended.

p. 188-189, exercise 2. Read only. "Implied Meaning in Advertisements"

p. 189 Exercise 3 "Implied Humor in Jokes"

Joke 1: Yvonne has devoted her efforts to succeeding at everything she does but has failed to understand that friendship is about connecting with others.

Joke 2: The mom suggests to her children that for Halloween she does not need a costume because she is portraying herself—a busy mother of three.

Joke 3: The elderly man suggests that the way he kept peact in his marriage was to always go along with whatever his wife wanted.

Joke 4: To understand this joke, it is necessary to know that Stephen King is the popular author who wrote a best-selling novel called _The Shining_.

p. 190-192 Exercise 4, "Implied Meaning in Cartoons"

Cartoon 1: The inference relates to the persistence of unwanted spam in electronic communication. Even the stranded men in the cartoon can't escape the constant stream of useless messages.

Cartoon 2: Although this woman wants to make up for her impact on the environment by planting a tree, she will fail because by driving she creates further damage. Moreover, her car appears to be one that is not fuel efficient. Aside from the environmental issue that is the point of the cartoon, one might infer from the position of the steering wheel and spelling of "centre" that the setting is England or another country in which one drives on the left side of the road.

p. 193 Exercise 5 "Recognizing Connotation in Familiar Words"

1. a   2. B   3. A   4. B   5. B   6. A   7. B   8. A   9. B   10. A

11. b   12. B   13. A   14. B   15. A   16. A   17. A   18. A   19. A   20. A

p. 193-194 Exercise 6, " Choosing Connotative Words"
(Answers will vary)

Positive	Negative
1. youngster	brat
2. leader	dictator
3. pure	clueless
4. helpful	overbearing
5. calm	dull

p. 194-195 Exercise 7, "Connotations in Textbooks"

1. negative; sounds self-serving
2. negative; suggests life- threatening bleeding or dangerous loss of money
3. negative, suggesting lowly worms or snakes

P. 195-196. Read about Euphemisms and Politically Correct Language, and Figurative Language.
p. 196 Exercise 8, "Understanding Idioms"

1. constantly busy, early and late
2. to have luck; to make money
3. extraordinarily happy; elated
4. to add substance or bulk
5. is quite expensive

p. 196-186. Read "Similes, Metaphors, Literary Analogies, Hyperbole, Personification, and Verbal Irony."
p. 198 Exercise 9, "Discovering Figurative Language in Essays"

1. A   2. B   3. A   4. A   5. A   6. A   7. B
8.   You can see, feel, hear, smell and taste the barrio
9. To add actual sounds heard in a barrio
10. The words are positive and add to the feeling of warmth.

p. 199 Exercise 10, "Figurative Language in Textbooks"
1. metaphor for the United States at the time of the Civil War.
2. lived large: Idiom for doing things in a grand manner or to an extreme
    A bear of a man: idiom for large in stature; rough
3. simile for feeling apprehension or fear

p. 200-202 "Figurative Language in Poetry"   Exercise 11

p. 162-163, Exercise 11; Poem 1
1. slightly dark in color; lacking enough light; shadowy
2. (1)rivers "ancient as the world" means the rivers have existed since the beginning of the world; "(2)rivers "older than the flow of human blood in human veins" means that rivers existed before humans appeared on the earth. Although this example does not use "like" or "as," it is a simile because it directly compares unlike objects. [Note: to Lisa, that does not make sense, but I am including it here because it is in the teacher's manual] (3) Soul grown "deep like the rivers" appears twice. It suggests that people of African ancestry have an ancient history and depth of spirit.
3. (1) "when dawns were young" suggests a time early in the history of the world (2) "the singing of the Mississippi" means that the sound of the river was melodic (3) the Mississippi's "muddy bosom" means the swell of the river was dark with mud.
4. These locations refer to the ancient roots of the African people and the relocation of many Africans to the American South as slaves.
5. People of African ancestry have an ancient history and a depth of experience that is as old as the first humans.

Poem 2

1. To a June bee boy
2. Metaphor suggesting that dreams are an elusive ideal
3. Answers will vary but should relate to the image of a young boy chasing a bee. The bee teases and entices but will not be caught.
4. He is disappointed and confused that he cannot catch the bee, which symbolizes the sweetness of achieving a dream
5. Answers will vary but should include the idea that dreams tease us by seeming to be within easy reach but remain difficult to attain.

P. 202-203 "More Types of Inferences; Inferences from Facts"
Exercise 12, "Drawing Inferences from Facts"
1. Birds are significantly more endangered by glass windows than by guns in the U.S.
2. Greenhouse gasses are contributing to global warming and Americans are creating more of it.
3. Super Bowl Sunday is still the best day for chain pizza sales, although more people are cooking frozen ones at home. Maybe the frozen products are getting better!

p. 204 Read "Inferences About a Speaker or Narrator"
p. 204-205 Exercise 13, "Inferences from Dialogue"
Passage 1
1. V   2. V   3. I   4. V   5. V
Passage 2
1. V   2. V   3. I   4. I   5. I

p. 205 Read "Inferences Based on Action and Description"
p. 206, Exercise 14 (after explanation): 1. F   2. T   3. T

p.206-207, Read "Inferences Based on Action"   Exercise 15: 1. C   2. B   3. D

p. 207, Exercise 16, Inferences Based on Description of a Place: 1. T   2. T   3. F

p. 208 Read "Using Prior Knowledge to Make Inferences;
p. 208-210 Exercise 17, Inferring Time and Place

Passage A: 1. A   2. B   3. (clues are already underlined)
Passage B: 4. C   5. B   6. (clues are already underlined)
Passage C: 7. C   8. B   9. (clues are already underlined)

p.210-211 Read "Expanding Prior Knowledge" and "Drawing Conclusions"
p.211-213   Exercise 18, Drawing Conclusions

Passage A
Einstein's speech developed later than normal, causing his parents to question his intelligence. By prior knowledge, we know that Einstein was, in fact, a gifted thinker, especially in terms of physics. He learned three languages, but he lacked fluency.
Passage B
Sacco and Vanzetti were wrongly convicted of a crime because of ethnic prejudice.
The prosecutor insulted Italian defense witnesses. The judge and jury were referred to as "bigoted."
Another person confessed, and evidence surfaced that may have proved Sacco and Vanzetti innocent.

They were not allowed a retrial or acquittal. Vanzetti's sentencing speech discussed suffering because of his Italian heritage.

Passage C
In the mid-1800s, competition for domestic employment among women increased significantly and was far greater than the competition men experienced when applying for jobs as a laborer.

Studies show that the ratio of domestic servants to families was halved from 1800 to 1840. Records also list nearly 3 times the number of female applicants for household work as men applying to labor gangs between 1845-1850.

p.213-216 Exercise 19 "The Story of an Hour." Questions for this story will be found in the essay section of the book. Use your Table of Contents.

P. 216-217: Read "Summary Points."

p. 218-224 Selection 1, "A Dip in the Poole."
p. 221: 1. T   2. F   3. F   4. F   5. F

p.360-361 Check Your Comprehension
1. D   2. C   3. B   4. A   5. D   6. B   7. A   8. C   9. B   10. A

11. False   12. False   13. False   14. False   15. True

Build your Vocabulary, p. 224

1. A   2. B   3. A   4. D   5. C   6. C   7. D   8. B   9. A   10. B

p. 225-227, "Concept Prep for Philosophy and Literature" p. 227 Review Questions.
1. Asking questions to explore a subject from all sides
2. The people of Athens wanted a scapegoat for their military defeat.
3. Plato wrote down the teachings of Socrates.
4. SPA, for Socrates, Plato, and Aristotle (Answers will vary)
5. The development of the foundation for analytical reasoning and logic
6. A category of literature, such as essay, fiction, poetry, or drama
7. For religious instruction and for entertainment
8. To keep cultural truths alive by recounting the adventures of Odysseus during his return from the Trojan War
9. Essay
10. The protagonist is the main character, whom the antagonist tries to harm.

P. 228-234, Selection 2, "The Mountain Man"
P. 231, Skill Development: Inference
1. T   2. F   3. F   4. T   5. F

P. 232-233, Check Your Comprehension

1. B   2. A   3. B   4. D   5. C   6. B   7. D   8. C   9. C   10. C
11. T   12. F   13. T   14. T   15. T

P. 234 Build Your Vocabulary

1. D   2. A   3. A   4. D   5. C   6. B   7. B   8. C   9. B   10. A

p. 243-245 "Concept Prep for Political Science"

1. The union of states needed a stronger central authority.
2. The first declared independence from England and resolved to fight for it; the second set up the structure of our current government.
3. Nine, one chief and eight associates
4. Executive
5. Legislative
6. Senate
7. Democrats want expanded government programs; Republicans do not
8. Conservative
9. Capitalism
10. Communism

p. 246-248 Vocabulary Booster

1. script
2. postscript
3. scribble
4. prescription
5. Subscription
6. Transcript
7. graphic
8. inscription
9. inscription
10. circumscribe

Part II.
11. transcript
12. Ascribe
13. Graphic   14. polygraph
15. graph
16. Phonograph
17. Geography   18. telegraph
19. prescription
20. cinematography

Rosenthal, Summer 2013

Point of View

Learning Objectives
From this chapter, readers will learn to:

1 Identify the author's point of view
2 Distinguish facts and opinions
3 Identify the author's purpose for writing
4 Recognize the author's tone

Stocktrek Images/SuperStock

From Chapter 8 of *Bridging the Gap: College Reading*, Eleventh Edition. Brenda D. Smith. Copyright © 2014 by Pearson Education, Inc. Published by Pearson Education, Inc. All rights reserved.

TEXTBOOKS AND THE AUTHOR'S POINT OF VIEW

If you are like many people, you might assume that textbooks contain facts rather than opinions, that historical accounts are based on fact and do not vary from one author to another, and that textbooks are free from an author's bias. Nothing could be further from the truth. Textbooks are replete with interpretation, opinion, and slanted—rather than balanced—views. In short, they reflect the author's point of view and the "politically correct" winds of change.

For example, in your world civilization textbook, you will read about the wealthy and cosmopolitan Persian Empire, whose kings were righteous rulers believed to be elected by the gods. About 2,500 years ago, the Persian Empire was at its height, with spectacular public buildings and palaces at the capital, Persepolis, located in what is now Iran. Yes, *you* will read about the splendor of the empire, but twenty-first-century inhabitants of the region will not. Read what these textbook authors have to say about the way historical facts about that region are treated:

> Islam denigrates the earlier cultures of its converts, just as it was noted that Christianity can. Everything before Islam was, in Arabic, *jahiliya*, "from the age of ignorance." This leaves little room in these peoples' historical consciousness for their pre-Islamic past, so they often lack interest in it. For example, despite Persia's brilliant antique history, for contemporary Iranians the glory began with the coming of Islam. Many people in Muslim countries view their own ancient cultural landscapes without interest. They may even discourage tourists from viewing pre-Islamic ruins.
>
> —Edward Bergman and William Renwick,
> *Introduction to Geography*, 2nd ed.

In other violent changes of regime, such as the Communist takeover of the Russian Empire, new leaders have also thrown out the old history books and written new ones to reflect the new political thinking. Even in American history books, you now see more about women and minorities—not because historical records have recently been unearthed, but in response to public demand. Thus, no purity rule applies to textbook writing.

The slant may start with, but is not limited to, what is included in the book; it continues with the author's interpretation. For example, the view of government in political science texts varies with liberal and conservative authors. Global warming, cloning, and stem cell replacement therapy can be opinion-laden topics in biology texts. And although the name of the first U.S. president does not vary from one American history book to another, the emphasis on the importance of Washington's administration might vary, depending on the author's point of view.

In short, *everything you read is affected by the author's point of view, purpose, tone, and presentation of facts and opinions.*

WHAT IS THE AUTHOR'S POINT OF VIEW?

Learning Objective 1

Identify the author's point of view

An author's opinions and theories concerning factual material will influence the presentation of the subject matter. Although the author of a British textbook might describe American history during Revolutionary times as a colonial uprising on a

distant continent, an American author would praise the heroic struggle for personal freedom and survival. Each of the two authors would write from a different **point of view** and express particular opinions because they have different ways of looking at the subject.

Recognizing the author's point of view is part of understanding what you read. Sophisticated readers seek to identify the beliefs of the author to know "where he or she is coming from." When the point of view is not directly stated, the author's choice of words and information provide clues for the reader.

What Is Bias?

The terms *point of view* and *bias* are very similar and are sometimes used interchangeably. When facts are slanted, though not necessarily distorted, to reflect the author's personal beliefs, the written material is said to reflect the author's bias. Thus, a **bias** is simply an opinion or position on a subject. As commonly used, however, *bias* has a negative connotation suggesting narrow-mindedness and prejudice, whereas *point of view* suggests thoughtfulness and openness. Perhaps you would like to refer to your own opinion as a point of view and to those of others, particularly if they disagree with you, as biases!

EXAMPLE Read the following passage and use the choice of information and words to identify the author's point of view or bias:

> As president, Richard Nixon enjoyed the pomp and circumstance of office. He liked to listen to the presidential song, "Hail to the Chief," and to review at strict attention ranks of marching soldiers. Nixon's vaguely royal pretensions seemed harmless enough initially, but after Watergate many people began to feel that an all-too-royal president was endangering democratic practice.
>
> —Morris P. Fiorina et al.,
> *The New American Democracy,* 3rd ed.

What is the author's point of view? Underline clues that support your answer.

EXPLANATION   The author feels that former President Nixon began to think that he was king of the country rather than president of a democracy. This is suggested by the passage and by phrases such as *pomp and circumstance, royal pretensions, all-too-royal,* and *endangering democratic practice.*

EXERCISE 1

Recognizing an Author's Point of View

Read the following passages, and use the choice of information and words to identify the author's point of view or bias.

PASSAGE 1

Commercial fishing vessels, which can catch massive amounts of fish using dragnets, have emptied coastal waters of fish, often with the help of government subsidies. No longer is the sea an inexhaustible source of food, as 60 percent of all fishing regions are now showing a decline in catch.

—Christian Goergen,
Politics in a Globalized World

What is the author's point of view? Underline clues that support your answer.

_____

_____

_____

PASSAGE 2

Unless you are willing to argue that single mothers are lazier than others, it will be hard to deny that circumstances and government policies matter for poverty. Single mothers are the largest group among the poor, because they are caught between a rock and a hard place. They need to take care of their children—often without support from a father—but without support from others, they also need to work to make money. Especially if they are young and do not have a good education, it will be very hard to find a job that pays enough for childcare and a decent living. Thus, many women are forced to rely on the welfare system.

—Christian Goergen,
Politics in a Globalized World

What is the author's point of view? Underline clues that support your answer.

_____

_____

_____

EXERCISE 2

EXERCISE 2 ## Comparing Points of View of Different Authors

Read the following two descriptions of Mary Stuart, queen of Scotland, from two different history books. Although both include positive and negative comments, the second author obviously finds the subject more engaging and has chosen to include more positive details.

Portrait of Mary Stuart, Queen of Scots (16th century), Anonymous. Scala/Art Resource, New York

PASSAGE A

Mary Stuart returned to Scotland in 1561 after her husband's death. She was a far more charming and romantic figure than her cousin Elizabeth, but she was no stateswoman. A convinced Catholic, she soon ran head-on into the granitelike opposition of Knox and the Kirk. In 1567 she was forced to abdicate, and in the following year she fled from Scotland and sought protection in England from Elizabeth. No visitor could have been more unwelcome.

—Joseph R. Strayer et al.,
The Mainstream of Civilization, 4th ed.

PASSAGE B

Mary Stuart was an altogether remarkable young woman, about whom it is almost impossible to remain objectively impartial. Even when one discounts the flattery that crept into descriptions of her, one is inclined to accept the contemporary evidence that Mary was extraordinarily beautiful, though tall for a girl—perhaps over six feet. In addition to beauty, she had almost every other attractive attribute in high degree: courage, wit, resourcefulness, loyalty, and responsiveness, in short everything needful for worldly greatness save discretion in her relations with men and a willingness to compromise, if need be, on matters of religion. She was a thoroughgoing Roman Catholic, a good lover, and a magnificent hater.

—Shepard B. Clough et al.,
A History of the Western World

1. How are the two descriptions alike? _____

   _____

2. How do the two descriptions differ? _____

   _____

3. Which clues signal that the author of the second description is more biased

   than the first? _____

   _____

4. What is the suggested meaning in the following phrases:

   a. "no stateswoman" _____

   b. "granitelike opposition" _____

   c. "more unwelcome" _____

   d. "save discretion in her relations with men" _____

   e. "thoroughgoing Roman Catholic" _____

WHAT IS THE READER'S POINT OF VIEW?

Thus far we have considered only the author's point of view. However, to recognize a point of view, a reader must know enough about the subject to realize that there is another opinion beyond the one being expressed. Therefore, prior knowledge and a slightly suspicious nature will open the mind to countless other views and alternative arguments.

On the other hand, prior knowledge can lead to a closed mind and rigid thinking. Existing opinions affect the extent to which readers accept or reject what they read. If their beliefs are particularly strong, sometimes they refuse to hear what is said or they hear something that is not said. Research has shown that readers will actually "tune out" new material that expresses views drastically different from their own. For example, if you were reading that the AIDS virus should not be a concern for most middle-class Americans, would you be "tuned in" or "tuned out"?

EXAMPLE Read the following passage on smoking from the point of view of a nonsmoker. Next, reread it from the point of view of a smoker. Finally, answer the questions.

> Smoke can permanently paralyze the tiny cilia that sweep the breathing passages clean and can cause the lining of the respiratory tract to thicken irregularly. The body's attempt to rid itself of the smoking toxins may produce a deep, hacking cough in the person next to you at the lunch counter. Console yourself with the knowledge that these hackers are only trying to rid their bodies of nicotines, "tars," formaldehyde, hydrogen sulfide, resins, and who knows what. Just enjoy your meal.
>
> —Robert Wallace,
> *Biology: The World of Life*

1. Is the author a smoker? Underline the clues suggesting your answer. _____
   _____

2. What is your view on smoking? _____
   _____

3. Reading this passage in the guise of a nonsmoker, what message is conveyed to you? _____
   _____

4. Assuming the role of a smoker, what message is conveyed to you? _____
   _____

5. What is the main point the author is trying to convey? _____
   _____

EXPLANATION Although it is possible that both the smoker and nonsmoker would get exactly the same message, it is more likely that the nonsmoker would be disgusted by the health risks, whereas the smoker would find the author guilty of exaggeration and discrimination. The main point is that smoking causes permanent physical damage. The attitude suggests that the author is probably not a smoker.

EXERCISE 3

Identifying Points of View

Read the following passages and answer the questions about point of view.

PASSAGE A: COLUMBUS

> On August 3, 1492, Columbus and some ninety mariners set sail from Palos, Spain, in the *Niña, Pinta,* and *Santa Maria.* Based on faulty calculations, the Admiral estimated Asia to be no more than 4500 miles to the west (the actual distance is closer to 12,000 miles). Some 3000 miles out, his crew became fearful and wanted to return home. But he convinced them to keep sailing west. Just two days later, on October 12, they landed on a small island in the Bahamas, which Columbus named San Salvador (holy savior).

A fearless explorer, Columbus turned out to be an ineffective administrator and a poor geographer. He ended up in debtor's prison, and to his dying day in 1506 he never admitted to locating a world unknown to Europeans. Geographers overlooked his contribution and named the Western continents after another mariner, Amerigo Vespucci, a merchant from Florence who participated in a Portuguese expedition to South America in 1501. In a widely reprinted letter, Vespucci claimed that a new world had been found, and it was his name that caught on.

—James Kirby Martin et al.,
America and Its Peoples

1. Which paragraph sounds more like the Columbus you learned about in elementary school? _____

   _____

2. What is the author's position on Columbus? Underline clues for your answer.

   _____

   _____

3. What is your view of Columbus? What has influenced your view? _____

   _____

   _____

4. What is the main point the author is trying to convey? _____

   _____

   _____

PASSAGE B: SURVIVING IN VIETNAM

Vietnam ranks after World War II as America's second most expensive war. Between 1950 and 1975, the United States spent $123 billion on combat in Southeast Asia. More importantly, Vietnam ranks—after our Civil War and World Wars I and II—as the nation's fourth deadliest war, with 57,661 Americans killed in action.

Yet, when the last U.S. helicopter left Saigon, Americans suffered what historian George Herring terms "collective amnesia." Everyone, even those who had fought in 'Nam, seemed to want to forget Southeast Asia. It took nearly ten years for the government to erect a national monument to honor those who died in Vietnam.

Few who served in Vietnam survived unscathed, whether psychologically or physically. One of the 303,600 Americans wounded during the long war was 101st Airborne platoon leader James Bombard, first shot and then blown up by a mortar round during the bitter Tet fighting at Hue in February 1968. He describes his traumatic experience as feeling the bullet rip into your flesh, the shrapnel tear the flesh from your bones and the blood run down your leg. . . . To put your hand on your chest and to come away with your hand red with your own blood, and to feel it running out of your eyes and out of your mouth, and seeing it spurt out of your guts, realizing you were dying. . . . I was ripped open from the top of my head to the tip of my toes. I had forty-five holes in me.

Somehow Bombard survived Vietnam.

Withdrawing U.S. forces from Vietnam ended only the combat. Returning veterans fought government disclaimers concerning the toxicity of the defoliant Agent Orange. VA hospitals across the nation still contain thousands of para- and quadriplegic Vietnam veterans, as well as the maimed from earlier wars. Throughout America the "walking wounded" find themselves still embroiled in the psychological aftermath of Vietnam.

—James Divine et al.,
America: Past and Present

1. What is the author's own view of the war? Underline clues for your answer.

   _____

   _____

2. What is your own position on the Vietnam War? _____

   _____

   _____

3. What is the purpose of Bombard's quotation? _____

   _____

   _____

4. How do you feel about war after reading this passage? _____

   _____

   _____

5. What is the main point the author is trying to convey? _____

   _____

   _____

BRAIN BOOSTER

Male and Female Brains and Their Points of View

Culture and environment obviously are important in shaping gender roles. However, neuroscience reveals that there are biological differences in male and female brains that influence thinking and behavior. Females have two X chromosomes, each containing 1,500 genes. Males have 1 X chromosome and 1 Y chromosome, which contains 100 genes. Many of the genes on the X chromosome govern verbal skills and other aspects of thinking. For this reason and others involving chemical differences, females generally tend to be better at language and seeing details, and males tend to excel at recognizing the gist of a situation.

What does this mean in college or at work? Males and females might bring different points of view to a problem or an interpretation of a reading selection simply because of different brain wiring. So, working groups are often more successful at finding solutions when they are made up of both males and females. Test this in your next team project or group exercise.

—Adapted from John J. Medina, Brain Rules.
© 2008 John J. Medina. Pear Press: Seattle, WA

WHAT ARE FACT AND OPINION?

Learning Objective 2

Distinguish facts and opinions

For both the reader and the writer, a point of view is a position or belief that logically evolves over time through gained knowledge and experience and is usually based on both facts and opinions. For example, what is your position on city curfews for youth, on helping the homeless, and on abortion? Are your views on these issues supported solely by facts? Do you recognize the difference between the facts and the opinions used in your thinking?

Both facts and opinions are used persuasively to support positions. You have to determine which is which and then judge the issue accordingly. A **fact** is a statement based on actual evidence or personal observation. It can be checked objectively with empirical data and proved to be true. By contrast, an **opinion** is a statement of personal feeling or judgment. It reflects a belief or an interpretation of evidence, rather than evidence itself; it cannot be proved true. Look for "should" statements such as, "High school students *should* aspire to earning a college degree." Also notice other value words such as *good, better, immoral, risky,* to name just a few. Adding the quoted opinion of a well-known authority to a few bits of evidence does not improve the data, yet this is an effective persuasive technique. Even though you may believe an opinion is valid, it is still an opinion.

EXAMPLE

Fact: Freud developed a theory of personality.

Fact: Freud believed that the personality is divided into three parts.

Opinion: Freud constructed the most complete theory of personality development.

Opinion: The personality is divided into three parts: the id, the ego, and the superego.

Authors mix facts and opinions, sometimes in the same sentence, to win you over to a particular point of view. Persuasive tricks include quoting a source of facts who then voices an opinion or hedging a statement with "It is a fact that" and attaching a disguised opinion. Recognize that both facts and opinions are valuable, but be able to distinguish between the two. The questions listed in the Reader's Tip can help you.

Reader's Tip | Questions to Uncover Bias

- What is your opinion on the subject?
- What is the author's opinion on the subject?
- What are the author's credentials for writing on the subject?
- What does the author have to gain?
- Does the author use facts or opinions as support?
- Are the facts selected and slanted to reflect the author's bias?

EXERCISE (4) **Differentiating Between Facts and Opinions**

Read each statement, and indicate *F* for fact and *O* for opinion.

————— 1. Regarding the drugs that can cause death from overdose, the dangers have been blown wildly out of proportion.

> —Jeffrey Reiman,
> *The Rich Get Richer and the Poor Get Prison:*
> *Ideology, Class, and Criminal Justice,* 7th ed.

————— 2. A misdemeanor is a crime punishable by less than one year in prison.

> —Adapted from John J. Macionis,
> *Social Problems*

————— 3. The most controversial tax is a general sales tax, which is levied by all but a few states on the sale of most goods, sometimes exempting food and drugs.

> —Adapted from David B. Magleby et al.,
> *Government by the People,* Teaching and
> Learning Classroom Edition, 6th ed.

————— 4. Phosphorus, found in detergents, causes an overgrowth of algae, which then consume all the available oxygen in the water, making it incapable of supporting any flora or fauna.

> —Ricky W. Griffin and Ronald J. Ebert,
> *Business,* 8th ed.

————— 5. Witnesses who identify culprits (from photos or police lineups) within 10 seconds are 90% accurate, whereas those who take longer than 12 seconds are only 50% accurate.

> —Lester A. Lefton and Linda Brannon,
> *Psychology,* 9th ed.

————— 6. When you feel anger, your heart rate increases and so does the temperature of your skin; and when you feel fear, your heart rate increases but your skin temperature actually decreases.

> —Stephen M. Kosslyn and Robin S. Rosenberg,
> *Psychology: The Brain, the Person, the World,* 2nd ed.

_____ 7. Convicted juveniles, like adult offenders, often gain early and undeserved release from jail.

—Judy Sheindlin,
*Don't Pee on My Leg and Tell Me It's Raining:
America's Toughest Family Court Judge Speaks Out*

_____ 8. Repairing the meetinghouse, building a school, aiding a widowed neighbor—such were the proper uses of wealth.

—Gary B. Nash et al.,
The American People, 6th ed., Vol. 1

_____ 9. Although there are a large number of Web browsers, some developed by Internet giants such as Microsoft, the dominant Web browser is Google, which has gained dominance by offering the most efficient search engine on the Web.

—Paul R. Gregory,
Essentials of Economics, 6th ed.

_____ 10. Americans are poorly informed about politics.

—Gary Wasserman,
The Basics of American Politics, 12th ed.

EXERCISE 5

Discerning Fact and Opinion in Textbooks

The following passage from a history text describes Sigmund Freud. Notice the mixture of facts and opinions in developing a view of this scientist. Mark the items that follow with *F* for fact and *O* for opinion.

PASSAGE A

Sigmund Freud was a disciplined man, precise and punctual in his habits. In many ways, his life was typical of the life of a Viennese bourgeois professional at the end of the nineteenth century. His day was like a railway timetable, scheduled to the minute—whether seeing patients, dining with his family, or taking his daily constitutional. He even calculated his pleasures, counting as his only indulgence the 20 cigars he smoked every day.

The order in Freud's life seemed curiously at odds with his dedication to the study of disorder. He was a man of science, a medical doctor specializing in *organic* diseases of the nervous system. Early in his career, he began to question *physiological* explanations for certain nervous disorders and to search for another reason for the disorders of the mind. His exploration took him to Paris in 1885 to study with the leading French neurologist, Jean Martin Charcot (1825–1893), whose work on hysteria had won him an international reputation.

Surrounded by hysterics in Charcot's clinic, Freud wondered whether organic physical illnesses could be traced to psychological problems. Freud explored the value of hypnosis as a technique for uncovering the secret workings of the mind. He learned that emotions alone could produce physical symptoms such as blindness and paralysis. By hypnotizing patients, Freud caught glimpses of the world of the unconscious as a vast and hidden terrain. He approached the new territory as an explorer.

Freud created a new science of the unconscious, psychoanalysis, when he rejected physiological causes for nervous disorders in favor of psychological ones. He intended psychoanalysis as a theory of personality and a method of treatment or therapy. That was a dramatic break with existing theories of madness and mental disorder. On his seventieth birthday, Freud looked back over his own career and described his achievement: "The poets and philosophers before me discovered the unconscious; what I discovered was the scientific method by which the unconscious can be studied."

—Mark Kishlansky et al.,
Civilization in the West, 6th ed.

_____ 1. Freud smoked 20 cigars each day.

_____ 2. He lived the life of a typical Viennese professional of his era.

_____ 3. The order in Freud's life was at odds with his dedication to the study of disorder.

_____ 4. Freud was a medical doctor specializing in organic disorders of the nervous system.

_____ 5. Freud created the science of psychoanalysis.

The following passage from a business text discusses Winston Churchill's leadership capabilities. Notice the mixture of facts and opinions in developing a view of this former British leader. Mark the items that follow with *F* for fact and *O* for opinion.

PASSAGE B

Successful leaders often have the experience of prevailing in the face of adversity and learning from earlier failures. Leaders' skills also must match the circumstances. Winston Churchill's career provides a classic example.

Churchill began his remarkable political career in 1901 when he became a member of the House of Commons at the age of 26. Prior to his entry into Parliament he had seen combat as a cavalry officer in India, Cuba, and the Sudan and was awarded several medals for valor. He rose quickly in politics and governmental service, becoming the First Lord of the Admiralty (civilian head of the British Navy) in 1911. One of Churchill's decisions about deployment of naval forces in 1915 during World War I resulted in failure and marked the end of his fast-track career. Churchill returned to combat, serving as an infantry officer in 1917. After World War I Churchill returned to public office but was essentially relegated to the sidelines of politics. His calls for rearmament, warnings about the intentions of the Nazis between 1933 and 1939, and criticisms of the government's attempts to appease the Nazis were ignored. When things looked the worst in May 1940, the country turned to the 65-year-old Churchill for leadership as Prime Minister. It is said that Churchill "stood out as the one man in whom the nation could place its trust."

In June 1940 Britain had been at war with Germany for a year. British soldiers had been driven out of France and narrowly escaped capture through an evacuation from Dunkirk. France surrendered on June 22, and the United States had not yet entered World War II. The Battle of Britain, which involved heavy bombing of Britain's major cities, was about to begin, and it appeared that Germany would invade Britain. The outcome looked bleak. Churchill's hats, cigars, and two-fingered "v" for victory signs were distinctive, as well as symbolic, and endeared him to his followers. There were other qualities about Churchill as well that made him well-suited for the challenges of leadership during these difficult times. Two specific examples of his personal risk-taking are described as follows:

Churchill as Prime Minister frequently and deliberately ran terrible personal risks. But the people admired him for it, and loved his offhand disregard for danger. Once, when a German bomb landed near his car and nearly tipped it over, he joked, "Must have been my beef that kept the car down"—a reference to his pudginess.

Winston Churchill was another who liked to leave his underground air-raid shelter in Whitehall for the streets the moment bombs began falling. Attempts were made to stop him, because the risk of getting one's head blown off or losing a limb from shrapnel was great. . . . "I'll have you know," thundered Churchill, "that as a child my nursemaid could never prevent me from taking a walk in the Green Park when I wanted to do so. And, as a man, Adolf Hitler certainly won't."

At the end of World War II in 1945, Churchill lost his bid for reelection because he was unresponsive to the needs for social change after the war. He returned to office again as Prime Minister from 1951 to 1955, but his performance was limited by age and health problems. In general, his service as a peace-time Prime Minister did not measure up to his service during war time.

—Charles R. Greer and Warren Richard Plunkett,
Supervision: Diversity and Teams in the Workplace, 10th ed.

_____ 1. Churchill began his political career at the age of 26 in the House of Commons.

_____ 2. Things looked the worst for England in May 1940.

_____ 3. France surrendered to Germany on June 22, 1940, but the United States had not yet entered the war.

_____ 4. Churchill was a frequent and deliberate risk-taker.

_____ 5. Churchill was a better leader during the war than during peacetime.

WHAT IS THE AUTHOR'S PURPOSE?

Learning Objective 3

Identify the author's purpose for writing

A textbook author can shift from an objective and factual explanation of a topic to a subjective and opinionated treatment of the facts. Recognizing the author's purpose does not mean that you won't buy the product; it just means that you will be a more cautious, well-informed consumer.

An author always has a **purpose** in mind when putting words on paper. A textbook reader expects that the author's purpose is to inform or explain objectively—

and, in general, this is true. At times, however, an author can slip from factual explanation to opinionated treatment of the facts, or persuasion. The sophisticated reader recognizes this shift in purpose and becomes more critical in evaluating the content. For example, a persuasive paragraph for or against more air quality control regulations should alert you to be more skeptical than you would be while reading a paragraph that only explains how air quality control works.

Just as we know that a textbook is generally intended to inform, we expect an election campaign speech to try to persuade. So, consider the context of a reading selection—the type of publication—as an important clue to its purpose. In addition, analyze the tone and the kinds of information presented, and determine the author's point of view on the topic. As always, think about the main point being made but also why the author wants to make it.

The author can have a single purpose or more than one such as the following:

inform	argue	entertain
explain	persuade	narrate
describe	condemn	shock
enlighten	ridicule	investigate

Read the following passage to determine the author's purpose.

EXAMPLE

love, *n.* A temporary insanity curable by marriage or by removal of the patient from the influences under which he incurred the disorder. This disease, like caries and many other ailments, is prevalent only among civilized races living under artificial conditions; barbarous nations breathing pure air and eating simple food enjoy immunity from its ravages. It is sometimes fatal, but more frequently to the physician than to the patient.

—Ambrose Bierce,
The Devil's Dictionary

EXPLANATION   The author defines love in a humorous and exaggerated manner for the purpose of entertaining the reader.

EXERCISE 6

Determining the Author's Purpose

Read the following passage and answer the questions about the author's purpose.

ISABELLA KATZ AND THE HOLOCAUST: A LIVING TESTIMONY

No statistics can adequately render the enormity of the Holocaust, and its human meaning can perhaps only be understood through the experience of a single human being who was cast into the nightmare of the Final Solution. Isabella Katz was the eldest of six children—Isabella, brother Philip, and sisters Rachel, Chicha, Cipi, and baby Potyo—from a family of Hungarian Jews. She lived in the ghetto of Kisvarda, a provincial town of 20,000 people, where hers was a typical Jewish family of the region—middle-class, attached to Orthodox traditions, and imbued with a love of learning.

Point of View

In 1938 and 1939 Hitler pressured Hungary's regent, Miklós Horthy, into adopting anti-Jewish laws. By 1941 Hungary had become a German ally, and deportations and massacres were added to the restrictions. Isabella's father left for the United States, where he hoped to obtain entry papers for his family, but after Pearl Harbor, Hungary was at war with America and the family was trapped. In the spring of 1944, when Hitler occupied Hungary, the horror of the Final Solution struck Isabella. On March 19 Adolf Eichmann, as SS officer in charge of deportation, ordered the roundup of Jews in Hungary, who numbered some 650,000. On May 28, Isabella's nineteenth birthday, the Jews in Kisvarda were told to prepare for transportation to Auschwitz on the following morning. Isabella recalled:

> And now an SS man is here, spick-and-span, with a dog, a silver pistol, and a whip. And he is all of sixteen years old. On his list appears the name of every Jew in the ghetto. . . . "Teresa Katz," he calls—my mother. She steps forward. . . . Now the SS man moves toward my mother. He raises his whip and, for no apparent reason at all, lashes out at her.

En route to Auschwitz, crammed into hot, airless boxcars, Isabella's mother told her children to "stay alive":

> Out there, when it's all over, a world's waiting for you to give it all I gave you. Despite what you see here . . . believe me, there is humanity out there, there is dignity. . . . And when this is all over, you must add to it, because sometimes it is a little short, a little skimpy.

Isabella and her family were among more than 437,000 Jews sent to Auschwitz from Hungary.

When they arrived at Auschwitz, the SS and camp guards divided the prisoners into groups, often separating family members. Amid the screams and confusion, Isabella remembered:

> We had just spotted the back of my mother's head when Mengele, the notorious Dr. Josef Mengele, points to my sister and me and says, "Die Zwei" [those two]. This trim, very good-looking German, with a flick of his thumb and a whistle, is selecting who is to live and who is to die.

Isabella's mother and her baby sister perished within a few days.

> The day we arrived in Auschwitz, there were so many people to be burned that the four crematoriums couldn't handle the task. So the Germans built big open fires to throw the children in. Alive? I do not know. I saw the flames. I heard the shrieks.

Isabella was to endure the hell of Auschwitz for nine months.

The inmates were stripped, the hair on their heads and bodies was shaved, and they were herded into crude, overcrowded barracks. As if starvation, forced labor, and disease were not enough, they were subjected to unspeakable torture, humiliation, and terror, a mass of living skeletons for whom the difference between life and death could be measured only in an occasional flicker of spirit that determined to resist against impossible odds. Isabella put it this way:

> Have you ever weighed 120 pounds and gone down to 40? Something like that—not quite alive, yet not quite dead. Can anyone, can even I, picture it? . . .

Our eyes sank deeper. Our skin rotted. Our bones screamed out of our bodies. Indeed, there was barely a body to house the mind, yet the mind was still working, sending out the messages "Live! Live!"

In November, just as Isabella and her family were lined up outside a crematorium, they were suddenly moved to Birnbäumel, in eastern Germany—the Russians were getting nearer, and the Nazis were closing down their death camps and moving the human evidence of their barbarism out of reach of the enemy. In January, as the Russians and the frigid weather closed in, the prisoners were forced to march through the snows deeper into Germany, heading toward the camp at Bergen-Belsen. Those who could not endure the trial fell by the side, shot or frozen to death. On January 23, while stumbling through a blizzard with the sound of Russian guns in the distance, Isabella, Rachel, and Chicha made a successful dash from the death march and hid in an abandoned house. Two days later Russian soldiers found them. Philip had been sent to a labor camp, and Cipi made it to Bergen-Belsen, where she died.

Isabella later married and had two children of her own, making a new life in America. Yet the images of the Holocaust remain forever in her memory. "Now I am older," she says, "and I don't remember all the pain. . . . That is not happiness, only relief, and relief is blessed. . . . And children someday will plant flowers in Auschwitz, where the sun couldn't crack through the smoke of burning flesh."

—Richard L. Greaves et al.,
Civilizations of the World, 3rd ed.

1. What is the author's purpose for including this story in a history textbook?

   _____

   _____

2. What does the author mean by "its human meaning can perhaps only be understood through the experience of a single human being"? _____

   _____

   _____

   _____

3. Why does the author include Isabella's quotations? _____

   _____

   _____

4. Why does the author include Isabella's quotation about the SS man? _____

   _____

   _____

5. What is Isabella's purpose in relating her story? _____

   _____

   _____

6. Is the passage predominantly developed through facts or opinions? Give an example of each. _____

_____

_____

7. How does the passage influence your thinking about the Holocaust? _____

_____

_____

_____

WHAT IS THE AUTHOR'S TONE?

The author's purpose directly affects the **tone,** the author's attitude toward the topic. If the purpose is to criticize, the tone will probably be condemning and somewhat mean-spirited. If the purpose is to entertain, the tone may be humorous and playful. To put it in simple terms, the tone of an author's writing is similar to the tone of a speaker's voice. For listeners, telling the difference between an angry tone and a romantic tone is easy; you simply notice the speaker's voice. Distinguishing among humor, sarcasm, and irony, however, may be more difficult. **Humorous** remarks are designed to be comical and amusing, whereas **sarcastic** remarks are designed to cut or inflict pain. As discussed earlier **ironic** remarks express the opposite of the literal meaning and show the incongruity between the actual and the expected. Making such precise distinctions requires a careful evaluation of what is said. Because the sound of the voice is not heard in reading, clues to the tone must come from the writer's presentation of the message. Your job is to look for clues to answer the question "What is the author's attitude toward the topic?" The list in the Reader's Tip shows the many ways a writer can express tone.

Reader's TIP Recognizing an Author's Tone

The following words with explanations can describe an author's tone or attitude:

- **Absurd, farcical, ridiculous:** laughable or a joke
- **Apathetic, detached:** not caring
- **Ambivalent:** having contradictory attitudes or feelings
- **Angry, bitter, hateful:** feeling bad and upset about the topic
- **Arrogant, condescending:** acting conceited or above others
- **Awestruck, wondering:** filled with wonder
- **Cheerful, joyous, happy:** feeling good about the topic
- **Compassionate, sympathetic:** feeling sorrow at the distress of others
- **Congratulatory, celebratory:** honoring an achievement or festive occasion

- **Cynical:** expecting the worst from people
- **Depressed, melancholy:** sad, dejected, or having low spirits
- **Disapproving:** judging unfavorably
- **Formal:** using an official style; of a high social class, genteel
- **Frustrated:** blocked from a goal
- **Hard:** unfeeling, strict, and unrelenting
- **Humorous, jovial, comic, playful, amused:** being funny
- **Incredulous:** unbelieving
- **Indignant:** outraged
- **Intense, impassioned:** extremely involved, zealous, or agitated
- **Ironic:** stating the opposite of what is expected; having a twist at the end
- **Irreverent:** lacking respect for authority
- **Mocking, scornful, caustic, condemning:** ridiculing the topic
- **Objective, factual, straightforward, critical:** using facts without emotions
- **Optimistic:** looking on the bright side
- **Outspoken:** speaking one's mind on issues
- **Pessimistic:** looking on the negative side
- **Prayerful:** religiously thankful
- **Reverent:** showing respect
- **Righteous:** morally correct
- **Romantic, intimate, loving:** expressing love or affection
- **Sarcastic:** saying one thing and meaning another
- **Satiric:** using irony, wit, and sarcasm to discredit or ridicule
- **Sensational:** overdramatized or overhyped
- **Sentimental, nostalgic:** remembering the good old days
- **Serious, sincere, earnest, solemn:** being honest and concerned
- **Straightforward:** forthright, direct
- **Subjective, opinionated:** expressing opinions and feelings
- **Tragic:** regrettable or deplorable
- **Vindictive:** seeking revenge

Try being an author yourself. Imagine that you have been waiting a half-hour for one of your friends to show up for a meeting, and you can wait no longer. You decide to leave a note. On your own paper, write your friend three different notes— one in a sympathetic tone, one in an angry tone, and one in a sarcastic tone. Notice in doing this how your tone reflects your purpose. Which note would you really leave and to which friend?

EXAMPLE Identify the tone of the following passage:

> When I actually went south, and actually saw signs that said "white" and "colored" and I actually could not drink out of that water fountain, or go to that ladies' room, I had a real emotional reaction. I remember the first time it happened, was at the Tennessee State Fair. And I had a date with this, this young man. And I started to go

to the ladies' room. And it said "white and colored" and I really resented that. I was outraged. So, it, it had a really emotional effect. . . . My response was, who's trying to change it, change these things. And I recall talking to a number of people in the dormitories at school and on campus, and asking them if they knew any people who were trying to—to bring about some type of change. And I remember being, getting almost depressed, because I encountered what I thought was so much apathy. At first I couldn't find anyone, and many of the students were saying, why are you concerned about that?

> Diane Nash, Interview at www.teachersdomain.org/resources
> In *Women and the Making of America,*
> Mari Jo Buhle, Teresa Murphy, and Jane Gerhard

The author's tone is _____

    a. ambivalent.
    b. congratulatory.
    c. indignant.

EXPLANATION   The author's tone is indignant (*c*). The repeated use of the word *actually*, as if she can't believe what she is experiencing, and the word *outraged* reflect the writer's emotions. In addition, her disappointment at finding no one who shares her intense concern about this issue further conveys the continued feelings of anger and indignation.

EXERCISE 7

Identifying Tone

Mark the letter that identifies the tone for each of the following examples. Refer to the Reader's Tip to define unfamiliar words.

_____ 1. Must I recycle everything? I don't want any more gifts of brown, "earth friendly" stationery. I want to exercise my right to burn my newspapers and throw my soda can in the trash.

    a. objective
    b. nostalgic
    c. angry

_____ 2. In the last few decades, health experts and environmentalists looked to birth control to save us from a growing world population that already exceeds 5.5 billion. Yet, as recently as 1914, the distribution of birth control information was illegal. In that year, Margaret Higgins Sanger, founder of the magazine *The Woman Rebel*, was arrested and indicted for sending birth control information through the mail. Surprisingly, again today some factions are pressing to limit women's access to birth control.

    a. optimistic
    b. ironic
    c. sentimental

_____ 3. The Golden Age or heyday of Hollywood was in the 1930s. Americans, economically crippled by the Great Depression, went to movies for fantasy escapes into worlds created by entertainers such as Clark Gable, Greta Garbo, and the Marx Brothers.

    a. objective
    b. nostalgic
    c. bitter

_____ 4. Doublespeak hides the truth, evades the issues, and misleads. No one gets fired these days. They disappear due to downsizing, work-force adjustments, and head-count reductions. After eliminating 8,000 jobs, an automobile company called it "a volume-related production schedule adjustment." Perhaps the families of the workers called it an "involuntary lifestyle reduction."

    a. sensational
    b. impassioned
    c. bitter

_____ 5. In his early thirties, Beethoven's gradual hearing loss became total. This prevented him from playing the piano properly but not from continuing to write music. His three most complex and acclaimed symphonies were written when he was stone deaf. He never heard them played.

    a. ironic
    b. sarcastic
    c. opinionated

EXERCISE 8

Identifying the Author's Tone in Paragraphs

Read the following passages to determine the author's tone and attitude toward the subject.

PASSAGE A: THE FENCE

My fingers wanted to reach through the wire fence, not to touch it, not to feel it, but to break it down, with what I did not understand. The burning was not there to be understood. Something was burning, the side of me that knew I was treated different, would always be treated different because I was born on a particular side of a fence, a fence that separated me from others, that separated me from the past, that separated me from the country of my genesis and glued me to the country I did not love because it demanded something of me I could not give. Something was burning now, and if I could have grasped the source of that rage and held it in my fist, I would have melted that fence.

—Benjamin Alire Saénz,
Exile, El Paso, Texas

Point of View

1. What is the author's tone? _____

_____

_____

2. Underline the words and phrases that suggest this tone.
3. What is the author's point of view? _____

_____

_____

4. What is your own point of view on the subject? _____

_____

_____

5. What is the main point the author is trying to convey? _____

_____

_____

The first day of freshman basketball tryouts, I learned that coaching girls is different. I was demonstrating the correct way to set a cross screen. I positioned my legs shoulder-width apart and crossed my hands—fists clenched—over my groin to protect myself from the injury that all men fear. I paused, confused, understanding from the girls' bewildered looks that something was wrong. The other coach, a 15-year veteran of coaching girls, recognized my rookie mistake and bailed me out. He raised his arms and covered his chest, and I knew that I had entered alien territory.

—Brendan O'Shaughnessy,
"It's a Whole New Ballgame for Veteran Coach,"
Chicago Tribune, December 1, 2002

1. What is the author's tone? _____

_____

2. Underline the words and phrases that suggest this tone.
3. What is the author's point of view? _____

_____

_____

4. What is your own point of view on the subject? _____

_____

_____

5. What is the main point the author is trying to convey? _____

_____

_____

PASSAGE C: WHY WOMEN SMILE

After smiling brilliantly for nearly four decades, I now find myself trying to quit. Or, at the very least, seeking to lower the wattage a bit.

Smiles are not the small and innocuous things they appear to be: Too many of us smile in lieu of showing what's really on our minds. Despite all the work we American women have done to get and maintain full legal control of our bodies, not to mention our destinies, we still don't seem to be fully in charge of a couple of small muscle groups in our faces.

Our smiles have their roots in the greetings of monkeys, who pull their lips up and back to show their fear of attack, as well as their reluctance to vie for a position of dominance. And like the opossum caught in the light by a clattering garbage can, we, too, flash toothy grimaces when we make major mistakes. By declaring ourselves non-threatening, our smiles provide an extremely versatile means of protection.

—Amy Cunningham,
"Why Women Smile"

1. What is the author's tone? _____

_____

_____

2. Underline the words and phrases that suggest this tone.

3. What is the author's point of view? _____

_____

_____

4. What is your own point of view on the subject? _____

_____

_____

5. What is the main point the author is trying to convey? _____

_____

_____

POINTS OF VIEW IN EDITORIAL CARTOONS

Editorial cartoons vividly illustrate how an author or an artist can effectively communicate point of view without making a direct verbal statement. Through their drawings, cartoonists have great freedom to be extremely harsh and judgmental. For example, they take positions on local and national news events and frequently depict politicians as crooks, thieves, or even murderers. Because the accusations are implied rather than directly stated, the cartoonist communicates a point of view but is still safe from libel charges.

EXAMPLE   Study the cartoon to determine what the cartoonist believes and is saying about the subject. Use the following steps to analyze the implied meaning and point of view:

1. Glance at the cartoon for an overview.

2. Answer the question "What is this about?" to determine the general topic.

   _____

   _____

   _____

3. Study the details for symbolism. Who or what is represented by the images shown? _____

   _____

   _____

4. With all the information in mind, explain the main point that the cartoonist is trying to get across. _____

   _____

   _____

5. What is the tone of the cartoon? _____

   _____

   _____

6. What is the cartoonist's purpose? _____

   _____

   _____

7. What is the cartoonist's point of view or position on the subject? What is your point of view? _____

   _____

   _____

   _____

Mike Lane/PoliticalCartoons.com

EXPLANATION　　Global warming is the topic of the cartoon, as suggested by the question on the back of the newspaper. The carefree polar bear sunbathes as the polar ice shelf cracks beneath the lounge chair. As the sun beams and the ice melts, the bear acclimates with sun shades, suntan oil, and an iced drink from the "KOOL-R." The main point of the cartoon is that we, like the polar bear, are ignoring the reality of global warming, and we will suffer the disastrous consequences. The question "What global warming?" suggests that we are in as much denial as the polar bear. The tone is sarcastic and pleading. The cartoonist's purpose is to spur us into action before it is too late.

EXERCISE 9

Interpreting an Editorial Cartoon

Use the same steps to analyze the message and answer the questions about the cartoon.

1. What is the general topic of this cartoon? _____

_____

2. What is represented by the objects such as the circular slide, the hoop, and

the tires? _____

_____

_____

_____
_____
_____
_____

3. What is the main point the cartoonist is trying to convey? _____
_____
_____
_____

4. What is the cartoonist's purpose? _____
_____
_____

5. What is the tone of the cartoon? _____
_____
_____

6. What is the cartoonist's point of view? _____
_____
_____
_____

7. What is your point of view on the subject? _____
_____
_____
_____

Cartoons are fun but challenging because they require prior knowledge for interpretation. To understand current news cartoons, you have to be familiar with the latest happenings. Look on the editorial page of your newspaper to enjoy world events from a cartoonist's point of view. If you prefer viewing them online, the home pages of some Internet service providers include links to the day's best cartoons; or you can do a Google search for cartoon sites.

As stated in the beginning of the chapter, even in college textbooks, authors' attitudes and biases slip through. Your responsibility as a reader is to be alert for signs of manipulation and to be ready—by noticing not only what is said but also what is not said—to question interpretations and conclusions. Sophisticated readers draw their own conclusions based on their own interpretation of the facts.

SUMMARY POINTS

1. How can I identify the author's point of view?
- In reading, *point of view* refers to the author's opinions and way of looking at the topic. The author's point of view, like the reader's point of view, can influence the presentation of facts and information in the text.
- Similar to making reasonable inferences, identifying the author's point of view requires analyzing word choice and selection of details in light of your own opinions and schemata.
- Analyze the use of facts and opinions, identify the author's tone, and determine the author's purpose in writing to reveal the author's point of view on the subject.

2. How can I distinguish facts and opinions?
- Analyze details in light of the definition of fact, something that can be proved objectively, and of opinion, something representing a feeling or judgment and that cannot be proved objectively.
- Be on the look-out for emotional language, "should" statements, and value words.

3. How can I identify the author's purpose for writing?
- Identifying the author's purpose is intertwined with analyzing tone, fact and opinions, and the author's point of view. The type of publication can also be a clue.

4. How can I recognize the author's tone?
- *Tone* refers to the author's attitude toward the subject. It is like a speaker's tone of voice.
- Be alert to words or phrases that reflect feelings, opinions, or beliefs. Remember that the tone might also be neutral or objective and not imply any opinion on the topic.

MyReadingLab™   For more help with Point of View, go to your learning path in MyReadingLab at www.myreadinglab.com

SELECTION 1   Philosophy

Pᴿᴇᴠɪᴇᴡ the next selection to predict its purpose and organization and to formulate your learning plan.

Activate Schema

Have you ever struggled with a decision?
What was your last important decision?
How did you arrive at a choice?
What is your next major decision?

Establish a Purpose for Reading

Life is about deciding. Whether the choice is seeing a movie or going bowling, or something of greater consequence like going to college or looking for a job, we want to make good decisions. Read to learn what causes us to hesitate and how to set standards for decision making that will last a lifetime.

Increase Word Knowledge

What do you know about these words?

vacillate	alternatives	project	stymied	obstacle
obeisance	mantras	facilitate	architecture	recidivism

Your instructor may give a true-false vocabulary review before or after reading.

Integrate Knowledge While Reading

Questions have been inserted in the margin to stimulate your thinking while reading. Remember to

Predict	Picture	Relate	Monitor	Correct	Annotate

I can relate to this!

((•─ **Scan this QR Code to hear this reading**

Dᴇᴄɪsɪᴏɴ

A Native American said he had two dogs fighting inside himself, one mean and the other good. When asked which one wins, he replied, "Whichever one I feed the most."

I will. I won't. I'll go. I'll stay. I should. I shouldn't. Yes. No. Yes. Maybe. At times
5 we teeter on the cliff of decision. We feel stressed by indecision as we vacillate through "decisions and revisions which a minute will reverse" (T. S. Eliot). If our thinking has been solid, usually the decision will follow. When it doesn't, we can assist it through a three-step process by considering the goals, alternatives, and probable outcomes of each alternative.

10 • Step 1: State the goal. (What is the desired result of our decision and action?)
   • Step 2: List the alternatives. (What are the possible plans of action—Plan A, Plan B, etc.?)
   • Step 3: Describe the probable outcome of each action plan. (Plan A, Plan B, etc.)

DIFFICULTIES IN DECIDING

Although the three-step process may appear simple, our mind does not work like a
15 machine, nor do other factors over which we have no control always work out as expected. Frequently we struggle to formulate goals, to assess the data, and to project possible outcomes. Let's look at some of the difficulties we can run into.

We struggle with several common roadblocks in making decisions. There is fear: What if we are wrong? Sometimes habits are so strong or convenient that we
20 continue our former ways even in the face of new information. Furthermore, some of us are so stymied by over thinking that we never act at all. And, at times, if we want something badly enough, conflicting motives stop our thinking.

A student captures some of the feelings, tensions, insights, and results of a decision in which she had conflicting motives:

Do any of these apply to me?

Roadblocks such as fear, habits, over thinking, and conflicting motives
affect decision making.
Jack Hollingsworth/Getty Images

25 My mind screamed NO! My thoughts argued with each other repeatedly. The fear had my speech and body paralyzed. Only my mind was functioning, tossing the negative messages like liquid mercury separating when put on a hard surface. I closed my eyes when I heard the Justice of the Peace say, "I now pronounce you man and wife." I started to cry! My new husband

30 mistook those tears as joyful tears. Only I knew of the estranged feelings that existed, knowing instantly that I had done myself a violent injustice. The vivid echoing memory of those vows creates a haunting mirage distressing all functions of my well-being.

I was a young know-it-all of seventeen. A typical sample of a teenager.

35 I had my mind made up to disband my family. I was spiteful. I wanted to prove my parents wrong! This dishonoring ill attitude that existed is still unexplainable to this day. I know I longed for some acceptance.

Fifteen years too late, the reflection is clear why I accepted those vows. I fell in love with my husband's family. His mom and dad loved me back.

40 I had a new family that loved me just the way I was. Yeah, I really felt important being a wife and daughter-in-law. These roles turned stale real fast. This was the beginning of my devastating trials in the adult world.

I've often thought of what my life would be like if I had made a different choice. This choice resulted in a brutal, costly divorce. It left me finan-

45 cially and emotionally distraught. An important part of my life was wasted and a long recovery was ahead of me. I can't replace the precious time lost, but I've learned to balance and weigh all my choices.

HOW TO DECIDE

Face Fear

If fear is the greatest obstacle to deciding, then courage and calm help us to decide. If we can free ourselves from obeisance to others, if we can strike strongly out on

50 our own and let the chips and opinions fall where they may, we increase our decision-making power. An example of high praise given to a citizen activist was "He put his body where his words were." Courage is not bottled and sold, but it can be bought with hard work. We can change our thinking with mantras such as "I think it's right; I'll do it; others can do what they want." Easier said than done, but courage can build

55 with practice.

Firm Our Foundation

When the decision is important and we have the time, the more thorough we are in our thinking preparation, the easier and better our decision will be. If we have covered our thinking bases, we have gone a long way toward deciding. We can make our thoughts objective and visible by writing them down.

60 A good way to capture our thoughts and facilitate decision making is to make a list of pros and cons. Pick any decision issue you wish (changing jobs, asking someone out on a date, breaking up with someone, taking a certain course, and so forth). Write it down on the chart that follows; then write all the thoughts for and against that decision. Evaluate the items for importance by indicating a weight of 1 to 10 in

65 the box alongside each item, using 10 if it is extremely important and 1 if it is of negligible importance. Now simply total the boxes and watch the scales of decision begin to tip in one direction.

Decision Issue:				
PROS	**Weight**	**CONS**	**Weight**	
Total		Total		

Call on Character

Sometimes, no matter what we know, the decision is hard because the results may be hurtful to us or to those we care about, or because the decision pits our greed against
70 our good. When our character is in conflict, then we dig deep and decide who we are and who we want to become; we reach for principles, motivation, and values; we real-ize that our choices define us, that we become what we choose. To help us through these trying decisions, we can turn to Marcus Aurelius, Roman emperor, warrior and philosopher. He tells us to perform each action as if it were our last. Similarly, Igna-
75 tius of Loyola, soldier and founder of the Jesuits, tells us to imagine ourselves on our deathbed and then choose as if the choice were the last event in our life.

Does character refer to moral values?

In cases of character conflict, we can "push" the decision by focusing on the positive side and then, when we are able, decide quickly so as not to prolong the pain of conflicting choice.

Feelings: A Boost Toward Decision

80 Hegel thinks that "nothing great in the world has been accomplished without pas-sion." That same passion can sometimes be that extra push toward a decision. Many of us make decisions not knowing that our feelings are driving our thoughts. If, how-ever, we are highly aware of our feelings, and if we give them input but not control, we can use feelings as part of the deciding process. Antonio Domasio is studying the
85 emotional architecture of the brain, watching the "split-second emotional assess-ments of situations that unfold so quickly that we're usually not aware of the process. . . . Emotions turn out to be essential to our rational decision-making proc-esses. If we didn't have those gut responses, we'd get caught in an endless cycle of analysis. . . . It's not that I'm saying the emotions decide things for you, it's that the
90 emotions help you concentrate on the right decision."

How does this relate to impulse control?

Image the Action

Another help in deciding is to form an image of ourselves doing the action. For in-stance if we cannot decide to go to a stern school authority or a terrifying boss, we can visualize ourselves walking down the hallway toward the person's office. When we can do this without significant anxiety, then we can visualize ourselves knocking
95 on the door, then walking in, and finally, saying the difficult message. It is important to be relaxed at each step before we image the next one. Imaging can prepare us for difficult decisions and actions.

Role-Play into Reality

After we have imaged it, then we can act it out, or role-play it. Delancy Street, a community prison in San Francisco, used role-playing to change thinking. Male
100 prisoners had to get haircuts, wear suits, and even walk "normally." They were asked to act as if they were successful, good citizens. This acting seemed to change their thinking, for their recidivism rate was quite low. About 80 percent of the role-

players entered society and stayed there; apparently, many became the citizens whom they role-played.

105　　We too can draw upon the power of acting to help ourselves carry out a decision. When the decision demands change and we don't seem to have the power to decide, we may be able to role-play the action. At first we will probably feel stiff, but repetition will make it easier; consequently, it will become easier to think about acting that way routinely. Finally, we will have the strength to do what we have been
110　role-playing, and then our minds and our bodies will work together. By playing the role we can become the role.

(1,496 words)

How can I apply these ideas?

—From Gary R. Kirby and Jeffery R. Goodpaster, *Thinking*, 4th ed., © 2007, pp. 321–327. Reproduced in print and electronic formats by permission of Pearson Education, Inc., Upper Saddle River, New Jersey.

Recall

Stop to self-test, relate, and react.

Your instructor may choose to give you a true-false comprehension review.

WRITE ABOUT THE SELECTION　MyReadingLab™

Complete this **Exercise** on **myreadinglab.com**

"It is our choices, Harry, that show what we truly are, far more than our abilities." Professor Dumbledore said this in J. K. Rowling's book, *Harry Potter and the Chamber of Secrets*. What is your point of view on this statement?

Response Suggestion: List at least five important decisions that have shaped your life—when a different choice would have made a big difference in who you are today.

SKILL DEVELOPMENT: EXPLORE POINT OF VIEW

Form a collaborative group and brainstorm a list of difficult decisions members have made or that they are facing. Choose the thorniest one, and consider the following questions:

- Which of the obstacles mentioned in the article do you think are most likely to interfere with a decision on this issue?
- Which method mentioned in the article do you think would be most useful?
- What decision do the members of the group think is the best? Why?
- Did group members have different points of view on these questions? Is there more than one reasonable point of view?

CHECK YOUR COMPREHENSION   MyReadingLab™

After reading the selection, answer the following questions with *a, b, c,* or *d.* To help you analyze your strengths and weaknesses, the question types are indicated.

Main Idea _____ 1. Which is the best statement of the main idea of this selection?

  a. People have difficulty making decisions for several common reasons.

  b. Many people fail to think clearly about the consequences of their choices.

  c. It is important to consider our emotions but not let them control our choices.

  d. Obstacles in decision making can be overcome with practice in several areas.

Detail _____ 2. Which of the following is *not* one of the obstacles to decision making mentioned by the author?

  a. Fear of making the wrong choice

  b. Thinking too much and too long about the alternatives

  c. Lack of confidence

  d. Force of habit

Detail _____ 3. When thinking through a difficult decision, the author recommends

  a. asking a trusted friend for advice.

  b. relying completely on our "gut" response.

  c. weighing the pros and cons by writing them down.

  d. considering the effect on our family and friends first.

Main Idea _____ 4. The main point of the section "Call on Character" is that

  a. we should act in accordance with our most positive values.

  b. our choices should be determined by what benefits us most.

  c. consulting a religious leader for advice is helpful.

  d. we should act quickly.

Detail _____ 5. Antonio Domasio's research on emotions and the brain revealed that

  a. emotions interfere with good decision making.

  b. emotions have an important role in making good decisions.

  c. emotions tend to overshadow our thought processes.

  d. we are always aware of how our emotions inform our thinking.

Inference _____ 6. The author includes the student's story about her marriage to

  a. demonstrate how important some decisions are.

  b. show that it would have been better if she had taken her parents' advice.

  c. prove that fear can be a powerful factor in making a good decision.

  d. illustrate the point that conflicting motives may interfere with clear thinking.

Inference _____ 7. The author might use which of the following as an example of a decision that especially involves examining character?

    a. Choosing either a career in medicine or the law

    b. Confronting a friend who is drinking excessively or ignoring it to preserve the friendship

    c. Choosing whether to join a school club or take a job

    d. Deciding whether to live at home or move into an apartment

Inference _____ 8. The student who made a poor decision to marry did so because

    a. she was blinded by her love for the man she married.

    b. she found acceptance and love in her husband's family that she did not experience in her own.

    c. she was too young to make a wise choice.

    d. she was pregnant and thought it would be better for the child if she married.

Inference _____ 9. You are struggling with the decision of whether to ask your boss for the promotion you feel you've earned or be content with your current position. Which course of action would the author most likely recommend?

    a. Picturing yourself approaching your boss' office, knocking on the door, and stating your case

    b. Reflecting on the emotions of frustration and resentment you have surrounding this issue

    c. Dressing as you would be expected to dress if you had the more responsible job

    d. Asking co-workers what they would do in your situation

Inference _____ 10. We can infer that the Delancy Street experiment

    a. was successful with prisoners in other facilities.

    b. would only work with nonviolent inmates.

    c. changed the guards' opinions of the prisoners.

    d. made the men feel and behave like the successful citizens they were pretending to be.

Answer the following with *T* (true) or *F* (false):

Inference _____ 11. The author's three-step method is intended for use in every decision-making situation.

Detail _____ 12. The author believes that courage can be learned with practice.

Detail _____ 13. The author states that feelings should have no part in decision making.

Inference _____ 14. It is reasonable to infer that the author would not approve of researching facts in a library or on the Internet prior to making a decision.

Inference _____ 15. The author believes that the ability to make good decisions can be learned.

SELECTION

1

BUILD YOUR VOCABULARY   MyReadingLab™

Complete
this **Exercise** on
myreadinglab.com

According to the way the italicized word was used in the selection, indicate *a*, *b*, *c*, or *d* for the word or phrase that gives the best definition. The number in parentheses indicates the line of the passage in which the word is located.

_____ 1. *"vacillate* through decisions" (5)
   a. suffer
   b. change one's mind
   c. race
   d. struggle

_____ 2. "the goals, *alternatives"* (8)
   a. options
   b. results
   c. actions
   d. problems

_____ 3. *"project* possible outcomes" (16–17)
   a. prefer
   b. choose
   c. criticize
   d. predict

_____ 4. *"stymied* by over thinking" (21)
   a. pleased
   b. frightened
   c. blocked
   d. energized

_____ 5. "the greatest *obstacle"* (48)
   a. barrier
   b. frustration
   c. emotion
   d. evil

_____ 6. *"obeisance* to others" (49)
   a. respect
   b. obeying
   c. listening
   d. submission

_____ 7. *"mantras* such as" (53)
   a. familiar rules
   b. repeated words or phrases
   c. figures of speech
   d. proverbs

_____ 8. *"facilitate* decision making" (60)
   a. challenge
   b. block
   c. ease
   d. complete

_____ 9. *"architecture* of the brain" (85)
   a. outbursts
   b. failings
   c. effects
   d. structure

_____ 10. "their *recidivism* rate" (102)
   a. unhappiness
   b. success
   c. employment
   d. return to crime

SELECTION 2   Science

PREVIEW the next selection to predict its purpose and organization and to formulate your learning plan.

Activate Schema

Do long-time residents in your area say that the climate has changed?
How would your area be affected by rising sea levels or warmer average temperatures?

Establish a Purpose for Reading

The issue of global warming is being discussed by individuals and governments all around the world. Read to find out about the evidence of its existence, the causes, and the effects.

Increase Word Knowledge

What do you know about these words?

ecosystems	prodigious	deforestation	marginal	curtailed
permafrost	perversely	bog	ecologists	temperate

Your instructor may give a true-false vocabulary review before or after reading.

Integrate Knowledge While Reading

Questions have been inserted in the margin to stimulate your thinking while reading. Remember to

Predict	Picture	Relate	Monitor	Correct	Annotate

MyReadingLab™

GLOBAL WARMING
Watch a video on global warming via your ebook at www.myreadinglab.com and then answer the related questions in the VIDEO LINK section or via MyReadingLab.

THE ROLE OF HUMANS IN GLOBAL WARMING

Environmental problems arise when human activities interfere with the natural functioning of ecosystems. Human industrial processes release toxic substances and produce more nutrients than nutrient cycles can efficiently process. Through massive consumption of fossil fuels, we have disrupted the natural cycles of carbon, sulfur, and nitrogen, causing acid deposition and global warming (an amplification of the greenhouse effect).

5

((•─ **Scan this QR Code to hear this reading**

Are humans the only factor?

Some scientists disagree?

OVERLOADING THE CARBON CYCLE CONTRIBUTES TO GLOBAL WARMING

Much of Earth's carbon is in long-term storage in reservoirs. One such reservoir is fossil fuels. Fossil fuels form from the buried remains of plants and animals. Over
10 millions of years, the carbon in the organic molecules of these organisms is transformed by high temperatures and pressures into coal, oil, or natural gas. When people burn fossil fuels to supply energy for heat, light, transportation, manufacturing, and agriculture, CO_2 is released into the atmosphere. By freeing carbon from the fossil fuel reservoir, humans are increasing the amount of CO_2 in the
15 atmosphere.

Without human intervention, the carbon in fossil fuels would stay locked away. Since the Industrial Revolution, however, we have increasingly relied on the energy stored in these fuels. As a result of our prodigious consumption of fossil fuels, the amount of CO_2 in the atmosphere has increased by more than 36% since 1850, from
20 280 parts per million (ppm) to 381 ppm. Atmospheric CO_2 continues to increase at a rate of 1.5 ppm per year.

Carbon dioxide is also added to the atmosphere by deforestation, which destroys tens of millions of acres of forests each year. When forests are cut and burned, the carbon stored in the bodies of trees returns to the atmosphere. The rate of defor
25 estation is especially rapid in the tropics, where rain forests are being converted to marginal agricultural land.

Altogether, human activities release almost 7 billion tons of carbon (in the form of CO_2) into the atmosphere each year. About half of this carbon is captured by the global carbon cycle—that is, it is absorbed into the plants, soil, and the
30 oceans. The remaining 3.5 billion tons remains in the atmosphere, fueling global warming.

Greenhouse Gases Trap Heat in the Atmosphere

Atmospheric CO_2 acts something like the glass in a greenhouse: It allows solar energy to pass through and reach Earth's surface, but it absorbs and is heated by the longer-wavelength energy that then radiates from the surface back into the atmo-
35 sphere. This greenhouse effect traps some of the sun's energy as heat and keeps Earth's atmosphere warm enough to support life.

Most climate scientists have concluded that the greenhouse effect has been intensified by human activities that produce CO_2 and other greenhouse gases such as methane, chlorofluorocarbons (CFCs), water vapor, and nitrous oxide. Historical
40 temperature records have revealed a global warming trend. The average global temperature has increased since 1860, paralleling the increase in atmospheric CO_2 (see Figure 1). Nineteen of the 20 hottest years on record have occurred since 1980, and the 6 hottest years were all after 1998.

A large, international group of climate scientists known as the Intergovernmen-
45 tal Panel on Climate Change (IPCC) predicts that, if greenhouse gas emissions are not curtailed, the average surface air temperature of Earth will increase by 3.6°F to 8.1°F (2.0°C to 4.5°C) by 2100. To put this change in perspective, average air temperatures during the peak of the last Ice Age (20,000 years ago), when much of North America was under a thick sheet of ice, were only about 9°F (5°C) lower than
50 at present.

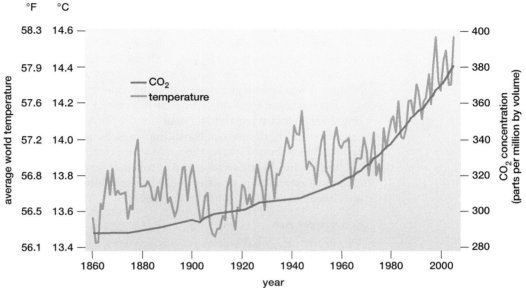

Figure 1 Global warming parallels CO₂ increases
The CO₂ concentration of the atmosphere (blue line) has increased steadily since 1860. Average global temperatures (red line) shows a parallel increase.

Global Warming Will Have Severe Consequences

Although the precise consequences of global warming are difficult to predict, disruptions that will affect living things are nearly certain. In fact, Earth has already begun to experience them. For example, scientists have documented effects of warming on glaciers and polar ice caps, on weather patterns, and on the living inhab-
55 itants of ecosystems. The speed and magnitude of these changes are expected to increase as warming continues.

A Global Meltdown Is Under Way

Throughout the world, ice is melting. Glaciers are retreating and disappearing. In Glacier National Park, where 150 glaciers once graced the mountainsides, only 35 remain, and scientists estimate that none will remain 30 years from now. Green-
60 land's ice sheet is melting at twice the rate of a decade ago, releasing 53 cubic miles (221 cubic kilometers) of water into the Atlantic annually. As glaciers and polar ice melt, global sea levels are rising. Increasing sea levels threaten to flood coastal cities, with island nations being especially vulnerable because inhabitants displaced by rising waters may have nowhere to go.
65   In addition to the meltdown of glaciers and ice caps, the permanently frozen soils of far northern lands are also melting. In Alaska, thawed permafrost allows tons of mud to wash into rivers and destroy salmon spawning grounds. Perversely, permafrost thawing due to global warming can cause even more global warming—the thawing releases additional CO₂ into the atmosphere as previously frozen organic
70 matter decomposes. In Siberia, a region of frozen soil the size of France and Germany combined is melting, creating a gigantic bog that could release billions of tons of CO₂ and methane (an even more potent greenhouse gas) into the atmosphere.

Weather Is Growing More Extreme

Climate scientists predict that global warming will increase the incidence of extreme weather events. Increasing evidence suggests that the weather is already being
75 affected. During the past 35 years, both the intensity and the duration of hurricanes has increased by 50%. The number of Category 4 and 5 hurricanes (the highest categories of wind speed and destruction) has doubled.

Even as some areas suffer from an increase in severe storms, other areas are getting drier. Scientists at the National Center for Atmospheric Research report that
80 since the 1970s, the area of Earth impacted by severe drought has doubled from about 15% to about 30%. As the world warms further, droughts in these regions will last longer and be more severe. Agricultural disruption resulting from the newly emerging extremes in weather could be especially disastrous for poor nations that are already barely able to feed themselves.

Ecosystems Are Affected

85 The impact of global warming on ecosystems could be profound. On land, plant distributions will change as rainfall and temperature change. For example, sugar maples may disappear from northeastern U.S. forests, and southeastern forests could be partially replaced by grasslands. In the sea, coral reefs, highly productive ecosystems already stressed by human activities, are likely to suffer further damage from
90 warmer waters, because reef-building corals are harmed by even small increases in water temperature.

Each change would be related to another.

Around the world, ecologists are discovering changes related to warming. The growing season in Europe has increased by more than 10 days during the past 28 years. In Europe and North America, spring flowers are blooming earlier. Birds in
95 many temperate regions begin nesting a week or more earlier than they did a few decades ago. The geographic ranges of many species of butterflies and birds have shifted toward the poles. Among the tropical organisms with expanding ranges are disease-carrying organisms such as malaria-transmitting mosquitoes, suggesting that diseases currently restricted to the tropics will soon be present in temperate regions
100 as well. Overall, the accumulated data from scientific investigations around the world provide strong evidence that warming-related biological changes are well under way.

(1,210 words)

—From Teresa Audesirk et al.,
Life on Earth, 5th ed.

Recall

Stop to self-test, relate, and react.

Your instructor may choose to give you a true-false comprehension review.

WRITE ABOUT THE SELECTION   MyReadingLab™

Complete
this **Exercise** on
myreadinglab.com

How can the behavior of individuals reverse a problem as large as global warming?

Response Suggestion: Brainstorm the ways in which your everyday activities contribute to global warming, and list them in one column. Next to each item, write one way you can reduce that impact on the environment.

 VIDEO LINK   MyReadingLab™

Complete
this **Exercise** on
myreadinglab.com

Now that you have read the selection and viewed the video on global warming, check your understanding by answering with *T* (true) or *F* (false):

_____ 1. While acknowledging increases in average temperatures in the United States, this video does not blame human activity.

_____ 2. Among the effects of global warming forecast in the video are rising water temperatures and more violent storms affecting the southeastern U.S. and more heat-related deaths in the Midwest.

_____ 3. The video predicts colder than usual temperatures in the northeastern and western states.

_____ 4. The authors of the reading selection would disagree with comments in the video regarding rising sea levels and melting glaciers.

_____ 5. The video warns that the window of opportunity to change warming trends is closing.

SKILL DEVELOPMENT: EXPLORE POINT OF VIEW

Form a collaborative group to discuss the following questions:

- Some people argue that global warming is a natural phenomenon rather than the product of human activity. Is the evidence presented by the authors convincing?
- Do the members of the group agree with the view presented in the selection?
- What do the group members do to protect the environment?
- Does your college use environmentally friendly practices for paper disposal and energy use? How might students encourage environmentally friendly practices on campus?

SELECTION 2

CHECK YOUR COMPREHENSION   MyReadingLab™

After reading the selection, answer the following questions with *a, b, c,* or *d*. To help you analyze your strengths and weaknesses, the question types are indicated.

Main Idea _____ 1. Which is the best statement of the main idea of this selection?
  a. If people don't act soon, global warming will devastate Earth.
  b. Greenhouse gases trap heat in the atmosphere.
  c. Human activities cause global warming by throwing the carbon cycle out of balance.
  d. Glacial and polar ice is melting rapidly.

Detail _____ 2. According to the article, about _____ of the global carbon emissions remain in the atmosphere.
  a. three-fourths
  b. one-half
  c. one-third
  d. one-fourth

Detail _____ 3. Experts predict that if greenhouse gas emissions are not reduced, the average air temperature will increase 3.6° to 8.1°F in the next 100 years as opposed to a 9° increase over the last _____ years.
  a. 1 million
  b. 500,000
  c. 20,000
  d. 100

Inference _____ 4. The authors use the statistics on increases in average air temperature to
  a. dramatize the rapid change taking place recently.
  b. alarm the reader about the melting ice caps.
  c. show that the change has been gradual and steady over time.
  d. minimize concern over the effects of greenhouse gases.

Inference _____ 5. Based on the information in the article, which would *not* be a contributor to global warming?
  a. Gasoline-powered automobiles
  b. Wind-powered generators
  c. Clearing of trees for housing or farms
  d. Factories

Inference _____ 6. We can infer from the line graph that
  a. the concentration of CO_2 in the atmosphere and air temperature are unrelated.
  b. the atmospheric CO_2 and air temperature did not rise in the years before 1860.
  c. the increase in atmospheric CO_2 and air temperature is a natural process.

d. something has occurred in the last fifty years or so to cause a rapid rise in air temperature and atmospheric CO_2.

Detail _____ 7. According to the article, global warming could be especially harmful to poorer nations because

a. they cannot afford the cost of reducing their carbon emissions.
b. they will have to sell their natural resources to wealthier countries.
c. the United States and other nations will be unable to provide as much foreign aid.
d. more severe droughts will decrease their ability to grow food crops.

Detail _____ 8. The carbon cycle is a natural phenomenon that ordinarily balances

a. carbon dioxide (CO_2) and emissions from manufacturing.
b. carbon releases from deforestation and greenhouse gases.
c. carbon emissions and their absorption into oceans, plants, and soil.
d. CO_2, methane, and greenhouse gases.

Inference _____ 9. From the details presented in the article, we can infer that

a. the scenic views that visitors see now in national parks and other undeveloped areas are different from those previous generations viewed.
b. views of glaciers and rivers have changed little in the last several decades.
c. wildlife is not seriously threatened by rising average air temperatures.
d. there is no need for concern about the effects of global warming on agriculture.

Main Idea _____ 10. The main point of the section "Ecosystems Are Affected" is that global warming

a. will change the amount of rainfall.
b. affects many natural systems.
c. changes the distribution of plant and animal life.
d. affects the oceans and marine life.

Answer the following with *T* (true) or *F* (false):

Inference _____ 11. Global warming could introduce diseases into North America and Europe that have not usually been seen there.

Detail _____ 12. Natural gas is a fossil fuel.

Detail _____ 13. Experts believe that global warming and the severity of hurricanes are unrelated.

Inference _____ 14. Wider ranges of butterflies and birds will not affect other animal populations.

Detail _____ 15. Since the 1970s, the land area experiencing severe drought has doubled.

SELECTION 2

BUILD YOUR VOCABULARY   MyReadingLab™

Complete
this **Exercise** on
myreadinglab.com

SELECTION 2

According to the way the italicized word was used in the selection, indicate *a, b, c,* or *d* for the word or phrase that gives the best definition. The number in parentheses indicates the line of the passage in which the word is located.

_____ 1. "functioning of *ecosystems*" (2)
   a. interrelated communities of organisms
   b. environmental lobbying groups
   c. industrial and manufacturing plants
   d. natural cycles

_____ 2. "our *prodigious* consumption" (18)
   a. shameful
   b. unnatural
   c. extremely large in amount
   d. restrained

_____ 3. "by *deforestation*" (22)
   a. a disease affecting trees
   b. a natural loss of forests
   c. planting of trees
   d. cutting of entire forests

_____ 4. "*marginal* agricultural land" (26)
   a. useless
   b. difficult to cultivate
   c. fertile
   d. free

_____ 5. "are not *curtailed*" (46)
   a. produced
   b. increased
   c. lessened
   d. neutralized

_____ 6. "thawed *permafrost*" (66)
   a. ice
   b. glaciers
   c. snow-covered areas
   d. frozen subsoil

_____ 7. "*Perversely*, permafrost thawing" (67)
   a. in a serious manner
   b. in a determined, undesirable way
   c. additionally
   d. favorably

_____ 8. "a gigantic *bog*" (71)
   a. lake
   b. river or stream
   c. marsh, swamp
   d. glacier

_____ 9. "*ecologists* are discovering" (92)
   a. scientists who study the relationship between organisms and their environment
   b. scientists who study weather
   c. scientists who study plants
   d. scientists who study insects

_____ 10. "in many *temperate* regions" (95)
   a. moderate in temperature
   b. very warm
   c. tropical
   d. excessively cold

SELECTION 3 | Health

PREVIEW the next selection to predict its purpose and organization and to formulate your learning plan.

Activate Schema

What have you heard about the use of steroids by professional athletes?
Do you know of student athletes who have taken these drugs?
What do you think is the best way to discourage teens from taking steroids?
Do you think young athletes are aware of the negative effects of steroids?

Establish a Purpose for Reading

Read to learn more about steroids and other performance-enhancing drugs.

Increase Word Knowledge

What do you know about these words?

heightened	promote	extent	euphoria	adverse
atrophy	alternatives	alleged	OTC	disclose

Your instructor may give a true-false vocabulary review before or after reading.

Integrate Knowledge While Reading

Questions have been inserted in the margin to stimulate your thinking while reading. Remember to

Predict	Picture	Relate	Monitor	Correct	Annotate

((•─ **Scan this QR Code to hear this reading**

STEROIDS

Public awareness of anabolic steroids recently has been heightened by media stories about their use by amateur and professional athletes, including Arnold Schwarzenegger during his competitive bodybuilding days. Anabolic steroids are artificial forms of the male hormone testosterone that promote muscle growth
5 and strength. These ergogenic drugs are used primarily by young men who believe the drugs will increase their strength, power, bulk (weight), speed, and athletic performance.

Former Olympic and world track and field champion Marion Jones was forced to forfeit all medals and prizes dating back to the year 2000 after admitting to taking performance-enhancing drugs.
Doug Mills/AP Images

EXTENT OF ABUSE

Most steroids are obtained through the black market. It once was estimated that approximately 17 to 20 percent of college athletes used them. Now that stricter drug-testing policies have been instituted by the National College Athletic Association (NCAA), reported use of anabolic steroids among intercollegiate athletes has dropped to 1.1 percent. However, a recent survey among high school students found a significant increase in the use of anabolic steroids since 1991. Little data exist on the extent of steroid abuse by adults. It has been estimated that hundreds of thousands of people age 18 and older abuse anabolic steroids at least once a year. Among both adolescents and adults, steroid abuse is higher among males than among females. However, steroid abuse is growing most rapidly among young women.

Why would use be increasing more among young women?

TWO AVAILABLE FORMS

Steroids are available in two forms: injectable solution and pills. Anabolic steroids produce a state of euphoria, diminished fatigue, and increased bulk and power in both sexes. These qualities give steroids an addictive quality. When users stop, they can experience psychological withdrawal and sometimes severe depression that in some cases leads to suicide attempts. If untreated, such depression associated with steroid withdrawal has been known to last for a year or more after steroid use stops.

EFFECTS

Adverse effects occur in both men and women who use steroids. These drugs cause mood swings (aggression and violence) sometimes known as "roid rage," acne, liver tumors, elevated cholesterol levels, hypertension, kidney disease, and immune system disturbances. There is also a danger of transmitting AIDS through shared needles. In women, large doses of anabolic steroids may trigger the development of masculine attributes such as lowered voice, increased facial and body hair, and male pattern baldness; they also may result in an enlarged clitoris, smaller breasts, and changes in or absence of menstruation. When taken by healthy males, anabolic steroids shut down the body's production of testosterone, which causes men's breasts to grow and testicles to atrophy.

This effect seems ironic.

PENALTIES

35 To combat the growing problem of steroid use, Congress passed the Anabolic Steroids Control Act of 1990. This law makes it a crime to possess, prescribe, or distribute anabolic steroids for any use other than the treatment of specific diseases. Anabolic steroids are now classified as a Schedule III drug. Penalties for their illegal use include up to five years' imprisonment and a $250,000 fine for the first offense, and
40 up to ten years' imprisonment and a $500,000 fine for subsequent offenses.

TRENDS

A new and alarming trend is the use of other drugs to achieve the supposed performance-enhancing effects of steroids. The two most common steroid alternatives are gamma hydroxybutyrate (GHB) and clenbuterol. GHB is a deadly, illegal drug that is a primary ingredient in many performance-enhancing formulas. GHB does
45 not produce a high. However, it does cause headaches, nausea, vomiting, diarrhea, seizures and other central nervous system disorders, and possibly death. Clenbuterol is used in some countries for veterinary treatments, but it is not approved for any use—in animals or humans—in the United States.

New attention was drawn to the issue of steroids and related substances when
50 St. Louis Cardinals slugger Mark McGwire admitted to using a supplement containing androstenedione (andro), an adrenal hormone that is produced naturally in both men and women. Andro raises levels of the male hormone testosterone, which helps build lean muscle mass and promotes quicker recovery after injury. McGwire had done nothing illegal, since the supplement can be purchased OTC (with estimated
55 sales of up to $800 million a year). Also, its use is legal in baseball, although it is banned by the National Football League, the NCAA, and the International Olympic Committee. A recent study found that when men take 100 mg of andro three times daily, it increases estrogen levels up to 80 percent, enlarges the prostate gland, and increases heart disease risk by 10 to 15 percent. This finding may or may not affect
60 its use in major league baseball—no decision has yet been made.

It was legal, but was it right?

Although andro has been banned by many sports organizations, visits to the locker rooms of many teams belonging to these organizations would disclose large containers of other alleged muscle-building supplements, such as creatine. Although they are legal, questions remain whether enough research has been done concerning
65 the safety of these supplements. Some people worry that they may bring consequences similar to those of steroids, such as liver damage and heart problems.

(805 words)

—Rebecca J. Donatelle,
Health: The Basics, 6th ed.

Recall

Stop to self-test, relate, and react.

Your instructor may choose to give you a true-false comprehension review.

WRITE ABOUT THE SELECTION   MyReadingLab™

Complete
this **Exercise** on
myreadinglab.com

Describe the effects and danger of steroids and the newer performance-enhancing alternatives.

Response Suggestion: Describe the available forms with their effects and dangers, and then do the same for GHB, clenbuterol, and andro.

SKILL DEVELOPMENT: EXPLORE POINT OF VIEW

Form a collaborative group and discuss the members' points of view on the use of performance-enhancing drugs by professional athletes. Decide on one position, either in favor or against allowing legal performance-enhancing drugs in professional sports, and list the supporting reasons. Join with another group that took the opposite position and debate the issue. Which side has the better argument?

CHECK YOUR COMPREHENSION   MyReadingLab™

After reading the selection, answer the following questions with *a*, *b*, *c*, or *d*. In order to help you analyze your strengths and weaknesses, the question types are indicated.

Main Idea _____ 1. Which is the best statement of the main idea of this selection?

a. Readers should push for harsher legal penalties for the use of steroids and related drugs.

b. Those contemplating the use of steroids and related drugs should be careful to learn the laws concerning their use.

c. Although steroids and related drugs offer short-term advantages to athletes, serious medical risks are associated with their use.

d. Although some medical dangers exist, media coverage of celebrities' use of steroids and other drugs has greatly exaggerated these dangers.

Detail _____ 2. Anabolic steroids can be defined as

a. having no ergogenic characteristics.

b. artificial forms of the male hormone testosterone.

c. drugs that contain high levels of GHB.

d. drugs that contain estrogen, which stimulates breast development.

Detail _____ 3. According to the passage, the use of steroids has been most effectively decreased in college athletes by

a. stricter policies of drug testing by college athletic associations.

b. the increased availability of other less dangerous drugs.

c. increased public awareness of health dangers of steroid use.

d. reluctance on the part of college athletes to use a drug popular with high school students.

Inference _____ 4. The author suggests that AIDS can be contracted by steroid users who

a. use the drug for a prolonged period of time.

b. experience psychological withdrawal symptoms.

c. share needles with other users.

d. have already experienced hypertension or kidney disease.

Detail _____ 5. According to the passage, the Anabolic Steroids Control Act of 1990 does all of the following *except*

a. criminalize prescribing steroids to enhance athletic performance.

b. increase the penalty for repeat offenses.

c. remove steroids from the Schedule III drug category.

d. allow steroids to be used for the treatment of specific diseases.

Inference _____ 6. U.S. policy regarding the use of clenbuterol might best be defined as

a. more stringent than that of some other countries.

b. acceptable for treatment of animals but not for treatment of humans.
c. likely to permit legalization for most uses in the near future.
d. allowing its use by athletes as long as they have been warned of the possible dangers.

Detail _____ 7. Androstenedione (andro) can most accurately be defined as

a. a drug that decreases testosterone.
b. a hormone that strengthens bones.
c. a drug that can be obtained only by prescription.
d. an adrenal hormone produced by men and women.

Inference _____ 8. The reader can conclude that if Mark McGwire had been a football player at the time he used andro,

a. his use of the drug would have been considered legal.
b. his use of the drug would have been considered illegal.
c. the supplements would have been provided free by the NFL.
d. the legality of his drug use would have been determined by the St. Louis Cardinals.

Inference _____ 9. The passage implies that steroid use may cause

a. a decrease in breast size for both men and women.
b. an increase in breast size for both men and women.
c. no changes in sexual characteristics for men or for women.
d. the growth of some male sex characteristics in women and the growth of some female sexual characteristics in men.

Detail _____ 10. Of the drugs mentioned in the passage, the only one explicitly cited as promoting faster recovery after injury is

a. creatine.
b. andro.
c. GHB.
d. clenbuterol.

Answer the following with *T* (true) or *F* (false):

Detail _____ 11. The slang term "roid rage" refers to the enhanced sense of athletic competitiveness caused by the use of steroids.

Inference _____ 12. Steroids produce euphoria (a high) among users, but GHB does not.

Detail _____ 13. According to the passage, the rate of increase in abuse of steroids is highest among young women.

Inference _____ 14. The reader can conclude that creatine is also a steroid.

Detail _____ 15. The most dangerous symptom associated with steroid withdrawal is physical exhaustion.

BUILD YOUR VOCABULARY   MyReadingLab™

Complete
this **Exercise** on
myreadinglab.com

According to the way the italicized word was used in the selection, select *a, b, c,* or *d* for the word or phrase that gives the best definition. The number in the parentheses indicates the line of the passage in which the word is located.

_____ 1. "has been *heightened*" (1)
  a. intensified
  b. examined
  c. rubbed
  d. lessened

_____ 2. "*promote* muscle growth" (4)
  a. graduate
  b. discredit
  c. encourage
  d. idealize

_____ 3. "*extent* of steroid abuse" (14)
  a. exit
  b. discussion
  c. amount
  d. decline

_____ 4. "state of *euphoria*" (19)
  a. gloom
  b. depression
  c. sleepiness
  d. bliss

_____ 5. "*Adverse* effects" (25)
  a. reverse
  b. wonderful
  c. negative
  d. positive

_____ 6. "to *atrophy*" (34)
  a. shrink
  b. enlarge
  c. hurt
  d. change

_____ 7. "steroid *alternatives*" (42)
  a. difficulties
  b. choices
  c. medications
  d. disorders

_____ 8. "purchased *OTC*" (54)
  a. or through contracts
  b. only the cheapest
  c. openly through countries
  d. over the counter

_____ 9. "would *disclose*" (62)
  a. negate
  b. withhold
  c. cover
  d. expose

_____ 10. "*alleged* muscle-building supplements" (63)
  a. supposed
  b. illegal
  c. dangerous
  d. hidden

SELECTION 3

VOCABULARY BOOSTER

Say, What?

Roots	dic, dict: "say"	locu, loqui: "speak"
	lingu: "tongue"	

Words with *dic, dict:* "say"

When Stephen became the supervisor and began to tell his co-workers how to do their jobs, he soon discovered that they did not respond well to his *dictatorial* management style.

- **dictate:** to say or read out loud for transcription; to command with authority

  Sarena's parents *dictated* the nonnegotiable conditions of her upcoming slumber party: no boys, no alcohol.

- **dictator:** a ruler using absolute power without hereditary right or consent of the people

  Fidel Castro, who staged a coup to oust former president Batista of Cuba, was a *dictator* who has remained in power for many years.

- **diction:** that aspect of speaking or writing dependent on the correct choice of words; the voice quality of a speaker or singer

  Listening to public speakers with fine *diction* is much easier than trying to decipher the words of those whose speech is not clear and distinct.

- **contradict:** to state the opposite of or deny; to imply denial with actions

  Mark's wild lifestyle seems to *contradict* his claim of being the quiet, studious type.

- **indict:** to charge with a crime; to seriously criticize or blame

  The grand jury *indicted* the alleged computer hacker for breaking into banking system computers to illegally move funds electronically.

- **predict:** to declare in advance or foretell the future

  Meteorologists *predict* the weather based on facts, experience, and use of complex meteorological instruments.

- **dictionary:** a reference book of alphabetically arranged words and their meanings

  Word-processing computer programs usually contain a *dictionary* and can run a spelling check on documents.

Words with *locu, loqui:* "speak"

The defendant's attorney was skilled in fluent, forceful, and persuasive speech, so it came as no surprise that his closing statement was *eloquent* enough to convince the jury of his client's innocence.

- *elocution:* the study and practice of public speaking; a style of speaking or reading out loud

  Julianne was taking speech classes for all her electives, hoping that the *elocution* practice would help in the frequent presentations required in her chosen career of public relations.

- *locution:* a word or phrase as used by a particular person or group

  In the late 1960s and early 1970s, hippies used *locutions* such as "groovy" or "way out, man."

- *colloquial:* characteristic of informal speech or writing; conversational

  Choosing the word "nope" instead of "no" is an example of using a *colloquial* expression.

- *soliloquy:* the act of speaking to oneself; a speech in a drama in which a character reveals innermost thoughts

  Aspiring actors often use *soliloquies* from Shakespeare's plays as audition monologues.

- *loquacious:* tending to talk too much or too freely; garrulous

  When meeting new people, Nadia often becomes nervous and *loquacious*, and tends to chatter on and on about unimportant things.

- *circumlocution:* a roundabout or indirect way of speaking; using more words than necessary

  After all the *circumlocution* in Sydney's story, such as what she was wearing, what she had to eat, and what time they left, we finally got to hear whether or not she liked her blind date.

SELECTION 3

Words with *lingu:* "tongue"

When you visit the doctor, it is customary for the nurse to take your *sublingual* temperature and your blood pressure.

- *linguistics:* the study of language

  Phonetics is the branch of *linguistics* involving the study of the production of speech sounds and the written symbols representing them.

- *multilingual:* able to speak several languages with some ease

  Some public schools in the United States are experiencing a need for *multilingual* teachers due to the influx of immigrants who do not yet speak English.

Review

Part I

Choose the best antonym from the list for each of the words below.

acquit or discharge	confirm	dialogue	directness	elected ruler
formal speech	obey	recall	silent	unconvincing

Point of View

1. contradict _____   6. dictator _____

2. circumlocution _____   7. indict _____

3. dictate _____   8. eloquent _____

4. predict _____   9. soliloquy _____

5. loquacious _____   10. colloquial _____

Part II

From the list, choose the word that best completes each of the sentences below.

locution	dictionary	indict	dictate	linguistics
diction	elocution	sublingual	dictatorial	contradict

11. His outstanding performance in the classroom seemed to _____ his rather ordinary test scores.

12. Studies indicate that multiples such as twins and triplets often communicate with their own unique words and phrases, or forms of _____.

13. To help with the study of technical vocabulary, a specialized _____ would be a useful purchase.

14. With infants, health-care professionals often opt for another means of assessing fever in lieu of a _____ temperature reading.

15. Several colleges offer a camera for _____ practice in speech labs.

16. The number of white collar criminals that courts are choosing to _____ has increased.

17. Virginia tried very hard not to give unwanted child-rearing instructions to her son and daughter-in-law because she remembered how she resented her own mother's _____ attitude.

18. A speaker with clear, distinct _____ is more easily understood than one with a regional accent.

19. Her friends are wondering how much longer she will remain in a relationship with a domineering person who seems to _____ rather than communicate.

20. Some researchers in the field of _____ specialize in the study of the development of regional dialects.

CREDITS

Note: Not all exercises are assigned, but all answers are shown.

Exercise 1

Passage 1:   Commercial fishing, along with governmental support of it, has had an unnatural and harmful ecological impact throughout the world.
Passage 2:   The author has empathy for the plight of single working mothers.

Exercise 2
1. Both say Mary Stuart was charming and a very devout Catholic.
2. The first is more critical; the second has more positive detail.
3. He suggests that he is biased, and his choice of words and attitude show it.
4. (as follows):
a. not a politician
b. strong opposition
c. not wanted
d. not secretive about her lovers
e. religiously narrow minded

Exercise 3
Passage A:
1. Both are critical, but the first gives the usual facts.
2. He was a fearless explorer but no administrator or intellect.
3. Answers will vary.
4. Columbus made many mistakes and is a tarnished hero.

Passage B:
1. The war was costly in human life, suffering, and money.
2. Answers will vary. (AWV)
3. To personalize the pain of war and get a negative reaction from the reader.
4. AWV
5. The Vietnam War created suffering and a tragic waste of human life.

Exercise 4
1. O   2. F   3. O   4. F   5. F   6. F   7. O   8. O   9. O   10. O

Exercise 5   Passage A: 1. F   2. O   3. O   4. F   5. F
Passage B: 1. F   2. O   3. F   4. O   5. O

Exercise 6, Determining the Author's Purpose.

1. To feel the terror rather than only learn the facts (emotional appeal).

2. One person's suffering is stronger than facts on thousands. The story creates a personal image.

3. For us to become eye witnesses. Her language is simple and innocent.

4. To visualize the cruelty of a 16-year-old versus innocent people.

5. For us to remember, so that such crimes do not happen again.

6. Fact: dates, places, numbers, and factual description; Opinion: Mother's quotation on human dignity.

7. AWV

Exercise 7, Identifying Tone.   1. C   2. B   3. B   4. C   5. A

Exercise 8, Identifying the Author's Tone in Paragraphs.

Passage A

1. Possible: angry, distressed, intense, indignant, outspoken.

2. Underline: <u>My fingers wanted to reach through the wire fence; to break it down; Something was burning...that separated me from others; ...that separated me from the country...could not give; rage; fist; I would have melted that fence.</u>

3. He sees the border fence as a symbol of separation—one that is keeping him from belonging to any country.

4. AWV

5. The author feels caught between two worlds and is not a part of either, due to circumstances beyond his control.

Passage B:

1. Humorous

2. Underline: <u>coaching girls is different; the injury that all men fear; my rookie mistake; I had entered alien territory.</u>

3. Coaching girls is different than coaching boys.

4. AWV

5. As a rookie girls' basketball coach, the author made some mistakes by trying to coach girls the way he had coached boys.

Passage C:

1. Angry, sad, disillusioned

2. Underline: <u>trying to quit; to lower the wattage a bit; maintain full legal control of our bodies, not to mention our destinies; fully in charge of a couple of small muscle groups in our faces; like the opossum; flash toothy grimaces; declaring ourselves non-threatening.</u>

3. Women should not feel forced to smile.

4. AWV

5. Women feel forced to smile even when they don't feel like it.

Exercise 9, Interpreting an Editorial Cartoon.

1. College Application procedures.
2. These items liken the college application process to getting through a series of obstacles successfully. As in the course depicted, college applicants must prove themselves successful. In the case of college, this is done by things such as providing evidence of class rank, rather than jumping through a hoop, but the cartoonist is drawing a parallel between the two.
3. Completing college applications is a series of challenges, with an element of chance mixed in (note the roulette wheel), most of which are rather rough on the student.
4. To compare the college application process to completing an obstacle course.
5. Possible answers: sarcastic, sympathetic to college students, mocking, satiric.
6. He views the college application procedure as overly difficult and likely to harm rather than help a student.
7. AWV

Selection 1, "Decision"
1. D   2. C   3. C   4. A   5. B   6. D   7. B   8. B   9. A   10. D
11. False   12. True   13. False   14. False   15. True
Build Your Vocabulary
1. B   2. A   3. D   4. C   5. A   6. D   7. B   8. C   9. D   10. D

Selection 2, "The Role of Humans in Global Warming"
1. C   2. B   3. C   4. A   5. B   6. D   7. D   8. C   9. A   10. B
11. True   12. True   13. False   14. False   15. True
Build Your Vocabulary
1. A   2. C   3. D   4. B   5. C   6. D   7. B   8. C   9. A   10. A

Selection 3, "Steroids"
1. C   2. B   3. A   4. C   5. C   6. A   7. D   8. B   9. D   10. B
11. False   12. True   13. True   14. False   15. False
Build Your Vocabulary
1. A   2. C   3. C   4. D   5. C   6. A   7. B   8. D   9. D   10. A

Vocabulary Booster
Part I:
1. confirm 2. Directness 3. Obey 4. Recall 5. Silent 6. elected ruler
7. quit or discharge 8. Unconvincing 9. Dialogue 10. formal speech
Part II:
1. contradict 12. Locution 13. Dictionary 14. Sublingual 15. elocution
16. indict 17. Dictatorial 18. Diction 19. Dictate 20. linguistics

Critical Thinking

Learning Objectives

From this chapter, readers will learn to:

1 Define critical thinking
2 Recognize barriers to critical thinking
3 Recognize arguments
4 Analyze and evaluate arguments
5 Define inductive and deductive reasoning
6 Practice thinking critically
7 Define creative thinking

Bathyscaphe. Copyright © 2012 Jacek Yerka. Licensed by MGL/www.mgllicensing.com

WHAT IS THINKING?

Thinking is an organized and controlled mental activity that helps you solve problems, make decisions, and understand ideas. To think is not simply to ponder; it is demanding, challenging, and rewarding work requiring skill and confidence.

All thinkers experience confusion, mental blocks, and failure at times. When faced with such adversity, poor thinkers get frustrated. They initially have trouble knowing where to begin and tend to jump haphazardly from one part of the problem to another. Lacking confidence, they eventually give up. Good thinkers, on the other hand, are strategic. They form a plan and systematically try different solutions. They work with confidence, persistently stick with the task, and find solutions.

EXERCISE 1

Problem Solving

Experience the thinking processes of good thinkers by solving the following problem. Warm up your thinking skills, formulate a plan, believe that you can do it (I did it, so can you!), be persistent, and solve this problem. Have fun with it!

Record your solution patterns as you "pour water" into empty glasses. If one approach fails, try another. This is not a trick but a problem that can be systematically solved—without throwing water away or estimating amounts. Use the illustration shown below to stimulate your thinking.

Rowena has three unmarked glasses of different sizes: 3 ounces, 5 ounces, and 8 ounces. The largest glass is full, and the other two glasses are empty. What can Rowena do to get 4 ounces of liquid into each of the two larger glasses?

—Adapted from Vincent Ryan Ruggiero,
The Art of Thinking, 7th ed.

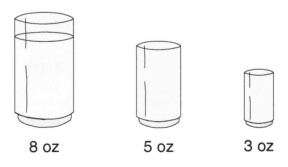

8 oz   5 oz   3 oz

There are several ways to solve this problem.

1. _____

_____

_____

_____

2. _____
   _____
   _____
   _____

3. _____
   _____
   _____
   _____

If you worked on the exercise at length, you have now experienced the rigors of earnest thinking. Did you work strategically? What was your plan? What were the frustrations? Were you persistent? Did you believe in your ability to find a solution? Did you enjoy using thinking for problem solving?

Problems in real life are usually expressed as questions that need an action plan. For example, how would you respond if company executives decided that your job required you to solve the following problems?

- How can workers be enticed to car pool?
- How can awards be distributed to employees to mark each five years of service?
- How can a dead elephant be removed from the parking lot after an unfortunate media event?

You would, of course, work systematically to find solutions to the stated problems.

What does all this have to do with critical thinking? Assuming it was your managers who identified the bigger issues regarding the need for car pooling, five-year awards, and elephant removal, they were the ones who did the critical thinking, and you were the one who got to do the problem solving.

WHAT IS CRITICAL THINKING?

Learning Objective 1

Define critical thinking

Critical thinking—deliberating in a purposeful, organized manner to assess the value of old and new information—precedes problem solving and defines the problems to be solved. Critical thinkers search, compare, analyze, clarify, evaluate, and conclude. They build on previous knowledge, recognize both sides of an issue, and evaluate the reasons and evidence in support of each. And they often deal with issues that can be controversial and can be seen from several different viewpoints. The words "how can" usually begin a problem-solving question, whereas "should" begins a critical thinking question.

For example, imagine the critical thinking needed to answer the controversial question "Should state legislators vote to take away the driver's licenses of students ages 16 through 18 who drop out of school?" Supporters would say that such a law would reduce the number of high school dropouts; detractors would contend it would violate the rights of students; and others would dismiss the idea on the basis

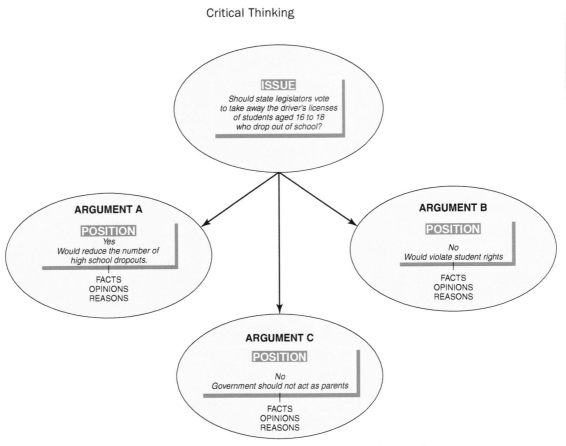

Depending on your position, many different arguments can be constructed for a single issue.

that government should not be in the parenting business. After forming a position, each side would line up evidence to build a persuasive argument to use in lobbying legislators. Both the developers of the arguments and the legislators would be critical thinkers. For the 16- to 18-year-old dropouts, the stakes would be high. The diagram above illustrates the parts and possibilities.

Some professors speak of critical thinking as if it were a special discipline rather than an application of many known skills. Keep reading to discover how "old friends" like *topic, main idea, details,* and *point of view* can connect with new terminology to become powerful vehicles of persuasion. In this chapter, we discuss a few new techniques for identifying and evaluating the support in an argument.

Critical Thinking Skills and College Goals

Many colleges cite the ability to think critically as one of the essential academic outcomes of a college education. An educated person is expected to think systematically, to evaluate, and to draw conclusions based on logic. At your college, an emphasis on critical thinking probably crosses the curriculum and thus becomes a part of every college course. When an instructor returns a paper to you with notes like "good logic" or "not enough support" written on it, the comments are referring

Reader's Tip — Four Habits of Effective Critical Thinkers

- **Be willing to plan.** Think first and write later. Don't be impulsive. Develop a habit of planning.
- **Be flexible.** Be open to new ideas. Consider new solutions for old problems.
- **Be persistent.** Continue to work even when you are tired and discouraged. Good thinking is hard work.
- **Be willing to self-correct.** Don't be defensive about errors. Figure out what went wrong, and learn from your mistakes.

to critical thinking. The same is true if you make a class presentation and are told either that your thesis is very convincing or that you are missing vital support. See the Reader's Tip for four habits of effective critical thinkers.

Critical thinking instruction has its own specialized vocabulary, often using seemingly complex terms for simple ideas. As you work through this chapter, you will become familiar with the critical thinking application of the following terminology:

analogy	argument	assertion	believability	conclusion	consistency
deduction	fallacy	induction	premise	relevance	reliability

Barriers to Critical Thinking

Learning Objective 2

Recognize barriers to critical thinking

Some people are mired in their own belief systems and do not want to rethink, change, or be challenged. They may be gullible and thus easily persuaded by a slick presentation or an illogical argument. For many people, the following barriers interfere with critical thinking:

1. **Frame of reference.** Each of us has an existing belief system that influences the way we deal with incoming information. We interpret new experiences according to what we already believe. We are culturally conditioned to resist change and feel that our own way is best. We refuse to look at the merits of something our belief system rejects, such as the advantages of legalizing drugs, for example.
2. **Wishful thinking.** We talk ourselves into believing things that we know are not true because we want them to be true. We irrationally deceive ourselves and engage in self-denial. For example, we might refuse to believe well-founded claims of moral corruption leveled at our favorite relative or a politician we voted for.
3. **Hasty moral judgments.** We tend to evaluate someone or something as good or bad, right or wrong, and remain fixed in this thinking. Such judgments are often prejudiced, intolerant, emotional, and self-righteous. An example of this

type of barrier to thinking critically would be the statement "Abortion should never be legal."

4. **Reliance on authority.** An authority such as a clergy member, a doctor, or a teacher is an expert source of information. We give authorities and institutions such as churches or governments the power to think for us and thus block our own abilities to question and reason.

5. **Labels.** Labels ignore individual differences and lump people and things into categories. Labels oversimplify, distort the truth, and usually incite anger and rejection. For example, to say, "People who love America and people who do not" forces others to take sides as a knee-jerk reaction. Stereotyping is a kind of labeling.

EXERCISE 2

Identifying Types of Barriers

Read the numbered statements below and identify with *a*, *b*, *c*, or *d* the type of barrier the statement best represents:

a. Wishful thinking
b. Frame of reference or hasty moral judgment
c. Reliance on authority
d. Labels

EXAMPLE

The new drug will not be helpful because the Federal Drug Administration (FDA) has not yet approved it.

EXPLANATION   The answer is c, reliance on authority, which in this case is a government agency. A critical thinker might argue that the FDA is slow to test and respond to new drugs, and that many drugs are used safely and successfully in other countries before the FDA grants approval for Americans.

_____ 1. Since attendance is not taken for each class session, unlimited absences are acceptable for the course.

_____ 2. According to the director of writing assistance, students are more likely to feel comfortable with peer tutors than with college instructors.

_____ 3. City dwellers are an impatient lot; they are rude and in a hurry.

_____ 4. Offering financial assistance to people who have fallen on hard times keeps them from learning to be independent.

RECOGNIZING AN ARGUMENT

Learning Objective 3

Recognize arguments

Just as we may have barriers to critical thinking, we also need to recognize that not every statement is an argument. **Assertions** such as "I like soy milk" or "We had a huge overnight snowfall, and my car is covered" are nonargumentative statements that are intended to inform or explain. An **argument,** on the other hand, is an assertion that supports a conclusion and is intended to persuade. The difference is intent and purpose. For example, the statement "The grass is wet because it rained last night" is an explanation, not an argument. To say, however, "You should water the grass tonight because rain is not predicted for several days" constitutes an argument. In the latter case, the conclusion of watering the grass is based on a "fact," the forecast, and the intent is to persuade by appealing to reason. To identify arguments, use inferential skills and recognize the underlying purpose or intent of the author.

EXERCISE 3

Identifying Arguments

Practice recognizing arguments by identifying each of the following statements with *A* (argument) or *N* (nonargumentative statement of information).

EXAMPLE

The foods in salad bars sometimes contain preservatives to keep them looking fresh and appealing.

> **EXPLANATION**   This is not an argument. It is not intended to move you to action. It is a statement of fact similar to "It sometimes snows at night."

_____ 1. Brown eyes and brown hair are genetically dominant over blue eyes and blond hair.

_____ 2. Since summer enrollment is low, the college should initiate a parking fee to offset lost income.

_____ 3. Student employment should first be offered to those who have demonstrated the most significant financial need.

_____ 4. Americans own more radios than they do television sets.

_____ 5. College students should date people their own age.

STEPS IN ANALYZING AND EVALUATING AN ARGUMENT

Learning Objective 4

Analyze and evaluate arguments

Analyzing an argument through critical thinking and evaluation combines the use of most of the skills that have been taught in this text. The amount of analysis depends on the complexity of the argument. Some arguments are simple; others are lengthy and complicated. The following is a four-step procedure that you can use to guide your critical thinking:

1. Identify the position on the issue.
2. Identify the support in the argument.
3. Evaluate the support.
4. Evaluate the argument.

Step 1: Identify the Position on the Issue

To identify the position on an issue or the conclusion in persuasive writing, use your main-idea reading skills. First, determine the topic that is the issue by asking yourself, "What is the passage primarily about?" Then ask, "What is the author

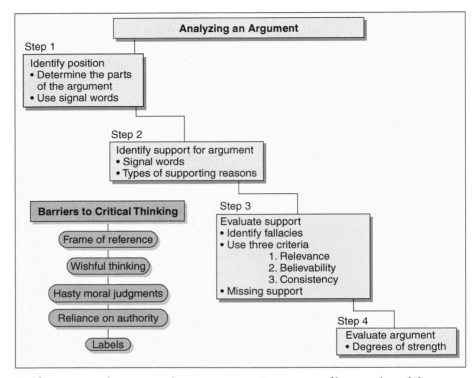

Use four sequential steps to analyze an argument. Be cautious of barriers that inhibit critical thinking.

trying to convey about the issue?" If you're not sure, examine the details and determine what point they support. Your answer will be a statement of the position that is being argued—in other words, the main point, thesis, or conclusion. For example, on the topic or issue of searching school lockers for weapons, one position or main point might be that it can prevent violence and a contrasting position or main point might be that it is an invasion of privacy.

In a college course on critical thinking or logic, the parts of an argument that you would be asked to identify would probably be called the **conclusion** and the **premises**. The conclusion is the position on the issue or the main point, and the premises are the supporting points. For example, an argument now exists on the death of Alexander the Great more than 2,300 years ago. The conclusion that some epidemiologists have reached is that he died of West Nile virus rather than typhoid or malaria. One premise states that he became paralyzed before he died, and paralysis is a symptom of the brain infection that marks West Nile virus. Another premise holds that Alexander saw ravens pecking one another, and some fell dead in front of him, and ravens are among the types of birds that are particularly susceptible to West Nile virus.

When reading an argument, be aware of the author's bias and your own biases. Do not allow your own beliefs to cloud your thinking. Guard against falling for the barriers to critical thinking that include limited frame of reference, wishful thinking, hasty moral judgments, reliance on authority, and labeling. Be sensitive to emotional language and the connotation of words. Cut through the rhetoric, and get to the heart of the matter.

EXAMPLE   Read the following passage, and identify the position on the issue that is being argued:

> The technology for television has far exceeded the programming. Viewers are recipients of crystal clear junk. Network programming appeals to the masses for ratings and advertising money and thus offers little creative or stimulating entertainment.

EXPLANATION   Several debatable issues about television are suggested by this passage. They include the abundance of technological advancement, the power of ratings, and the importance of advertising money. The topic or issue, however, concerns the quality of network programming. Although it is not directly stated, the argument or central issue is "Network television programming offers little creative or stimulating entertainment."

Signal Words   We have said that the position on the issue may be stated as the thesis or main point. However, it does not necessarily appear at the beginning of an argument. Instead, it might be embedded within the passage or stated at the end as a conclusion. Look for the following key words that may be used to signal the central issue:

| as a result | finally | in summary | therefore |
| consequently | for these reasons | it follows that | thus, should |

EXAMPLE   What is the position on the issue that is being argued in the following passage?

> Although a year in a U.S. prison costs more than a year at Harvard, almost no one leaves prison rehabilitated. Prisoners meet and share information with other hardened criminals to refine their "skills." It seems reasonable, therefore, to conclude that prisons in the United States are societal failures.

EXPLANATION   The position on the issue of prison rehabilitation in this argument is directly stated in the last sentence. Note the inclusion of the signal word *therefore.*

EXERCISE 4   **Identifying the Position on the Issue**

Read the following sentence groups, and indicate the number of the sentence that states the position on the issue.

1. (1)Ten is the new twenty. (2)In modern America, the stage of late childhood has all but disappeared. (3)Parents allow their under-thirteens to play video games rated for mature audiences and to view movies intended for teens or adults.

   Position on issue: _____

2. [1]Online courses are often a time-saver for students who live far from campus. [2]The majority of institutions offering these classes are accredited and have experienced faculty. [3]Consider taking courses online because of the many advantages that come with this option for learning.

Position on issue: _____

3. [1]The amount of time a doctor spends with a patient has declined over the past few decades. [2]Managed care has led to quantity over quality when it comes to patient appointments. [3]Doctors see a prescribed number of patients within an allotted time period, regardless of the medical issues involved.

Position on issue: _____

4. [1]We are fast becoming a nation of perfectionists. [2]We trim our body fat, color our hair, and pump our muscles. [3]Our teeth are whitened, our bodies dieted and exercised, and, in some cases, "perfection" is even attempted via surgery.

Position on issue: _____

5. [1]Some parts of the country encourage this support by providing curbside collection of recyclables at no cost to the consumer. [2]Other places charge the same amount to collect recycled products as they do for general refuse. [3]If policies that entice consumers to recycle were implemented nationwide, our country's rate of recycling would certainly increase greatly.

Position on issue: _____

Step 2: Identify the Support in the Argument

In a college logic course, after identifying the position on the issue of an argument, you would be asked to identify and number the premises, or support statements. For example, in an argument about searching high school lockers, a proponent's first premise or support statement might be that *guns and knives are always found in searches*. Other premises, such as *the school owns the lockers* and *metal detectors at the school's entrance miss harmful, illegal drugs*, would have added further supporting evidence. In short, to identify the premises, simply identify significant supporting details for the main point.

Signal Words Supporting reasons may be directly stated or may be signaled. The key words that signal support for an argument are in some cases the same as those that signal significant supporting details. They include the following:

because	if	assuming that
since	first, second, finally	given that

EXAMPLE

What happens when the passage about U.S. prisons is rewritten so that signal words introduce supporting details? Read the following:

One can conclude that prisons in the United States are societal failures. First, almost no one leaves prison rehabilitated. Second, prisoners meet and share information with other hardened criminals to refine their "skills." Taxpayers should also consider that a year in prison costs more than a year at Harvard.

EXPLANATION   The argument is the same with or without the signal words. In a longer passage, the signal words usually make it easier to identify the significant supporting details or reasons.

EXERCISE 5

Identifying Support for the Argument

Read the following sentence groups. Record the number of the sentence that states the position on the issue that is being argued and the numbers of the support statements.

1. (1)Radar detectors on cars warn drivers of police surveillance. (2)At the beep, drivers slow down to avoid tickets. (3)Such devices should be banned because they promote driving beyond the legal speed limit.

   Position on issue: _____ Support: _____

2. (1)Major game reserves in Africa such as the Ngorongoro Crater are in protected areas, but many lie adjacent to large tracts of land with no conservation status. (2)Animals that migrate off the reserves compete with humans for food and are endangered. (3)Thus, clear boundaries between areas for animals and people would minimize friction.

   Position on issue: _____ Support: _____

3. (1)Some state laws prohibit the sale of obscene material to minors. (2)Consequently, in these states musicians who sell CDs with obscene lyrics should be prosecuted. (3)Such lyrics brutalize women and are audio pornography.

   Position on issue: _____ Support: _____

4. (1)Doctors should try to make a patient's visit to the office less humiliating. (2)First, you see a receptionist who tells you to fill out forms and wait your turn. (3)Next, the nurse takes your blood pressure and extracts blood while you look at the diplomas on the wall. (4)Finally, you are led into a cold room to strip down and wait still longer for the doctor to appear for a few expensive minutes of consultation.

   Position on issue: _____ Support: _____

5. (1)In most companies, college graduates get higher-paying jobs than those who do not attend college. (2)As the years go by in a company, promotions and their accompanying raises tend to go primarily to the college graduates. (3)Thus, it can be concluded that a college degree is worth money.

   Position on issue: _____ Support: _____

Reader's Tip — Types of Support for Arguments

- **Facts:** objective truths
  Ask: How were the facts gathered? Are they true?

- **Examples:** anecdotes to demonstrate the truth
  Ask: Are the examples true and relevant?

- **Analogies:** comparisons to similar cases
  Ask: Are the analogies accurate and relevant?

- **Expert opinions:** words from a recognized expert
  Ask: What are the credentials and biases of the expert?

- **Causal relationship:** saying that one thing caused another
  Ask: Is it an actual cause or merely an association?

- **Common knowledge claim:** assertion of wide acceptance
  Ask: Is it relevant? Does everyone really believe it?

- **Statistics:** numerical data
  Ask: Do the numbers accurately describe the phenomenon?

- **Personal experiences:** personal anecdotes
  Ask: Is the experience applicable to other situations?

Types of Supporting Reasons Readers would probably prefer support for an argument to be in the simple form of a smoking gun with fingerprints on it, but such conclusive evidence is usually hard to find. Evidence comes in many different forms and may be tainted with opinion. The Reader's Tip that follows contains some categories of "evidence" typically used as supporting reasons in an argument. Each type, however, has its pitfalls and should be immediately tested with an evaluative question.

Step 3: Evaluate the Support

As a reader, you will decide to accept or reject the author's conclusion based on the strength and acceptability of the reasons and evidence. Keep in mind that although strong arguments are logically supported by valid reasons and evidence, weak, invalid arguments also may be supported by the crafty use of reason and evidence. Your job is to assess the validity of the support.

Teachers of logic warn students to beware of fallacies when they evaluate the support for an argument. A **fallacy** is an inference that appears to be reasonable at first glance, but closer inspection proves it to be unrelated, unreliable, or illogical. For example, to say that something is right because everybody is doing it is not a convincing reason for accepting an idea. Such "reasoning," however, can be compelling and is used so frequently that it is labeled a *bandwagon fallacy.*

Logicians have categorized, labeled, and defined more than two hundred types of fallacies or tricks of persuasion. For critical thinkers, however, the emphasis should be less on memorizing a long list of fallacy types and more on understanding how such irrelevant reasoning techniques can manipulate logical thinking. Fallacies are tools employed in constructing a weak argument that critical thinkers should spot. In a court of law, the opposing attorney would shout "Irrelevant, Your Honor!" to alert the jury to the introduction of fallacious evidence.

Evaluate the support for an argument according to three criteria: (1) **relevance,** (2) **believability,** and (3) **consistency.** The following list of fallacies common to each area can sensitize you to the "tools" of constructing a weak argument.

1. **Relevance fallacies: Is the support related to the conclusion?**
   - *Ad hominem.* An attack on the person rather than the issue is used in the hope that the idea will be opposed if the person is opposed.
     Example: Do not listen to Mr. Hite's views on education because he didn't even finish high school.
   - **Bandwagon.** Everybody is doing it, and you will be left out if you do not quickly join the crowd.
     Example: Everybody around the world is drinking Coke, so you should too.
   - **Misleading analogy.** Two things are compared, suggesting that they are similar when they are in fact distinctly different.
     Example: College students are just like elementary school students; they need to be taught self-discipline.
   - **Straw person.** A distorted or exaggerated form of the opponent's argument is introduced and dismissed as ridiculous.
     Example: When a teenage daughter is told she cannot go out on the weeknight before a test, she replies, "It's unreasonable to say that I can never go out on a weeknight."
   - **Testimonials.** Respected celebrities make strong, convincing claims, though they are not actually experts.
     Example: A famous actor endorses a medication to treat headaches.
   - **Transfer.** An association with a positively or negatively regarded person or thing lends the same association to the argument (also called guilt or virtue by association).
     Example: A local politician quotes President Lincoln in a speech as if to imply that Lincoln would have agreed with and voted for the candidate.

2. **Believability fallacies: Is the support believable or highly suspicious?**
   - **Incomplete facts** or **card stacking.** Factual details are omitted to misrepresent reality.
     Example: Buy stock in this restaurant chain because it is under new management and people eat out a lot.
   - **Misinterpreted statistics.** Numerical data are applied to unrelated populations that the numbers were never intended to represent.
     Example: More than 20 percent of people exercise daily and thus do not need fitness training.

- **Overgeneralizations.** Examples and anecdotes are asserted as if they apply to all cases rather than a select few.
  Example: High school students do little work during their senior year and thus are overwhelmed at college.
- **Questionable authority.** A testimonial suggests that people who are not experts actually do have authority in a certain area.
  Example: Dr. Lee, a university sociology professor, testified that the DNA reports were 100 percent accurate.

3. **Consistency fallacies: Does the support hold together, or does it fall apart and contradict itself?**

  - **Appeals to emotions.** Highly charged language is used for emotional manipulation.
    Example: Give money to our organization to help these children—these starving orphans—who are in desperate need of medical attention.
  - **Appeals to pity.** Pleas to support the underdog are made on behalf of a person or issue.
    Example: Please give me an A for the course because I need it to get into law school.
  - **Circular reasoning** or **begging the question.** Support for the conclusion merely restates the conclusion.
    Example: Drugs should not be legalized because it should be against the law to take illegal drugs.
  - **Oversimplification.** An issue is reduced to two simple choices, without consideration of other alternatives or "gray areas" in between.
    Example: The choices are very simple in supporting our foreign-policy decision to send troops. You are either for America or against it.
  - **Slippery slope.** Objections to an issue are raised because unless dealt with, it will lead to greater evil and disastrous consequences.
    Example: Support for assisting the suicide of a terminally ill patient will lead to the ultimate disposal of the marginally sick and elderly.

EXERCISE 6

Identifying Fallacies

Identify the type of fallacy in each of the following statements by indicating *a, b,* or *c*:

_____ 1. Hollywood movie stars and rock musicians are not experts on the environment and should not speak out on environmental policy.

    a. testimonial
    b. *ad hominem*
    c. bandwagon

_____ 2. Prayer in school is like cereal for breakfast. They both get the morning off to a good start.

    a. circular reasoning
    b. appeal to emotions
    c. misleading analogy

_____ 3. The advocate for rezoning of the property concluded by saying, "George Washington was also concerned about land and freedom."

    a. transfer
    b. *ad hominem*
    c. straw person

_____ 4. The explanation for the distribution of grades is simple. College students either study or they do not study.

    a. misinterpreted statistics
    b. oversimplification
    c. appeal to pity

_____ 5. Your written statement agreeing with my position will enable me to keep my job.

    a. misinterpreted statistics
    b. appeal to pity
    c. card stacking

_____ 6. Everyone in the neighborhood has worked on the new park design and agreed to it. Now we need your signature of support.

    a. bandwagon
    b. appeal to emotions
    c. begging the question

_____ 7. Democrats go to Washington to spend money with no regard for the hardworking taxpayer.

    a. circular reasoning
    b. bandwagon
    c. overgeneralization

_____ 8. The suicide rate is highest over the Christmas holidays, which means that Thanksgiving is a safe and happy holiday.

    a. misinterpreted statistics
    b. card stacking
    c. questionable authority

_____ 9. The workers' fingers were swollen and infected, insects walked on their exposed skin, and their red eyes begged for mercy and relief. We all must join their effort.

    a. oversimplification
    b. appeal to emotions
    c. overgeneralization

_____ 10. Our minister, Dr. Johnson, assured the family that our cousin's cancer was a slow-growing one so that a brief delay in treatment would not be detrimental.

    a. transfer
    b. straw person
    c. questionable authority

Determine Missing Support   Arguments are written to persuade and thus include the proponent's version of the convincing reasons. Therefore, writers might leave out or gloss over evidence that would contradict their points. In analyzing an argument, remember to ask yourself, "What is left out?" Be an advocate for the opposing point of view, and guess at the evidence that would be presented. Decide if evidence was consciously omitted because of its adverse effect on the conclusion. For example, a businessperson arguing for an increased monthly service fee might neglect to mention how much of the cost reflects administrative raises and profit.

Step 4: Evaluate the Argument

Important decisions are rarely made quickly or easily. A period of incubation is often needed for deliberating among alternatives. Allow yourself time to go over arguments, weighing the support and looking at the issues from different perspectives. Good critical thinkers are persistent in seeking solutions.

One researcher, Diane Halpern, expresses the difficulty of decision making by saying, "There is never just one war fought. Each side has its own version, and rarely do they agree."[1] As a reader, you are obligated to consider all factors carefully in seeking the truth. Halpern uses a picture of a table that represents the position on an issue and compares the legs of the table to four different degrees of support. Use them to evaluate the strength of an argument.

---

[1]Diane Halpern, *Thought and Knowledge,* 2nd ed. (Hillsdale, NJ: Lawrence Erlbaum, 1989), p. 191.

The Strength of an Argument

Strong Argument

- Strong, related reasons provide support.
- Many weak reasons can provide support.
- A few weak reasons do not adequately support.
- Unrelated reasons give no support.

Weak Argument

Remember, in critical thinking there is no "I'm right, and you're wrong." There are, however, strong and weak arguments. For instance, you might agree with the author's conclusion but find the support insufficient to make a strong argument. On the other hand, you might disagree with the author's position but acknowledge that he or she constructed a strong argument. Strong, relevant, believable, and consistent reasons build a good argument.

EXERCISE 7

Evaluating Your Own Decision Making

Now that you are familiar with the critical thinking process, analyze your own thinking in making the important recent decision of where to attend college. No college is perfect; many factors must be considered. The issue or conclusion is that you have decided to attend the college where you are now enrolled. List relevant reasons and/or evidence that supported your decision. Evaluate the strength of your reasoning. Are any of your reasons based on fallacies?

Position: My decision to attend this college was based on the following:

1. _____
   _____

2. _____
   _____

3. _____
   _____

4. _____
   _____

5. _____
   _____

How would you evaluate your own critical thinking in making a choice among colleges? Perhaps you relied heavily on information from others. Were those sources credible?

INDUCTIVE AND DEDUCTIVE REASONING

Learning Objective 5

Define inductive and deductive reasoning

In choosing a college, did you follow an inductive or deductive reasoning process? Did you collect extensive information on several colleges and then weigh the advantages and disadvantages of each? Those who follow an **inductive reasoning** process start by gathering data, and then, after considering all available material, they formulate a conclusion. Textbooks based on this plan give details first and lead you into the main idea or conclusion. They strive to put the parts into a logical whole and thus reason "up" from particular details to a broad generalization. This is sometimes called "bottom-up" reasoning.

Deductive reasoning, on the other hand, follows the opposite pattern. With this type of reasoning, you start with the conclusion derived from a previous experience and apply it to a new situation. Perhaps your college choice is a family tradition; your parents are alumni, and you have always expected to attend that school. Perhaps you are attending the college closest to where you live. Although your thinking may have begun with the conclusion, you probably have since discovered many reasons why the college is right for you. When writers use a deductive pattern, they first give a general statement and then enumerate the reasons. This is also known as "top-down" thinking.

Despite the formal distinction between inductive and deductive reasoning, in real life we switch back and forth as we think. Our everyday observations lead to conclusions that we then reuse and modify to form new conclusions.

Inductive Reasoning	Deductive Reasoning
(2) Conclusion	(1) CONCLUSION
⬆	⬇
(1) DATA, REASONS, EVIDENCE	(2) Data, Reasons, Evidence

APPLYING THE FOUR STEPS OF CRITICAL THINKING

Learning Objective 6

Practice thinking critically

The following is an example of how the four-step format can be used to evaluate an argument. Read the argument, analyze it according to the directions for each step, and then read the explanation of how the critical thinking process was applied. Remember that critical thinking takes time, concentrated effort, and persistence.

THE ARGUMENT: EXTRATERRESTRIAL LIFE

(1)Surely life exists elsewhere in the universe. (2)After all, most space scientists today admit the possibility that life has evolved on other planets. (3)Besides, other planets in our solar system are strikingly like Earth. (4)They revolve around the sun, they borrow light from the sun, and several are known to revolve on their axes, and to be subject to the same laws of gravitation as Earth. (5)What's more, aren't those who make light of extraterrestrial life soft-headed fundamentalists clinging to the foolish notion that life is unique to their planet?

—Joel Rudinow and Vincent Barry,
Invitation to Critical Thinking, 3rd ed.

- **Step 1.** Identify the position on the issue. What is the topic of this argument, and what is the main point the writer is trying to convey? Although many ideas may be included, what is the central concern being discussed and supported? Record the number for the sentence that states the position on the issue.

  _____

- **Step 2.** Identify the support in the argument. What are the significant supporting details that support the position that is being argued? Record the numbers for supporting statements.

  _____

- **Step 3.** Evaluate the support. Examine each supporting assertion separately for relevance, believability, and consistency. Can you identify any as fallacies that are intended to sell a weak argument? List each sentence that expresses a fallacy and identify the type of fallacy. Then identify the type of supporting information you feel is missing.

  Evaluation: _____

  _____

  _____

  Missing support: _____

  _____

  _____

- **Step 4.** Evaluate the argument. What is your overall evaluation of the argument? Is the argument convincing? Does the argument provide good reasons and/or evidence for believing the thesis?

Explanation of the Four Steps

- **Step 1.** *Identify the position on the issue.* The position, assertion, thesis, main point, or conclusion is directly stated in the first sentence. Good critical thinkers would note, however, that "life" is not clearly defined as plant, animal, or human.
- **Step 2.** *Identify the support in the argument.* This argument contains three main premises or significant supporting details, in the following sentences:
  Sentence 2: Space scientists admit the possibility that life has evolved on other planets.

Sentence 3: Other planets in our solar system are strikingly like Earth.
Sentence 5: Those who make light of extraterrestrial life are soft-headed fundamentalists clinging to the foolish notion that life is unique to this planet.

- **Step 3.** *Evaluate the support.* The first supporting detail, sentence 2, is a vague appeal to authority that does not reveal who "most space scientists" are. Do the scientists work for NASA? The second premise, sentence 3, is also vague and presented as a misleading comparison. Other planets may be round, but they have different temperatures and different atmospheres. The third supporting statement, sentence 5, is an oversimplified, personal attack on those who may not agree with the argument. Scientific support for this argument seems to be missing. The support is weak in all three areas: relevance, believability, and consistency.

- **Step 4.** *Evaluate the argument.* This is a weak argument. There may be good reasons to believe that life exists on other planets, but this argument fails to provide them. The possibility of extraterrestrial life might be argued through statistics from astronomy and a specific definition of "life."

EXERCISE 8

Applying the Four Steps to Different Arguments

Read the following three arguments, and apply the four-step format for evaluation. Using the sentence numbers, identify the position on the issue and the support. Then evaluate the argument.

ARGUMENT 1: CHILD CRIMINAL OFFENDERS

(1)Centuries ago, when there was little or no distinction between children and adults in daily life, children who committed crimes were treated exactly as adult offenders were treated. (2)More recently, they have been treated quite differently; they are given special consideration for first offenses, receive lighter sentences for second and subsequent offenses, and are placed in special reform schools and rehabilitation centers rather than in prisons. (3)But many people have begun to question the wisdom of that special consideration. (4)They reason that the crime in question, and not the criminal's age, should dictate the punishment. (5)Children who kill are either guilty of murder or not guilty.

—Adapted from Vincent Ryan Ruggiero,
The Art of Thinking, 7th ed. pp. 18, 237, 229. Published by
Longman. © 2004 by Pearson Education, Inc., Glenview, IL.

- **Step 1.** Identify the position on the issue. _____
- **Step 2.** Identify the support in the argument. _____
- **Step 3.** Evaluate the support. Examine each supporting assertion for relevance, believability, and consistency. List each sentence that expresses a fallacy and identify the type of fallacy. Then identify the type of supporting information you feel is missing.

Evaluation: _____
_____
_____

Missing support: _____

_____

- **Step 4.** Evaluate the argument. What is your overall evaluation and why?

_____

_____

ARGUMENT 2: INVASION OF PRIVACY

(1)When you call 911 in an emergency, some police departments have a way of telling your telephone number and address without your saying a word. (2)The chief value of this, say the police, is that if the caller is unable to communicate for any reason, the dispatcher knows where to send help. (3)But don't be duped by such paternalistic explanations. (4)This technology is a despicable invasion of privacy, for callers may be unaware of the insidious device. (5)Even if they are, some persons who wish anonymity may be reluctant to call for emergency help. (6)Remember that the names of complainants and witnesses are recorded in many communities' criminal justice systems. (7)A fairer and more effective system seemingly would include an auxiliary number for 911 callers who wish anonymity.

—Joel Rudinow and Vincent E. Barry,
Invitation to Critical Thinking, 3rd ed.

- **Step 1.** Identify the position on the issue. _____
- **Step 2.** Identify the support in the argument. _____
- **Step 3.** Evaluate the support. Examine each supporting assertion for relevance, believability, and consistency. List each sentence that expresses a fallacy and identify the type of fallacy. Then identify the type of supporting information you feel is missing.

Evaluation: _____

_____

_____

_____

Missing support: _____

_____

_____

- **Step 4.** Evaluate the argument. What is your overall evaluation and why?

_____

_____

_____

ARGUMENT 3: BAN BOXING

[1]As a practicing physician, I am convinced that boxing should be banned. [2]First, boxing is a very visible example that violence is accepted behavior in our society—outside the ring as well as inside. [3]This sends the wrong message to America's youth. [4]Second, boxing is the only sport where the sole object is to injure the opponent. [5]Boxing, then, is morally offensive because its intent is to inflict brain injuries on another person. [6]Third, medical science can't take someone who has suffered repeated blows to the head and restore that person to normal function. [7]This causes many physicians to conclude that our society should ban boxing. [8]Boxing is morally and medically offensive. [9]So as a physician, I believe boxing should be banned.

—From Robert E. McAfee,
"Regulation Won't Work: Ban Boxing" as appeared in *USA Today*.
December 20, 1990. Reprinted by permission of the author.

- **Step 1.** Identify the position on the issue. _____
- **Step 2.** Identify the support in the argument. _____
- **Step 3.** Evaluate the support. Examine each supporting assertion for relevance, believability, and consistency. List each sentence that expresses a fallacy and identify the type of fallacy. Then identify the type of supporting information you feel is missing.

  Evaluation: _____
  _____
  _____

  Missing support: _____
  _____
  _____

- **Step 4.** Evaluate the argument. What is your overall evaluation and why?

  _____
  _____
  _____

ARGUMENT 4: DETECT ONLINE ROMANCE

[1]The following story is proof that surveillance software should be considered ethically correct. [2]The software is cheap. [3]Its legality has not been questioned. [4]It is available from a host of companies. [5]Computer spying woke me up to reality, as the story explains.

[6]"I'm not doing anything wrong, believe me," she'd said for weeks. But he didn't buy it. He'd read her e-mail, listened in on her phone conversations. He watched the chats, too. Fifty bucks bought him software to slip into the family computer and secretly record his wife's every move.

So it's 5 A.M., she's sleeping upstairs, he ventures onto the computer. He starts up the software and finds a series of black-and-white snapshots taken of the screen while she was online. She calls herself "rita_neb" and her every come-on, every flirtation, every misspelling, is saved. The correspondent is some guy in Nebraska, and the talk is not just flirting but, you know, graphic—and Greg Young begins to cry. His 22-year marriage is over.

—Bill Hancock, "Spying at Home:
A New Pastime to Detect Online Romance,"
Computers and Security, October 1, 2000

- **Step 1.** Identify the position on the issue. _____
- **Step 2.** Identify the support in the argument. _____
- **Step 3.** Evaluate the support. Examine each supporting assertion for relevance, believability, and consistency. List each sentence that expresses a fallacy and identify the type of fallacy. Then identify the type of supporting information you feel is missing.

Evaluation: _____

_____

_____

Missing support: _____

_____

_____

- **Step 4.** Evaluate the argument. What is your overall evaluation and why?

_____

_____

_____

_____

ARGUMENT 5: FILM VIOLENCE

(1)I walked out of the movie after a half hour. (2)It was either leave or throw up. (3)In an early scene, a wolf attacks two young men, killing one and badly slashing the other. (4)No gory detail is left to the imagination. (5)Yet, somehow, many people around me in the theater found the visual assault enjoyable as they laughed and laughed.

(6)Chicago film critic Roger Ebert reported that in viewing another film on two separate occasions, he observed both audiences laughing in scenes showing a woman beaten, raped, and cut up. (7)One respectable-looking man next to him kept murmuring, (8)"That'll teach her." (9)Ebert found that reaction frightening. Like any powerful experience, film viewing has the capacity to brutalize us. (10)No one should be permitted to poison the air the rest of us breathe. (11)Neither should a filmmaker have the right to poison the social climate.

—Adapted from Vincent Ryan Ruggiero,
The Art of Thinking, 7th ed.

- **Step 1.** Identify the position on the issue. ‗‗‗‗‗‗‗

- **Step 2.** Identify the support in the argument. ‗‗‗‗‗‗‗

- **Step 3.** Evaluate the support. Examine each supporting assertion for relevance, believability, and consistency. List each sentence that expresses a fallacy and identify the type of fallacy. Then identify the type of supporting information you feel is missing.

  Evaluation: ‗‗
  ‗‗‗
  ‗‗‗
  ‗‗‗
  ‗‗‗

  Missing support: ‗‗‗‗‗‗‗‗‗‗‗‗‗‗‗‗‗‗‗‗‗‗‗‗‗‗‗‗‗‗‗‗‗‗
  ‗‗‗

- **Step 4.** Evaluate the argument. What is your overall evaluation and why?

  ‗‗‗
  ‗‗‗
  ‗‗‗

CREATIVE AND CRITICAL THINKING

Learning Objective 7

Define creative thinking

A chapter on critical thinking would not be complete without an appeal for creative thinking. You might wonder, "Are critical thinking and creative thinking different?" **Creative thinking** refers to the ability to generate many possible solutions to a problem, whereas critical thinking refers to the examination of those solutions for the selection of the best of all possibilities. Both ways of thinking are essential for good problem solving.

Diane Halpern uses the following story to illustrate creative thinking:

Many years ago when a person who owed money could be thrown into jail, a merchant in London had the misfortune to owe a huge sum to a money-lender. The money-lender, who was old and ugly, fancied the merchant's beautiful teenage daughter. He proposed a bargain. He said he would cancel the merchant's debt if he could have the girl instead.

Both the merchant and his daughter were horrified at the proposal. So the cunning money-lender proposed that they let Providence decide the matter. He told them that he would put a black pebble and a white pebble into an empty money-bag and then the girl would have to pick out one of the pebbles. If she chose the black pebble, she would become his wife and her father's debt would be canceled. If she chose the white pebble, she would stay with her father and the debt would still be canceled. But if she refused to pick out a pebble, her father would be thrown into jail and she would starve.

Reluctantly the merchant agreed. They were standing on a pebble-strewn path in the merchant's garden as they talked, and the money-lender stooped down to pick up two pebbles. As he picked up the pebbles the girl, sharp-eyed with fright, noticed that he picked up two black pebbles and put them into the money-bag. He then asked the girl to pick out the pebble that was to decide her fate and that of her father.

—Diane Halpern,
Thought and Knowledge, 2nd ed.

If you were the girl, what would you do? Think creatively, and, without evaluating your thoughts, list at least five possible solutions. Next think critically to evaluate your list, and then circle your final choice.

1. _____

2. _____

3. _____

4. _____

5. _____

In discussing the possible solutions to the problem, Halpern talks about two kinds of creative thinking, vertical thinking and lateral thinking. **Vertical thinking** is a straightforward and logical way of thinking that would typically result in a solution like, "Call his hand and expose the money-lender as a crook." The disadvantage of this solution is that the merchant is still in debt, so the original problem has not been solved. **Lateral thinking,** on the other hand, is a way of thinking *around* a problem or even redefining the problem. Edward DeBono suggests that a lateral thinker might redefine the problem from "What happens when I get the black pebble?"[2] to "How can I avoid the black pebble?" Using this new definition of the problem and other seemingly irrelevant information, a lateral thinker could come up with a winning solution. When the girl reaches into the bag, she should fumble and drop the stone she selects on the "pebble-strewn path." The color of the pebble she dropped could then be determined by looking at the one left in the bag. Since the remaining pebble is black, the dropped one that is now mingled in the path must have been white. Any other admission would expose the money-lender as a crook. Probably the heroine thought of many alternatives, but thanks to her ability to generate a novel solution and evaluate its effectiveness, the daughter and the merchant lived happily free of debt.

DeBono defines vertical thinking as "digging the same hole deeper" and lateral thinking as "digging the hole somewhere else."[3] For example, after many years of researching a cure for smallpox, Dr. Edward Jenner stopped focusing on patients who were sick with the disease and instead began studying groups of people who never seemed to get smallpox. Shortly thereafter, using this different perspective, Dr. Jenner discovered the clues that led him to the smallpox vaccine.

---

[2]E. DeBono, *New Think: The Use of Lateral Thinking in the Generation of New Ideas* (New York: Basic Books, 1968), p. 195.

[3]E. DeBono, "Information Processing and New Ideas—Lateral and Vertical Thinking," in S. J. Parnes, R. B. Noller, and A. M. Biondi, eds., *Guide to Creative Action: Revised Edition of Creative Behavior Guidebook* (New York: Scribner's, 1977).

The Creative Brain

Studies in neuroscience demonstrate that creativity involves both conscious and unconscious brain activity. Many ground-breaking inventions have started with dreams or seemingly "out-of-nowhere" ideas. The key word here is "seemingly" because creative insights begin with conscious attention to a problem and a desire to solve it. When the background work of identifying a problem and gathering information has been done, our brains can work behind the scenes, unconsciously, to uncover a solution.

To pave the way for creative insights, first identify a problem and collect as much information about it as possible from many sources. Try to look at the problem from many points of view. Then—this step is key—let the whole thing incubate. Do something else that takes your mind completely to another focus. When you're least expecting it, your unconscious mind just might give birth to a surprise, maybe in a dream, in the hazy period before becoming fully awake, in the shower, while exercising, or driving to school or work. As soon as possible, write it down. Examine the idea, refine it, and test it. You might have a great way to approach your term paper or even a new invention.

Adapted from 12 Brain/Mind Learning Principles in Action: Developing Executive Functions of the Human Brain, *2nd Ed.*
Renate Caine, et al.

Creative and critical thinking enable us to see new relationships. We blend knowledge and see new similarities and differences, a new sequence of events, or a new solution for an old problem. We create new knowledge by using old learning differently.

SUMMARY POINTS

1. What is the definition of critical thinking?
- Critical thinking is thinking in a purposeful, organized manner. It requires assessing the value of old and new information.
- Critical thinking defines problems to be solved.
- "Should" often begins a critical thinking question; "how can" usually begins the next step, problem solving.

2. What are common barriers to critical thinking?
- **Frame of reference barriers:** Failure to consider ideas outside of our belief system
- **Wishful thinking:** Refusal to accept ideas that we do not like or accepting only those we hope are true
- **Hasty moral judgments:** Quick judgments based on personal prejudices or emotions.
- **Reliance on authority:** Blindly accepting what an authority figure tells us without questioning or examining its merit
- **Labels:** Putting people and ideas into rigid categories and ignoring individual differences. Stereotyping is an example

3. How can I recognize an argument?
- An argument contains an assertion that is intended to persuade the reader or listener.
- An assertion, on the other hand, is a nondebatable statement that is intended to inform or explain.

4. What are the steps to analyzing and evaluating an argument?
1. Identify the issue (called the *conclusion*), the author's position on the topic, using main idea skills. Look for common signal words that indicate the conclusion.
2. Identify the supporting evidence. These details are called *premises*. Use common signal words to help locate them. Typical supporting evidence includes facts, examples, analogies, expert opinions, causal relationships, common knowledge claims, statistics, and personal experiences.
3. Evaluate the support by questioning the evidence provided. Ask, "Is it relevant to the conclusion?" "Is it believable?" and "Does it consistently support the same conclusion?" Be alert to common logical fallacies and consider what evidence is missing that might contradict the conclusion or further support it.
4. Evaluate the entire argument. Consider the strength of the argument on the basis of the evidence provided. Unrelated reasons make a very weak argument. A few weak reasons also provide inadequate support. Many weak reasons can constitute a relatively strong argument. Strong, related reasons create a very strong, solid argument. Remember that you are evaluating the strength of the argument, not whether you agree with the conclusion.

5. What are inductive and deductive reasoning?
- Inductive reasoning begins by examining the details, the evidence, and from them arriving at a logical conclusion.
- Deductive reasoning begins with a given conclusion and then provides evidence to support it.

6. How should I practice critical thinking?
- Critical thinking requires time, systematic concentrated effort, re-reading, and re-examination of the argument presented.
- Avoid the barriers to critical thinking.
- Follow the four steps.
- Be persistent even when the thinking is difficult!

7. What is the definition of creative thinking?
- Creative thinking is the generation of many possible solutions to a problem.
- It is sometimes called *lateral thinking* as opposed to *vertical thinking,* which relies on logic.

MyReadingLab For more help with critical thinking, go to your learning path in MyReadingLab at www.myreadinglab.com

SELECTION 1   Essay

P REVIEW the next selection to predict its purpose and organization and to formulate your learning plan.

Activate Schema

Why are most politicians good-looking?
Did looks help Mitt Romney win the Republican presidential nomination in 2012?

Establish a Purpose for Reading

Recall a time when you might have discriminated against a person or people on the basis of appearance. Then reflect on whether you have been discriminated against because you were not nicely dressed. Do well-groomed customers receive better service from salespeople and restaurant staff? Read the selection to discover how we subconsciously favor good looks.

Integrate Knowledge While Reading

Questions have been inserted in the margin to stimulate your thinking while reading. Remember to

| Predict | Picture | Relate | Monitor | Correct | Annotate |

MyReadingLab™

THE MAGIC NUMBER OF BEAUTY
Watch a video on beauty via your ebook at www.myreadinglab.com and then answer the related questions in the VIDEO LINK section or via MyReadingLab.

Scan this QR code to hear this reading

Is this all true? Is it fair?

THE IMPORTANCE OF BEING BEAUTIFUL

Unlike many people, I was neither shocked nor surprised when the national Israeli TV network fired a competent female broadcaster because she was not beautiful. I received the news with aplomb because I had just finished extensive research into "person perception," 5 an esoteric branch of psychology that examines the many ways in which physical attractiveness—or lack of it—affects all aspects of your life.

Unless you're a 10—or close to it—most of you will respond to my findings with at least some feelings of frustration or perhaps 10 disbelief. In a nutshell, you can't overestimate the importance of being beautiful. If you're beautiful, without effort you attract hordes of friends and lovers. You are given higher school grades than your smarter—but less appealing—classmates. You compete successfully for jobs against men or women who are better qualified but less 15 alluring. Promotions and pay raises come your way more easily. You are able to go into a bank or store and cash a check with far less hassle than a plain Jane or John. And these are only a few of the many advantages enjoyed by those with a ravishing face and body.

"We were surprised to find that beauty had such powerful effects," confessed
20 Karen Dion, a University of Toronto social psychologist who does person perception research. "Our findings also go against the cultural grain. People like to think that success depends on talent, intelligence, and hard work." But the scientific evidence is undeniable.

In large part, the beautiful person can attribute his or her idyllic life to a
25 puzzling phenomenon that social scientists have dubbed the "halo effect." It defies human reason, but if you resemble Jane Fonda or Paul Newman it's assumed that you're more generous, trustworthy, sociable, modest, sensitive, interesting, and sexually responsive than the rest of us. Conversely, if you're somewhat physically unattractive, because of the "horns effect" you're stigmatized as being mean, sneaky,
30 dishonest, antisocial, and a poor sport to boot.

The existence of the halo/horns effect has been established by several studies. One, by Dion, looked at perceptions of misbehavior in children. Dion provided 243 female university students with identical detailed accounts of the misbehavior

Success in the modeling industry is largely based on physical attractiveness.
Everett Collection Inc./Alamy

349

of a seven-year-old school child. She described how the youngster had pelted
35 a sleeping dog with sharp stones until its leg bled. As the animal limped away,
yelping in pain, the child continued the barrage of stones. The 243 women were
asked to assess the seriousness of the child's offense and to give their impression of
the child's normal behavior. Clipped to half of the reports were photos of seven-
year-old boys or girls who had been rated "high" in physical attractiveness; the
40 other half contained photos of youngsters of "low" attractiveness. "We found," said
Dion, "that the opinions of the adults were markedly influenced by the appearance
of the children."

One evaluator described the stone thrower, who in her report happened to be
an angelic-looking little girl, in these glowing terms: "She appears to be a perfectly
45 charming little girl, well mannered and basically unselfish. She plays well with
everyone, but, like everyone else, a bad day may occur. . . . Her cruelty need not be
taken too seriously." For the same offense, a homely girl evoked this comment from
another evaluator: "I think this child would be quite bratty and would be a problem
to teachers. She'd probably try to pick a fight with other children. . . . She would be
50 a brat at home. All in all, she would be a real problem." The tendency throughout the
243 adult responses was to judge beautiful children as ordinarily well behaved and
unlikely to engage in wanton cruelty in the future; the unbeautiful were viewed as
being chronically antisocial, untrustworthy, and likely to commit similar transgres-
sions again.

55 The same standards apply in judging adults. The beautiful are assumed innocent. John Jurens, a colorful private investigator, was once consulted by a small
Toronto firm which employed 40 people. Ten thousand dollars' worth of merchan-
dise had disappeared, and it was definitely an inside job. After an intensive investigation, which included the use of a lie detector, Jurens was certain he had caught the
60 thief. She was 24 years old and gorgeous—a lithe princess with high cheekbones,
green eyes and shining, long black hair. The employer dismissed Jurens's proof with
the comment, "You've made a mistake. It just can't be her." Jurens commented sadly,
"A lot of people refuse to believe that beautiful can be bad."

David Humphrey, a prominent Ontario criminal lawyer, observed, "If a
65 beautiful woman is on trial, you practically have to show the judge and jury a
movie of her committing the crime in order to get a conviction." The halo and
horns effect often plays an important role in sentencing by courts. After spending
17 days observing cases heard in an Ontario traffic court, Joan Finegan, a graduate
psychology student at the University of Western Ontario, concluded that pleasant
70 and neat-looking defendants were fined an average of $6.31 less than those who
were "messy."

CAREERS

If you're a good-looking male over six feet tall, don't worry about succeeding at
your career.

75 A study of university graduates by the *Wall Street Journal* revealed that well-
proportioned wage earners who were six-foot-two or taller earned 12 percent
more than men under six feet. "For some reason," explained Ronald Burke, a York
University psychologist and industrial consultant, "tall men are assumed to be
dynamic, decisive, and powerful. In other words, born leaders." A Toronto consultant for Drake Personnel, one of the largest employment agencies in Canada,
80 recalled trying to find a sales manager for an industrial firm. He sent four highly

How might the halo or horn effect influence child development?

350

SELECTION 1

qualified candidates, only to have them all turned down. "The fifth guy I sent over was different," said the consultant. "He stood six-foot-four. He was promptly hired."

The well-favored woman also has a distinct edge when it comes to getting a job she's after. "We send out three prospects to be interviewed, and it's almost always 85 the most glamorous one that's hired," said Edith Geddes of the Personnel Centre, a Toronto agency that specializes in female placements. "We sometimes feel bad because the best qualified person is not chosen." Dr. Pam Ennis, a consultant to several large corporations, observed. "Look at the photos announcing promotions in the *Globe and Mail* business section. It's no accident that so many of the women hap-90 pen to be attractive and sexy-looking." Ennis, an elegant woman herself, attributes at least part of her career success to good looks. Her photograph appears on the brochures she mails out to companies soliciting new clients. "About eight out of 10 company presidents give me an appointment," she said. "I'm sure that many of them are curious to see me in person. Beauty makes it easier to establish rapport."

How can you capitalize on this observation?

OLD AGE

95 An elderly person's attractiveness influences the way in which he or she is treated in nursing homes and hospitals. Doctors and nurses give better care to the beautiful ones.

Lena Nordholm, an Australian behavioral scientist, presented 289 doctors, nurses, social workers, speech therapists, and physiotherapists with photos of eight attractive and unattractive men and women. They were asked to speculate about 100 what kind of patients they would be. The good-lookers were judged to be more cooperative, better motivated, and more likely to improve than their less attractive counterparts. Pam Ennis, the consultant, commented, "Because the doctor feels that beautiful patients are more likely to respond to his treatment, he'll give them more time and attention."

105 We like to think we have moved beyond the era when the most desirable woman was the beauty queen, but we haven't. Every day we make assumptions about the personality of the bank teller, the delivery man, or the waitress by their looks. The way in which we attribute good and bad characteristics still has very little to do with fact. People seldom look beyond a pleasing façade, a superficial attractiveness. But 110 the professors of person perception are not discouraged by this. They want to educate us. Perhaps by arming us with the knowledge and awareness of why we discriminate against the unattractive, we'll learn how to prevent this unwitting bigotry. Just maybe, we can change human nature.

Should you fight this or use it?

(1,371 words)

—From Sidney Katz,
"The Importance of Being Beautiful," originally appeared in *Today*,
July 24, 1982. © 1982 by Sidney Katz.

Recall

Stop to self-test, relate, and react.

Your instructor may choose to give you a true-false comprehension review.

SKILL DEVELOPMENT: THINK CRITICALLY

Apply the four-step format for evaluating the argument. Use the perforations to tear this page out for your instructor.

- **Step 1.** Identify the position on the issue. State the main point the author is arguing.

  _____

  _____

- **Step 2.** Identify the support in the argument. Make a lettered list of the major assertions of support.

  A. _____

  B. _____

  C. _____

  D. _____

  E. _____

  F. _____

  _____

  G. _____

  H. _____

  I. _____

- **Step 3.** Evaluate the support using the letters you listed in Step 2. Comment on relevance, believability, and consistency for the assertions you listed in Step 2. Label any fallacies. What support do you feel is missing?

  A–B: _____

  C–D: _____

  E: _____

  F–I: _____

  Missing support: _____

  _____

  _____

  _____

- **Step 4.** Evaluate the argument. What is your overall evaluation and why? Comment on the strength of the argument. _____

  _____

  _____

What is your opinion on the issue? _____

_____

_____

WRITE ABOUT THE SELECTION   MyReadingLab™

Complete
this **Exercise** on
myreadinglab.com

How do you plan to use the ideas from this selection to your benefit and apply the author's documented awareness of discrimination according to looks?

Response Suggestion: Discuss this from two points of view: the way you manage yourself and the way you perceive and assess others.

VIDEO LINK   MyReadingLab™

Complete
this **Exercise** on
myreadinglab.com

Now that you have read the selection and viewed the video on "The Magic Number of Beauty", check your understanding by answering with *T* (true) or *F* (false):

_____ 1. The research showed that the ratio of 1:1.618 is the key to the perception of a beautiful face.

_____ 2. The "Magic Number" refers to the height of the forehead and width of the face.

_____ 3. The research described in the video explains the "halo/horns" effect discussed in the reading selection.

_____ 4. The research shown in the video is the work of a surgeon who rebuilds damaged faces.

_____ 5. The "Magic Number" appears to apply only to Caucasians

CHECK YOUR COMPREHENSION   MyReadingLab™

Complete this **Exercise** on **myreadinglab.com**

Answer the following questions about the selection:

1. Why do we like to believe that success depends on talent, intelligence, and hard work? _____

   _____

   _____

   _____

2. How does the study of the misbehaving seven-year-old prove the existence of the halo/horns effect? _____

   _____

   _____

   _____

3. What does the statement "you get the top score" mean? _____

   _____

   _____

   _____

4. What evidence shows that the beautiful are treated differently in legal matters?

   _____

   _____

   _____

5. Why do you think tall men are assumed to be born leaders? _____

   _____

   _____

6. What does the author mean by "Beauty makes it easier to establish rapport"?

   _____

   _____

   _____

7. For the elderly, why can looks be a life-and-death matter? _____

   _____

   _____

   _____

SELECTION 2   Essay

P<small>REVIEW</small> the next selection to predict its purpose and organization and to formulate your learning plan.

Activate Schema

Contact sports such as football, ice hockey, soccer, wrestling, boxing,—even basketball and baseball are often in the news for violent incidents. Are these incidents just a natural result of competitive play or has the drive to win gone beyond the bounds of good sportsmanship? Should stricter rules be in place to protect players? Should the rules be different for professional and youth athletes? Have the fans contributed to the situation?

Establish a Purpose for Reading

Read to find out where this author stands on the controversial subject of violence in sports and why. Read critically to judge the merits of his argument and decide if you agree.

Integrate Knowledge While Reading

Questions have been inserted in the margins to stimulate your thinking while reading. Remember to

Predict	Picture	Relate	Monitor	Correct	Annotate

GIVE THE REF A GAVEL

((•─ **Scan this QR code to hear this reading**

Points to author's experience

Strong language!

In the N.F.L., hit lists are nothing new. In 1986 the Green Bay Packers targeted players by marking numbers on their sideline towels. One number marked was 9, that of the Chicago Bears quarterback Jim McMahon: he was slammed to the turf by defensive end Charles Martin of the Packers, damaging an already injured shoulder.
5 Mr. McMahon decided not to sue or press charges—I was one of his lawyers at the time—even though Mr. Martin's hit was blatantly premeditated.

Sports bounties—fees paid to team members for injuring opposing players on the field of play—are old news, too. In a nationally publicized 2005 case, a youth baseball coach offered $25 to an 8-year-old to throw at the face of his own teammate—
10 a poor hitter with autism—to knock him out of a playoff game. The recently exposed New Orleans Saints cabal, then, is more than just a contemporary pro football story.

The Saints' bounty program, in operation from 2009 to 2011 and run by the team's defensive coordinator at the time, Gregg Williams, paid bonuses to more than
15 20 Saints players for injuring key members on opposing teams through violent hits. This ruthless criminal conspiracy should be punished beyond the N.F.L. fines and

Gregg Williams, (center) Defensive Coordinator for the New Orleans Saints, ran the team's bounty program that paid bonuses to players that injured key members of opposing teams through violent hits.

Suzi Altman/ZUMA Press/Newscom

suspensions that loom. Yet, tragically, it may not be. American criminal courts have largely adopted a hands-off approach to on-field injuries, because judges deem them too messy to resolve amid the inevitable conflicting testimony. Another obstacle is
20 our culture's macho conception of sports, where players on the field are expected to "man up" in the face of threats to their safety, however extreme.

Do I agree?

Contact sports should not, of course, be routinely second-guessed by crowded courts. But should a vicious attack meant to severely injure or paralyze be over-looked just because it happened on the field of play and not in the locker room or
25 parking lot? Canada doesn't think so: In October 2000, a Canadian court convicted the Boston Bruins hockey player Marty McSorley for his brutal stick attack on an opponent's head with just seconds left in the game.

A 2000 hockey attack in the United States did manage to produce a convic-tion, but only because it occurred just seconds *after* the game-ending buzzer. In that
30 case, the victim, a teenager in a high school game, was blindsided and left paralyzed. The Illinois court would have been powerless, though, had the attack occurred seconds before.

Why would criminal laws be better?

Many states now have civil tort laws that immunize contact sports from the usual injury claims—but not from aberrant misconduct. Yet little criminal law
35 applies to the same on-field mayhem. (In fact, in 1980, a proposed federal Sports Violence Act aimed at pro sports was defeated in Congress.)

There is simply no reason football and other sports at pro, college and even high school levels should any longer treat malicious on-field actions as beyond criminal prosecution. Video technology now gives courts the tools to intervene. Almost every
40 game in America, from Pop Warner football to the N.F.L., is videotaped either by legions of frenzied parents or multiple network television cameras. Now society

needs to shed the grotesque "manning up" mentality of abusive competition as a character builder.

45 Those who participated in the Saints' bounty pool should be prosecuted as well as fined or suspended. Had such behavior occurred in a school cafeteria or on the subway or in a dark alley, this is exactly what would happen. But because it was on television as part of a Sunday entertainment ritual, it may get a pass.

The author's position?

Rather than wait for our courts to gradually wake up, state legislatures should accelerate the process by adopting laws defining and criminalizing something we 50 can call "flagrant sports battery." This could protect not just N.F.L. players, but athletes in high school and college. These laws would not apply to customary hard hits, personal fouls or the normally accepted aggressive play that is part of the game. But they would proscribe aberrant conduct like hit lists and bounties, and penalize other malicious actions. For instance, the Tennessee Titans' Albert Haynesworth 55 raking his cleats across the face of a defenseless player in 2006 (it took 30 stitches to close the wounds).

A second position?

The hands-off mentality that immunizes sports from criminal law is enabling more mayhem in America, not less. One wonders whether such tolerance might have even contributed to the look-the-other-way approach allegedly taken by Penn 60 State in the face of the highly publicized child abuse scandal that subsequently tainted its football program. America must take a civilized stand against aberrant conduct on the field as well as off. It would be criminal not to.

(771 words)

By Eldon L. Ham

Recall

Stop to talk, write, and think about the selection.

Your instructor may choose to give you a true-false comprehension review.

SKILL DEVELOPMENT: THINK CRITICALLY

Apply the four-step format for evaluating an argument. Use the perforations to tear this page out for your instructor.

- **Step 1.** Identify the position on the issue. State the main point the author is arguing.

  _____

  _____

- **Step 2.** Identify the support in the argument. Make a lettered list of the major assertions of support.

  A. _____

  _____

  _____

B. _____

_____

C. _____

_____

D. _____

_____

_____

E. _____

_____

F. _____

_____

_____

G. _____

_____

H. _____

_____

I. _____

_____

J. _____

_____

_____

K. _____

_____

L. _____

_____

- **Step 3.** Evaluate the support using the letters you listed in Step 2. Comment on relevance, believability, and consistency for the assertions you listed. Label any fallacies. What support do you feel is missing?

_____

_____

_____

_____

_____

_____

_____

_____

_____

_____

_____

_____

Missing support? _____

_____

_____

• **Step 4.** Evaluate the argument. What is your overall evaluation and why?

_____

_____

_____

_____

_____

_____

_____

_____

_____

_____

_____

_____

What is your opinion on this issue? _____

WRITE ABOUT THE SELECTION MyReadingLab™

Complete
this **Exercise** on
myreadinglab.com

After evaluating the argument presented in this essay and considering your own opinion, how would you support your position? Write a persuasive essay that clearly states your position on sports violence and supports it with strong evidence.

Response Suggestion: Begin by writing a position statement. Next, list all of the evidence you think would support your point. Then, apply Step 3 and evaluate the evidence. Select your most convincing evidence, and add to it if necessary to construct your essay. Be sure to re-read and revise the essay to present a strong argument.

CHECK YOUR COMPREHENSION   MyReadingLab™

After reading the selection, answer the following questions with *a, b, c,* or *d.* To help you analyze your strengths and weaknesses, the question types are indicated.

Main Idea _____ 1. What is the author's main point?

    a. Criminal laws should be in place to limit violence in sports.

    b. Violence in sports is caused by too much emphasis on winning.

    c. Football is the most violent American sport.

    d. Teams that reward players for violence against opponents should be punished.

Detail _____ 2. What is the author's background?

    a. He is a lawyer and professor of law.

    b. He is the legal representative of several professional football teams.

    c. He is a former football player for the Chicago Bears.

    d. He is a medical authority on sports injuries.

Detail _____ 3. What was the court's decision in Jim McMahon's case?

    a. The court found Charles Martin guilty.

    b. Charles Martin and the Green Bay Packers were found innocent of wrong-doing.

    c. The court was unable to come to a decision.

    d. McMahon did not press charges.

Detail _____ 4. What are sports bounties?

    a. Extra payments for players who help identify potential new team members.

    b. Payments for mentoring new, young players.

    c. Rewards given to players by their teams to hurt opposing players.

    d. Payments to players who identify teammates who violate the rules.

Main Idea _____ 5. Which item best describes the topic of this essay?

    a. Violence in professional football

    b. Violence and competition

    c. A solution to excessive sports violence

    d. Violence in American society

Inference _____ 6. Why was "Give the Ref a Gavel" selected as the essay's title?

    a. The author wants to give sports referees legal authority to convict athletes.

    b. It creates curiosity about the connection between sports and the law.

    c. It clearly states the author's position on sports violence.

    d. It declares sports violence as the topic of the essay.

Detail _____ 7. What was the outcome of the case in which a youth baseball coach told a player to injure an autistic teammate?

    a. The coach was suspended from coaching youth baseball.
    b. The coach was praised by the parents of most players on the team.
    c. The coach was found guilty in a court of law.
    d. The essay does not say what happened in this case.

Detail _____ 8. The author believes one reason for sports violence in the United States is that

    a. sports fans say it makes games more interesting to watch.
    b. it is a natural part of the game.
    c. American culture expects violent, aggressive behavior in sports because it proves a player's masculinity.
    d. violence is necessary to win and winning is the main goal.

Detail _____ 9. The hockey player who injured another player in a United States incident in 2000 was convicted because

    a. the victim's injuries were so severe.
    b. the incident happened in a high school game.
    c. the incident occurred after the end of the game.
    d. Illinois has strict laws against on-field sports violence.

Inference _____ 10. Which of the following situations does the author believe should *not* be subject to criminal punishment?

    a. Any serious injury that occurs during the course of a game
    b. Violent behavior that involves high school athletes
    c. Bounty systems that reward players for hurting opposing players
    d. Malicious behavior by an athlete that occurs off the field of play

Answer the following with *T* (true) or *F* (false).

Inference _____ 11. The Canadian legal system is stricter regarding violent behavior during the course of a game.

Detail _____ 12. The author believes that violent behavior in sports should be handled only by fines and suspensions.

Inference _____ 13. The author mentions that the youth baseball player was autistic to appeal to the reader's emotions.

Inference _____ 14. The author believes that the Packers and Charles Martin were at fault in Jim McMahon's injury.

Inference _____ 15. By calling the New Orleans Saints bounty system a "cabal," the author intended to put it in a negative light.

SELECTION 2

SELECTION 3 Essay

SELECTION 3

PREVIEW the next selection to predict its purpose and organization and to formulate your learning plan.

Activate Schema

What happy memories do you have of your childhood?
Who were the class bullies when you were in school?

Establish a Purpose for Reading

The author is making an argument about how boys become men. Read to understand his argument, weigh the support, and to determine your position on the issue.

Integrate Knowledge While Reading

Questions have been inserted in the margin to stimulate your thinking while reading. Remember to

| Predict | Picture | Relate | Monitor | Correct | Annotate |

How Boys Become Men

Scan this QR Code to hear this reading

Is this definition of manhood learned or genetically programmed?

Two nine-year-old boys, neighbors and friends, were walking home from school. The one in the bright blue windbreaker was laughing and swinging a heavy-looking book bag toward the head of his friend, who kept ducking and stepping back. "What's the matter?" asked the kid with the bag, whooshing it over his head. "You
5 chicken?"

His friend stopped, stood still and braced himself. The bag slammed into the side of his face, the thump audible all the way across the street where I stood watching. The impact knocked him to the ground, where he lay mildly stunned for a second. Then he struggled up, rubbing the side of his head. "See?" he said proudly.
10 "I'm no chicken."

No. A chicken would probably have had the sense to get out of the way. This boy was already well on the road to becoming a *man*, having learned one of the central ethics of his gender: Experience pain rather than show fear.

Women tend to see men as a giant problem in need of solution. They tell us that
15 we're remote and uncommunicative, that we need to demonstrate less machismo and more commitment, more humanity. But if you don't understand something about boys, you can't understand why men are the way we are, why we find it so difficult to make friends or to acknowledge our fears and problems.

Boys live in a world with its own Code of Conduct, a set of ruthless, unspoken,
20 and unyielding rules:

Don't be a goody-goody.

Never rat. If your parents ask about bruises, shrug.

Never admit fear. Ride the roller coaster, join a fistfight, do what you have to do.
Asking for help is for sissies.

25 Empathy is for nerds. You can help your best buddy, under certain circumstances. Everyone else is on his own.

Never discuss anything of substance with anybody. Grunt, shrug, dump on
teachers, laugh at wimps, talk about comic books. Anything else is risky.

Boys are rewarded for throwing hard. Most other activities—reading, befriend-
30 ing girls, or just thinking—are considered weird. And if there's one thing boys don't
want to be, it's weird.

More than anything else, boys are supposed to learn how to handle themselves.
I remember the bitter fifth-grade conflict I touched off by elbowing aside a bigger
boy named Barry and seizing the cafeteria's last carton of chocolate milk. Teased for
35 getting aced out by a wimp, he had to reclaim his place in the pack. Our fistfight, at
recess, ended with my knees buckling and my lip bleeding while my friends, sympathetic but out of range, watched resignedly.

When I got home, my mother took one look at my swollen face and screamed.
I wouldn't tell her anything, but when my father got home I cracked and confessed,
40 pleading with them to do nothing. Instead, they called Barry's parents, who restricted
his television for a week.

The following morning, Barry and six of his pals stepped out from behind a
stand of trees. "It's the rat," said Barry.

I bled a little more. *Rat* was scrawled in crayon across my desk.
45 They were waiting for me after school for a number of afternoons to follow.
I tried varying my routes and avoiding bushes and hedges. It usually didn't work.

Does this code of conduct cross cultural boundaries?

A soccer game turns violent.
Paul A. Souders/Corbis

SELECTION 3

I was as ashamed for telling as I was frightened. "You did ask for it," said my best friend. Frontier Justice has nothing on Boy Justice.

50 In panic, I appealed to a cousin who was several years older. He followed me home from school, and when Barry's gang surrounded me, he came barreling toward us. "Stay away from my cousin," he shouted, "or I'll kill you."

After they were gone, however, my cousin could barely stop laughing. "You were afraid of *them?*" he howled. "They barely came up to my waist."

55 Men remember receiving little mercy as boys; maybe that's why it's sometimes difficult for them to show any.

"I know lots of men who had happy childhoods, but none who have happy memories of the way other boys treated them," says a friend. "It's a macho marathon from third grade up, when you start butting each other in the stomach."

60 "The thing is," adds another friend, "you learn early on to hide what you feel. It's never safe to say 'I'm scared.' My girlfriend asks me why I don't talk more about what I'm feeling. I've gotten better at it, but it will *never* come naturally."

You don't need to be a shrink to see how the lessons boys learn affect their behavior as men. Men are being asked, more and more, to show sensitivity, but they dread the very word. They struggle to build their increasingly uncertain work lives

65 but will deny they're in trouble. They want love, affection, and support but don't know how to ask for them. They hide their weaknesses and fears from all, even those they care for. They've learned to be wary of intervening when they see others in trouble. They often still balk at being stigmatized as weird.

Some men get shocked into sensitivity—when they lose their jobs, their wives,

70 or their lovers. Others learn it through a strong marriage, or through their own children.

It may be a long while, however, before male culture evolves to the point that boys can learn more from one another than how to hit curve balls. Last month, walking my dog past the playground near my house, I saw three boys encircling a fourth,

75 laughing and pushing him. He was skinny and rumpled, and he looked frightened. One boy knelt behind him while another pushed him from the front, a trick familiar to any former boy. He fell backward.

When the others ran off, he brushed the dirt off his elbows and walked toward the swings. His eyes were moist and he was struggling for control.

80 "Hi," I said through the chain-link fence. "How ya doing?"

"Fine," he said quickly, kicking his legs out and beginning his swing.

(995 words)

—Jon Katz,
"How Boys Become Men." Reprinted by
permission of Sterling Lord Literistic, Inc.

Is there an age at which male friendships do change and become more supportive?

SELECTION 3

Recall

Stop to self-test, relate, and react.

Your instructor may choose to give you a true-false comprehension review.

SKILL DEVELOPMENT: THINK CRITICALLY

Apply the four-step format for evaluating the argument. Use the perforations to tear out this page for your instructor.

- **Step 1.** Identify the position on the issue. State the main point the author is arguing.

  _____

  _____

  _____

- **Step 2.** Identify the support in the argument. Make lettered lists of the major assertions of support.

  I. Boys grow up under a ruthless code of conduct that includes the following:

     A. _____

     _____

     B. _____

     _____

     C. _____

     _____

     D. _____

     _____

     E. _____

     _____

     F. _____

     _____

     G. _____

     _____

  II. As a consequence of the code of conduct, men exhibit the following behaviors:

     A. _____

     _____

     B. _____

     _____

     C. _____

     _____

     D. _____

     _____

SELECTION 3

- **Step 3.** Evaluate the support using the letters you listed in Step 2. Comment on relevance, believability, and consistency for the assertions you listed in Step 2. Label any fallacies. What support do you feel is missing?

  _____

  _____

  _____

- **Step 4.** Evaluate the argument. What is your overall evaluation and why?

  _____

  _____

  _____

  _____

  _____

  What is your opinion on the issue? _____

  _____

  _____

WRITE ABOUT THE SELECTION MyReadingLab™

Complete
this **Exercise** on
myreadinglab.com

How might men get shocked into sensitivity through loss or marriage or children? Can this happen to women also?

Response Suggestion: Discuss an example of this kind of shock. What kind of sensitivity resulted?

CHECK YOUR COMPREHENSION   MyReadingLab™

After reading the selection, answer the following questions with *a*, *b*, *c*, or *d*. To help you analyze your strengths and weaknesses, the question types are indicated.

⚙
Complete
this **Exercise** on
myreadinglab.com

Inference _____ 1. What is the best statement of the main idea of this selection?

    a. It is more difficult for boys than for girls to learn how to become responsible and fair-minded adults.

    b. Boys in today's world face a set of unspoken rules that put them in conflict with their parents.

    c. Boys grow up learning a code of conduct that affects adult male behavior.

    d. Boys in today's world are much more likely to break the unspoken rules because the rules limit their personal growth.

Inference _____ 2. In telling the story of the two nine-year-old boys, the narrator is trying to explain

    a. what it is like to walk home from school with a friend.

    b. that courage is not easy to explain to school-age children.

    c. the kind of experiences that make boys into less sensitive men.

    d. why boys often behave with violence toward one another.

Inference _____ 3. When the narrator mentions the "central ethics of his gender," he is referring to

    a. traditions of justice and honor for men.

    b. fundamental rules of male behavior.

    c. assessments of male moral character.

    d. rules that govern his own adult life.

Inference _____ 4. The narrator indicates that the "Code of Conduct" is a set of rules that

    a. fathers teach to their sons.

    b. are unwritten yet understood.

    c. teach leadership and commitment.

    d. are emphasized by teachers.

Detail _____ 5. According to the narrator, one of the worst things a boy can do is be

    a. different.

    b. uncommunicative.

    c. aggressive.

    d. friendly.

Inference _____ 6. The narrator tells the story about himself in fifth grade primarily to illustrate that

    a. he had been an unusually fearful boy.

    b. his cousin liked protecting him from other boys.

    c. he had violated the Code of Conduct and suffered the consequences.

    d. his school had a lot of boys who picked on him.

SELECTION 3

Inference _____ 7. The narrator says, "I was as ashamed for telling as I was frightened" to illustrate that he

    a. grew tired of getting beaten up by classmates.
    b. thought his parents would get mad at him.
    c. felt pressure to live by the Code of Conduct.
    d. knew he had started it all by elbowing Barry.

Inference _____ 8. The narrator uses the phrase "macho marathon" to suggest that the way boys treat each other in school

    a. seems to be never-ending.
    b. is physically exhausting.
    c. feels like a kind of workout.
    d. is ultimately channeled into organized sports.

Detail _____ 9. According to the author, men are most likely to

    a. readily admit when they are in trouble.
    b. hide weaknesses.
    c. intervene when others are in trouble.
    d. communicate feelings.

Inference _____ 10. The story the narrator tells at the end, about the four boys on the playground, seems meant to show that the

    a. narrator had been shocked into sensitivity.
    b. narrator feels that male culture is evolving.
    c. boys of today are like boys have always been.
    d. boys who were playing were not really hurt.

Answer the following with *T* (true) or *F* (false):

Inference _____ 11. The author concludes that men who learn not to fear pain as they are growing up build strong moral character in the process.

Inference _____ 12. The narrator realized that the best solution was for Barry's father to be contacted about the fight.

Inference _____ 13. The selection suggests that men dislike talking about their feelings because they learned not to talk about feelings when they were boys.

Detail _____ 14. According to the author, although progress is slow, male culture is clearly evolving and becoming generally more sensitive.

Inference _____ 15. The response "Fine" in the last line of the selection indicates that the young boy understands the "central ethic of his gender."

SELECTION 3

VOCABULARY BOOSTER

Lights, Camera, Action!

Roots	*luc, lum:* "light"	*photo:* "light"
	act, ag: "to do"	

Words with *luc, lum:* "light"

Mexican Christmas lanterns called *luminarias*—bags with sand and a lit candle inside—line streets and driveways not only in the Southwest but all over America at Christmas.

- *lucid:* clear; glowing with light; easily understood; sane

  The patient's statements were not *lucid* when she was brought into the psychiatric treatment center.

- *luminescence:* the giving off of light without heat

  A fluorescent light bulb or tube is a *luminescent* fixture that gives off light but remains cool when the mercury vapor inside the tube is acted upon by electrons.

- *luminous:* radiating or reflecting light; well lighted; shining; enlightened

  Due to the neon lighting on most of its buildings, Las Vegas is one of the most *luminous* cities in the United States at night.

- *luminary:* a celestial body; a person who is a shining example in a profession

  Muhammad Ali is still a *luminary* in the boxing world.

- *illuminate:* to supply with light; light up; to make lucid or clarify

  Let me *illuminate* the facts for you before you take misinformed action.

- *elucidate:* to make lucid or clear; explain

  Mario had to successfully *elucidate* details about his new invention to investors in order to get funding.

- *translucent:* allowing light to pass through without being transparent

  The Martinez family chose a *translucent* frosted glass that would provide privacy for the renovated bathroom.

Words with *photo:* "light"

The wrinkles and discolored skin on Brooke's face and hands were signs of *photo-aging* from spending years in the sun without sunscreen protection.

- *photogenic:* having features that look attractive in a photograph

  The supermodel was extremely *photogenic*, and she could also act.

- *photography:* a process of producing images on sensitized surfaces by the chemical action of light or other forms of radiant energy

  Sensitized film in a camera receiving sunlight or flash lighting by opening the camera's aperture or eye is a form of *photography.*

- *photogrammetry:* the process of making surveys and maps through the use of aerial photographs

  The surveying firm had its own small airplane for taking aerial photos to use in the *photogrammetry* project for the National Park Service.

- *photosensitivity:* quality of being photosensitive; abnormal sensitivity of the skin to ultraviolet light

  Some prescription drugs can cause *photosensitivity,* requiring avoidance of the sun or use of a sunscreen.

- *telephoto lens:* a camera lens that produces a large image of distant or small objects

  George's *telephoto lens* made it possible to get close-up pictures of the inaccessible waterfall.

- *photocopy:* a duplicate of a document or print made on specialized copying equipment

  Xerox, the name of the first and most well-known *photocopy* machine manufacturer, is the word commonly used to mean "copy."

Words with *act, ag:* "to do"

The *actors* and *actresses* were waiting offstage for their cues to go onstage during Act Three of the play.

- *act:* anything done, being done, or to be done; a formal decision, law, or statute; a main division of a play

  A clown performing a magic *act* entertained the children at the six-year-old's birthday party.

- *activate:* to make active; to place a military unit on active status

  Before using her new credit card, Sheila *activated* it by calling a telephone number to notify the lender that she had received the card.

- *activism:* the practice of achieving political or other goals through actions of protest or demonstration

  During the 1960s, *activism* was used to protest the Vietnam War and civil rights injustices in the United States.

- *agent:* a representative working on behalf of another

  Toby's *agent* promised to get him a film role before the end of the year.

- *agency:* an organization that provides a particular service; the place of business of an agent

  The FBI is an *agency* of the U.S. government.

- *agenda:* a list or outline of things to be done or matters to be acted or voted upon

  A vote for a new accounting firm to represent the company was on the *agenda* for the annual stockholders' meeting.

- *acting:* serving as a temporary substitute during another's absence; the art of performing in plays, films, etc.

  While the city mayor was out on maternity leave, one of the council members served as *acting* mayor.

Review

Part I

Indicate whether the following statements are true *(T)* or false *(F)*:

_____ 1. If you enjoy working with figures, a position as an Internal Revenue *agent* might be a job to consider.

_____ 2. When she began to date another man, her boyfriend considered her behavior an *act* of betrayal.

_____ 3. Some home security systems are *activated* by movement.

_____ 4. Your local township surely has an *agency* devoted to helping the homeless find shelter.

_____ 5. *Photogenic* students do not look attractive in most pictures.

_____ 6. A *telephoto lens* is used to reduce the size of the object being photographed.

_____ 7. When high-ranking executives leave their positions, companies ordinarily appoint someone to serve as an *acting* authority until a suitable replacement can be found.

_____ 8. The word *photocopy* is a synonym for the word *plagiarize.*

_____ 9. Someone who has just experienced a trauma might not be totally *lucid.*

_____ 10. People in the business of nature *photography* probably have little interest in the outdoors.

Part II

Choose an antonym from the list for each of the words below.

activism	photoaging	illuminate	photosensitivity
agent	luminous	activate	luminary

11. unknown _____

12. reacting to dark _____

13. positive effects of

    sun on skin _____

14. adversary _____

15. apathy _____

16. turn off _____

17. dull _____

18. to darken _____

CREDITS

Video screen captures reproduced with permission of BBC Motion Gallery Education: Creativity; TOMS Shoes: Changing the World; The Effects of Stress; The New Entrepreneur; DNA and the Criminal Justice System; Illiteracy in the United States; Global Warming; The Magic Number of Beauty; The American Diet.

Ruggiero, Vincent Ryan, from *The Art of Thinking*, 7th ed.; pp. 18, 237, 229. Published by Longman. Copyright © 2004 by Pearson Education, Inc. Reprinted by permission of Pearson Education, Inc., Glenview, IL.; Ruggiero, Vincent Ryan, from *The Art of Thinking*, 7th ed.; pp. 18, 237, 229. Published by Longman. Copyright © 2004 by Pearson Education, Inc. Reprinted by permission of Pearson Education, Inc., Glenview, IL.;

Answer Key to "Critical Thinking" in *Bridge to College Reading*

Note: Not all exercises are assigned, but all answers are given.

Exercise 1. Problem Solving.

1. Fill the 3 oz. glass and empty it into the 5 oz. glass. Fill it a second time and empty as much as will fit in the 5 oz. glass. Now the 3 oz. glass contains 1 oz., the 5 oz. glass has 5 oz., and the 8 oz. glass has 2 oz.

2. Empty 5 oz. into the 8 oz. glass. Then empty the 3 oz. glass. Now the 3 oz. glass is empty, the 5 oz. glass contains 1 oz., and the 8 oz. glass contains 7 oz.

3. Fill the 3 oz. glass from the 8 oz. glass. Empty 3 oz. into the 5 oz. glass. Now the 3 oz. glass will be empty and the 5 and 8 oz. glasses each contain 4 oz.

Exercise 2. Identifying Types of Barriers.

Example: 1. A   2. C   3. D   4. B

Exercise 3. Identifying Arguments

Example: 1. N   2. A   3. A   4. N   5. A

Exercise 4. Identifying the Position on the Issue

1. Sentence 2   2. Sentence 3   3. Sentence 2   4. Sentence 1   5. Sentence 3

Exercise 5. Identifying Support for the Argument

1. Position: Sentence 3   Support: Sentences 1, 2
2. Position: Sentence 3   Support: Sentences 1, 2
3. Position: Sentence 2   Support: Sentences 1, 3
4. Position: Sentence 1   Support: Sentences 2, 3, 4
5. Position: Sentence 3   Support: Sentences 1, 2

Exercise 6. Identifying Fallacies

1. B   2. C   3. A   4. B   5. B   6. A   7. C   8. A   9. B   10. C

Exercise 7. Evaluating Your Own Decision Making. Answers will vary.

Exercise 8. Applying the Four Steps to Different Arguments.

Argument 1: Child Criminal Offenders
Step 1: Sentence 4. Step 2: Sentences 1, 2, 3, 5
Step 3. Evaluation: 1 and 2 are factual explanations. Sentence 3 is bandwagon. Sentence 5 is oversimplification. The support is weak in all 3 areas: relevance, believability and consistency.
Missing Support: Statistical data about actual criminal cases with children.
Step 4: The argument lacks evidence. It is supported only with opinions.

Argument 2: Invasion of Privacy.

Step 1: Sentence 7. Step 2: Sentences 4, 5, 6.

Step 3. Evaluation: Sentence 4 is opinion and "despicable" and "insidious" are emotional words. Sentence 5 might be true, but types of callers should be included. Sentence 6 is vague and appeals to emotions. The support states both the values and the potential harm. It contains unnecessarily emotional language but is still relevant and believable.

Missing support. Statistics on fear of calling and why

Step 4. Argument has merit because it calls for additional numbers for callers who want it but now a complete change of the existing system. It is a moderately strong argument.

Remaining answers are not given here.

Vocabulary Lessons

Pronunciation Key

Pronunciation Key

Learning how to pronounce words will make you more likely to use the words you learn. Sometimes you may even know a word by sound and not recognize the way it is spelled; after you sound out the word, you may realize that you know it. The pronunciation guide on the opposite page will help you sound out the words in this text. The pronunciations are given in the Word List for each chapter.

The symbols used here are found in several dictionaries. There are slight differences in pronunciation symbols used in dictionaries, but a pronunciation guide is usually found in the front of a dictionary and at the bottom of each page. If you are unsure of how to pronounce a word, ask your instructor or another knowledgeable person to say the word for you. You can also hear the words for this text on the book's Web site.

Accent Marks and Stress

An important skill in pronouncing words is learning how to decipher accent marks. The primary accent mark (′) is a dark mark. Any word that has more than one syllable will have a primary accent mark. This mark tells you which syllable to add stress to when you pronounce it. For example, in the word *replace* [ri plās′], more emphasis is put on the second syllable as illustrated by the primary accent mark.

In words that have more than two syllables, there is sometimes a secondary accent mark (′). This mark is lighter than the primary accent mark. This mark symbolizes a stress on the syllable but not as strong a stress as on the syllable with the primary accent mark next to it. For example, in the word *appetizer* [ap′ ə tī′ zer], the third syllable has some stress symbolized by the secondary accent mark, but the first syllable has the strongest stress as shown by the primary accent mark.

Pronunciation Differences

The pronunciations given in dictionaries are considered the standard pronunciations, although some words can be pronounced more than one way, and both are considered correct. For example, consider the word *Caribbean* [kar′ ə bē′ ən, kə rib′ ē ən]. You will hear different pronunciations by English speakers worldwide. British, Canadian, Australian, and American speakers may not even understand each other at times due to different pronunciations of the same word. Even within a country, people do not sound the same. Regional differences are found throughout the United States; Texans, New Yorkers, and Californians do not always sound the same. Differences in pronunciations are also due to other factors such as education and age. The dynamics of language make learning new words and learning about words an exciting enterprise.

VOWEL SOUNDS

Symbol	Examples
a	**a**ct, b**a**t
ā	d**ay**, **age**
âr	**air**, d**are**
ä	f**a**ther, st**a**r
e	**e**dge, t**e**n
ē	sp**ee**d, mon**ey**
ə*	**a**go, syst**e**m, eas**i**ly, c**o**mpete, foc**u**s
ēr	d**ear**, p**ier**
i	f**i**t, **i**s
ī	sk**y**, b**i**te
o	n**o**t, w**a**sp
ō	n**o**se, **o**ver
ô	l**a**w, **o**rder
oi	n**oi**se, enj**oy**
o͞o	tr**ue**, b**oo**t
oo	p**u**t, l**oo**k
y͞oo	c**u**te, **u**nited
ou	l**ou**d, c**ow**
u	f**u**n, **u**p
ûr	l**ear**n, **ur**ge, butt**er**, w**or**d

*This symbol, the schwa, represents the sound of unaccented vowels. It sounds like "uh."

CONSONANT SOUNDS

Symbol	Examples
b	**b**ack, ca**b**
ch	**ch**eap, ma**tch**, pic**t**ure
d	**d**oor, hea**d**
f	**f**an, lea**f**, **ph**one
g	**g**ive, do**g**
h	**h**er, be**h**ave
j	**j**ust, pa**g**e
k	**k**ing, ba**k**e, **c**ar
l	**l**eaf, ro**ll**
m	**m**y, ho**m**e
n	**n**ote, rai**n**
ng	si**ng**, ba**n**k
p	**p**ut, sto**p**
r	**r**ed, fa**r**
s	**s**ay, pa**ss**
sh	**sh**ip, pu**sh**
t	**t**o, le**t**
th	**th**in, wi**th**
TH	**TH**at, ba**TH**e
v	**v**alue, li**v**e
w	**w**ant, a**w**ay
y	**y**es, on**i**on
z	**z**oo, ma**z**e, ri**s**e
zh	plea**s**ure, vi**s**ion

Composition

The Midterm

Composition

The Midterm

Review Tips

Next week is the in-class essay midterm. To help you prepare for it, this sheet reviews some of the important concepts we have covered so far this semester. You will be writing about one of the four short stories we have read in the last two weeks. You will be explaining how the story is significant to today's world even though it was written more than one hundred years ago.

Amy E. Olson

1. Make your **thesis** clear. The reader should know what your proposal is within the first or second paragraph of your essay. Your **intention** is to convince your reader that this short story is still important to read because it relates in one or more ways to society today.

2. You may need to **refute** other points of view. Think about ways an opponent might disagree with you and show how his or her view isn't as strong as yours.

3. Make your examples **vivid**. Pick scenes from the story that dramatically support your view. Pick examples from today's world that clearly show a connection to the events or ideas in the short story.

4. Remember the importance of **coherence** as you organize your essay. Pick a method of organization that allows the reader to clearly follow each of your points, and make sure each of your examples relates to your thesis.

5. Watch your **diction**. Your choice of words helps to set the tone of your essay. This is a formal essay, so you should avoid using slang words or other informal types of language.

6. You will need to **cite** passages from the story in your paper. As you **annotate** the story, look for lines and scenes that will help to make your point. Write comments in the margins, star important passages, and underline sections you may want to quote or **paraphrase**. You do not want to **plagiarize** any passages, so be sure to record the page number in parentheses after any quotations or paraphrases you use. Stealing other people's words or ideas is a serious offense that can get you expelled from college. Below are examples of quoting and paraphrasing to remind you of the correct formats.

Quotation: Use the writer's own words, and put the words in quotation marks.

The reader becomes skeptical of the narrator's sanity when he reveals his reason for committing murder: "Whenever it fell upon me, my blood ran cold; and so by degrees—very gradually—I made up my mind to take the life of the old man, and thus rid myself of the eye forever" (Poe 2).

Paraphrase: Put the writer's words into your own words, and do not use quotation marks.

The narrator says he isn't mad, but the reader begins to wonder how sane he can be when he reveals that he slowly decides to kill the old man because he is terrorized by the old man's eye (Poe 2).

If you take the time to prepare for the in-class essay by rereading the short stories, marking important passages in the stories, and thinking about how the stories relate to today's world, you should have no problem in writing your essay.

Predicting

For each set, write the definition on the line next to the word to which it belongs. If you are unsure, return to the reading, and underline any context clues you find. After you've made your predictions, check your answers against the Word List at the end of the chapter. Place a checkmark in the box next to each word whose definition you missed. These are the words you'll want to study closely.

Set One

to disprove	a plan	consistency	clear or dramatic
a proposal that is defended by argument			

❑ 1. **thesis** (line 8) _____

❑ 2. **intention** (line 9) _____

❑ 3. **refute** (line 11) _____

❑ 4. **vivid** (line 13) _____

❑ 5. **coherence** (line 15) _____

Set Two

to quote as an example or expert	the choice and use of words	to make notes or comments on
to use the words or ideas of someone else as one's own		to express in other words

❑ 6. **diction** (line 18) _____

❑ 7. **cite** (line 20) _____

❑ 8. **annotate** (line 20) _____

❑ 9. **paraphrase** (line 22) _____

❑ 10. **plagiarize** (line 23) _____

Self-Tests

1 Circle the correct meaning of each vocabulary word.

1. cite:	to exaggerate	to quote
2. diction:	choice of words	choice of type size
3. plagiarize:	to quote	to steal
4. paraphrase:	to use an author's words	to express in other words
5. refute:	to disprove a statement	to agree with a statement
6. annotate:	to write a book	to make notes in a book
7. coherence:	illogical organization	orderly relationship
8. vivid:	brilliant	dull
9. intention:	a plan	clueless
10. thesis:	a proposal	a refusal

2 Match a word to each example. Use each word once.

VOCABULARY LIST

annotate	vivid	paraphrase	diction	plagiarize
cite	refute	thesis	intention	coherence

1. Shirley Jackson's story begins pleasantly: "The morning of June 27th was clear and sunny, with the fresh warmth of a full-summer day" (3). _____

2. a neon green skirt worn with a dazzling pink blouse _____

3. According to Austen, it isn't how long it takes but how good it is that matters. _____

4. I *really want* a new car. I *desire* a new car. I *need* a new car. _____

5. To put it in my own words, ask not what your country can do for you, but what you can do for your country. _____

6. *Good example of the boy's home life; Clear relationship to incidents in par. 3* _____

7. Some people in the company believe the change in policy is causing problems, but they need to look ahead and see that, after some initial scheduling problems, all employees will have more time to spend on leisure pursuits. For example, when the rotation begins.... _____

8. More math classes need to be offered so that students can graduate on time. _____

9. The plan is to get up at 6:00 and be on the road by 6:30. _____

10. The architect did a great job of uniting the addition with the unique qualities of the 1930s cottage. _____

3 Finish the sentences using the vocabulary words. Use each word once.

VOCABULARY LIST

refuted	thesis	plagiarize	paraphrase	cite
vivid	diction	coherence	intention	annotate

1. My niece has a(n) _____ imagination. She can turn a tree and a stick into a castle and a wand and spend hours in her fairy kingdom.

2. The _____ of my research paper is that more Neighborhood Watch programs will make our city safer.

3. Because I was writing for children, I paid extra attention to my _____. I didn't want to use words they wouldn't understand.

4. I was confused when reading Isabel's paper because it lacked _____. First she told about a trip to a farm, and then she described her math test, and her topic was supposed to be about a favorite building.

5. It can be hard to _____ because you want to get the writer's idea correct, but you can't use any of the writer's key words or the same sentence pattern.

6. When I _____ a reading, I mark important scenes and note questions that I might want to bring up in a class discussions.

7. The _____ of the orientation meeting was to help students, not to confuse them.

8. I thought my idea for the party was the best, but after Tony _____ my points, I saw how expensive and impractical my plan was.

9. I didn't mean to _____, but I didn't take very good notes, and I used the author's words four separate times without putting quotation marks around those passages.

10. My sister says she is never late; however, I can _____ five times she was late in the last two weeks.

Identify the two vocabulary words represented in the photos.

Gerald Warnken, Jr.

Amy E. Olsen

1. _____

2. _____

Word Wise

Collocations

It is my *intention to* be the first in line at the Grand Opening Sale tomorrow.

You should be able to easily identify the *thesis statement* in each of the three essays we will be reading now that you know what to look for.

Interesting Etymologies

Plagiarize comes from the Latin *plagium,* "kidnapping," which comes from *plaga* meaning "net or snare." Obviously the meaning "to use the words or ideas of someone else as one's own" is an example of kidnapping. The word has been in use since the late 1500s.

Vivid comes from the Latin *vividus,* "spirited, lively," which comes from *vivus,* "alive." The word originated in the early 1600s. In reference to colors, its first use is recorded in 1665. The use of the word to mean "active or lively" when referring to the imagination or an interest in something is first reported in 1853.

Interactive Exercise

Read the paragraph below, and use it to help you complete the sentence starters.

The sky was gray, and thunder sounded in the distance. It was almost nightfall, and Helena was far from a place to rest. She had hoped to make it to her aunt's house before dark, but the adventure by the river had slowed her down. She hadn't expected to meet a family of trolls underneath the bridge. She had always thought the stories about trolls were ridiculous, but today she discovered that they could be true. The trolls had actually been quite nice. They even offered her homemade cookies. Though she hadn't really believed in trolls, if she did, she wouldn't have imagined them baking cookies. A streak of lightening lit up the sky, and the next blast of thunder sounded closer. Then the rain began to pour. Helena ran to a nearby tree, whose branches protected her from the rain. She took the last chocolate chip cookie out of her pocket and nibbled on it as she contemplated what to do next.

1. If I was going to annotate this paragraph, I would comment on _____ _____

2. If I was writing a review of this story, my thesis would be _____ _____

3. In my review, I would cite the following sentence: _____ because _____

4. The writer's intention is _____

5. I feel the writer's coherence is _____

6. The diction in the passage shows _____

7. The most vivid part of the paragraph is _____

8. I would paraphrase the sentence "She hadn't expected to meet a family of trolls underneath the bridge" this way: _____

9. It would be difficult for someone to refute my review because _____ _____

10. It is wrong to plagiarize because _____

HINT

Study Often

Don't try to fit all of your studying into one session before a test. Look at your notes for a class often. Review them the day you write them while the information is fresh in your mind in case you want to add further details. Also do a weekly review of your notes so that, as you learn new material, you can build on the old information. These same ideas apply to learning vocabulary. Look often at the flash cards and word maps you make. Even taking ten minutes a day to go over the words for that week will help you remember the meanings. While you are waiting for another class to start, for a friend who is late, or for the bus to come, take some of that time to review the words.

Word List

annotate
[an′ ō tāt′]

v. to make notes or comments on or in the margins (usually in reference to a book)

cite
[sīt]

v. 1. to quote as an example or expert
2. to give as support or proof

coherence
[kō hēr′ əns, kō her′-]

n. the quality of a logical or orderly relationship of parts; consistency; unity

diction
[dik′ shən]

n. 1. the choice and use of words in speech or writing
2. distinctness of speech

intention
[in ten′ shən]

n. a plan; an aim that guides action

paraphrase
[par′ ə frāz′]

v. to express in other words

n. a restatement of a passage using other words

plagiarize
[plā′ jə rīz′]

v. to use the words or ideas of someone else as one's own; to steal from another's writing

refute
[ri fyoo t′]

v. to disprove; to show that a person or statement is wrong by argument or proof

thesis
[thē′ sis]

n. a proposal that is defended by argument

vivid
[viv′ id]

adj. 1. clear; striking; dramatic
2. brilliant; having extremely bright colors
3. active; lively

Words to Watch

Which words would you like to practice with a bit more? Pick 3–5 words to study, and list them below. Write the word and its definition, and compose your own sentence using the word correctly. This extra practice could be the final touch to learning a word.

Word	Definition	Your Sentence
1. _____	_____	_____
2. _____	_____	_____
3. _____	_____	_____
4. _____	_____	_____
5. _____	_____	_____

Mathematics

Work It Out

Mathematics

Work It Out

Complete the questions on this introductory worksheet by the next class meeting. These topics will be the focus of the class for the first half of the semester. Bring any concerns you have about these exercises to the next class meeting, or stop by during my office hours.

1. The company's monthly **quota** is 800 units. Use the following graph to answer the questions about the company.

    A. How many months has the company met its allowance? _____

    B. Use **statistics** to show how far the company was below its quota for March. _____

    C. Which month was the company 50% below its quota? _____

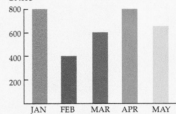

2. Use the following prices to figure out the **mean**, **median**, and mode for a pair of pants at a local department store.

    $12, $20, $20, $25, $30, $44, $59

    A. Mean, or average (add up all the numbers and divide by the number of items) _____

    B. Median (or middle number) _____

    C. Mode (the number that appears the most often) _____

3. **Calculate** what the **variable** x and the variable y stand for in the following equations.

    A. $3 + x + 6 = 14$ $x = $ _____

    B. $4y + 11 = 27$ $y = $ _____

    C. $2x - 6 = 60$ $x = $ _____

4. Use the lines to the right to answer the following questions.

    A. Next to each line, indicate whether the line is **horizontal**, vertical, or diagonal.

    B. Use the variable A to indicate where two lines **intersect** and the variable B to show where three lines cross.

    C. Label the **parallel** lines C.

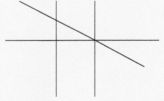

5. Which of the following shapes is **symmetrical**? _____

    Does the balanced shape cause a different reaction in you than the other shape? If it does, why do you think that might be so? _____

A.

B.

Predicting

For each set, write the definition on the line next to the word to which it belongs. If you are unsure, return to the reading, and underline any context clues you find. After you've made your predictions, check your answers against the Word List at the end of the chapter. Place a checkmark in the box next to each word whose definition you missed. These are the words you'll want to study closely.

Set One

numerical facts   the middle number in a specified sequence of numbers   the average   to figure
a part of a total amount or an allowance

- ❑ 1. **quota** (line 4) _____
- ❑ 2. **statistics** (line 7) _____
- ❑ 3. **mean** (line 10) _____
- ❑ 4. **median** (line 10) _____
- ❑ 5. **calculate** (line 16) _____

Set Two

balanced   lines that go in the same direction and never meet   to cross   parallel to level ground
a symbol that represents a changeable amount

- ❑ 6. **variable** (line 16) _____
- ❑ 7. **horizontal** (line 21) _____
- ❑ 8. **intersect** (line 23) _____
- ❑ 9. **parallel** (line 25) _____
- ❑ 10. **symmetrical** (line 26) _____

Self-Tests

1 Put a T for true or F for false next to each sentence.

_____ 1. If a person decides to take a statistics class, it would help to be good at math.

_____ 2. It is a good idea to calculate how much your purchases will be before you check out to make sure you have enough money.

_____ 3. The mean for the three ages 11, 19, and 33 is 21.

_____ 4. Having a small triangle on one side of a picture and five large circles on the other side would be a symmetrical arrangement.

_____ 5. The weather in the United States is rarely variable.

_____ 6. Elevators usually travel horizontally.

_____ 7. The parallels between pyramid designs in Egypt and Central America have caused some people to speculate that the pyramids were built by aliens.

_____ 8. When a vertical and a horizontal line cross, they intersect.

_____ 9. It could be difficult to fill one's quota of strawberries to be picked if the person stops to eat several every five minutes.

_____ 10. The median number in the following series is 9: 2, 4, 9, 12, 15, 23, 35.

2 Complete each sentence using the vocabulary words. Use each word once.

VOCABULARY LIST

calculate	horizontal	intersect	quota	symmetrical
mean	median	parallel	statistics	variable

1. The most recent _____ show that enrollment is up 20% in all math classes this semester compared with the last two semesters.

2. Our study showed that people were more attracted to the display with the _____ design than to the one with the irregular pattern.

3. From my past experiences of driving north, I _____ that it will take us nine hours to reach Grandma's house.

4. When I worked in retail, my hours were _____. I started anywhere between 7 a.m. and 6 p.m., and I worked from four to eight hours a day.

5. The new road has been designed to _____ the town, so tourists have to come right through downtown, and we hope that will cause them to stop and do some shopping or spend the night.

6. As soon as I got my _____ of donations for the auction, I quit asking. Even though it is for a worthy cause, I am not really comfortable asking businesses to contribute items.

Dan A. Tallorin

7. The _____ house price in our city has dropped 30% in the last year.

8. I was offered a(n) _____ transfer at work. I would have stayed at the same level but would have been in a different department. Because I like the people I work with now, I turned it down.

9. The _____ structures, so perfectly spaced in the park, make for an ideal passageway.

10. I calculated the _____ for my math test scores by dividing the sum of my scores by the number four (that is how many tests we have had), and I am averaging 87%.

3 Complete the following analogies.

VOCABULARY LIST

parallel	horizontal	intersect	median	symmetrical
mean	quota	calculate	statistics	variable

1. long : short :: vertical : _____

2. skyscrapers : tall :: interest rates : _____

3. old : elderly :: compute: _____

4. boring : exciting :: unbalanced : _____

5. 10, 15, 20, 24, 43, 56 = 22 : _____ :: poodle : dog

6. portion : _____ :: silence : hush

7. hem : a skirt :: _____ : a circle

8. railroad tracks : _____ :: fog : weather

9. house : home :: average : _____

10. government : _____ :: cook : stove

Identify the two vocabulary words represented in the drawings.

1. _____

2. _____

Word Wise

Collocations

The pilot took a *calculated risk* and landed the plane in an onion field minutes before running out of fuel.

The *median income* for a job as a teacher in my state is $35,000 a year.

I am enjoying the story line about the *parallel universe* more than the one about life on Earth in the recent Tremendous Team comic book series.

Word Pairs

Symmetrical/Asymmetrical: Symmetrical means "balanced." Asymmetrical means "unbalanced; irregular." The symmetrical building attracted people to its graceful design. The asymmetrical building shocked people and displeased several of them.

Connotations and Denotations

Quota: denotation—"the number or percentage of people of a specified type allowed into a group." In recent years, quota systems have upset people, and *quota* has taken on a negative connotation for many people. How do you feel when you hear that a college or other organization must fulfill a quota for admitting people?

Interactive Exercise

Answer the following questions to practice using the vocabulary words.

Imagine you eat lunch out Monday through Friday for a week. On Monday, you have a tuna sandwich that costs $6.60; on Tuesday, teriyaki chicken for $6.00; on Wednesday, curry for $5.20; on Thursday, a burrito for $4.80; and on Friday, a slice of pizza for $2.40. Use this information to answer the following questions.

1. Calculate the median price of your five meals. _____

2. Calculate the mean price of your five meals. _____

3. Supply the answers for these statistics:

    A. One day you spend 50% less than on the previous day. Which day was that? _____

    B. One day you spent 10% more than on the following day. Which day was that? _____

4. If your quota for meals out a month is 18, and, so far this month, you have eaten out four other times besides the five times this week, what percentage of your quota have you used up? _____

5. Calculate what the variable x stands for in these equations:

    A. Monday's meal $+$ Friday's meal $+ x = \$15.00$
       $x =$ _____ (which day's meal)
    B. A burrito $+$ curry $- x = \$ 7.60$
       $x =$ _____ (which food item)

Answer the following questions about the sketch of the house.

6. How many horizontal lines are in the frame of the house? _____

7. How many sets of parallel lines are in the frame of the house? _____

8. What are two symmetrical elements of the house? _____ _____

9. What area of the front yard does the entrance pathway intersect? _____

HINT

Multiple Meanings

Most words have more than one meaning. For some words, one meaning is used more often than the others, but for other words, two or three of their meanings are equally used. For example, a bat is "a wooden club used to hit a ball" or "a mammal that flies, usually at night." Both meanings for bat are frequently used. However, among the meanings for *cure* as a noun, most people would know "a means of healing" and possibly "a process of preserving meat, fish, etc. by smoking, salting, or the like," but the meaning of "the office or district of a curate or parish priest" is not seen as often. If you ever see a word used in a way you are not familiar with, check a dictionary to see if it has another meaning you do not know. You may be surprised at how many meanings even a short and seemingly simple word may have. *Webster's Collegiate Dictionary* lists twenty-four meanings for the word *so*. Be prepared for the fun and challenges that multiple meanings provide.

Word List

calculate
[kal′ kyə lāt′]
v. to figure; to compute; to evaluate

horizontal
[hôr′ i zon′ tl, hor′-]
adj. 1. parallel to level ground
2. flat; at the same level

intersect
[in′ tər sekt′]
v. to cross; to meet at a point; to cut through

mean
[mēn]
n. the result found by dividing the sum of a set of numbers by the number of items in the set; the average

adj. holding a middle position

median
[mē′ dē ən]
n. the middle number in a specified sequence of numbers (if the sequence has an even number of numbers, the average of the two middle numbers)

adj. relating to or located in the middle

parallel
[par′ ə lel′]
adj. 1. lines that go in the same direction and never meet
2. alike in some form

n. a likeness

quota
[kwō′ tə]
n. 1. a part of a total amount; an allotment; an allowance
2. the number or percentage of people of a specified type allowed into a group

statistics
[stə tis′ tiks]
n. 1. (used with a plural v.) data; numerical facts
2. (used with a singular v.) the science that deals with the study of numerical data

symmetrical
[si me′ tri kəl]
adj. regular in arrangement of matching parts; balanced

variable
[vâr′ ē ə bəl]
n. 1. a symbol that represents a changeable amount
2. something that may change

adj. changeable; inconstant

Words to Watch

Which words would you like to practice with a bit more? Pick 3–5 words to study, and list them below. Write the word and its definition, and compose your own sentence using the word correctly. This extra practice could be the final touch to learning a word.

Word	Definition	Your Sentence
1. _____	_____	_____
_____		
2. _____	_____	_____
_____		
3. _____	_____	_____
_____		
4. _____	_____	_____
_____		
5. _____	_____	_____
_____		

Word Parts I

From Chapter 5 of *Academic Vocabulary: Academic Words*, Fifth Edition. Amy E. Olsen. Copyright © 2013 by Pearson Education, Inc.
All rights reserved.

Word Parts I

Look for words with these **prefixes, roots**, and/or **suffixes** as you work through this course. Learning basic word parts can help you figure out the meanings of unfamiliar words.

prefix: a word part added to the beginning of a word that changes the meaning of the root
root: a word's basic part with its essential meaning
suffix: a word part added to the end of a word; indicates the part of speech

Word Part	Meaning	Examples and Definitions
Prefixes		
ambi-	both, around	*ambivalence:* having conflicting feelings; feeling both ways *ambiance:* the atmosphere around a person
mag-	great, large	*magnitude:* greatness *magnify:* to make larger
post-	after, behind	*posterity:* future generations; those that come after *postdoctoral:* pertaining to study done after receiving a doctorate
Roots		
-duc-	to lead	*conducive:* leading toward *induce:* lead one to do
-lev-	lift, light, rise	*alleviate:* to lighten; to reduce *elevator:* a device that lifts people
-pon-, -pos-	to put, to place	*proponent:* one who puts one's point forward *juxtaposition:* an act of placing close together
-not-	mark	*annotate:* to mark or make notes on *denote:* to be a mark or sign of
-vi-, -viv-	life, to live	*vivid:* filled with life; dramatic *revive:* to bring back to life
Suffixes		
-dom (makes a noun)	state, condition, or quality of	*martyrdom:* the state of suffering *freedom:* the condition of being free
-tude (makes a noun)	state or quality of	*magnitude:* the quality of being great *gratitude:* the state of being thankful

Self-Tests

1 Read each definition, and choose the appropriate word. Use each word once. The meaning of the word part is underlined to help you make the connection. Refer to the Word Parts list if you need help.

VOCABULARY LIST

survive	attitude	ambidextrous	levitate	postbellum
wisdom	conductor	deposit	denote	magnum

1. capable of using <u>both</u> hands _____
2. occurring <u>after</u> a war _____
3. the person who <u>leads</u> the orchestra _____
4. <u>to put</u> money in the bank _____
5. to be a <u>mark</u> or sign of _____
6. to continue <u>to live</u> _____
7. a <u>large</u> wine bottle _____
8. a <u>state</u> of mind about something _____
9. the <u>quality of</u> having good judgment _____
10. to float or <u>lift</u> a person or thing _____

2 Finish the sentences with the meaning of each word part. Use each meaning once. The word part is underlined to help you make the connection.

VOCABULARY LIST

after	great	lead	life	rise
condition	put	mark	state of	around

1. She received a <u>post</u>humous award: it was given to her the year _____ she died.
2. My free<u>dom</u> is important to me. It is a(n) _____ that I don't take for granted.
3. I moved the <u>lev</u>er to make the door _____.
4. I use a pen when I an<u>not</u>ate a book so I can easily see every _____ I make.
5. My friends tried to se<u>duce</u> me into going to the movies, but they couldn't _____ me astray; I stayed home and studied.
6. His answers were <u>ambi</u>guous: he kept dancing _____ my questions.
7. I trans<u>pos</u>ed the numbers on my check: I _____ the "1" before the "2" and ended up being nine dollars short.
8. Their house is <u>magni</u>ficent; everything about it is _____.
9. Katy is a con<u>viv</u>ial person; she is so sociable and full of _____.
10. In ancient Rome, captives often lived a life of servi<u>tude</u>; they spent the rest of their lives in a(n) _____ slavery.

3 Finish the story using the word parts below. Use each word part once. Your knowledge of word parts, as well as the context clues, will help you create the correct words. If you do not understand the meaning of a word you have made, check the dictionary for the definition or to see whether the word exists.

WORD PARTS

lev	ambi	viv	mag	duc
tude	post	pos	not	dom

A Revealing Walk

After three days of snow and a six-hour power outage, the (1)_____ance in the apartment was rather unpleasant. We had been cooped up for too long. One roommate was beginning to make rude remarks about my hair, while I was insulting his taste in clothing. Our other roommate was curled up in the corner with a book in front of his face trying to ignore us. We were all suffering from bore(2)_____ and needed something to amuse ourselves.

Amy E. Olsen

I decided it was best to ex(3)_____e myself to the elements as the snow was beginning to melt. When I first ventured out, I wondered what could have in(4)_____ed me to come out in the cold, but then I remembered our bickering, and I thought the walk was still a good idea. Little did I realize that the walk would be a(n) (5)_____able one. The air was fresh, and it felt good to be moving. As I looked at the splendor of the snow-covered trees, the (6)_____nitude of the problems in the apartment began to seem so small. Then I saw the flowers poking out of the snow. Their beauty re(7)_____ed my spirits. To see life blooming again made me happy. Maybe the long winter we had been having would soon be over. I felt such grati(8)_____ to the lovely flowers. The return of life made me think about (9)_____erity and what I most wanted to leave for future generations. Maybe the re(10)_____ance of a few flowers in the snow to the big issues of life and death wouldn't hit most people, but for some reason those flowers made me look at the world in a whole new way.

4 Pick the best definition for each underlined word using your knowledge of word parts. Circle the word part in each of the underlined words.

a. the state of having enough

b. a person who puts one's point forward

c. liveliness

d. the condition of being famous

e. surrounding

f. showing a great spirit

g. a raised area of earth along a river

h. to lead or bring in

i. marks or symbols used in a particular field

j. examination of a body after death

_____ 1. Diana's <u>vivacity</u> kept the party alive: she danced and laughed all night.

_____ 2. The <u>levee</u> wasn't high enough to keep the water from flooding the houses.

_____ 3. The <u>postmortem</u> revealed that the man had been poisoned.

_____ 4. The musical <u>notations</u> confused me at the beginning of my piano class, but after a few weeks, I could easily read them.

_____ 5. The <u>magnanimous</u> donation helped us build the hospital sooner than we expected.

_____ 6. Keri didn't let <u>stardom</u> go to her head. Even after appearing in three blockbuster movies, she was still the same sweet girl when she came home for the holidays.

_____ 7. I found the <u>ambient</u> music in the restaurant annoying instead of relaxing.

_____ 8. Four years after his retirement, the community decided it was time to <u>induct</u> Phillips into the local Sports Hall of Fame.

_____ 9. We have a <u>plentitude</u> of food with the pizza I got and the chicken you brought.

_____ 10. She was a <u>proponent</u> of the new park from the beginning; she continually let people know that the neighborhood kids needed a safe place to play.

5 A good way to remember word parts is to pick one word that uses a word part and understand how that word part functions in the word. Then you can apply that meaning to other words that have the same word part. Use the words to help you match the word part to its meaning.

Set One

_____ 1. **ambi-:** ambiguous, ambivalent, ambiance

_____ 2. **mag-:** magnificent, magnify, magnitude

_____ 3. **-dom:** martyrdom, freedom, wisdom

_____ 4. **-duc-:** induce, conductor, seduce

_____ 5. **-vi-, -viv-:** viable, vivid, revive

a. life, to live

b. to lead

c. state, condition, or quality of

d. both, around

e. great, large

Set Two

_____ 6. **-pon-, -pos-:** proponent, juxtaposition, deposit

_____ 7. **-lev-:** levity, levitate, elevator

_____ 8. **post-:** posterity, postdoctoral, posthumously

_____ 9. **-not-:** annotate, denote, notation

_____ 10. **-tude:** magnitude, gratitude, multitude

f. lift, light, rise

g. state or quality of

h. after, behind

i. to put, to place

j. mark

Interactive Exercise

Use the dictionary to find a word you don't know that uses the word part listed below. Write the meaning of the word part, the word, and the definition. If your dictionary has the etymology (history) of the word, see how the word part relates to the meaning, and write the etymology after the definition.

Word Part	Meaning	Word	Definition and Etymology
EXAMPLE: *mag-*	great, large	magnifico	1. a Venetian nobleman 2. any person of high rank (from Latin "magnificus, magn(us)," large, great)
1. *ambi-*			
2. *-duc-*			
3. *-lev-*			
4. *post-*			
5. *-vi-* or *-viv-*			

Match each photograph to one of the word parts below, and write the meaning of the word part.

mag-   post-   -lev-   -vi-/-viv-   -dom

Amy E. Olsen

Amy E. Olsen

1. _____

2. _____

Word Wise

Context Clue Mini-Lesson

This lesson uses antonyms—words that mean the opposite of the unknown word—as the clues. Circle the antonyms you find for the underlined words and then write a word that is the opposite of the antonym as your definition of the word.

When I went to visit, Marsha's greeting was <u>cordial</u>. A few people had told me that she was often cold and unfriendly, but I did not find her so. We merrily chatted for an hour, when suddenly she cast an <u>aspersion</u> on my blouse. I thought she was going to compliment it when she mentioned the unusual color, but I was wrong. I was <u>dejected</u>. I had been so excited about making a new friend. What I had hoped to be the beginning of a new friendship turned out to be its <u>demise</u>.

Your Definition

1. Cordial _____

2. Aspersion _____

3. Dejected _____

4. Demise _____

HINT

Etymologies

An etymology is the history of a word. Some dictionaries will explain in an entry how the word came into existence. Words can be developed in several ways such as being made up, coming from a person's name, or evolving from foreign languages. Reading a word's etymology can sometimes help you remember the meaning. For example, the word **dismal** comes from the Latin *dies mali*. *Dies* is the plural of day and *mali* the plural of evil. In Middle English the word meant "unlucky days." There were two days in each month that were thought to be unfavorable, and it was believed a person shouldn't start anything important on those days. These days were even marked on calendars during the Middle Ages. For example, in March, the two days were the 1st and 28th, and in June, the days were the 10th and 16th. The word now means "causing depression or dread." It is easy to see how this definition came from the idea of unlucky days.

Not all words have interesting histories, but taking the time to read an etymology can be useful. If you get excited about word origins, there are books available on the subject that show how fascinating language can be.

Sociology

The Importance of Hello

From Chapter 7 of *Academic Vocabulary: Academic Words*, Fifth Edition. Amy E. Olsen. Copyright © 2013 by Pearson Education, Inc. All rights reserved.

Sociology

The Importance of Hello

Greetings are a **socialization** behavior that most people take for granted because greetings are so **pervasive** in society. But from a young age, people are taught the appropriate greetings for different circumstances.
5 Studying everyday life can help us better understand why we act the ways we do. Sociologist Erving Goffman points out that greetings are part of our face-to-face contacts, phone conversations, and letters.

Shutterstock

One area that greetings illuminate is **status**. For
10 example, which person says "hello" first and how someone is greeted can be part of the **stratification** system in a society. In the past, a man removed his hat and bowed to greet a prince or king; this behavior showed his lower rank in the society. This greeting became truncated over time. Later,
15 people began to greet equals by just lifting the hat and then by touching the hat. Finally, a motion toward the hat was enough of a greeting among friends.

Greetings also show cultural differences. In France, people kiss each other on the cheeks as a friendly, everyday greet-
20 ing, but this type of behavior is not the **norm** in the United States. In fact, activities that are acceptable in one country may seem odd or even be **taboo** in another country. Learning what is acceptable and what is prohibited is important for

Shutterstock

travelers, especially for those conducting international business. In the United Sates, most business intro-
25 ductions begin with a firm, short (three- to four-second) handshake. In Europe, business associates also shake hands, but the handshake is usually more formal. Business greetings in Europe rarely display the friendly backslaps that are sometimes seen in the United States. In Japan, people customarily bow as a greeting, and many business people have learned to look carefully at how the bow is done. The depth of a bow reflects the status between the two people. In Arab countries, men often greet each other with a hand
30 on the right shoulder and a kiss on each cheek. Though a handshake is usually used when meeting people from other regions, it may be done with two hands and be more of a handhold. In Latin American countries, male friends hug each other when they meet, and women kiss each other on the cheeks. In business settings, the handshake is typically the norm at first; however, after a third or fourth meeting, a hug might be given. Visitors are generally allowed some flexibility in greeting ceremonies, but because greetings are
35 so ingrained, a native of a country may be **ostracized** if he or she fails to follow proper behavior.

Linguist C. A. Ferguson, as an informal experiment, decided to **deviate** from **conventional** greeting behavior at work. For two days in a row, he didn't respond to his secretary's "good morning." He reported that the atmosphere was unpleasant on the first day and tense on the second day. By the third day, to **alleviate** the stress and save their working relationship, he discontinued the experiment. What people
40 say and do in what may seem like simple greetings can have more importance than people imagine.

Predicting

For each set, write the definition on the line next to the word to which it belongs. If you are unsure, return to the reading, and underline any context clues you find. After you've made your predictions, check your answers against the Word List at the end of the chapter. Place a checkmark in the box next to each word whose definition you missed. These are the words you'll want to study closely.

Set One

standing, especially social standing	a standard	the act of developing levels of class
a learning process	having the quality to spread throughout	

☐ 1. **socialization** (line 1) _____

☐ 2. **pervasive** (line 2) _____

☐ 3. **status** (line 9) _____

☐ 4. **stratification** (line 11) _____

☐ 5. **norm** (line 20) _____

Set Two

excluded	to relieve	forbidden from use	to move away from a set behavior	customary

☐ 6. **taboo** (line 22) _____

☐ 7. **ostracized** (line 35) _____

☐ 8. **deviate** (line 36) _____

☐ 9. **conventional** (line 36) _____

☐ 10. **alleviate** (line 39) _____

Self-Tests

1 Put a T for true or F for false next to each statement.

_____ 1. A group might consider ostracizing someone with an unpleasant odor.

_____ 2. Ox-drawn carts are pervasive in American society.

_____ 3. A massage can help to alleviate stress.

_____ 4. One's status in society is often determined by one's job.

_____ 5. Spending the weekend skiing in Switzerland is the norm for most students.

_____ 6. Riding a pogo stick is a conventional method of transportation.

_____ 7. Blowing bubbles with one's gum is considered taboo in the classroom.

_____ 8. There is no type of stratification in the military.

_____ 9. A flooded road can cause people to deviate from an intended route.

_____ 10. Socialization can take place at the dinner table.

2 Finish the reading using the vocabulary words. Use each word once.

VOCABULARY LIST

alleviate	norm	pervasive	deviate	socialization
status	taboo	conventional	ostracized	stratification

Not Just Toys

The (1)_____ process begins at an early age. Sometimes parents don't even realize how (2)_____ the process is. For instance, children are usually given (3)_____ toys for boys and girls. It was the (4)_____ for years for boys to play with cars and girls with dolls. In some families it would even have been (5)_____ for a boy to play with a doll. There were possible penalties for children who decided to (6)_____ from accepted social practices. A girl who enjoyed playing with cars or throwing a baseball may well have been (7)_____ by other girls who perceived her behavior as inappropriate.

Amy E. Olsen

Today a child's (8)_____ in a group may still be determined by his or her toys. However, (9)_____ more often comes from financial resources. One way to (10)_____ potential conflicts over expensive electronic toys is to introduce children to a variety of ways to play from simple tag to inexpensive board games. Children can also learn that saving for expensive games can be part of the fun of getting them.

Identify the two vocabulary words represented in the drawings.

Word Visions

1. _____

2. _____

3 Circle the word that best completes each sentence.

1. Some companies are beginning to question the (conventional, pervasive) wisdom that people work better under pressure.

2. To (deviate, alleviate) the pain, Elizabeth put ice on her sore knee.

3. I kept asking about the (norm, status) of the flight, but no one at the check-in counter was sure when the plane would take off.

4. It is usually considered (taboo, norm) to ask how much money a person makes.

5. When no one got a raise, discontent was the (conventional, pervasive) mood in the office.

6. I enrolled my son in preschool to help his (socialization, stratification).

7. We had to (deviate, alleviate) from the syllabus because it was worthwhile to attend the assembly.

8. In some countries, such as India, (stratification, taboo) has been important to how people are treated.

9. It is considered the (norm, taboo) to tip waiters in the United States, but that is not the custom in all countries.

10. Sarah was (ostracized, alleviated) from the cooking club when she brought in a peanut butter and jelly sandwich and called it gourmet food.

Word Wise

Collocations

The *conventional wisdom* has been that eating dessert will make a person fat, but it is more likely the portion size and type of dessert that will put on the pounds.

We had to *deviate from* the plan when Malina called in sick since we only had three people to give the presentation instead of four.

The *socialization process* starts early with children learning what actions are and are not acceptable in their family.

Connotations and Denotations

Conventional: denotation—"conforming to established standards." For some people the connotation of *conventional* is "boring." They think that "conforming to established standards" is old fashioned, and they would rather try something new or different. When you hear the word *conventional,* how do you react?

Interesting Etymologies

Ostracize comes from the Greek *ostrakon,* "tile or pottery." In ancient Greece when a city wanted to see if a man should be forced to leave because he was in trouble with the state, a vote was taken on tiles. If six thousand people voted "yes," the man was banished for a minimum of five years. Today ostracize has the same effect—"to exclude, by general consent, from society or from privileges"—but without the voting tiles.

Taboo comes from the Tongan word *tabu,* "marked as holy." Tongan is a Polynesian language spoken in the Tonga island group, which is located in the southern Pacific Ocean. Taboos were originally restrictions against mentioning certain matters in fear that they might anger the gods. The word came to mean "forbidden from use or mention" or "a prohibition excluding something from use." What is considered taboo changes depending on the society and the time period.

Interactive Exercise

Give two examples for each of the following.

1. Where can you see socialization taking place?

   _____   _____

2. What are pervasive problems in today's society?

   _____   _____

3. What jobs have a high status in American society?

   _____   _____

4. What institutions use stratification?

   _____   _____

5. What situations might cause someone to deviate from his or her regular behavior?

   _____   _____

6. What norms are found in the classroom?

   _____   _____

7. What topics are usually considered taboo at dinner parties?

   _____   _____

8. Why might someone be ostracized from a group?

   _____   _____

9. What are conventional Mother's or Father's Day gifts?

   _____   _____

10. What do you do to alleviate pain when you are sick?

    _____   _____

HINT

Word Groups

Putting words into related groups can help your mind organize new vocabulary. To create word groups, get a piece of paper, pick a category, and list as many of the vocabulary words whose definitions fit under that heading in a general way. You will, of course, need to know the shades of meaning the more frequently you use a word. Academic subjects are one way to organize some of the words. You want to come up with other categories as you study more words.

For example, here are four words that fit the category "the arts": vivid, parallel and symmetrical, (could be used to describe a painting); and taboo.

1. _____   3. _____
2. _____   4. _____

Other possible categories are "science words," "business words," and "undesirable characteristics."

Word List

alleviate
[ə lē′ vē āt′]

v. to relieve; to reduce

conventional
[kən ven′ shən əl]

adj. 1. customary
2. conforming to established standards

deviate
[dē′ vē āt′]

v. 1. to move away from a norm or set behavior
2. to cause to turn aside or to differ

norm
[nôrm]

n. a standard or pattern regarded as typical for a specific group

ostracize
[os′ trə sīz′]

v. to exclude, by general consent, from society or from privileges

pervasive
[pər vā′ siv, -ziv]

adj. having the quality to spread throughout; extensive

socialization
[so′ shə li zā′ shən]

n. the process whereby an individual learns the values and behaviors appropriate to his or her culture and status

status
[stā′ təs, stat′ əs]

n. 1. a relative position; standing, especially social standing
2. high standing
3. situation

stratification
[strat′ ə fi kā′ shən]

n. the act or process of developing levels of class or privilege

taboo
[tə boō′, ta-]

adj. forbidden from use or mention

n. a prohibition excluding something from use

v. to forbid or prohibit

Words to Watch

Which words would you like to practice with a bit more? Pick 3–5 words to study, and list them below. Write the word and its definition, and compose your own sentence using the word correctly. This extra practice could be the final touch to learning a word.

Word	Definition	Your Sentence
1. _____	_____	_____
2. _____	_____	_____
3. _____	_____	_____
4. _____	_____	_____
5. _____	_____	_____

Foreign Languages

Welcome Additions

Foreign Languages

Welcome Additions

More foreign words and phrases come into common English usage each year. Because English has always borrowed words from other languages, people aren't always aware that a word originated
5 in another place. For example, *banana* and *zombie* are African words, *cookie* and *yacht* come from the Dutch, and *yogurt* from Turkish. Other words may still sound foreign, but they are used every day when speaking English.

Amy E. Olsen

10   Imagine eating dinner **alfresco** on a pleasant evening. While you are enjoying the view from the patio, your waiter comes to tell you about the soup **du jour** and other daily specials. After you take a sip of the delicious French onion soup you ordered, you sit back and enjoy the **bon mot** your companion credits to Mark Twain: "I am opposed to millionaires, but it would be dangerous to offer me the position." You laugh at
15 the witty remark and then ask, "Who needs to be a millionaire?" You know you are living **la dolce vita** as you take pleasure in your excellent meal, good company, and lovely atmosphere. When your dessert arrives, the waiter lights a match, applies it to the banana flambé, and shouts, "**Voilà!**" The alcohol ignites, and the flames create a magnificent finale to your evening. Possibly without even being aware of it, you have just spent an evening filled with foreign phrases.

20   Foreign words also appear frequently in the media. The Latin phrase **carpe diem** was an important message in the 1989 Oscar-winning film *Dead Poet's Society*. The film is about a strict boys' school where an English professor
25 tries to teach his students to live life to the fullest. Carpe diem also appears on numerous calendars and motivational posters. To seize the day is a message we often forget in today's hectic world. The term **doppelganger** comes from German
30 for a ghostly double, and the concept has been explored in short stories by writers such as Edgar Allan Poe in "William Wilson" and by Robert Louis Stevenson in "Markheim." Writers have

Shutterstock

also claimed to have seen their doppelgangers. The English poet Shelly saw his shortly before he
35 drowned in Italy, while the German poet Goethe claimed to have seen his riding down a road. Even a single word can have an impact in a story, such as **nada** as used in "A Clean Well-Lighted Place" by Ernest Hemingway. Nothing can certainly come to mean something.

      It isn't necessarily a **faux pas** to not understand every foreign word or phrase currently in use, but to avoid possibly embarrassing moments, the wise person will want to learn at least a few of these
40 phrases. The multicultural **zeitgeist** of the twenty-first century asks all of us to grow along with the language.

Predicting

For each set, write the definition on the line next to the word to which it belongs. If you are unsure, return to the reading, and underline any context clues you find. After you've made your predictions, check your answers against the Word List at the end of the chapter. Place a checkmark in the box next to each word whose definition you missed. These are the words you'll want to study closely.

Set One

There it is!	a witty remark	out-of-doors	the good life	as served on a particular day

☐ 1. **alfresco** (line 10) _____

☐ 2. **du jour** (line 12) _____

☐ 3. **bon mot** (line 13) _____

☐ 4. **la dolce vita** (line 16) _____

☐ 5. **voilà** (line 18) _____

Set Two

nothing	the spirit of the time	seize the day	a mistake	a ghostly double or counterpart

☐ 6. **carpe diem** (line 21) _____

☐ 7. **doppelganger** (line 29) _____

☐ 8. **nada** (line 36) _____

☐ 9. **faux pas** (line 38) _____

☐ 10. **zeitgeist** (line 40) _____

Self-Tests

1 Match each word with its synonym in Set One and its antonym in Set Two.

Synonyms

Set One

_____	1. carpe diem	a. mood
_____	2. doppelganger	b. mistake
_____	3. bon mot	c. grab the chance
_____	4. zeitgeist	d. double
_____	5. faux pas	e. witticism

Antonyms

Set Two

_____	6. alfresco	f. old
_____	7. nada	g. Darn!
_____	8. la dolce vita	h. indoors
_____	9. voilà	i. everything
_____	10. du jour	j. dreariness

2 Finish the sentences using the vocabulary words. Use each word once.

VOCABULARY LIST

bon mot	nada	alfresco	dolce vita	doppelganger
carpe diem	voilà	faux pas	zeitgeist	du jour

1. The special _____ at the cafeteria was kidney pie; I decided to pass.

2. As we sat on the porch of our cabin overlooking the lake, we thought this was the _____.

3. Shortly before her death, Queen Elizabeth I is reported to have seen her _____ lying on a bed.

4. My cousin is the expert at the _____; she always knows the right thing to say to make people laugh.

5. After a busy semester, I was looking forward to doing _____ for a week.

6. Sometimes I get so involved in everything I need to get done that I forget to _____.

7. I think that having toilet paper stuck to one's shoe all night would be considered a(n) _____ at most parties.

8. In the 1920s, the _____ seemed to be to party as much as possible in order to forget World War I.

9. The play will be performed _____ to enhance the play's forest setting.

10. I kept trying, and, _____, my story was finally accepted for publication.

Identify the two vocabulary words represented in the photographs.

Word Visions

1. _____

2. _____

3 Connect the vocabulary words to the following items or situations. Use each word once.

VOCABULARY LIST

alfresco	carpe diem	du jour	doppelganger	voilà
bon mot	faux pas	la dolce vita	nada	zeitgeist

1. a pocket without any lira, pesos, or francs _____

2. French onion soup on Wednesdays _____

3. greed in the 1980s _____

4. under the stars _____

5. "There is only one thing in the world worse than being talked about, and that is not being talked about." —Oscar Wilde _____

6. I found my keys! _____

7. asking a woman whether her child is her grandchild _____

8. When the woman he has admired all semester asks to borrow a pen, the man asks her out. _____

9. Robert Louis Stevenson's character Markheim meets his evil self. _____

10. a three-course lunch followed by a nap _____

Word Wise

Collocations

I like to eat out on Fridays because the *soup du jour* is usually clam chowder—my favorite.

Interesting Etymologies

Doppelganger comes from the German *doppel,* "double," and *gänger,* "goer or walker." The meaning of doppelganger is "a ghostly double or counterpart of a living person." There is a theory that a person's double is somewhere out there. There is also the belief that a person will die soon after seeing his or her doppelganger. Famous people from Catherine the Great to Goethe have reported seeing their doppelganger. The doppelganger theme is popular in literature and film from Guy de Maupassant's short story "Lui" to the film *The Man with My Face.*

Interactive Exercise

Write a sentence that provides an example for each word. Try to relate the example to your life or your community to better help you remember the word. For some of the words, your examples may need to be fictitious.

Examples:
dolce vita <u>Most people in my town consider la dolce vita to be sailing on the lake on a sunny day.</u>

doppelganger <u>My husband and I met a hotel clerk who could have been the doppelganger for my sister-in-law. We both thought she looked and sounded just like Terri.</u>

Tony Olsen

1. alfresco _____

2. carpe diem _____

3. doppelganger _____

4. faux pas _____

5. voilà _____

6. bon mot _____

7. zeitgeist _____

8. dolce vita _____

9. du jour _____

10. nada _____

Word Part Reminder

Below are a few exercises to help you review word parts. Fill in the missing word part from the list, and circle the meaning of the word part found in each sentence.

Example: My daughter needs to learn that the proper place ⬭to put⬭ her trash is in the garbage can; she thinks it is all right to dis*pos*e of it on the floor of her room.

lev   vi   dom   mag

1. Darlene always makes a problem greater than it is; I get tired of the way she has to _____nify everything to make herself important.

2. For my brother, living the good life means a sixty-mile bike ride followed by a carton of chocolate ice cream, but for me la dolce _____ta is a hike in the woods and a big bowl of cherries.

3. I was so impressed when the magician made the woman rise four feet into the air. I had never seen a person _____itate before.

4. I can't imagine a worse condition than living in a country where people don't have any free_____s.

Word List

Word	Language	Part	Definition
alfresco [al fres′ kō]	Italian	*adv.* *adj.*	out-of-doors; in the open air outdoor
bon mot [bôn mō′]	French	*n.*	a witty remark or comment; witticism
carpe diem [kär′ pe dē′ em, kär′ pā dē′ əm]	Latin	*n.*	seize the day; enjoy the present
dolce vita [dōl′ chā vē′ tä]	Italian	*n.*	the good life (usually preceded by *la*)
doppelganger [dop′ əl gāng′ ər]	German	*n.*	a ghostly double or counterpart of a living person
du jour [də zhoor′, d o͞o-]	French	*adj.*	1. as prepared or served on a particular day 2. fashionable; current
faux pas [fō pä′]	French	*n.*	a mistake; a slip or blunder in manners or conduct; an embar- rassing social error
nada [nä′ dä]	Spanish	*n.*	nothing
voilà [vwä lä′]	French	*interj.*	There it is! (used to express success or satisfaction)
zeitgeist [tsīt′ gīst′, zīt′]	German	*n.*	the spirit of the time; the general feeling of a particular period of time

Words to Watch

Which words would you like to practice with a bit more? Pick 3–5 words to study, and list them below. Write the word and its definition, and compose your own sentence using the word correctly. This extra practice could be the final touch to learning a word.

Word	Definition	Your Sentence
1. _____	_____	_____
_____	_____	_____
2. _____	_____	_____
_____	_____	_____
3. _____	_____	_____
_____	_____	_____
4. _____	_____	_____
_____	_____	_____
5. _____	_____	_____
_____	_____	_____

Word Parts II

Word Parts II

Look for words with these **prefixes, roots**, and/or **suffixes** as you work through this course. Learning basic word parts can help you figure out the meanings of unfamiliar words.

prefix: a word part added to the beginning of a word that changes the meaning of the root
root: a word's basic part with its essential meaning
suffix: a word part added to the end of a word; indicates the part of speech

Word Part	Meaning	Examples and Definitions
Prefixes		
ex-	out, out of, former	*export:* to send or carry goods out of a country *exclude:* to keep out
per-	through, throughout, completely	*pervasive:* spreading throughout *perform:* to go through with; to complete
sym-	with, together	*symbiotic:* pertaining to the living together of two dissimilar organisms *symphony:* brings together a combination of sounds
Roots		
-flu-, -flux-	to flow	*affluence:* a flowing toward *influx:* an act of flowing in
-her-, -hes-	to stick	*coherent:* sticking to one point *adhesive:* sticky
-plac-	to please	*placate:* to please; to calm *placid:* pleasantly calm
-port-	to carry	*portfolio:* a case for carrying papers or drawings *portable:* easy to carry
-sta-, -sti-	to stand, to be in a place	*status:* standing; social position *destitute:* lacking; without support or standing
Suffixes		
-most (makes an adjective)	most	*utmost:* the most extreme *foremost:* the most important
-phobia (makes a noun)	fear of	*acrophobia:* a fear of heights *claustrophobia:* a fear of enclosed places

Self-Tests

1 Read each definition, and choose the appropriate word. Use each word once. The meaning of the word part is underlined to help you make the connection. Refer to the Word Parts list if you need help.

VOCABULARY LIST

pervade	fluid	foremost	complacent	exhale
sympathize	export	coherent	anthrophobia	stationary

1. to feel <u>with</u> someone _____
2. <u>pleased</u> with oneself often without an awareness of some problem _____
3. a substance that is capable of <u>flowing</u> _____
4. <u>sticking</u> to one point _____
5. to breathe <u>out</u> _____
6. the <u>most</u> important _____
7. a <u>fear of</u> people _____
8. <u>to carry out</u> of a country _____
9. to spread <u>throughout</u> _____
10. <u>standing</u> still; not moving _____

2 Finish the sentences with the meaning of each word part. Use each meaning once. The word part is underlined to help you make the connection.

VOCABULARY LIST

please	out of	together	completely	stick
flow	most	stand	fear of	to carry

1. Terry used <u>ex</u>tortion to get money _____ the man.
2. Her perfume <u>per</u>meated the room; the smell _____ took over the space.
3. Anthony is <u>flu</u>ent in five languages. The ability to speak another language just seems to _____ out of him.
4. I enjoy going to the <u>sym</u>phony. I like how all the instruments come _____ to make beautiful sounds.
5. To <u>plac</u>ate the hungry guests, Alexa thought she could _____ them with cheese and crackers before the main course was ready.
6. I did not know Tina suffered from ailuro<u>phobia</u> until Seeley jumped on her lap and she confessed to a _____ cats.
7. The ad<u>hes</u>ive tape really helped my package _____ together. My sister said it took her an hour to get it open.
8. I reveal my inner<u>most</u> secrets to my diary. I don't dare share my _____ secret feelings with anyone.
9. I asked the <u>por</u>ter at the train station _____ my bags to my car because I was tired of lifting them.
10. I am not going to let any ob<u>sta</u>cles (financial, emotional, or physical) _____ in the way of my completing college.

3 Finish the story using the word parts found below. Use each word part once. Your knowledge of word parts, as well as the context clues, will help you create the correct words. If you do not understand the meaning of a word you have made, check the dictionary for the definition or to see whether the word exists.

WORD PARTS LIST

her	ex	plac	sti	sym
per	most	flu	port	phobia

Crossing a Bridge

For years I suffered from aqua(1)_____.
My fear of water had been with me since I was a
teenager. I can remember swimming in the community
pool when I was in elementary school, but something
happened around the age of fourteen that led to an
intense fear of being in, on, or over water. I went to a
psychologist who suggested that my fear could be a(n)
(2)_____ptom of a larger problem, but I
wasn't willing to explore that idea.

Katy Tallorin

My fear (3)_____cluded my doing so many things. I once had the chance to
im(4)_____ some beautiful vases for my antique shop, but the man in Japan would
only sell to me personally, and I was afraid to fly over the Pacific Ocean. My fear also never
(5)_____mitted me to take hikes in the local woods with the rest of my family because I
would have had to cross several streams. I looked fondly at their photographs for years, and they kept
encouraging me to join them. And, of course, the swimming that I enjoyed as a child was absolutely
out of the question.

My son finally forced me to quit being so ob(6)_____nate and face my fear. He
reminded me that I had always ad(7)_____ed to the idea that he could do anything,
so he asked why couldn't I. He took me to a beautiful spot in the woods and showed me how
(8)_____id the water was under the bridge. It certainly did look calm, almost pleasant.
Then he showed me how to walk gently across the bridge. With a few in(9)_____ential
words, he coaxed me across. It was a major breakthrough! I was so proud of myself.

After two more years of gradual progress, I am ready to undertake a fabulous trip to the
southern(10)_____ point on the planet. I am planning a cruise to Antarctica. I will actually be spending two weeks on a ship. Now I truly believe fears can be overcome. I wish I hadn't
waited so long to face mine.

4 Pick the best definition for each underlined word using your knowledge of word parts. Circle the word part in each of the underlined words.

a. the maximum

b. conduct; how one carries oneself

c. tending to unify or stick together

d. sweetly or smoothly flowing

e. not to be pacified or pleased

f. cannot be passed through

g. stale or foul from standing, as in a pool of water

h. the former president

i. an abnormal fear of being alone

j. a pleasant arrangement of parts with each other

_____ 1. Because our dog has <u>monophobia</u>, we have to take her with us everywhere.

_____ 2. The bank's new lock is <u>impervious</u> to known methods of safe cracking.

_____ 3. The <u>symmetry</u> of the building made it appealing to most people.

_____ 4. I was proud of my son's <u>deportment</u> at the luncheon. He is usually loud, but he was quiet and well mannered.

_____ 5. The <u>ex-president</u> of the company had to face a barrage of questions from reporters about his actions after it was discovered that he had hidden money in a secret account.

_____ 6. I tried my <u>utmost</u> to keep the party a surprise, but the day before her graduation, I accidently mentioned ordering a cake, and Paloma guessed that there was something going on.

_____ 7. The <u>stagnant</u> pond had a horrible smell to it.

_____ 8. The singer's <u>mellifluous</u> voice kept the audience enchanted for two hours.

_____ 9. Because of the movie's <u>cohesive</u> structure, it was easy to understand how the different characters all came to know each other.

_____ 10. The little boy was <u>implacable</u>; nothing would quiet him until his mother stopped at the toy store.

5 A good way to remember word parts is to pick one word that uses a word part and understand how that word part functions in the word. Then you can apply that meaning to other words that have the same word part. Use the words to help you match the word part to its meaning.

Set One

_____ 1. **ex-:** export, exclude, ex-husband

_____ 2. **-flu-, -flux-:** fluid, fluctuate, influx

_____ 3. **-sta-, -sti-:** status, stationary, destitute

_____ 4. **-most:** utmost, foremost, southernmost

_____ 5. **-plac-:** placate, placid, complacent

a. to flow

b. to please

c. out, out of, former

d. to stand, to be in a place

e. most

Set Two

_____ 6. **per-:** pervasive, perennial, permutation

_____ 7. **-port-:** portfolio, portable, import

_____ 8. **sym-:** symbiotic, symmetrical, sympathy

_____ 9. **-her-, -hes-:** coherent, inherent, adhesive

_____ 10. **-phobia:** acrophobia, metrophobia, aquaphobia

f. fear of

g. to carry

h. through, throughout, completely

i. with, together

j. to stick

Interactive Exercise

Use the dictionary to find a word you don't know that uses each word part listed below. Write the meaning of the word part, the word, and the definition. If your dictionary has the etymology (history) of the word, see how the word part relates to the meaning, and write the etymology after the definition.

Word Part	Meaning	Word	Definition and Etymology
EXAMPLE:			
-flu-	to flow	fluvial	formed by the action of flowing water
			From Latin "fluvius," river; from "fluere," to flow
1. ex-			
2. per-			
3. -port-			
4. -sta-			
5. sym-			

Word Visions

Match each photograph to one of the word parts below, and write the meaning of the word part.

sym-   -flu-/-flux-   -her-/-hes-   -port-   -phobia

Gerald Warnken, Jr.

Amy E. Olsen

1. _____

2. _____

Word Wise

Internet Activity: Writing a Book Review

A perfect place to practice your newly acquired vocabulary is on the Internet. You can share your thoughts with others and use new words by writing a book review at Amazon.com. This online store has a space for you to write reviews of the books it sells. Go to the site and type in the name of a book you would like to review. You can pick a book you enjoyed reading or one that you disliked. It can be a work of fiction or nonfiction. You may even want to rate one of your textbooks. If Amazon sells the book, it will come up in a list of books. Go to the page for the book you want, and click on the "Create your own review" link. You will need to supply an e-mail address and a password before you can begin your review. Click on the "review guidelines" to read Amazon's rules for writing a review. You will be asked to rate the book from 1 to 5 stars, supply a title for your review, and then write the review. Use at least five of the vocabulary words you are learning in your review. You can use your real name on the review or create a pen name. Read through the directions for both to decide which you want to do. Most reviews are posted within two days. Once your review is posted, let your classmates know what book you reviewed. You can then read each others' reviews and practice reading the vocabulary words in new contexts. Your instructor may ask you to print out your review to display it in class or to read it aloud. Have fun sharing your opinions with the world and getting a chance to use your new knowledge in a real-life setting.

HINT

Test-Taking Strategies

Studying is essential to do well on a test, but for some people that isn't enough to ease the stress that testing can bring. A few strategies may help you deal with test anxiety.

- Get a good night's rest, and eat a healthy breakfast, lunch, or dinner before the exam.
- Exercise before the exam. Take a walk or do some stretching to help you relax.
- When you get to the classroom, take a few deep breaths and visualize yourself in a soothing spot such as hiking in a forest or taking a bath. Also picture yourself as being successful at the test; don't focus on any negatives.
- Read each question carefully. Look for important words in a question such as "the least" or "always."
- If the test is multiple-choice, read each of the choices before making your decision. Be aware of choices such as "all of the above" or "none of the above."
- If the test is a fill-in-the-blank, try putting each choice in the blank and see which sounds best.
- If you get stuck on a question in a matching test, go on to the next one. When you finish answering the questions that are easy for you, see which questions and choices are left. With fewer choices, the answers should be easier to find (for example, look at Self-Tests 2 and 3 in this chapter).

Being a bit nervous can help during a test by keeping you alert, but too much stress can ruin even the most prepared student's chances of success. If text anxiety becomes a serious problem for you, check with the counselors at your college for advice.

Word Parts III

From Chapter 16 of *Academic Vocabulary: Academic Words*, Fifth Edition. Amy E. Olsen. Copyright © 2013 by Pearson Education, Inc.
All rights reserved.

Word Parts III

Look for words with these **prefixes**, **roots**, and/or **suffixes** as you work through this course. Learning basic word parts can help you figure out the meanings of unfamiliar words.

prefix: a word part added to the beginning of a word that changes the meaning of the root

root: a word's basic part with its essential meaning

suffix: a word part added to the end of a word; indicates the part of speech

Word Part	Meaning	Examples and Definitions
Prefixes		
meta-	change	*metamorphosis:* a change in form *metabolism:* chemical changes in an organism
multi-	many, much	*multitude:* an indefinite number; many *multicolored:* many-colored
para-	next to, almost, beyond, abnormal	*paraphrase:* to restate almost like the original *parallel:* next to each other without ever meeting
Roots		
-ann-, -enn-	year	*biannual:* happening twice each year *perennial:* lasting through many years
-mut-	change	*permutation:* the act of changing *mutant:* a new type of organism due to a change
-sequ-	to follow	*sequential:* to follow in order *sequel:* anything that follows; a continuation
-tract-	to drag, to pull, to draw	*abstract:* to draw or pull out *tractor:* a vehicle used to pull things
-trib-	give	*tribute:* something given or done to show respect *contribute:* to give along with others
Suffixes		
-oid (makes an adjective)	like, resembling	*paranoid:* resembling paranoia (a suspicion of others) *humanoid:* resembling humans
-ure (makes a verb)	action or process	*procure:* process of getting something *failure:* action of failing

Self-Tests

1 Read each definition, and choose the appropriate word. Use each word once. The meaning of the word part is underlined to help you make the connection. Refer to the Word Parts list if you need help.

1. the <u>process</u> of making something safe _____

2. star<u>like</u> _____

3. lasting 100 <u>years</u> _____

4. to <u>give</u> out _____

5. a person trained to work <u>next to</u> a lawyer or teacher _____

6. <u>to draw</u> or <u>pull</u> out _____

7. the <u>change</u> in location of a disease in the body _____

8. having <u>many</u> skills _____

9. to <u>change</u> a penalty to a less severe form _____

10. the <u>following</u> of one thing after another _____

VOCABULARY LIST

asteroid	commute
secure	sequence
distribute	centennial
multitalented	abstract
paraprofessional	metastasis

2 Finish the sentences with the meaning of each word part. Use each meaning once. The word part is underlined to help you make the connection.

VOCABULARY LIST

draw	many	give	process	almost
year	resemble	change	follow	changes

1. And<u>roids</u> are popular characters in science fiction movies because they _____ human beings; therefore, they are easy to costume.

2. The <u>mut</u>ant ant was able to carry twice as much as a normal ant. The _____ made it a valuable addition to the colony.

3. I at<u>tribute</u> much of my success as a musician to my fifth-grade music teacher; I _____ him credit for teaching me about the discipline of practicing and the beauty of creating new sounds.

4. The <u>sequel</u> continues to _____ Nita's adventures, but now she is three years older and entering college.

5. My <u>para</u>phrase was _____ like the original quote, but I made sure to use enough of my own words and style to avoid plagiarizing.

6. I was able to pro<u>cure</u> the special chocolates my husband likes, but the _____ wasn't easy. I had to call ten places to find where I could order them.

7. I like the way the writer uses a <u>meta</u>phor to compare the woman's face to a banana. The way he _____the usual use of the word *banana* clearly shows that the woman has a long, thin face.

8. My husband usually forgets our <u>anni</u>versary, but he remembered this _____.

9. The store was able to _____ me in with an at<u>tract</u>ive window display.

10. Because I work for a <u>multi</u>national corporation, I could be transferred to _____ countries.

3 Finish the story using the word parts. Use each word part once. Your knowledge of word parts, as well as the context clues, will help you create the correct words. If you do not understand the meaning of a word you have made, check the dictionary for the definition or to see whether the word exists.

WORD PARTS LIST

multi	sequ	trib	oid	ann
meta	para	mut	tract	ure

The Baking Battle

Amy E. Olsen

It was time for the town's (1)_____ual cooking contests, and this year I was going to participate for the third time. This year I was going to con(2)_____ute my extraordinary brownies. I was paran(3)_____ that someone would discover my secret ingredients, so when I went shopping for them, I bought fifty other items. No one who saw me at the store would be able to figure out which ingredients were going into the brownies. My brownies had gone through several per(4)_____ations over the years, but I now felt they were perfect. I carefully followed the proced(5)_____ I had established for making the ultimate brownie. The whole process had to be just right. Finally, the brownies were ready for their (6)_____morphosis. Into the oven they went to change from sticky batter to delicious delights.

In the afternoon, I took my brownies to the judging area. There I met my other competitors. I was upset to see June Elaine with a pan of brownies. She had won so many times in (7)_____ple categories, including cakes, casseroles, and wheat breads. She even won the chili cook-off one year. The judges tasted all fifteen entries twice. Then they adjourned to another room to discuss their choices. They still hadn't emerged after thirty minutes. I thought they were trying to pro(8)_____ the suspense, but I didn't need them to draw it out any longer. I was so nervous. They finally came out and said, "We have an unusual situation this year. We have been unable to decide between two of the entries. Con(9)_____ently, we are going to break with tradition and give two first place awards." I held my breath. I was one of the winners! The other, of course, was June Elaine. I didn't care that we both won first place. I was actually proud to have my brownies in the same league as hers. I even hoped that my entries from now on would (10)_____llel her success.

4 Pick the best definition for each underlined word using your knowledge of word parts. Circle the word part in each of the underlined words.

a. the process of expressing disapproval

b. resembling the truth but unproven

c. a quality given to a person or thing

d. unchangeable

e. a person who changes a literary work from one form to another

f. beyond the usual

g. a comment that doesn't follow the preceding one

h. to draw away

i. happening every two years

j. involving the use of many methods of communication

_____ 1. The Internet has helped to spread several <u>factoids</u>; people read the same stories about killer bananas or ways to earn thousands of dollars and think the stories are real.

_____ 2. Mina is studying <u>paranormal</u> activities, such as clairvoyance and extrasensory perception.

_____ 3. I enjoyed the <u>multimedia</u> presentation. The use of various types of visuals and sounds made the presentation extremely interesting.

_____ 4. The board had to <u>censure</u> the secretary for putting inappropriate remarks in the minutes.

_____ 5. An <u>attribute</u> that immediately comes to mind when I think of Carol is friendliness.

_____ 6. Unfortunately, Verda was <u>immutable</u> about her vacation plans, and she went to the mountains to ski even though there wasn't any snow.

_____ 7. I found it hard to understand the speaker because his speech was filled with one <u>non sequitur</u> after another. His ideas just didn't connect.

_____ 8. The Olympics are a <u>biennial</u> celebration of athletics worldwide.

_____ 9. I put the rusted statue in the garage; now it won't <u>detract</u> from the appeal of the house.

_____ 10. My uncle is a <u>metaphrast</u>; he changes short stories into poems.

5 A good way to remember word parts is to pick one word that uses a word part and understand how that word part functions in the word. Then you can apply that meaning to other words that have the same word part. Use the words to help you match the word part to its meaning.

Set One

_____ 1. **multi-:** multitude, multiply, multifaceted

_____ 2. **meta-:** metamorphosis, metaphor, metabolism

_____ 3. **-tract-:** abstract, tractor, attractive

_____ 4. **-sequ-:** sequential, sequel, consequence

_____ 5. **-oid:** humanoid, paranoid, android

a. to follow

b. change

c. many, much

d. to drag, to pull, to draw

e. like, resembling

Set Two

_____ 6. **para-:** parallel, parasite, paranormal

_____ 7. **-trib-:** tribute, contribute, attribute

_____ 8. **-mut-:** permutation, commute, mutation

_____ 9. **-ann, -enn-:** annals, anniversary, perennial

_____ 10. **-ure:** procure, failure, procedure

f. give

g. year

h. action or process

i. change

j. next to, almost, beyond, abnormal

Interactive Exercise

Use the dictionary to find a word you don't know that uses each word part listed below. Write the meaning of the word part, the word, and the definition. If your dictionary has the etymology (history) of the word, see how the word part relates to the meaning, and write the etymology after the definition.

Word Part	Meaning	Word	Definition and Etymology
EXAMPLE:			
-sequ-	to follow	sequela	an abnormal condition resulting from a previous disease. From Latin "sequela," what follows
1. -ann-			
2. meta-			
3. multi-			
4. -mut-			
5. -tract-			

Match each photograph to one of the word parts below, and write the meaning of the word part.

Word Visions

multi-   -mut-   -sequ-   -tract-   -oid

Amy E. Olsen

1. _____

Amy E. Olsen

2. _____

Word Wise

Internet Activity: For Further Reading and Research

When readings capture your attention, turn to the Internet for more information. When you see a vocabulary word you have been studying on a Web site, note how it is used. You will also likely come across new words where you can practice your context-clue skills to discover a meaning. Here are a few sites to get you started in your quest for further information.

For more on immigration, Genghis Khan, the Mayans, Julius Caesar, Karl Marx, or the former Soviet Union, try historychannel.com. At the History Channel's Web site, type in the time period, person, or event that interests you, and you will find a wide choice of articles to click on.

For science information, visit *National Geographic* magazine at nationalgeographic.com or the Discovery Channel site at discovery.com. For technology information, try the site for *Wired* magazine: wired.com.

To explore the art and entertainment worlds, try salon.com for articles on a variety of creative interests from art to movies.

For a list of challenging words and how many times a word has appeared in the *New York Times* in the past year with an example of the word in context, visit nytimes.com/learning/students/wordofday.

For dictionary entries, a word-of-the-day feature, and word-related games, give the Merriam-Webster Online dictionary at m-w.com a look.

HINT

Marking Words When Reading

When you read for fun, it can be counterproductive to stop and look up every word you don't know—you will become frustrated with reading instead of enjoying it. Looking for context clues is the best way to find the meaning of an unknown word, but sometimes this method doesn't work. There are various ways of keeping track of unfamiliar words; try these methods to see which fits your style.

- Keep a piece of paper and a pen next to you, and write down the word and page number.
- Keep a piece of paper next to you, and rip it into small pieces or use sticky notes. Put a piece between the pages where the word you don't know is located. For added help, write the word on the paper.
- If the book belongs to you, circle the words you don't know and flip through the book later to find them.
- If the book belongs to you, dog-ear the page (turn the corner down) where the word you don't know is located. This method is useful when you don't have paper or a pen handy.
- Repeat the word and page number to yourself a few times. Try to connect the page number to a date to help you remember it.

When you are done reading for the day, get your dictionary and look up the words you marked. The last two methods work best if you don't read many pages before you look up the words or if there are only a few words you don't know. Using these methods will help you learn new words without harming the fun of reading. Note: If you come across a word you don't know several times and not knowing its meaning hinders your understanding of what is going on, then it's a good idea to stop and look up the word.

Political Science

Searching for the Ideal

From Chapter 18 of *Academic Vocabulary: Academic Words*, Fifth Edition. Amy E. Olsen. Copyright © 2013 by Pearson Education, Inc. All rights reserved.

Political Science

Searching for the Ideal

Political systems have come in many forms over the course of human history. The quest for a **utopian** form of government has run the **gamut** from monarchies to democracies. Ancient Rome and the Soviet Union are two
5 examples separated by time and place that show the similarities and differences in how governments are run.

Julius Caesar Shutterstock

After the rule of a tyrannical king, the Romans formed a **republic** around 500 B.C. The senators of the republic worked together to make decisions regarding laws.
10 This system worked well until Rome began to expand, and it became harder to control the many lands Rome had conquered. Eventually military power became more important than laws. In 62 B.C. Julius Caesar proposed a triumvirate with himself, the general Pompey, and the rich banker Crassus. These three men ruled Rome through bribery, fear, and other methods. When the trium-
15 virate collapsed, Pompey and Caesar went to war. Caesar won and became "Dictator for Life"; there was even talk of making Caesar a king. Rome had gone from a republic to a **totalitarian** government. Caesar did make improvements for the people such as fixing the taxation system, making living conditions easier in the conquered territories, and changing the calendar. Still, his authoritarian
20 rule was not appreciated, and seeing no other way to **oust** him, a group of nobles murdered Caesar in the Senate on the Ides of March (March 15) in 44 B.C.

Karl Marx Monument in Chemnitz, Germany
Dorling Kindersley

In the 1800s the world was changing due to the rise of industrialism. The **milieu** was ripe for new ideas. Many peo-
25 ple lived in slums and worked long hours in harsh conditions. Karl Marx was the voice for this class. In 1867 he published *Das Kapital,* explaining the class struggle between the poor and the rich. The **proletariat** consisted of the workers who could gain power from the **bourgeoisie**, the property-owning
30 capitalist class, only by revolution. Marx felt this revolution would take place in Germany or England where capitalism was well established, but it was Russia in 1917 that saw the start of communism. Lenin and Trotsky led the fight for workers' rights with Lenin becoming dictator of the newly named
35 Union of Soviet Socialist Republics (USSR). After Lenin's death in 1924, Stalin became dictator. Stalin began many reforms, but he also silenced all opposition. A totalitarian government was born again.

The USSR was dissolved in 1991, and the **ideology** underlying communism has been shaken. Capitalism continues to thrive worldwide, although some workers still fight for fair wages and **ethical**
40 treatment. Humankind continues its search for an ideal form of government.

Predicting

For each set, write the definition on the line next to the word to which it belongs. If you are unsure, return to the reading, and underline any context clues you find. After you've made your predictions, check your answers against the Word List at the end of the chapter. Place a checkmark in the box next to each word whose definition you missed. These are the words you'll want to study closely.

Set One

the entire range	resembling an ideal place	to remove
a government that uses dictatorial control		a state where power rests with the citizens

❑ 1. **utopian** (line 2)_____

❑ 2. **gamut** (line 3)_____

❑ 3. **republic** (line 8)_____

❑ 4. **totalitarian** (line 16)_____

❑ 5. **oust** (line 20)_____

Set Two

the working class	environment	pertaining to right and wrong conduct
a system of beliefs or ideas		the property-owning class

❑ 6. **milieu** (line 24)_____

❑ 7. **proletariat** (line 28)_____

❑ 8. **bourgeoisie** (line 29)_____

❑ 9. **ideology** (line 38)_____

❑ 10. **ethical** (line 39)_____

Self-Tests

1 Circle the correct meaning of each vocabulary word.

1. utopian:	idealized	realized
2. republic:	power with a dictator	power with the people
3. bourgeoisie:	middle class	working class
4. ideology:	set of natural laws	system of beliefs
5. oust:	to remove	to add
6. gamut:	range	one and only
7. milieu:	emptiness	surroundings
8. proletariat:	working class	middle class
9. totalitarian:	liberal	authoritarian
10. ethical:	unfair	fair

2 Write the vocabulary word on the line next to the example it best fits. Use each word once.

Set One

VOCABULARY LIST

oust	ideology	utopian	gamut	totalitarian

1. Reg told his bike racing team that he would order all the team's clothing in the sizes he thought people needed. What kind of leader is he? _____

2. The team voted to remove Reg as manager. What did it decide to do? _____

3. Reg cried and laughed on being told to go. What did his emotions show? _____

4. Reg then formed a team built on the beliefs that the manager is always right, and everyone should train seven days a week. What are his beliefs called? _____

5. He also believes that the team members will never argue and that the team will win every race. What is his outlook on life? _____

Set Two

VOCABULARY LIST

bourgeoisie	republic	proletariat	milieu	ethical

6. Ava owns a house on a lake. What group is she part of, in Marxist theory? _____

7. Lou rents an apartment and works as a waiter. What group does he belong to, following Marxist theory? _____

8. Ava and Lou get to vote for the president of their country. What kind of political system does their country have? _____

9. Lou and Ava became friends at a soccer game. They believe sports are fun when people treat each other fairly and athletes don't use illegal substances to improve performance. To what type of standards do they adhere? _____

10. They both work in busy places. What is one's environment called? _____

Identify the two vocabulary words represented in the drawings.

Word Visions

1. _____   2. _____

3 Complete the reading using each word once.

VOCABULARY LIST

ethical	milieu	ideology	utopian	bourgeoisie
proletariat	oust	republic	gamut	totalitarian

The Survey

For my political science class, I took a survey asking students what life would be like in their
(1)_____ society. I was surprised at some of the responses. The answers ran the
(2)_____ from governments that gave citizens complete freedom to those with strict controls. I was surprised at first by the woman who favored a(n) (3)_____ form of government,
but the more I talked to her, the more I saw that she didn't like making decisions. Most people felt that
the (4)_____ treatment of others was essential in a perfect society. Most students favored
a(n) (5)_____ and liked the idea of citizens making decisions about laws. Most people
didn't want a class society. Several students thought it was unfair how the (6)_____ had
manipulated workers for years. A few even felt that, in an ideal society, everyone would belong to the
(7)_____ and work together for the good of society, although several noted that this system
hadn't been historically successful. Most people saw the (8)_____ in a perfect society as one
of peace. One man wrote on his survey, "I'd (9)_____ any whiners, and then life would be
great." I also asked people to give me one word that fit in their political (10)_____. Among the
words I collected were *equality, respect,* and *compromise.* The survey helped me write an excellent paper.

➤ Word Wise

Collocations

The game brought out a *gamut of emotions* from sadness and anger to eventual happiness.
Ethical standards are required in certain fields, such as medicine, law, and finance.
What represents the *ethical treatment* of animals has been controversial in recent years.

Word Pairs

Bourgeoisie/Proletariat: Bourgeoisie in Marxist theory means "the property-owning capitalist
class." Proletariat, also in Marxist theory, refers to "the workers who do not own property and who
must sell their labor to survive." On a Saturday afternoon, the bourgeoisie enjoy a relaxing stroll
through the park, while the proletariat continue to toil in the factories.

Interesting Etymologies

Utopian: The noun Utopia comes from Greek *ou,* "not," plus *topos,* "a place" and means "nowhere." The word was coined by Thomas More in 1516 to use as the title of his book about an
imaginary ideal island society. A utopia (lowercase) is "any ideal place," and the adjective utopian
means "resembling utopia."

Interactive Exercise

Give two examples for each of the following situations.

EXAMPLE: **milieu** at a sporting event   _fans cheering_   _a scoreboard flashing_

1. **milieu** at a party _____ _____

2. **proletariat** actions _____ _____

3. **ideology** of a dictator _____ _____

4. characteristics of a **utopian** society _____ _____

5. circumstances that would cause a company to **oust** its president _____ _____

6. actions of a **totalitarian** government _____ _____

7. showing a **gamut** of emotions _____ _____

8. **bourgeoisie** behavior _____ _____

9. actions in a **republic** _____ _____

10. **ethical** standards in the medical profession _____ _____

HINT

Banned Books

Freedom of expression has not always been a right granted to all people in all places. Over the centuries, several books have been banned because of their content or wording. Many of the books that are now considered classics were banned at one time. A person doesn't have to like every book that is printed, but keeping an open mind about what one is asked to read in college or what one chooses to read later in life helps to foster creativity, critical thinking, and understanding in an individual.

The following are a few books that have been banned previously (Are any a surprise to you?):

Of Mice and Men by John Steinbeck   _The Color Purple_ by Alice Walker
The Catcher in the Rye by J. D. Salinger   _James and the Giant Peach_ by Roald Dahl
The House of Spirits by Isabel Allende   _To Kill a Mockingbird_ by Harper Lee
Beloved by Toni Morrison   _Bless Me Ultima_ by Rudolfo Anaya
Lord of the Flies by William Golding   _Harry Potter_ (the series) by J. K. Rowling

Word List

bourgeoisie
[boor′ zhwä zē′]

n. 1. in Marxist theory, the property-owning capitalist class
2. the middle class

ethical
[eth′ i kəl]

adj. 1. pertaining to right and wrong conduct; fair
2. adhering to principles of conduct that are considered correct, especially related to certain professions

gamut
[gam′ ət]

n. the entire scale or range

ideology
[ī′ dē ol′ ə jē, id′ ē-]

n. a system of beliefs or ideas, often political, held by a person, group, or institution

milieu
[mil yoo′]

n. environment; surroundings

oust
[oust]

v. to remove; to force out

proletariat
[prō′ lə târ′ ē ət]

n. 1. in Marxist theory, the workers who do not own property and who must sell their labor to survive
2. the lowest or poorest class

republic
[ri pub′ lik]

n. 1. a state where power rests with the citizens
2. a state where the head of government is usually an elected president

totalitarian
[tō tal′ i târ′ ē ən]

adj. 1. pertaining to a government that uses dictatorial control and forbids opposition
2. authoritarian

n. an adherent of totalitarian principles or government

utopian
[yoo tō′ pē ən]

adj. 1. resembling utopia, an ideal place
2. involving idealized perfection

Words to Watch

Which words would you like to practice with a bit more? Pick 3–5 words to study, and list them below. Write the word and its definition, and compose your own sentence using the word correctly. This extra practice could be the final touch to learning a word.

Word	Definition	Your Sentence
1. _____	_____	_____
2. _____	_____	_____
3. _____	_____	_____
4. _____	_____	_____
5. _____	_____	_____

Computer Science

Concerns to Consider

From Chapter 20 of *Academic Vocabulary: Academic Words*, Fifth Edition. Amy E. Olsen. Copyright © 2013 by Pearson Education, Inc.

Computer Science

Concerns to Consider

Technology, especially the computer, is rapidly changing the world. The **ubiquitous** nature of the computer is probably not even realized by most people. We see them in our homes, in schools, and in libraries, but computer technology can be
5   found in cars, cell phones, and even appliances like washing machines. With the increased reliance on technology, some people are **wary** of the changes and wonder if society is moving too quickly. Other people embrace the changes and look forward to the benefits of each new innovation.

Amy E. Olsen

10   One concern deals with privacy. Many people today enjoy the ease of shopping, banking, and paying bills online. However, if your personal information is not securely **encrypted**, problems can arise. Without encoding private information, unscrupulous people can access credit card num-
15   bers, bank accounts, or other personal information. Your money can easily be stolen but, even worse, so can your identity. If this happens, the criminal can use your name to commit crimes from theft to murder. It can take years and loads of paperwork to get your good name back. Another area that worries some people is the idea of **embedding** computer chips in clothing and possibly in a person's hand or brain. Researchers are looking at attaching global positioning systems (GPS) to jackets
20   and putting miniature cameras into necklaces. A person could simply push buttons on one's sleeve to listen to music or text a message. One may even be able to swipe a hand over a scanner to pay for a bill instead of using a credit card. The question is whether the benefits of having less to carry outweigh the possible loss of privacy. Some people can be considered **paranoid** in their concern that someone is constantly watching them; on the other hand, George Orwell's idea of Big Brother, as
25   presented in his novel *1984,* could become a reality.

Another area of concern is language. Some people are afraid that English is being corrupted by the **jargon** computers have created. New words and new ways of using words have come from computers. We now "surf" the Web and use a "mouse" to move the cursor. Abbreviations are especially popular. E-mailing—and even more so text messaging—have developed shorthand
30   languages. With the use of terms like OIC (oh, I see) and 2G2BT (too good to be true), many people feel that the English language has become unintelligible. Conversely, those who regularly use new methods of communication consider them fast and easy ways to stay in touch with family and friends.

Some people have **qualms** about individuals interacting too often with computers and becom-
35   ing out of touch with real people. People who **telecommute** and live alone may not see or speak to a live person all week. This divide may even become greater as computers become more **humanoid**. Computer scientists are developing computers that can sense your mood. These computers would use cameras and microphones to examine facial expressions and listen to sounds. They would also use touch to see how a person handles the mouse. If the computer sensed that you were upset, it would
40   try to cheer you up, possibly by telling a joke or sympathizing with you. If you continually pushed the mouse hard, the computer might take this as a signal of frustration. The computer could then offer

to help with your problem. Many people would love a computer friend who would be readily available for support. Others have genuine concerns about isolation and the inability of people to
45 communicate with one another.

What one person sees as a wonderful innovation, such as having a refrigerator that tells you that you are out of milk and eggs or offers you recipe suggestions based on what is in the refrigerator, another person sees as an infringement. Some people
50 are afraid that the more computers can do for us the less we will be able to think for ourselves. None of us can be **complacent** as we face the challenges and enjoy the benefits new technologies bring. We will all need to do more than THT (think happy thoughts) if we are to deal with the pros and cons of each new
55 development.

Amy E. Olsen

Predicting

For each set, write the definition on the line next to the word to which it belongs. If you are unsure, return to the reading, and underline any context clues you find. After you've made your predictions, check your answers against the Word List at the end of the chapter. Place a checkmark in the box next to each word whose definition you missed. These are the words you'll want to study closely.

Set One

put into a code	showing unreasonable suspicion	fixing deeply into something	watchful
existing everywhere			

❑ 1. **ubiquitous** (line 2) _____

❑ 2. **wary** (line 7) _____

❑ 3. **encrypted** (line 13) _____

❑ 4. **embedding** (line 18) _____

❑ 5. **paranoid** (line 23) _____

Set Two

to work from home by using a computer linked to one's company	feelings of doubt	self-satisfied
the language of a particular profession or group	resembling human beings	

❑ 6. **jargon** (line 27) _____

❑ 7. **qualms** (line 34) _____

❑ 8. **telecommute** (line 35) _____

❑ 9. **humanoid** (line 36) _____

❑ 10. **complacent** (line 51) _____

Self-Tests

1 Circle the correct meaning of each vocabulary word.

1. embed:	to implant	to extract
2. telecommute:	to work in an office	to work from home
3. humanoid:	having animal traits	having human characteristics
4. jargon:	unintelligible talk	simple language
5. ubiquitous:	existing everywhere	found nowhere
6. complacent:	worried	untroubled
7. wary:	cautious	hasty
8. encrypt:	to put into a code	to share
9. paranoid:	suspicious	trusting
10. qualm:	certainty	uneasiness

2 Complete the following sentences using the vocabulary words. Use each word once.

VOCABULARY LIST

humanoid	telecommute	encrypt	complacent	paranoid
jargon	ubiquitous	wary	embedded	qualm

1. We had become _____ about updating the security software on our computer, so we shouldn't have been surprised when we found a virus on it.

2. My major _____ about going camping this weekend is the weather. There is supposed to be a huge snowstorm in the mountains.

3. I enjoy science fiction shows with _____ characters, such as Data from *Star Trek: The Next Generation* or the Cylons in *Battlestar Galactica*.

4. The geologist carefully dug out the fossil that had been _____ in the side of the cliff for millions of years.

5. So much computer _____ is based on abbreviations that I'm often unsure of what someone is trying to tell me.

6. My friend is _____ that someone is listening to his phone conversations, so sometimes we have to speak in code.

7. I was afraid to buy anything online because I thought my credit card number would be stolen, but after I read how carefully sites _____ information these days, I have been successfully shopping electronically for months.

8. Computer terms have become so _____ that my five-year-old said he wanted an "e-hug" from me instead of a real hug.

9. I am _____ of ads that claim to be able to make me look twenty years younger or make me rich in one month.

10. I'm glad my job lets me _____; I hated dealing with the horrible traffic every morning and evening when I had to drive to work.

3 Match each vocabulary word to the appropriate situation or example. Use each word once.

1. a vase surrounded by foam in a box to ship _____
2. hard drive, CD-ROM, BFF, L8R _____
3. being able to work in one's pajamas _____
4. cell phones, reality television _____
5. The Terminator _____
6. #jf4^)6*9j _____
7. possible feeling after riding a roller coaster _____
8. constantly looking over one's shoulder _____
9. reaction to an e-mail from an unfamiliar company _____
10. barely studying for a third test because you got A's on the first two _____

VOCABULARY LIST

wary	telecommute
encrypt	complacent
paranoid	jargon
embed	humanoid
qualm	ubiquitous

Identify the two vocabulary words represented in the drawings.

Word Visions

1. _____

2. _____

Word Wise

Internet Activity: How Often Is It Used?

Here is an activity that illustrates different contexts for the vocabulary words and emphasizes the enormity of the Internet. Type a vocabulary word into a search engine such as Google or Yahoo. See how many times the word is found. Read through the first entries to examine how the word is used. Open a site that seems interesting and look for the word to see it in its full context. For example, the word *telecommute* turned up 3,320,000 results. Among the first ten entries, it was used in the contexts of companies friendly to telecommuting and how to convince your boss to let you telecommute. Sometimes you will get a lot more results. *Thesis* turned up 77,700,000 results. Have fun seeing what is out there. Share your finds with classmates. What words did people pick to look up? Which word had the fewest results and which the most? Did anyone find an exciting site?

Your word: _____ Number of results: _____
A sample context: _____
Name of the Web site you visited: _____

Interactive Exercise

Answer the following questions about the vocabulary words.

1. Do you feel that your private information is safely encrypted when you shop online or use the Internet for banking or other personal transactions? Explain why or why not.
   _____

2. What is something that is ubiquitous on your college campus?
   _____

3. What is a situation where it would be wise to be wary? _____

4. If you had a computer chip embedded in your hand, what features would you like it to provide?
   _____

5. Would you like a job where you could telecommute? Explain why or why not.
   _____

6. What would be an action of a paranoid? _____

7. What is something people shouldn't be complacent about? _____

8. What are two qualms freshmen usually have when they enter college?
   _____

9. Would you prefer to own a computer that looks humanoid or one that looks like a machine? Why?
   _____

10. Give two examples of jargon you might use in a typical day. Where do the words come from (the Internet, text messaging, or your job)?
    _____

Word Part Reminder

Below are a few exercises to help you review word parts. Fill in the missing word part from the list, and circle the meaning of the word part found in each sentence.

trib	oid	multi	sequ

1. He looked and acted so much like a human that I was shocked to learn that Nathan is
   an andr_____.

2. I enjoyed getting to follow the further adventures of Detective Lewis Thor in the
   _____el to the first novel, where he solved a murder on the Oregon coast.

3. We will give out one thousand brochures on child safety this weekend. By
   dis_____uting that many, we will help a lot of people.

4. There were many reasons I failed to make it to the study session, but, among
   my _____tude of problems, the main one was that my car wouldn't start.

Word List

complacent
[kəm plā′ sənt]

adj. pleased with oneself, often to a dangerous degree; self-satisfied; untroubled

embed
[em bed′]

v. 1. to fix deeply into something; to implant
2. to envelop or enclose

encrypt
[en kript′]

v. 1. to put into a code
2. to change a file or e-mail message by using a code so it will be meaningless to unauthorized users if intercepted while traveling over a network

humanoid
[hyōō′ mə noid′]

adj. resembling human beings; having human characteristics

n. a being with human form; an android

jargon
[jär′ gən, -gon]

n. 1. the language of a particular profession or group
2. unintelligible talk

paranoid
[par′ ə noid′]

adj. showing unreasonable or abnormal distrust or suspicion

n. one afflicted with paranoia

qualm
[kwäm, kwôm]

n. 1. a feeling of doubt or misgiving; uneasiness
2. a feeling of sickness, faintness, or nausea

telecommute
[tel′ i kə myōōt′]

n. to work from home by using a computer linked to one's company

ubiquitous
[yōō bik′ wi təs]

adj. existing or being everywhere, especially at the same time

wary
[wâr′ ē]

adj. cautious; watchful

Words to Watch

Which words would you like to practice with a bit more? Pick 3–5 words to study, and list them below. Write the word and its definition, and compose your own sentence using the word correctly. This extra practice could be the final touch to learning a word.

Word	Definition	Your Sentence
1.		
2.		
3.		
4.		
5.		

Education

What's Your Personality?

Education

What's Your Personality?

It is obvious that people react differently in the same situations and that people have different job and hobby preferences. In an effort to understand the reasons for these differences, researchers began
5 to classify people's behaviors into categories called personality types. Katherine Briggs and her daughter Isabel Briggs-Myers, beginning in the 1920s, developed one of the most famous personality tests. They based their studies on the Swiss psychologist Carl
10 Jung's (1875–1961) work. Jung felt people had **inherent** preferences and that, to lead a successful

Flying Colors Ltd./Digital Vision/Getty Images

life, a person needed to follow his or her **inclinations** instead of trying to change them. Briggs and her daughter took Jung's ideas and began to study thousands of people to come up with questions that could lead to personality profiles. By 1956 they had developed a test that the Educational Testing
15 Service (ETS), the group that administers the Scholastic Aptitude Test (SAT), was willing to publish. There was some initial resistance to the test since neither woman was a psychologist, but their work prevailed, and since then the Myers-Briggs Type Indicator (MBTI) has been given to millions of people.

    One area most personality tests examine is how people prefer to interact with others. The questions aim to see whether a person is an **introvert** or **extrovert**. Introverts tend to be shy, and they do not enjoy
20 dealing with people. They prefer having a few friends to spend time with, and they like working alone. Extroverts, on the other hand, relish meeting people, having lots of friends, and working with others. In school, introverts and extroverts often look at being involved in group projects differently, with extroverts usually welcoming working with others.

    Another area of difference is how people perceive the world. Some people are known as "sensors."
25 They like to get information in a **sequential** order, they like facts, and they like hands-on activities. These are the people who prefer to use their five senses to gather information. They are the **tactile** people who want to touch something to test its reality. The other group is called "intuitive." They are fine with getting information in ran-
30 dom order, and they enjoy dealing with **abstract** ideas. In educational settings, these differences can lead to problems. Most elementary school teachers, about 70%, are sensory types, and most people are sensory types, also about 70%. The predominance of sensory early-learning teachers works
35 well for most young students, but about 77% of college professors are the intuitive type. For many sensors, a college lecture given by an intuitive, who freely makes random observations and uses generalities, becomes frustrating. They want an outline; they want order. They want concrete ex-
40 amples. This difference makes **academia** difficult for some personality types.

Shutterstock

Another difference is whether people are "thinkers" or "feelers" when they make decisions. Thinkers are very logical. They tend to be detached, and their goal is fairness. Feelers are more concerned with how the results of a decision will affect other people. They are concerned with harmony over justice. The last
45 type of difference features the "judgers" and the "perceivers." Judgers like an orderly environment. They make a plan and stick to it. Perceivers prefer to be spontaneous. They don't like to make firm decisions. For this type, what works one day might not be the right thing to do the next day.

The MBTI asks questions that help people create a personality profile that includes the four ways of interacting with the world. Two possible personality types are the ISTJ (Introvert, Sensor, Thinker,
50 Judger) and the ENFP (Extrovert, Intuitive, Feeler, Perceiver). These two types deal with situations differently, and they relate to each other differently, which can sometimes lead to arguments and stressful situations. It can be helpful to understand these differences to better get along with each other and to better know oneself. For instance, a person can create a **scenario** involving an educational situation and imagine how he or she would act based on a given personality profile. Personality profiles, however,
55 don't try to confine the individual. They allow for the **multifaceted** nature of each person, but they can help a person see one's inclinations. An awareness of why one behaves a certain way can assist a person in a variety of life's activities from education and career choices to romance and money management.

Predicting

For each set, write the definition on the line next to the word to which it belongs. If you are unsure, return to the reading, and underline any context clues you find. After you've made your predictions, check your answers against the Word List at the end of the chapter. Place a checkmark in the box next to each word whose definition you missed. These are the words you'll want to study closely.

Set One

| in order   existing in someone as a permanent quality   preferences   an outgoing person   a shy person |

☐ 1. **inherent** (line 11) _____

☐ 2. **inclinations** (line 12) _____

☐ 3. **introvert** (line 19) _____

☐ 4. **extrovert** (line 19) _____

☐ 5. **sequential** (line 25) _____

Set Two

| an imagined series of events   an idea not related to a specific example |
| many-sided   the world of higher education   pertaining to the sense of touch |

☐ 6. **tactile** (line 27) _____

☐ 7. **abstract** (line 30) _____

☐ 8. **academia** (line 40) _____

☐ 9. **scenario** (line 53) _____

☐ 10. **multifaceted** (line 55) _____

Self-Tests

1 Match each term with its synonym in Set One and its antonym in Set Two.

Synonyms

Set One

_____ 1. academia   a. concrete

_____ 2. scenario   b. natural

_____ 3. tactile   c. university

_____ 4. inclination   d. preference

_____ 5. inherent   e. plan

Antonyms

Set Two

_____ 6. abstract   f. simple

_____ 7. extrovert   g. extrovert

_____ 8. multifaceted   h. concrete

_____ 9. sequential   i. random

_____ 10. introvert   j. introvert

2 Finish the following sentences. Use each word once.

VOCABULARY LIST

inherent	academia	introvert	sequential	extrovert
multifaceted	inclination	tactile	abstract	scenario

1. An extreme _____ might spend a year alone and not miss the company of other people.

2. Some people say that those in _____ are too far removed from daily life and live in an "ivory tower."

3. A study was just published that suggests kindness is _____ in all people.

4. A local professor's _____ ideas on time travel have won him a Science Foundation award.

5. My husband is the _____ in the family. He can visit with people for hours, while I prefer to sit in the corner reading a book.

6. In one _____ I take seven classes and attend summer session to graduate early, while in another I head to Europe for six months and graduate late. I know which sounds better to me.

7. Kids love the new _____ display at the Children's Museum. It lets them touch objects found in rivers and oceans.

8. The City Council's _____ plan to restructure the city's departments will begin in departments starting with "A" and continue in order through the alphabet.

9. My first _____ was to clean my son's room, but I stopped myself and decided he needs to learn to pick up after himself.

10. Sayuri wants to be a _____ person, so she plans to major in biology and literature, as well as learn to play the piano and become an expert at fencing.

3 For each set, complete the analogies.

Set One

VOCABULARY LIST

scenario	inherent	inclination	introvert	academia

1. faulty : flawed :: innate : _____

2. likes big parties : extrovert :: avoids crowds : _____

3. detective : murder scene :: professor : _____

4. menu : restaurant :: _____ : movie

5. aversion : snakes :: _____ : sleeping in

Set Two

VOCABULARY LIST

sequential	multifaceted	abstract	extrovert	tactile

6. sunset : visual :: a shower : _____

7. troll : mean :: _____ : sociable

8. cow : animal :: economic problems : _____

9. yell : whisper :: _____ : random

10. barber : cut :: dentist : _____

Identify the two vocabulary words represented in the photographs.

Word Visions

Gerald Warnken, Jr.

1. _____

Milt Olsen

2. _____

Word Wise

Internet Activity: Web Search

Do a Web search for three of the words below. Record a sentence from a Web site that uses the word. Also provide the address (URL) for each Web site. Consider how seeing a word in another context strengthens your retention of its meanings.

scenario	academia	introvert	extrovert	inherent	inclination

1. _____

_____

2. _____

_____

3. _____

_____

Interactive Exercise

Finish each of the sentence starters using at least one of the vocabulary words in each sentence. Feel free to add word endings to the vocabulary words as needed (i.e., -s, -ed, -ly).

EXAMPLE:
An obstacle I have had to overcome in college is _*my inclination to complete assignments at the last minute.*_

1. I would describe myself as _____ because _____

   _____

2. I would describe one of my friends as _____ because _____

   _____

3. An obstacle I have had to overcome is _____

   _____

4. I like it when my professors _____

5. My favourite subject in college is _____ because _____

   _____

6. When I am assigned to work with a group, I feel_____

   _____

7. I make decisions _____

8. One aspect of college that I really enjoy is _____

   _____

9. When I started college, I was surprised to see _____

   _____

10. The information in this chapter's reading is relevant to my life because _____

   _____

HINT

A World of Words

Keep your eyes open for new words. You will certainly encounter new words in the textbooks you read in college and in the lectures your professors give, but new words can be found everywhere. Don't turn off your learning when you leave the classroom. When you see a new word in a newspaper or on the Web or even on a billboard, use the strategies you have learned in this book: Look for context clues around the new word, try to predict the meaning, and check the dictionary if you aren't sure of the meaning. No matter where you are or at what age you may be, your vocabulary can continue to grow.

Word List

abstract
[adj. and v. ab
strakt′, ab′ strakt,
n. ab′ strakt]

adj. 1. an idea not related
to a specific example
2. not easily understood;
complex
v. 1. to take out; to
extract
2. to summarize
n. a summary

academia
[ak′ ə dē′ mē ə]

n. the world of higher
education; a scholastic
environment or life

extrovert
[ek′ strə vûrt′]

n. an outgoing person

inclination
[in′ klə nā′ shən]

n. 1. a liking or preference
2. a tendency toward a
certain action or
condition; a leaning

inherent
[in hēr′ ənt, -her′]

adj. existing in someone or
something as a permanent
quality; innate; natural

introvert
[in′ trə vûrt′]

n. a shy person

multifaceted
[mul′ tē fas′ i tid, tī-]

adj. many-sided; versatile;
complex

scenario
[si när′ ē ō′, si när′-]

n. 1. an imagined series of
events; a projected plan
with several possibilities
2. an outline of the plot of
a play, movie, etc.

sequential
[si kwen′ shəl]

adj. characterized by a regular
order of parts; in order;
following

tactile
[tak′ til, -tīl]

adj. pertaining or perceptible to
the sense of touch; concrete

Words to Watch

Which words would you like to practice with a bit more? Pick 3–5 words to study, and list them below. Write the word and its definition, and compose your own sentence using the word correctly. This extra practice could be the final touch to learning a word.

Word	Definition	Your Sentence
1.		
2.		
3.		
4.		
5.		

Film

Well Worth Watching

From Chapter 24 of *Academic Vocabulary: Academic Words*, Fifth Edition. Amy E. Olsen. Copyright © 2013 by Pearson Education, Inc. All rights reserved.

Film

Well Worth Watching

Classic Movie Corner

If you are looking for a great movie to spend time with this weekend, here are two classics that won't disappoint you, even if you have seen them before.

5 *Wild Strawberries* (1957)

The Everett Collection

Ingmar Bergman's *Wild Strawberries* has been **hailed** as a masterpiece, and it is a film that deserves its reputation. Bergman wrote
15 and directed the film. The movie takes viewers into the mind of Isak Borg, an elderly gentleman, as he embarks on a long car trip to receive an honorary degree. The **cinematography** brilliantly uses black-and-white contrasts to show his
20 disturbed thoughts. **Surreal** dream sequences take us into his past and into his **disconcerted** mind. Clocks without hands and an examination room with strange questions are among the unusual experiences Dr. Borg faces. The
25 **juxtapositions** of old age and youth (both Borg's youth and the young people he meets on his journey) force us, as well as the doctor, to examine life and our actions. As this is a film you will want to discuss after viewing, invite your
30 friends over to share ideas on what the dream sequences might mean and what Bergman may have wanted people to gain from seeing the movie.

35 The film stars Victor Sjostrom, Bibi Andersson, Ingrid Thulin, Gunnar Bjornstand, and Max Von Sydow. Swedish. 90 minutes.

Psycho (1960)

The Everett Collection

Alfred Hitchcock's films are a must for the **connoisseur** of the suspense **genre**, and *Psycho* is one of his best films. Whether you have seen it
40 once, twice, or a hundred times, it is worth another viewing, and if you have never seen it, it is about time you did. Hitchcock was marvelously **attuned** to the darker sides of human nature, and he was able to convey the fears and desires of lust
45 and greed in fascinating images. In the famous shower scene, for example, Hitchcock uses **montage** to create the suspense. Through careful editing, he creates tension in the audience while barely showing the plunging knife touch the
50 victim. In fact, Hitchcock put seventy-eight short shots together to create the scene. For many people, *Psycho* **epitomizes** the suspense movie. It holds all the thrills an audience expects from the unexpected. Hitchcock masterfully used lighting,
55 camera movements, and music to create the terror one craves in a suspense movie, unlike many of the disappointing horror films of today that reveal too much, too fast, and too predictably. Norman Bates continues to reign as one of the scariest
60 characters in film history.

The film stars Anthony Perkins, Vera Miles, John Gavin, Martin Balsam, John McIntire, and Janet Leigh. American. 108 minutes.

Predicting

For each set, write the definition on the line next to the word to which it belongs. If you are unsure, return to the reading, and underline any context clues you find. After you've made your predictions, check your answers against the Word List at the end of the chapter. Place a checkmark in the box next to each word whose definition you missed. These are the words you'll want to study closely.

Set One

fantastic	approved enthusiastically	disturbed
the art of motion picture photography	acts of placing close together	

❑ 1. **hailed** (line 9) _____

❑ 2. **cinematography** (line 18) _____

❑ 3. **surreal** (line 20) _____

❑ 4. **disconcerted** (line 21) _____

❑ 5. **juxtapositions** (line 25) _____

Set Two

a style	a film editing technique	a person who can judge the best in a field
serves as a typical or perfect example of	adjusted	

❑ 6. **connoisseur** (line 39) _____

❑ 7. **genre** (line 39) _____

❑ 8. **attuned** (line 44) _____

❑ 9. **montage** (line 48) _____

❑ 10. **epitomizes** (line 53) _____

Self-Tests

1 Circle the correct meaning of each vocabulary word.

1. hail:	welcome	ignore
2. connoisseur:	unsure of quality	judge of the best
3. genre:	a style	an exception
4. montage:	separate	combining to form a whole
5. attune:	adjust	clash
6. epitomize:	typify	conceal
7. disconcerted:	clear	confused
8. surreal:	unreal	factual
9. cinematography:	art of writing	art of motion picture photography
10. juxtaposition:	putting far apart	placing close together

Identify the two vocabulary words represented in the drawings.

1. _____

2. _____

2 Finish the sentences. Use each word once.

VOCABULARY LIST

epitomized	attuned	connoisseur	surreal	juxtaposition
montage	hailed	disconcerted	genre	cinematography

1. My father is a chocolate _____; he will eat nothing but the finest European chocolates.

2. The newspaper reviewer loved the concert; she _____ it as the best performance in the symphony's twenty-year history.

3. The _____ of scenes on a quiet beach with the freeway traffic really showed that the character needed to escape the pressures of the big city.

4. The vivid colors used in the film caused me to pay attention to the _____ over the other elements such as music and plot.

Amy E. Olsen

5. By being _____ to the latest trends, some producers can create a movie that capitalizes on a fad such as skateboarding or disco dancing.

6. It is easy to become _____ in today's multiplex theaters; I went to get popcorn and couldn't find my way back without asking an usher for directions.

7. On movie night we make a bowl of popcorn, and we each select a film from our favorite _____ to watch. I pick a musical, and my husband chooses an action film.

8. In *Battleship Potemkin,* Eisenstein's skillful editing of scenes showing the poor treatment of the sailors creates a powerful _____ that depicts the men's discontent.

9. The scene where the man threw the puppy off the roof _____ his evil nature.

10. It was a(n) _____ experience when I woke up in a hotel room and thought I was in my own bedroom.

3 These comments are overheard as people file out of the multiplex movie theater. Match each sentence to the word it best fits. Use each word once.

VOCABULARY LIST

genre	surreal	attune	disconcerted	juxtaposition
montage	hail	epitomize	connoisseur	cinematography

1. "The desert scenes were beautifully filmed. They really showed the richness of color in the sand and the sunsets." _____

2. "That was a great film! It's going to be the year's best movie!" _____

3. "Even though it was so strange, I liked it when everyone started flying around and speaking that strange language." _____

4. "Once I got used to the relaxed pace of the movie, I really enjoyed it." _____

5. "I am an expert on horror movies, and I can tell you this was not one of the director's best efforts." _____

6. "It really disturbed me when the movie began jumping back and forth between the past and the present." _____

7. "Next time we stay home and rent Westerns: those are my kind of movies." _____

8. "It was interesting how the blonde woman was standing next to old cars in so many scenes. I think the director was trying to make a point about stereotypes in America." _____

9. "That film is a perfect example of everything I dislike about musicals, especially having people break into a song every ten minutes." _____

10. "I liked the part where the director put the various shots of prison life together to show the boredom of the prisoners." _____

Word Wise

Collocations

I was *disconcerted by* Alfred's suggestion that I wasn't telling the whole truth about what I had done over the weekend.

Interesting Etymologies

Hail comes from the Middle English phrase *waes haeil,* "be healthy." The word *wassail,* a drink, also comes from this origin, and it is often drunk during times of well wishing in the December holidays. When a movie is hailed as great, there are well wishes there too. Hail means "to welcome; to call out to" and "to approve enthusiastically."

Interactive Exercise

Answer the following questions.

1. What is your favorite movie genre? _____

2. What might happen in a surreal dream? _____
_____

3. What would look unusual juxtaposed next to a piece of fruit? _____
_____

4. What are you a connoisseur of, or what would you like to be a connoisseur of? _____
_____

5. What can you do to be better attuned to the feelings of others? _____
_____
_____

6. Which movie star do you think epitomizes style? _____

7. What movie do you think has beautiful cinematography? _____
_____

8. What could happen in a movie to make you feel disconcerted? _____
_____
_____

9. What would you hail as a great achievement of humankind? _____
_____
_____

10. If you were to create a montage showing the first day of kindergarten, what are three images you would use? _____
_____
_____

HINT

Make It Yours

An important step in learning new vocabulary is to practice using the words. When you feel comfortable with a word's definition, start using the word in your writing and conversations. If you only try to memorize the word for a test, you will likely forget it after the test. Make your acquisition of new vocabulary meaningful by using the words in everyday situations. Also try to connect the word to prior knowledge or experiences. Are there situations you have been in in which the word would be appropriate? Try to integrate the word with your life as much as possible. You will impress your friends and family and feel good about yourself as you show people what you have learned.

Word List

attune
[ə toon', ə tyoon']

v. to adjust; to bring into harmony

cinematography
[sin' ə mə tog' rə fē]

n. the art or technique of motion picture photography

connoisseur
[kon' ə sûr', -soor']

n. a person who can judge the best in an art or other field

disconcerted
[dis' kən sûrt' əd]

adj. disturbed; disordered; confused

epitomize
[i pit' ə miz']

v. to serve as a typical or perfect example of; to typify

genre
[zhän' rə]

n. a class of artistic work (movie, book, etc.) having a particular form, content, or technique; a style

hail
[hāl]

v. 1. to approve enthusiastically
2. to cheer; to welcome; to call out to

juxtaposition
[juk' stə pə zish' ən]

n. an act of placing close together, especially for comparison or contrast

montage
[mon täzh']

n. 1. a film editing technique that presents images next to each other to convey an action, idea, or feeling
2. the combining of various elements to form a whole or single image

surreal
[sə rē' əl, -rēl']

adj. unreal; fantastic; having the quality of a dream

Words to Watch

Which words would you like to practice with a bit more? Pick 3–5 words to study, and list them below. Write the word and its definition, and compose your own sentence using the word correctly. This extra practice could be the final touch to learning a word.

Word	Definition	Your Sentence
1. _____	_____	_____
_____	_____	_____
2. _____	_____	_____
_____	_____	_____
3. _____	_____	_____
_____	_____	_____
4. _____	_____	_____
_____	_____	_____
5. _____	_____	_____
_____	_____	_____

Answer Key to Vocabulary Lessons, pages 359-449. (Pages are approximate)

"Composition: The Midterm"

Predicting Set One: 1. a proposal that is defended by argument 2. a plan 3. to disprove 4. clear or dramatic 5. consistency

Set Two:
6. the choice and use of words 7. to quote as an example or expert
8. to make notes or comments on 9. to express in other words
10. to use the words or ideas of someone else as one's own

Self-Test 1:
1. to quote 2. choice of words 3. to steal 4. to express in other words
5. to disprove a statement 6. to make notes in a book 7. orderly relationship
8. brilliant 9. a plan 10. a proposal

Self-Test 2:
1. cite 2. vivid 3. paraphrase 4. diction 5. plagiarize
6. annotate 7. refute 8. thesis 9. intention 10. coherence

Self-Test 3:
1. vivid 2. thesis 3. diction 4. coherence 5. paraphrase
6. annotate 7. intention 8. refuted 9. plagiarize 10. cite

Word Visions: 1. vivid 2. annotate
Read Word Wise, hint; Skip Interactive Exercise. Use Word list for definitions; skip Words to Watch.

"Mathematics: Work It Out"
Predicting: Set One: 1. a part of a total amount or an allowance 2. numerical facts
3. the average 4. the middle number in a specified sequence of numbers 5. to figure
Set Two: 6. a symbol that represents a changeable amount 7. parallel to level ground
8. to cross 9. lines that go in the same direction and never meet 10. balanced
Self -Test 1:
1. T 2. T 3. T 4. F 5. F 6. F 7. T 8. T 9. T 10. F
Self-Test 2:
1. statistics 2. symmetrical 3. calculate 4. variable 5. intersect
6. quota 7. median 8. horizontal 9. parallel 10. mean

Self-Test 3:
1. horizontal 2. variable 3. calculate 4. symmetrical 5. median
6. quota 7. intersect 8. parallel 9. mean 10. statistics
Word Visions: 1. symmetrical 2. parallel

"Word Parts I"

Self-Test 1: 1. ambidextrous   2. postbellum   3. conductor   4. deposit   5. denote
6. survive   7. magnum   8. attitude   9. wisdom   10. levitate

Self-Test 2: 1. after   2. condition   3. rise   4. mark   5. lead   6. around
7. put   8. great   9. life   10. state of

Self-Test 3:
1. ambi   2. dom   3. pos   4. duc   5. not   6. mag   7. viv   8. tude   9. post   10. lev

Self Test 4:
1. C   2. G   3. J   4. I   5. F   6. D   7. E   8. H   9. A   10. B

Self-Test 5: (Set One) 1. d   2. e   3. c   4. b   5. a
(Set Two) 6. I   7. f   8. h   9. j   10. g

Skip Interactive Exercise. Word Visions: 1. mag-, great, large   2. –lev-, lift, light, rise
Skip Word Wise (Read the HINT)

"Sociology: The Importance of Hello"

Predicting: Set One: 1. a learning process   2. having the quality to spread throughout
3. standing, especially social standing   4. the act of developing levels of class
5. a standard

Set Two: 6. forbidden from use   7. excluded
8. to move away from a set behavior   9. customary   10. to relieve
Self-Test 1:   1. T   2. F   3. T   4. T   5. F   6. F   7. T   8. F   9. T   10. T

Self-Test 2:   1. socialization   2. pervasive   3. conventional   4. norm
5. taboo   6. deviate   7. ostracize   8. status   9. stratification   10. alleviate

Word Visions: 1. stratification   2. taboo
Self-Test 3:   1. conventional   2. alleviate   3. status   4. taboo   5. pervasive
6. socialization   7. deviate   8. stratification   9. norm   10. ostracized
Read Word Wise; Skip Interactive Exercise, Hint, Use Word List, skip words to watch.
"Foreign Languages: Welcome Additions"

Predicting: Set One: 1. out-of-doors   2. as served on a particular day   3. a witty remark
4. the good life   5. There it is!

Set Two: 6. seize the day   7. a ghostly double or counterpart   8. nothing
9. a mistake   10. the spirit of the time

Self-Test 1:   1. C   2. D   3. E   4. A   5. B   6. H   7. I   8. J   9. G   10. F
Self-Test 2:   1. du jour   2. dolce vita   3. doppelganger   4. bon mot
5. nada   6. carpe diem   7. faux pas   8. zeitgeist   9. alfresco   10. voila

Word Visions: 1. alfresco   2. nada

Self-Test 3:   1. nada   2. du jour   3. zeitgeist   4. alfresco   5. bon mot   6. voila
7. faux pas   8. carpe diem   9. doppelganger   10. la dolce vita

Read Word Wise; Skip Interactive Exercise, Word Part Reminder, Words to Watch. Use Word List for definitions.

"Word Parts II"

Self-Test 1:   1. sympathize   2. complacent   3. fluid   4. coherent   5. exhale
6. foremost   7. anthrophobia   8. export   9. pervade   10. stationary

Self-Test 2:   1. out of   2. completely   3. flow   4. together   5. please
6. fear of   7. stick   8. most   9. to carry   10. stand

Self-Test 3:

1. phobia   2. sym   3. ex   4. port   5. per   6. sti   7. her   8. plac
9. flu   10. most

Self-Test 4: 1. I   2. F   3. J   4. B   5. H   6. A   7. G   8. D   9. C   10. E
Self-Test 5: 1. C   2. A   3. D   4. E   5. B   6. H   7. G   8. I   9. J   10. F

Skip Interactive Exercise, Word Visions: 1. –port-, to carry   2. –flu-, flux-, to flow
Read Word Wise/Hint

"Word Parts III"

Self-Test 1: 1. secure   2. asteroid   3. centennial   4. distribute   5. Paraprofessional
6. abstract   7. metastasis   8. multitalented   9. commute   10. sequence

Self-Test 2: 1. resemble   2. change   3. give   4. follow   5. almost   6. process
7. changes   8. year   9. draw   10. many

Self-Test 3:
1. ann   2. trib   3. oid   4. mut   5. ure   6. meta   7. multi   8. tract   9. sequ   10. para

Self-Test 4: 1. b   2. f   3. j   4. a   5. c   6. d   7. g   8. I   9. h   10. g
Self-Test 5: 1. c   2. b   3. d   4. a   5. e   6. j   7. f   8. I   9. g   10. h

Interactive Exercise: Skip. Word Visions: 1. multi-, many, much   2. –sequ-, to follow
Word Wise/Hint: Read!

"Computer Science: Concerns to Consider"

Predicting: Set One: **1.** existing everywhere   2. watchful   3. put into a code
4. fixing deeply into something   5. showing unreasonable suspicion

Set Two: 6. the language of a particular profession or group 7. feelings of doubt 8. to work from home by using a computer linked to one's company 9. resembling human beings 10. self-satisfied

Self-Test 1:
1. to implant 2. to work from home 3. having human characteristics
4. unintelligible talk 5. existing everywhere 6. untroubled 7. cautious
8. to put into a code 9. suspicious 10. uneasiness

Self-Test 2:
1. complacent 2. qualm 3. humanoid 4. embedded 5. jargon
6. paranoid 7. encrypt 8. ubiquitous 9. wary 10. telecommute

Self-Test 3:
1. embed 2. jargon 3. telecommute 4. ubiquitous 5. humanoid
6. encrypt 7. qualm 8. paranoid 9. wary 10. complacent
Word Visions: 1. telecommute 2. embed

Skip Word Wise, Interactive Exercise, Word Part Reminder, and Words to Watch. Use Word List for definitions.

"Political Science: Searching for the Ideal"

Predicting: Set One: 1. resembling an ideal place 2. the entire range
3. a state where power rests with the citizens 4. a government that uses dictatorial control
5. to remove
Set Two: 6. environment 7. the working class 8. the property-owning class
9. a system of beliefs or ideas 10. pertaining to right and wrong conduct

Self-Test 1: 1. idealized 2. power with the people 3. middle class 4. system of beliefs
5. to remove 6. Range 7. surroundings 8. working class 9. Authoritarian 10. fair
Self-Test 2: 1. totalitarian 2. oust 3. gamut 4. ideology 5. utopian
6. bourgeoisie 7. proletariat 8. republic 9. ethical 10. milieu
Word Visions: 1. oust 2. gamut
Self-Test 3: 1. utopian 2. gamut 3. totalitarian 4. ethical 5. republic
6. bourgeoisie 7. proletariat 8. milieu 9. oust 10. ideology
Read Word Wise; Skip interactive exercise; Read Hint, skip Words to Know; use Word List for definitions.

"Education: What's Your Personality?"

Predicting: **Set One:** 1. existing in someone as a permanent quality 2. preferences
3. a shy person 4. an outgoing person 5. in order

Set Two: 6. pertaining to the sense of touch 7. an idea not related to a specific example
8. the world of higher education 9. an imagined series of events 10. many-sided

Self-Test 1: 1. C   2. E   3. A   4. D   5. B   6. H   7. J   8. F   9. I   10. G

Self-Test 2: 1. introvert   2. academia   3. inherent   4. abstract   5. extrovert   6. scenario   7. tactile   8. sequential   9. inclination   10. multifaceted

Self-Test 3:

1. inherent   2. introvert   3. academia   4. scenario   5. inclination
6. tactile   7. extrovert   8. multifaceted   9. sequential   10. abstract

Word Visions: 1. tactile   2. Academia   **Word Wise: Skip; Interactive Exercise: Skip (But read the HINT);   Skip Words to Watch; Use Word List for Definitions**

"Film: Well Worth Watching"

Predicting: Set One: 1. approved enthusiastically   2. the art of motion picture photography
3. fantastic   4. disturbed   5. acts of placing close together

Set Two: 6. a person who can the judge the best in a field   7. a style
8. adjusted   9. a film editing technique   10. serves as a typical or perfect example of

Self-Test 1:

1. welcome   2. judge of the best   3. a style   4. combining to form a whole   5. adjust
6. typify   7. confused   8. unreal   9. art of motion picture photography
10. placing close together

Word Visions: 1. connoisseur   2. hail

Self-Test 2:

1. connoisseur   2. hailed   3. juxtaposition   4. cinematography   5. attuned
6. disconcerted   7. genre   8. montage   9. epitomized   10. surreal

Self-Test 3:

1. cinematography   2. hail   3. surreal   4. attune   5. connoisseur
6. disconcerted   7. genre   8. juxtaposition   9. epitomize   10. montage

Read Word Wise; Skip Interactive Exercise; Read Hint; Skip Words to Watch; Use Word List for Definitions.

Study Skills for College

How to Mark a Book

Mortimer Adler

Mortimer Adler (1902–2001) received his Ph.D. from Columbia University in 1928. A conservative thinker, Adler advocated education based on the "truths" found in the classical works of Western civilization. Many academic intellectuals have scorned his simple formulas for progress, but the larger culture has often embraced his ideas, as his post as chairman of the editorial board of the Encyclopedia Britannica *indicated. His Great Books project, for which he is widely known, resulted in the publication and wide circulation of handsome bound sets of important works of world literature. As you read his essay on how to mark a book, you will see a man who thought that the world is, or ought to be, clear and simple.*

1   You know you have to read "between the lines" to get the most out of anything. I want to persuade you to do something equally important in the course of your reading. I want to persuade you to "write between the lines." Unless you do, you are not likely to do the most efficient kind of reading.

    I contend, quite bluntly, that marking up a book is not an act of mutilation but of love.

    You shouldn't mark up a book which isn't yours. Librarians (or your friends) who lend you books expect you to keep them clean, and you should. If you decide that I am right about the usefulness of marking books, you will have to buy them. Most of the world's great books are available today, in reprint editions, at less than a dollar.

    There are two ways in which you can own a book. The first is the property right you establish by paying for it, just as you pay for clothes and furniture. But this act of purchase is only the prelude to possession. Full ownership comes only when you have made it a part of yourself, and the best way to make yourself a part of it is by writing in it. An illustration may make the point clear. You buy a beefsteak and transfer it from the butcher's ice-box to your own. But you do not own the beefsteak in the most important sense until you consume it and get it into your bloodstream. I am arguing that books, too, must be absorbed in your bloodstream to do you any good.

Confusion about what it means to *own* a book leads people to a false reverence for paper, binding, and type—a respect for the physical thing—the craft of the printer rather than the genius of the author. They forget that it is possible for a man to acquire the idea, to possess the beauty, which a great book contains, without staking his claim by pasting his bookplate inside the cover. Having a fine library doesn't prove that its owner has a mind enriched by books; it proves nothing more than that he, his father, or his wife, was rich enough to buy them.

There are three kinds of book owners. The first has all the standard sets and best-sellers—unread, untouched. (This deluded individual owns woodpulp and ink, not books.) The second has a great many books—a few of them read through, most of them dipped into, but all of them as clean and shiny as the day they were bought. (This person would probably like to make books his own, but is restrained by a false respect for their physical appearance.) The third has a few books or many—everyone of them dog-eared and dilapidated, shaken and loosened by continual use, marked and scribbled in from front to back. (This man owns books.)

Is it false respect, you may ask, to preserve intact and unblemished a beautifully printed book, an elegantly bound edition? Of course not. I'd no more scribble all over a first edition of *Paradise Lost* than I'd give my baby a set of crayons and an original Rembrandt! I wouldn't mark up a painting or a statue. Its soul, so to speak, is inseparable from its body. And the beauty of a rare edition or of a richly manufactured volume is like that of a painting or a statue.

But the soul of a book *can* be separated from its body. A book is more like the score of a piece of music than it is like a painting. No great musician confuses a symphony with the printed sheets of music. Arturo Toscanini reveres Brahms, but Toscanini's score of the C-minor Symphony is so thoroughly marked up that no one but the maestro himself can read it. The reason why a great conductor makes notations on his musical scores—marks them up again and again each time he returns to study them—is the reason why you should mark your books.

If your respect for magnificent binding or typography gets in the way, buy yourself a cheap edition and pay your respects to the author.

Why is marking up a book indispensable to reading? First, it keeps you awake. (And I don't mean merely conscious; I mean wide awake.) In the second place, reading, if it is active, is thinking, and thinking tends to express itself in words, spoken or written. The marked book is usually the thought-through book. Finally, writing helps you remember the thoughts you had, or the thoughts the author expressed. Let me develop these three points.

If reading is to accomplish anything more than passing time, it must be active. You can't let your eyes glide across the lines of a book and come up with an understanding of what you have read. Now an ordinary piece of light fiction, like say, *Gone With the Wind,* doesn't require the most active kind of reading. The books you read for pleasure can be read in a state of relaxation, and nothing is lost. But a great book, rich in ideas and beauty, a book that raises and tries to answer great fundamental questions, demands the most active reading of which you are capable. You don't absorb the ideas of John Dewey the way you absorb the crooning of Mr. Vallee. You have to reach for them. That you cannot do while you're asleep.

If, when you've finished reading a book, the pages are filled with your notes, you know that you read actively. The most famous *active* reader of great books I know is President Hutchins, of the University of Chicago. He also has the hardest schedule of business activities of any man I know. He invariably reads with a pencil, and sometimes, when he picks up a book and pencil in the evening, he finds himself, instead of making intelligent notes, drawing what he calls "caviar factories" on the margins. When that happens, he puts the book down. He knows he's too tired to read, and he's just wasting time.

But, you may ask, why is writing necessary? Well, the physical act of writing, with your own hand, brings words and sentences more sharply before your mind and preserves them better in your memory. To set down your reaction to important words and sentences you have read, and the questions they have raised in your mind, is to preserve those reactions and sharpen those questions.

Even if you wrote on a scratch pad, and threw the paper away when you had finished writing, your grasp of the book would be surer. But you don't have to throw the paper away. The margins (top and bottom, as well as side), the end-papers, the very space between the lines, are all available. They aren't sacred. And, best of all, your marks

473

and notes become an integral part of the book and stay there forever. You can pick up the book the following week or year, and there are all your points of agreement, disagreement, doubt, and inquiry. It's like resuming an interrupted conversation with the advantage of being able to pick up where you left off.

And that is exactly what reading a book should be: a conversation between you and the author. Presumably he knows more about the subject than you do; naturally, you'll have the proper humility as you approach him. But don't let anybody tell you that a reader is supposed to be solely on the receiving end. Understanding is a two-way operation; learning doesn't consist in being an empty receptacle. The learner has to question himself and question the teacher. He even has to argue with the teacher, once he understands what the teacher is saying. And marking a book is literally an expression of your differences, or agreements of opinion, with the author.

15   There are all kinds of devices for marking a book intelligently and fruitfully. Here's the way I do it:

1. *Underlining:* Of major points, of important or forceful statements.
2. *Vertical lines at the margin:* To emphasize a statement already underlined.
3. *Star, asterisk, or other doo-dad at the margin:* To be used sparingly, to emphasize the ten or twenty most important statements in the book. (You may want to fold the bottom corner of each page on which you use such marks. It won't hurt the sturdy paper on which most modern books are printed, and you will be able to take the book off the shelf at any time and, by opening it at the folded corner page, refresh your recollection of the book.)
4. *Numbers in the margin:* To indicate the sequence of points the author makes in developing a single argument.
20   5. *Numbers of other pages in the margin:* To indicate where else in the book the author made points relevant to the point marked; to tie up the ideas in a book, which, though they may be separated by many pages, belong together.
6. *Circling of key words or phrases.*
7. *Writing in the margin, or at the top or bottom of the page, for the sake of:* Recording questions (and perhaps answers) which a passage raised in your mind; reducing a complicated discussion to a simple statement; recording the sequence of major points right through the books. I use the end-papers at the back of the book

15

to make a personal index of the author's points in the order of their appearance.

The front end-papers are, to me, the most important. Some people reserve them for a fancy bookplate. I reserve them for fancy thinking. After I have finished reading the book and making my personal index on the back end-papers, I turn to the front and try to outline the book, not page by page, or point by point (I've already done that at the back), but as an integrated structure, with a basic unity and an order of parts. This outline is, to me, the measure of my understanding of the work.

If you're a die-hard anti-book-marker, you may object that the margins, the space between the lines, and the end-papers don't give you room enough. All right. How about using a scratch pad slightly smaller than the page-size of the book—so that the edges of the sheets won't protrude? Make your index, outlines, and even your notes on the pad, and then insert these sheets permanently inside the front and back covers of the book.

25 Or, you may say that this business of marking books is going to slow up your reading. It probably will. That's one of the reasons for doing it. Most of us have been taken in by the notion that speed of reading is a measure of our intelligence. There is no such thing as the right speed for intelligent reading. Some things should be read quickly and effortlessly, and some should be read slowly and even laboriously. The sign of intelligence in reading is the ability to read different things differently according to their worth. In the case of good books, the point is not to see how many of them you can get through, but rather how many can get through you—how many you can make your own. A few friends are better than a thousand acquaintances. If this be your aim, as it should be, you will not be impatient if it takes more time and effort to read a great book than it does a newspaper.

You may have one final objection to marking books. You can't lend them to your friends because nobody else can read them without being distracted by your notes. Furthermore, you won't want to lend them because a marked copy is a kind of intellectual diary, and lending it is almost like giving your mind away.

If your friend wishes to read your *Plutarch's Lives,* "Shakespeare," or *The Federalist Papers,* tell him gently but firmly to buy a copy. You will lend him your car or your coat—but your books are as much a part of you as your head or your heart.

Annotation

Annotation helps readers to read actively, interact with the author, remain connected to the text, and avoid zoning out. Many readers find that annotation contributes to improved comprehension and retention when reading college-level material.

Here is a checklist of some ways to mark a text.

1. Underline or highlight major points or important statements.

2. Use symbols such as stars or asterisks (*) or numbers to indicate text that is meaningful or key in some way.

3. Underline so as to identify the structure of the text: central theme/thesis statement, main ideas/topic sentences, major supporting details.

4. Make notes to identify logic patterns, such as numbering each reason identified by a transition, or that indicate cause/effect or comparison/contrast.

5. Make margin notes that restate key points or state inferences.

6. Make notes that carry on a "conversation" with the author: agreeing or disagreeing with points, or just reacting in some way.

7. Make marks to indicate where you lost interest.

8. Make question marks to identify confusing passages.

9. Circle key words or important vocabulary.

10. Circle unclear vocabulary.

11. **If you know that you will be summarizing and/or responding to the text, here's a nifty idea:** In the left margin, make notes of anything pertaining to the text. For example, make note of the main idea, or restate it in your own words. Number reasons, define vocabulary, or make note of organizational patterns. In the right margin, make connections to the text. Respond, question, agree or disagree, or react. When you are finished, your left margin should contain

information to help you write a summary, and the right margin will contain information to help you write a response.

Keep in mind that annotating and highlighting are meant to catch the most essential information, so you have to be selective. If you highlight the majority of the text, you won't be able to identify the really important concepts and ideas.

Annotation is also quite personal. You don't have to do the entire list shown above, nor should you be limited to it. Just keep a pencil in your hand and interact with the material in a way that is meaningful and will lead to understanding it better and remembering more.

Annotating What You Read

Annotating what you read is a helpful technique for comprehension and study. To *annotate* means to mark a selection and make notes to yourself. Below is a sample annotated passage from *The Big Change* by Frederick Lewis Allen, a historical book similar to the history textbooks for your college courses. Allen traces the causes and effects of the Great Depression of the 1920s and 1930s, one of the greatest economic crises to face the United States. In this excerpt the author explains how the Depression affected people, but he writes without expressing his opinions or emotions.

The Great Depression

Frederick Lewis Allen

Intro:
Historical
anecdote
traces be-
ginning of
Depression

1   On the morning of October, 24, 1929, the towering structure of American prosperity cracked wide open. For many days the prices of stocks on the New York Stock Exchange had been sliding faster and faster downhill; that morning they broke in a wild panic. The leading bankers of New York met at the (House of Morgan) to form a buying pool to support the market; Richard Whitney, brother of a leading Morgan partner, thereupon crossed the street to the great hall of the Stock Exchange and put in orders to buy United States Steel at 205; and for a time prices rallied. Pierpont Morgan had halted the Panic of 1907. Surely this panic, too, would yield to the organized confidence of the great men of the world of finance.

What?
Check

C & C
to past

2   But within a few days it was clear that they could no more stop the flood of selling than (Dame Partington) could sweep back the Atlantic Ocean. On it went, session after session. On the worst day, October 29, over sixteen million shares of stock were thrown on the market by frantic sellers. And it was not until November 13 that order was restored.

?

Under-
standable!

3   In the course of a few brief weeks, thirty billion dollars in paper values had vanished into thin air—an amount of money larger than the national debt at that time. The whole credit structure of the American economy had been shaken more severely than anybody then dared guess. The legend of Wall Street leadership had been punctured. And the Great Depression was on its way.

4   At first business and industry in general did not seem to have been gravely affected. Everybody assured everybody else that nothing really important had happened, and during the spring of 1930 there was actually a Little Bull Market of considerable proportions. But in May this spurt was at an end. And then there began an almost uninterrupted two-year decline, not only in security prices, but also—an infinitely more serious matter—in the volume of American business: a vicious circle of ebbing sales, followed by declining² corporate income, followed by attempts to restore that income by cutting³ salaries and wages and laying⁴ off men, which caused increased⁵ unemployment and further⁶ reduced sales, which led to increased ⁷business losses, which led to further ⁸wage cutting and further firing⁹ of men, and so on toward disaster.

?

Bad
Effect on
security
prices

Effects on
biz

5-In-
creased
unemploy-
ment

6-More
reduction
in sales

7-More biz
losses

8-More
wage cuts

9-More
firing

1-Lower
sales

2-Less
corporate
income

3-Cutting
salaries

4-Laying
off workers

Yes! Must
have been

5   During these bewildering years President Hoover at first tried to organize national optimism by summoning business executives to Washington to declare that conditions were fundamentally sound and that there would be no wage cutting. This didn't work. Then for a time he was inactive, trusting to the supposedly self-correcting processes of the market. These didn't work. Then, convinced that the financial panic which was simultaneously raging in Europe was the worst source of trouble,

he organized an international moratorium in war debts and reparations—a fine stroke of diplomacy which alleviated matters only briefly. Then he set up the Reconstruction Finance Corporation to bring federal aid to hard-pressed banks and businesses—while steadfastly refusing, as a matter of principle, to put federal funds at the disposal of individual persons who were in trouble. Just when it seemed as if recovery were at hand, in the winter of 1932–1933, the American banking system went into a tailspin; even the RFC solution hadn't worked. The result was one of the most remarkable coincidences of American history. It was on March 4, 1933—the very day that Hoover left the White House and Franklin D. Roosevelt entered it—that the banking system of the United States ground to a complete halt. An able and highly intelligent President, committed to orthodox economic theories which were generally considered enlightened, had become one of the tragic victims of the collapse of the going system.

> 4
>
> 5
>
> **BAM!**
>
> **Imagine!**
>
> **Summary—
> Result**

Actions by Pres. Roosevelt to start recovery

6   Whereupon Roosevelt, declaring in his cheerfully resolute Inaugural Address that "the only thing we have to fear is fear itself," swept into a tornado of action—successfully reopening the banks and initiating that lively, helter-skelter, and often self-contradictory program of reform, relief, and stimulation which was to keep the country in a dither during the middle nineteen-thirties and bring at least a measure of recovery.

Practice. Annotate one of the following essays from this textbook: "Teenagers Are Not Becoming More Violent" by Mike Males (p. 109), or "It's Not Just a Phase" by Katherine E. Zondlo (p. 120).

Outlining What You Read

Outlining is another technique that can help you comprehend and remember what you read. It can also help you plan an essay before you write it. Following is an outline of the excerpt from Frederick Lewis Allen.

The Great Depression

Thesis: The Great Depression which started in 1929 kept the United States in a dither through the middle nineteen-thirties.

Introduction: The events that led up to the Great Depression (1–3)
  I. The effects of the Stock Market Crash on October 29, 1929 (4)
    A. Positive effects
      1. Assurances that nothing really important had happened
      2. Rally in Bull Market
    B. Negative effects
      1. Decline in security prices
      2. A downward spiral of effects on American business
        a. Fewer sales
        b. Less corporate income
        c. Lower salaries and wages
        d. Laying off workers
        e. Increased unemployment
        f. More reduction in sales
        g. More business losses
        h. More wage cuts
        i. More firings
        j. Disaster
  II. Attempts to remedy the situation (4–5)
    A. Unsuccessful attempts by President Hoover
      1. Organizing national optimism
      2. Leaving the solution to the self-correcting process of the market
      3. Organizing an international moratorium in war debts and reparations
      4. Setting up the Reconstruction Finance Corporation
      5. Refusing to allow individuals to use federal funds

B. Actions by President Roosevelt
   1. Reopening banks
   2. Initiating program of reform, relief, and stimulation

Practice. Outline one of the following essays in this textbook: "From Forced Technology to High Tech/High Touch" by John Naisbitt (p. 320), or "Friends, Good Friends—And Such Good Friends" by Judith Viorst (p. 162).

Summarizing What You Read

Writing a summary of a passage is another effective way to check your comprehension of what you read and to have a brief version for review. A *summary* is a condensation of the original, expressing the meaning in your own words. You summarize what the author says, but do not include all the explanations and examples that are in the original. Neither should you include any of your own interpretations or comments; just stick to what the author says. A summary is brief, usually 10 to 20 percent the length of the original. Here are a few tips to help you write a summary:

1. Read the entire passage first without marking or taking notes or beginning to summarize.
2. Identify the author's main point. It may be stated as a thesis sentence or it may be implied.
3. Identify and mark the major divisions of the passage.
4. Summarize section by section, not line by line or sentence by sentence.
5. When you complete the summary, compare it with the original to make sure you have not misinterpreted the author.

Following is a summary of the passage by Frederick Lewis Allen.

The Great Depression began on October 29, 1929, with the collapse of the New York Stock Exchange. Leading bankers tried to stop the collapse but could not. For a short time it seemed that there had been no negative effects, but soon it was evident that the American economy had been badly shaken. The negative effects on security prices and on business continued to increase. Although President Hoover tried to correct the downward spiral of the economy, his efforts were unsuccessful, and he became a victim of the collapse. When Roosevelt became president, he instituted a cycle of reform, relief, and stimulation, but recovery was very slow. [107 words]

Practice. Write a summary of one of the following essays from this textbook: "Relationships 101" from *Time Magazine* (p. 137), or "No Shame in My Game" by Katherine S. Newman (p. 281).

SQ3R and Cornell Note-Taking

SQ3R and Cornell Note-Taking are two study techniques that can help you read and take notes from your lectures and your textbooks efficiently.

I.   *SQ3R: Survey, Question, Read, Recite and Review*

A. **Survey.** This is a preview of a chapter. There are certain things you look for as you survey.

    1. Title: Ask yourself, what do you already know about the topic? What might you expect to learn? Activate your schema.

    2. First Paragraph: This is an introduction and it may contain the author's plan of organization.

    3. Headings and subheadings. These are the topics or concepts that have been developed by the author; some are major and others are minor.

    4. Last paragraph or conclusion. This will tie together everything in the chapter. It may include a review, final conclusions, and a restatement of the thesis.

    5. Other things to look for in the survey: Graphs, charts, definitions, questions at the end of the chapter, length.

B. **Question.** Questions create curiosity, improve concentration, and give you a purpose for your reading. They turn you into an active reader.

    1. Turn all titles, subtitles and subheadings into questions. For example, if a heading says, "Characteristics of a Plant Cell," your question might be, "What are the characteristics of a plant cell?"

    2. Write your questions down. You now know what to look for as you read. If you use the Cornell Note-taking method, write your question in the narrow column on the left.

C. **Read.** Read one section at a time, trying to find the answer to the question.

    1. If, in your reading, you discover that a different question is being answered, adjust your question accordingly.

    2. Read for good understanding, and **write down your answer** in your own words. If you use the Cornell Note-taking Method, your answer will be written in the larger column on the right.

D. **Recite.** At the end of each section, look away and say OUT LOUD your question and answer.

> 1. Hearing yourself paraphrasing information helps to get the information into your long-term memory.
> 2. Check your recall against the book.
> 3. Without reciting, you may forget HALF of what you read after only one day.

D. **Review.** Do this regularly and over time.

> 1. After you have read the material, section by section, questioning, reading and reciting, you should look at the chapter as a whole. How do all the parts relate to each other?
> 2. Some students make a map or chart of the ideas at this point.
> 3. If you recite and review each week, you will understand and remember. Review whenever you study; don't just do homework and think you are finished. By reviewing, you will need less time for test preparation and your grades will improve!

II. *Cornell Note-taking Method. This method can be used for textbooks or lectures, or both.*

A. Using a piece of regular notepaper, draw a line down the page so that you have two columns. The left column should be narrow, and the right column twice as wide. Leave a space at the bottom blank.

B. The left column is where you should write down the questions that have been generated by the subheadings you read while you used the SQ3R method on your textbook.

C. The right column is where you should write down the answers to your questions. These answers should be in your own words, and you should devise ways of abbreviating words, such as leaving out vowels or using symbols.

D. At the blank space at the bottom, summarize the notes in your own words. By putting together all the information in two or three complete sentences, you truly internalize it and make it your own.

E. Alternatively, you can use this method for lectures. In this case, you take notes on the right side of the page. Questions are then written based on the notes you have written. The summary is written the same way as #D.

Conclusion: By using the Cornell Note-taking method in combination with SQ3R, you create a study sheet containing questions and answers that you can use to study for tests. It allows you to read your textbook ONCE, very thoroughly. It is time-consuming, but by doing it well the first time, you free yourself of the burden of rereading chapters, wondering what you are supposed to get out of the reading, and trying to re-learn material instead of reviewing it.

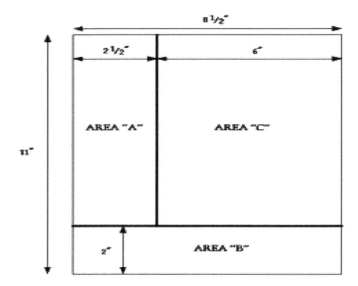

Organizing Details by Mapping

There are different ways to take notes from textbooks, so it is important to try different styles in order to know which ones work best for you in different situations. How complete your notes should be will depend on how much prior knowledge you have, what your purpose is, and the kind of test you will be taking. These study techniques will also help you in your writing classes because they can be used as pre-writing activities. A thorough outline or map will provide plenty of support for an essay.

The following paragraph on headaches will be used for both the mapping and the outlining activities.

It would be difficult to find anyone who has not suffered from a severe headache. However, not many people know there are three different types of headaches. Of these three types, the *tension* headache is the most common and least painful. This muscular headache is usually described as a dull ache in the scalp, jaw, neck, or shoulders. The second, more severe type, the *migraine* headache, affects twice as many women as it does men. The migraine, a combination of muscular and vascular contractions, is described as a throbbing pressure. Some sufferers see flashing lights or dots or lines just before their migraine strikes. Others have nausea and vomiting. The most severe and least common, the *cluster* headache, affects only 1.5 percent of the population, but it makes a person unable to function. The cluster headache focuses on eyes, neck, and temples. It is described as a hot branding poker rammed into the head. Its name comes from its tendency to hit quickly, one after the other.

-- Nancy Gottesman, from Reading Faster and Understanding More, Book 2, Fifth Ed.

The following scrambled list of phrases is taken from the paragraph. Find and underline the three most general terms.

More severe and affects twice as many women as men
Muscular—dull ache in scalp, jaw, neck, and shoulders
Tendency to hit quickly, one after another
Nausea and vomiting experienced by others
Tension headache
Focus on eyes, neck, and temples
Only 1.5 percent of population affected
Muscular and vascular contractions—throbbing pressure
Cluster headache
Migraine headache
Like a hot branding poker rammed into head
Victim unable to function
Most common and least painful
Flashing lights, dots, or lines seen before headache hits
Most severe and least common

Place the information in the list into the appropriate places on this mapping outline.

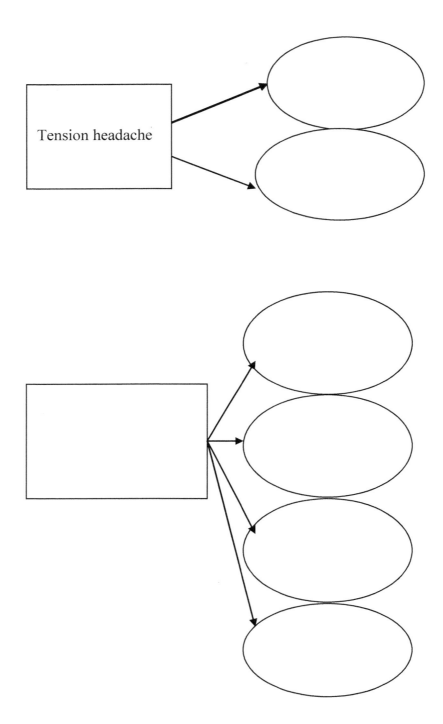

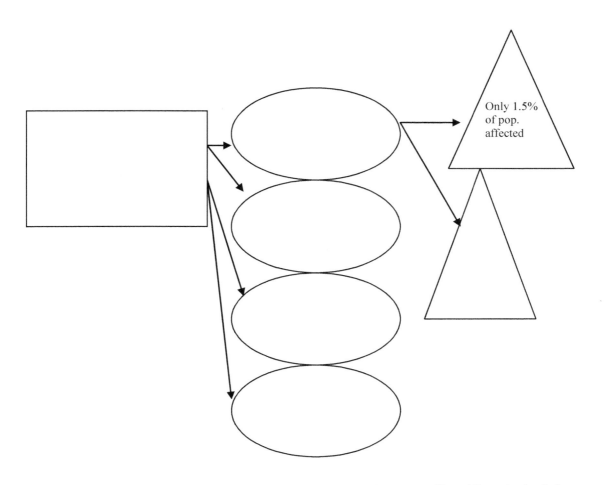

Source: *Reading Faster and Understanding More Book Two*, Fifth edition by Wanda Maureen Miller and Sharon Steeber de Orozco

Outlining

There are two types of outlines: topic outlines and sentence outlines. Topic outlines are made up of fragments, indenting, and labels (both letters and numbers). The main idea is written as the only complete sentence. In a topic outline, Roman numerals (I, II, III, IV, V) are comparable to the rectangles in the mapping outline. They represent the major details. Capital letters are comparable to the ovals in the mapping outline, and Arabic numbers (1, 2, 3) are comparable to triangles. For a long essay or chapter, you might find yourself going into fourth-level details with lowercase letters, fifth-level details with Arabic numbers in parentheses, or sixth-level details with lowercase letters in parentheses. Just remember that you alternate numbers and letters. Indent less important details to the right.

A sentence outline can be identical to the topic outline, except it uses complete sentences instead of fragments. You use the same indenting and the same labels to represent the same organization—most important to least important. Details that are parallel in importance have parallel indentation, parallel labels, and parallel wording. Some instructors, or employers asking for a business report, may require the more formal, sometimes more detailed sentence outline. A sentence outline requires writers to think even more clearly and express themselves in complete thoughts.

It is up to you what type of outline you wish to use, depending on your preference and your purpose. You can even mix the three types when you are writing study notes. What is important is that you use some method to organize your thoughts or the thoughts of the author as you make your way through a textbook. You can use these methods when reading, writing, listening, or speaking.

Practice Activity: On the next page, arrange the same information you used from the scrambled list on headaches, but this time create a **topic outline**. Place each item to the right of its appropriate label. Make sure the items in your outline are worded exactly like those in the scrambled list. Again, follow the order of the details in the paragraph. The topic outline should have the same basic organization and content that you used in the mapping outline. However, you will need to add a title and a main idea. The main idea should be expressed as a complete sentence.

Adapted from *Reading Faster and Understanding More, Book Two*, 5th edition by Wanda Maureen Miller and Sharon Steeber de Orozco.

_____
[title]

Main Idea: _____

_____
[Clue: Paraphrase the topic sentence, which is *not* the first sentence]

I. _____

    A. _____

    B. _____

II. _____

    A. _____

    B. _____

    C. _____

    D. _____

III. _____

    A. _____

        1. _____

        2. _____

    B. _____

    C. _____

    D. _____

Writing a Summary and/or a Response to an Essay, Story, or Textbook Selection

Summary Writing. The reader of your summary should be able to know, in general, what the passage was about.

- Include the title and author, preferably in the first sentence.
- Include the main idea/thesis/central point.
- Include key details…but not too many!
- Do not repeat information.
- Do not use the word "I" unless you are saying, "The last book I read was…." Do not give any opinions.
- Your summary should be in paragraph form, with complete sentences.
- Your summary could follow or comment on the logic pattern/pattern of organization of the passage itself.

Response Writing. Writing a response to what you read gives you a chance to reflect on your reading and connect with the author. There are many ways to do this. Some of them include the following:

- Write a quote (a few sentences) from the book that you liked. Be sure to record page numbers. Explain why these passages caught your attention.

- Make a prediction of what you think will happen next. Or, write a prediction of how you think the book will end. Then next time (or at the end of the book), say if your prediction was similar to what actually happened in the book.

- Did the book remind you of anything or anyone in your own life? What? Who? Write the event down (or a brief character description) and your personal event (or person that you know) that seemed similar. Be specific.

- Write a short statement of a few sentences that begins with "I noticed," "I wonder," "I agree," or "I disagree."

- Are you confused about what happened (or didn't happen) in the book? What events or characters do you not understand? Are there words or references you don't understand? What are they? Can you find answers to your questions? If so, write those down as well. They might form the basis for a future research project.

- Did the chapter evoke any emotions, such as laughter, smiles, tears, anger? Were you bored? Record some of your reactions. Be specific about what happened in the chapter that made you feel that way.

- Is there an idea or event in the book that makes you stop and think, or prompts questions? Identify the idea and explain your thoughts.

- Do you have a favorite character or least favorite character? Who it is? What does s/he do or say that makes you feel that way?

- Sometimes the location or the historical period depicted in the text may be worth thinking about. Tell what the setting is (time, place) and make observations as they pertain to such things as gender relations, race, family, social class, and ideology.

- After reading the entire book, think about whether you liked it or not. Would you recommend the book? Did it turn out the way you hoped it would? What did you think of the book overall?

Improving Reading Rate

Read in Phrases, Not for Words

Here is a technique that can start to improve both your rate and your comprehension right away: read in phrases (units of thought) instead of stopping on individual words. Consider this example:

> To / train / yourself / to / read / in / phrases, / use / the / natural /
> rhythm / of / the / language / to / help / you.

The slashes mark the places where many readers pause, whether they are aware of it or not. Too many students read word-by-word. The reader who pauses on every word in that sentence stops (or fixates) seventeen times. The person who reads in phrases, however, groups together chunks of words that make sense. A more effective reader might see the sentence this way:

> To train yourself / to read in phrases, / use the natural rhythm /
> of the language / to help you.

The slashes mark logical "bites" of meaning to take at one time. Did you notice how punctuation such as commas and periods also marks natural places to stop and read? The better reader would fixate only five times instead of seventeen times. This reader could be reading three times as fast—just because of reading in phrases instead of word-by-word.

TRY THIS: Put slashes after phrases in the following paragraph. Pay attention to what the words say so you can see which words belong together.

> When you read, hold the book about sixteen inches from your face. Try to create a mental picture of what you're reading, and your concentration (and memory) will automatically improve. Look for the six Ws that news reporters use: Who and What, Where and When, Why and How.

Use this approach on all your easier reading. As you get more practice, you'll be able to digest longer phrases at a time, and reading in phrases will soon become natural. You will probably find that it carries over into more difficult material. Be aware, however, that even the best readers read difficult materials word-by-word some of the time. Many reading experts believe word-by-word reading in such cases can even help the learning process, especially for memorizing. So don't try to speed-read your textbooks by straining to read in phrases. Other techniques, such as previewing and vocabulary building, are more likely to increase your speed when you study-read.

Avoid Margin Reading

Now that you know about the importance of reading in phrases of meaning instead of word-by-word, you can practice *fixating* on a whole phrase at a single glance. You will learn to rely more on your *peripheral vision.* This next technique also asks you to use your peripheral vision.

This is the technique of not "reading" the blank margins. If you always start fixating right on the first word of each line, you are including in your line of vision the blank margin, which contains no information. You are *margin reading.*

How do you stop wasting part of your fixation on the margin? Simply said, you start and stop your point of fixation about a half-inch—two or three words—in from each side margin. With your peripheral vision, you still see the information to the left or right of your new fixation point. So you don't lose anything except the meaningless blank space in the margin.

You may wish to try this technique right now with the rest of this page. Pencil in a light **line** going down the page on the left (under the **bolded** words) and on **the** right.

As you continue to read this page, remember to start fixating at the vertical line on the left side of the page. Then, move your eyes horizontally along the line of print as usual. Take your attention off the line of print when you get to the vertical line on the right side of the page. With a little practice, you won't need to draw vertical lines because avoiding margin reading will have become automatic. You may want to start with the narrower columns in a newspaper, and draw your own lines.

Avoid Regressing

Do you *regress* often when you read? That is, do you reread phrases, sentences, or even whole paragraphs, sometimes whole pages? If you find that you have passed your eyes over a page, recognizing the words but remembering nothing, then you may be in the habit of regressing. You may have programmed your brain to regress. You start to read and a message in your subconscious lazily says: "Oh, don't bother to tune in yet. Think about something else. You know you're just going to reread this. Tune in on the second reading."

What an obvious waste of time! To break the habit, reprogram your subconscious. Tell yourself: "You may read this only once. You will not have the luxury of rereading. A big rock will fall on your head if you regress. You have only one chance. Tune in." Or try reading with an index card in your hand. Use the card like a camera shutter to cover the lines you just read.

Even if you backslide and tune out, keep reading. Try to pick up the train of thought without regressing; you will be more successful than you think. Once your subconscious knows you have taken away the crutch of regressing, you will regress less.

Remember, both these tips—avoid margin-reading and avoid regressing—involve some skipping. So try them on your practice reading, not on your study reading.

Avoid/Break Other Bad Habits

There are some other bad habits you should avoid or break. These include:

Lip moving. If you are moving your lips while you read silently, you are reading one word per focus instead of an entire phrase. This means you are stuck at a speaking rate of 250 words per minute or lower. To break the habit, put a pencil between your lips while reading. If it falls out, you know you are moving your lips .If you feel hopelessly stuck on word-by-word reading, try this experiment. Preview an easy, interesting magazine article on a topic familiar to you. Then, as you read the article, count (one, two, three…) with your lips, while trying to keep your mind on the ideas in the article.

Finger pointing at each word to avoid losing your place limits your peripheral vision. It limits your thinking power. Your brain can move faster than your finger can. Instead of pointing your finger at each word to keep your place, run your finger down the margin while you read. Point at the *line* you are reading, not at each word. If you wish to break the habit of using your finger completely, hold the book firmly in both hands.

Squinting means you may have a vision problem. Adjust your light source. If the problem continues consider having your eyes checked. And of course, if you need reading glasses, use them!

Subvocalization is the habit of reading aloud inside your head. While subvocalization can be an effective way of study reading difficult material, it should be avoided when trying to read more quickly. Try to envision the action in a book as though you are watching a movie, instead of focusing on one word at a time.

Falling asleep while reading is common, and it could be the result of eye fatigue. However, it is more likely to be the result of poor reading/study habits. Learn to become an active reader by using the many reading strategies covered in your reading class, such as annotation, SQ3R, and note-taking.

If you have a known reading disability, you may be helped by putting a special plastic sheet over your page. The plastic sheet should be a color, such as blue, pink, or orange. See your disability advisor for more information.

--Adapted from *Reading Faster and Understanding More, Book 2*, by Wanda Maureen Miller and Sharon Steeber de Orozco

Phrase Exercise #1. These exercises have a "key phrase" on the left, followed by three phrases on the right. Find the same phrase as quickly as you can. Then slash it. Move on to the next line right away. Record your time, and check for errors.

Key Phrase		Time_____	Errors_____
1. **old rake**	gold rock	old rake	rate oak
2. **brown grass**	grown lass	brown grass	green grass
3. **hot sun**	hot sun	new home	hog sound
4. **water tap**	wooden top	water pipe	water tap
5. **spring bud**	spring bud	singing buddy	spring fever
6. **wild river**	ill diver	vile rival	wild river
7. **dry bush**	dry bush	day bed	high brush
8. **tall tree**	tall tree	late treat	tea time
9. **cold wind**	wild colt	cold wind	old window
10. **orange moon**	orange moon	arranged room	orchid moon
11. **swift stream**	stiff swing	some string	swift stream
12. **small trail**	tall sail	small trail	short trail
13. **rain cloud**	rain cloud	loud train	clear train
14. **open sky**	shy poet	open sky	open season
15. **wooden fence**	warm face	wooden fence	wood lot
16. **rough rock**	rude shock	tough cork	rough rock
17. **bright star**	right start	bright star	light year
18. **broken gate**	broken gate	grown gal	garden gate
19. **thick mud**	muddy stick	sick maid	thick mud
20. **bare hill**	rare bill	ill bear	bare hill

Phrase Exercise #2. Make a slash through the phrases identical to the key phrase.

Key Phrase	Time _____		Errors _____
1. red rug	bed bug	rude hug	red rug
2. dirty wall	thirty balls	dirty wall	flirty gal
3. light bulb	mighty bull	slight flub	light bulb
4. clean sink	pink cream	mean wink	clean sink
5. long hall	long hall	long sash	lame hand
6. sharp knife	short knave	nice harp	sharp knife
7. bread box	black bed	dread lox	bread box
8. old chair	cold choir	bold cheer	old chair
9. bright fire	bright fire	light briar	fair fight
10. soft couch	slight slouch	soft couch	some grouch
11. new broom	new broom	rude broom	nude brute
12. wide porch	poor wife	dire scorch	wide porch
13. table leg	labeled egg	maple peg	table leg
14. small dish	silly dash	all fish	small dish
15. green glass	last queen	green glass	genial lass
16. glowing lamp	rolling land	glowing lamp	bowling hand
17. cracked cup	cocker pup	cracked cup	crated rake
18. dinner bell	inner dell	ill winner	dinner bell
19. flower vase	flower vase	forward pace	lower base
20. hot toaster	low loafer	hot toaster	late boaster

Phrase Exercise #3   Make a slash through the phrases identical to the key phrase.

Key Phrase   Time _____   Errors _____

1. to save gas   to have gas   two gas savers   to save gas

2. controls pollution   central pollution   controls pollution   controlled pullout

3. owning a car   owning cars   owning a car   the owner's car

4. slow driving   slow driver   slow driving   slow drive

5. a seat belt   a neat belt   a seat belt   a near belt

6. car pool   car pooling   car pool   careful pal

7. pedal travel   pedal travel   pedal traveled   pedal drag

8. careful driver   careful driver   careful diver   scared of driving

9. radial tires   radial tires   radial tire   radical tire

10. make and model   made a model   make and model   maker's model

11. a popular item   a populous item   a popular item   a popular mite

12. having overdrive   having overhang   having overdrive   having overdone

13. lower rpm   lower rim   lower rpm   slower rpm

14. air filter   air filter   fair filter   air flight

15. natural resource   national resource   nature's resource   natural resource

16. harmful emissions   harmful omissions   harmless emissions   harmful emissions

17. wasting energy   wasteful energy   wasting energy   wasting energies

18. used the brakes   abused the brakes   fused the brakes   used the brakes

19. road tested   toad rested   rod tested   road tested

20. camping trip   camping trip   camping tent   camper rip-off

Phrase Exercise #4   Make a slash through the phrases identical to the key phrase.

Key Phrase   Time _____   Errors _____

1. six swimming swans	swats six swans	six sweet sins	six swimming swans
2. this covered wagon	the costly wigs	this covered wagon	that wagging dog
3. the dripping faucet	the file cabinet	the worst fault	the dripping faucet
4. downfall of man	downfall of man	fall of women	many funny clowns
5. a clean ashtray	a clean ashtray	clears an aisle	a betrayed clod
6. gangster movie	big motorcycle gang	picture of mother	gangster movie
7. smoke-filled lungs	smoke-filled lungs	dreadful smog	broken filling
8. polka-dot bikini	yellow dotted bikini	polka-dot bikini	danced the polka
9. down narrow streets	down narrow streets	marrow of bones	deft right turns
10. danced a jig	danced a jig	a rigged dance	a fancy jib
11. in slow motion	in slow motion	inside the track	an insolent action
12. a crossword puzzle	a crossword puzzle	a jigsaw puzzle	a puzzling word
13. handles with care	careful handling	handles with care	a hot handle
14. puts to sleep	a sleazy slut	but not there	puts to sleep
15. cooks your goose	cooks your goose	goose your crook	cupful of gin
16. prays for peace	prays for peace	pans of pears	preys on people
17. wins the war	war to win	wins the war	the won war
18. the lost letter	a lost letter	the better lot	the lost letter
19. treads on me	treads on me	reads this too	one dread night
20. rips it across	crosses the rip	trips it across	rips it across

--Adapted from *Reading Faster and Understanding More, Book 2*, by Wanda Maureen Miller and Sharon Steeber de Orozco

Skimming: Snatching Ideas on the Run

I. Introduction: Why Skim?

    A. **A good reader is a flexible reader.**

        1. Use different speeds for different purposes.

            a. Study reading vs. reading for fun

        2. Reasons to Skim

            a. Reread material you have already studied

            b. Sort out and discard, as with junk mail

            c. Look over potential reading material, such as a book or magazine

            d. When reading for pleasure, to pass over minor or uninteresting sections in order to follow the major plot in a light, easy novel

            e. To keep informed in a general way about the news

            f. To review your lecture notes after class

            g. To see which reference materials might be useful to a term paper

            h. To be able to discuss the general content of a reading assignment for a class when you didn't have time to really read it thoroughly

            i. Once learned, skimming leads to increased words per minute on usual reading materials.

II. What is Skimming?

    A. Skimming is not the same as careful reading.

    B. Skimming is purposeful **skipping** of words and sections to find the main idea.

    C. Skimming for main points requires a goal of 700-800 words per minute, or at least double (and possibly, triple!) your usual words per minute rate.

    D. Skimming works well when you need to cover a vast amount of reading quickly, when you have to pick out passages from material that contains a lot of details, with easy reading materials, or with material you consider relatively unimportant.

    E. **A 50% comprehension rate is expected.**

III. How to Skim

    A. Preview the material.

        1. Find the topic

        2. Length of material

        3. Logic patterns

        4. Organization of the material

        5. Read the title, the first paragraph, and look for the thesis statement. If it's not there, read the 2nd paragraph.

        6. Read the last paragraph. The thesis might be there as well.

    B. Look for main ideas in the first or second sentences of each paragraph.

    C. Read almost in a zigzag pattern down the page, skipping over more than one line at a time. With a newspaper article, read vertically down the column of print.

    D. Look for context clues that might signal a sequence of ideas, logic patterns, and connections being made. Look for important transitions.

    E. Be willing to miss a lot of information. Remember, you can always slow down. Right now you are trying to develop the ability to speed up.

    F. DO NOT READ EVERYTHING!

Sources: *Reading Faster and Understanding More* by Miller and Steeber de Orozco

The College Student by Walter Pauk

Essays and Stories for College Readers

The Baffling Question

Bill Cosby

Bill Cosby (1937–) dropped out of high school and entered the Navy, but eventually attended Temple University on a football scholarship and, upon graduation, began doing standup comedy. A series of Grammy-winning comedy records and hit movies and television shows followed, much of the comedy based on the commonplaces of family life. His fame as a symbol of American family life reached its peak in the 1980s when his weekly situation comedy, The Cosby Show (1984–1992), had an audience of sixty million viewers. In the essay printed below, an excerpt from his book Fatherhood *(1986), you can detect the influence of the patterns of spoken English in the pacing and development of ideas that were incorporated in comedy routines.*

1   So you've decided to have a child. You've decided to give up quiet evenings with good books and lazy weekends with good music, intimate meals during which you finish whole sentences, sweet private times when you've savored the thought that just the two of you and your love are all you will ever need. You've decided to turn your sofas into trampolines and to abandon the joys of leisurely contemplating reproductions of great art for the joys of frantically coping with reproductions of yourselves.

Why?

Poets have said the reason to have children is to give yourself immortality; and I must admit I did ask God to give me a son because I wanted someone to carry on the family name. Well, God did just that and I now confess that there have been times when I've told my son not to reveal who he is.

"You make up a name," I've said. "Just don't tell anybody who you are.

Immortality? Now that I have had five children, my only hope is that they all are out of the house before I die.

No, immortality was not the reason why my wife and I produced these beloved sources of dirty laundry and ceaseless noise. And we also did not have them because we thought it would be fun to see one of them sit in a chair and stick out his leg so that another one of them running by was launched like Explorer I. After which I said to the child who was the launching pad, "Why did you do that?"

"Do what?" he replied.

"Stick out your leg."

"Dad, I didn't know my leg was going out. My leg, it does that a lot."

If you cannot function in a world where things like this are said, then you better forget about raising children and go for daffodils. My wife and I also did not have children so they could yell at each other all over the house, moving me to say, "What's the problem?"

"She's waving her foot in my room," my daughter replied.

"And something like that *bothers* you?"

"Yes, I don't *want* her foot in my room."

"Well," I said, dipping into my storehouse of paternal wisdom, why don't you just close the door?"

"Then I can't see what she's doing!"

Furthermore, we did not have the children because we thought it would be rewarding to watch them do things that should be studied by the Menninger Clinic.

"Okay," I said to all five one day, "go get into the car."

All five then ran to the same car door, grabbed the same handle, and spent the next few minutes beating each other up. Not one of them had the intelligence to say, "Hey, *look*. There are three more doors." The dog, however, was already inside.

And we did not have the children to help my wife develop new lines for her face or because she had always had a desire to talk out loud to herself. "Don't tell *me* you're *not* going to do something when I tell you to move!" And we didn't have children so I could always be saying to someone, "Where's my change?"

Like so many young couples, my wife and I simply were unable to project. In restaurants we did not see the small children who were casting their bread on the water in the glasses the waiter had brought; and we did not see the mother who was fasting because she was both cutting the food for one child while pulling another from the floor to a chair that he would use for slipping to the floor again. And we did not project beyond those lovely Saturdays of buying precious little things after leisurely brunches together. We did not see that *other* precious little things would be coming along to destroy the first batch.

Questions for "The Baffling Question" by Bill Cosby

_____1. What does Bill Cosby expect couples to do when they don't have children?

    a. argue at restaurants, cope with reproductions of themselves, and visit museums.
    b. create great art, write good books, and cook beautiful meals.
    c. have quiet reading periods, listen to music, and speak in complete sentences during conversations.

_____2. Why would Cosby want his son to "not reveal who he is?"

    a. His son's name should be a secret; it's nobody else's business.
    b. His son had probably done something so bad that Cosby might be embarrassed by it.
    c. Cosby is such a celebrity that he doesn't want his son to be embarrassed by it.

_____3. In paragraph 15-16, Cosby says, "Furthermore, we did not have the children because we thought it would be rewarding to watch them do things that should be studied by the Menninger Clinic." The Menninger Clinic is a psychiatric institute that provides mental health treatment, research, and education. What does Cosby mean?

    a. He means that he would enjoy giving a reward to the Menninger Clinic.
    b. He means that his children's behavior is sometimes totally crazy.
    c. He means that it is rewarding to watch his children's growth at the Clinic.

_____4. What is the overall tone of this essay?

    a. sad
    b. stern
    c. disappointed
    d. humorous

_____5. The essay is organized to contrast what two things?

    a. immortality vs. mortality
    b. life with children vs. life without children
    c. insanity vs. sanity
    d. leisurely lunches vs. hectic dinners

_____6. In paragraph 18, Cosby describes what happened when five children try to get in the car at the same time. The paragraph ends with, "The dog, however, was already inside." What is being implied?

    a. The dog was already inside the car.
    b. The children were in the car with the dog.
    c. The children spent five minutes beating each other up instead of using all the doors.
    d. The dog was acting smarter than the children.

_____7. At the very end of the essay, Cosby says, "We did not see that *other* precious little things would be coming along to destroy the first batch." What is "the first batch?"

    a. the children
    b. the cookies they had baked
    c. the precious little things they had purchased after leisurely brunches
    d. their relationship

_____8. Why did Bill Cosby and his wife decide to have children?

    a. They thought it would make them immortal by continuing their genetic lineage.
    b. They had children so the children could yell at each other all over the house.
    c. They thought it would be rewarding to watch their children do crazy things.
    d. It would help his wife develop new lines on her face and make her talk to herself.
    e. They're not sure, but they do know they did not think ahead of what was to come.

_____9. What is the primary purpose of the essay?

    a. to inform
    b. to entertain
    c. to persuade

Why I Want a Wife

Judy Brady

Judy Brady (1937–), born in San Francisco, studied painting and received a B.F.A. in 1962 in art from the University of Iowa. Then she married and raised a family in a traditional housewife role. She later commented that her male professors had talked her out of pursuing a career in education. In the late 1960s, she became active in the women's movement and began writing articles on feminism and other social issues. In 1990, she was the editor of Women and Cancer, *an anthology by women. The essay "Why I Want a Wife" appeared in the first issue of* Ms. *magazine in 1972.*

1 I belong to that classification of people known as wives. I am A Wife. And, not altogether incidentally, I am a mother.

Not too long ago a male friend of mine appeared on the scene fresh from a recent divorce. He had one child, who is, of course, with his ex-wife. He is looking for another wife. As I thought about him while I was ironing one evening, it suddenly occurred to me that I, too, would like to have a wife. Why do I want a wife?

I would like to go back to school so that I can become economically independent, support myself, and, if need be, support those dependent upon me. I want a wife who will work and send me to school. And while I am going to school I want a wife to take care of my children. I want a wife to keep track of the children's doctor and dentist appointments. And to keep track of mine, too. I want a wife to make sure my children eat properly and are kept clean. I want a wife who will wash the children's clothes and keep them mended. I want a wife who is a good nurturant attendant to my children, who arranges for their schooling, makes sure that they have an adequate social life with their peers, takes them to the park, the zoo, etc. I want a wife who takes care of the children when they are sick, a wife who arranges to be around when the children need special care, because, of course, I cannot miss classes at school. My wife must arrange to lose time at work and not lose the job. It may mean a small cut in my wife's income from time to time, but I guess I can tolerate that. Needless to say, my wife will arrange and pay for the care of the children while my wife is working.

I want a wife who will take care of *my* physical needs. I want a wife who will keep my house clean, a wife who will pick up after me. I want a wife who will keep my clothes clean, ironed, mended, replaced when need be, and who will see to it that my personal things are kept in their proper place so that I can find what I need the minute I need it. I want a wife who cooks the meals, a wife who is a *good* cook. I want a wife who will plan the menus, do the necessary grocery shopping, prepare the meals, serve them pleasantly, and then do the cleaning up while I do my studying. I want a wife who will care for me when I am sick and sympathize with my pain and loss of time from school. I want a wife to go along when our family takes a vacation so that someone can continue to care for me and my children when I need a rest and change of scene.

5   I want a wife who will not bother me with rambling complaints   5
about a wife's duties. But I want a wife who will listen to me when I feel the need to explain a rather difficult point I have come across in my course of studies. And I want a wife who will type my papers for me when I have written them.

I want a wife who will take care of the details of my social life. When my wife and I are invited out by friends, I want a wife who will take care of the babysitting arrangements. When I meet people at school that I like and want to entertain, I want a wife who will have the house clean, will prepare a special meal, serve it to me and my friends, and not interrupt when I talk about the things that interest me and my friends. I want a wife who will have arranged that the children are fed and ready for bed before my guests arrive so that the children do not bother us. I want a wife who takes care of the needs of my guests so that they feel comfortable, who makes sure that they have an ashtray, that they are passed the hors d'oeuvres, that they are offered a second helping of the food, that their wine glasses are replenished when necessary, that their coffee is served to them as they like it. And I want a wife who knows that sometimes I need a night out by myself.

I want a wife who is sensitive to my sexual needs, a wife who makes love passionately and eagerly when I feel like it, a wife who makes sure that I am satisfied. And, of course, I want a wife who will not demand sexual attention when I am not in the mood for it. I want a wife who assumes the complete responsibility for birth control, because I do not want more children. I want a wife who will remain sexually faithful to me so that I do not have to clutter up my intellectual life with jealousies. And I want a wife who understands that *my* sexual needs may entail more than strict adherence to monogamy. I must, after all, be able to relate to people as fully as possible.

If, by chance, I find another person more suitable as a wife than the wife I already have, I want the liberty to replace my present wife with another one. Naturally, I will expect a fresh, new life; my wife will take the children and be solely responsible for them so that I am left free.

When I am through with school and have a job, I want my wife to quit working and remain at home so that my wife can more fully and completely take care of a wife's duties.

10   My God, who *wouldn't* want a wife?   10

Questions to "Why I Want a Wife" by Judy Brady

_____1. What is the narrator's tone?

a. sarcastic, almost bitter

b. accepting with good grace

c. resigned, giving up to the inevitable

d. sincere, honest

_____2. In the second paragraph, Brady says, "As I thought about him (a male friend, recently divorced, who is looking for another wife), while I was ironing one evening, it suddenly occurred to me that I, too, would like to have a wife." This sentence is ironic because

a. The author is ironing, a stereotypical task for a wife.

b. The author would like someone else to do her ironing for her.

c. The author means the opposite of what she is actually saying.

_____3. One way the author emphasizes the constant demands on a wife is by:

a. listing a few of them

b. repeating the phrase, "I want a wife" over and over again

c. saying how much she wishes she wasn't a wife

_____4. In paragraph 8, Brady writes, "And I want a wife who understands *my* sexual needs may entail more than strict adherence to monogamy." This means:

a. The wife has permission to take a lover.

b. This is a couple that will be loyal to each other.

c. The narrator may need monogamy more than the wife.

d. The narrator may need more than just one lover.

Note: **The following is an outline of paragraph 4. Fill in the blanks with the topic sentence/main idea sentence, and appropriate details, <u>all from the paragraph.</u>**

Paragraph 4: Find the topic sentence/main idea sentence and write it below.

I. Main Idea Statement/Sentence:

(5)_____

      A. keep my house clean

      B. pick up after me

      C. keep my clothes clean, ironed, mended, replaced

      D. keep my personal things in their proper place.

      E. cook the meals—a good cook.

          a. plan the menus (<u>use the paragraph and keep going!</u>)

          b (6). _____

          c. (7)_____

          d. (8)_____

          e. (9)_____

      F. care for me when I am sick

      a. sympathize with my pain and loss of time from school

      G. (10) _____

          a. continue to care for me and my children when I need a rest and change of scene.

Today's Kids Are, Like, Killing the English Language. Yeah, Right.

Kirk Johnson

Every generation, it seems, has some comment about the younger generation and the butchery it performs on the English language. Adults point to the speech of teenagers and see it as a sign of civilization in decline. School becomes the place where the problem is addressed and teenagers learn to use "proper" language, the language of grownups. In spite of these efforts, the language of youth persists, forcing us to ask the question, "What is language, anyway?" In this article from the August 9, 1998 issue of the New York Times, *Kirk Johnson offers a dynamic view of language, one in which language may be viewed as a logical and creative response to shifting social conditions, the cultural climate, and technological developments.*

1   As a father of two pre-teen boys, I have in the last year or so become a huge fan of the word "duh." This is a word much maligned by educators, linguistic brahmins and purists, but they are all quite wrong.

Duh has elegance. Duh has shades of meaning, even sophistication. Duh and its perfectly paired linguistic partner, "yeah right," are the ideal terms to usher in the millennium and the information age, and to highlight the differences from the stolid old 20th century.

Even my sons might stop me at this point and quash my hyperbole with a quickly dispensed, "Yeah, right, Dad." But hear me out:

"Today's Kids Are, Like, Killing the English Language. Yeah, Right." by Kirk Johnson, reprinted from the *New York Times*, August 9, 1998.

I have become convinced that duh and yeah right have arisen to fill a void in the language because the world has changed. Fewer questions these days can effectively be answered with yes or no, while at the same time, a tidal surge of hype and mindless blather threatens to overwhelm old-fashioned conversation. Duh and yeah right are the cure.

Good old yes and no were fine for their time—the archaic, black and white era of late industrialism that I was born into in the 1950's. The yes-or-no combo was hard and fast and most of all simple: It belonged to the Manichean red-or-dead mentality of the cold war, to manufacturing, to "Father Knows Best" and "It's a Wonderful Life."

5   The information-age future that my 11-year-old twins own is   5
more complicated than yes or no. It's more subtle and supple, more loaded with content and hype and media manipulation than my childhood—or any adult's, living or dead—ever was.

And duh, whatever else it may be, is drenched with content. Between them, duh and yeah-right are capable of dividing all language and thought into an exquisitely differentiated universe. Every statement and every question can be positioned on a gray scale of understatement or overstatement, stupidity or insightfulness, information saturation or yawning emptiness.

And in an era when plain speech has become endangered by the pressures of political correctness, duh and yeah right are matchless tools of savvy, winking sarcasm and skepticism: caustic without being confrontational, incisive without being quite specific.

With duh, you can convey a response, throw in a whole basket full of auxiliary commentary about the question or the statement you're responding to, and insult the speaker all at once! As in this hypothetical exchange:

Parent: "Good morning, son, it's a beautiful day."

10   *Eleven-year-old boy: "Duh."*   10

And there is a kind of esthetic balance as well. Yeah—right is the yin to duh's yang, the antithesis to duh's empathetic thesis. Where duh is assertive and edgy, a perfect tool for undercutting mindless understatement or insulting repetition, yeah right is laid back, a surfer's cool kind of response to anything overwrought or oversold.

New York, for example, is duh territory, while Los Angeles is yeah—right. Television commercials can be rendered harmless and inert by simply saying, "yeah, right," upon their conclusion. Local television news reports are helped out with a sprinkling of well-placed duhs, at moments of stunning obviousness. And almost any politician's speech cries out for heaping helpings of both at various moments.

Adolescent terms like "like," by contrast, scare me to death. While I have become convinced through observation and personal experimentation that just about any adult of even modest intelligence can figure out how to use duh and yeah right properly, like is different. Like is hard. Like is, like, dangerous.

Marcel Danesi, a professor of linguistics and semiotics at the University of Toronto who has studied the language of youth and who coined the term "pubilect" to describe the dialect of pubescence, said he believes like is in fact altering the structure of the English language, making it more fluid in construction, more like Italian or some other Romance language than good old hard-and-fast Anglo-Saxon. Insert like in the middle of a sentence, he said, and a statement can be turned into a question, a question into an exclamation, an exclamation into a quiet meditation.

15 Consider these hypothetical expressions: "If you're having broccoli for dinner, Mr. Johnson, I'm, like, out of here!" and "I was, like, no way!" and perhaps most startlingly, "He was, like, duh!"

In the broccoli case, like softens the sentence. It's less harsh and confrontational than saying flatly that the serving of an unpalatable vegetable would require a fleeing of the premises.

In the second instance, like functions as a kind of a verbal quotation mark, an announcement that what follows, "no way," is to be heard differently. The quote itself can then be loaded up with any variety of intonation—irony, sarcasm, even self-deprecation—all depending on the delivery.

In the third example—"He was, like, duh!"—like becomes a crucial helping verb for duh, a verbal springboard. (Try saying the sentence without like and it becomes almost incomprehensible.)

But like and duh and yeah right, aside from their purely linguistic virtues, are also in many ways the perfect words to convey the sense of reflected reality that is part of the age we live in. Image manipulation, superficiality, and shallow media culture are, for better or worse, the backdrop of adolescent life.

20 Adults of the yes-or-no era could perhaps grow up firm in their knowledge of what things "are," but in the Age of Duh, with images reflected back from every angle at every waking moment, kids swim

in a sea of what things are "like." Distinguishing what is from what merely seems to be is a required skill of an 11-year-old today; like reflects modern life, and duh and yeah right are the tools with which such a life can be negotiated and mastered.

But there is a concealed paradox in the Age of Duh. The information overload on which it is based is built around the computer, and the computer is, of course, built around—that's right—the good old yes-or-no binary code: Billions of microcircuits all blinking on or off, black or white, current in or current out. Those computers were designed by minds schooled and steeped in the world of yes or no, and perhaps it is not too much of a stretch to imagine my sons' generation, shaped by the broader view of duh, finding another path: binary code with attitude. Besides, most computers I know already seem to have an attitude. Incorporating a little duh would at least give them a sense of humor.

Everything Has a Name

Helen Keller

Helen Keller (1880–1968) was born in Tuscumbia, Alabama. As a result of illness, she lost her senses of sight and hearing at 19 months. Taught to speak, read, and write by Anne Sullivan, her teacher and lifelong companion, Keller graduated from Radcliffe (1904) at age 24. A symbol of personal strength and perseverance, Keller became a distinguished lecturer and writer. Her autobiography, The Story of My Life *(1902), was made into the award-winning film,* The Miracle Worker *(1959). This essay, excerpted from her autobiography, describes the moment when Keller understood the concept of language and reveals how that changed her life.*

1   The most important day I remember in all my life is the one on which my teacher, Anne Mansfield Sullivan, came to me. I am filled with wonder when I consider the immeasurable contrast between the two lives which it connects. It was the third of March, 1887, three months before I was seven years old.

On the afternoon of that eventful day, I stood on the porch, dumb, expectant. I guessed vaguely from my mother's signs and from the hurrying to and fro in the house that something unusual was about to happen, so I went to the door and waited on the steps. The afternoon sun penetrated the mass of honeysuckle that covered the porch, and fell on my upturned face. My fingers lingered almost unconsciously on the familiar leaves and blossoms which had just come forth to greet the sweet southern spring. I did not know what the future held of marvel or surprise for me. Anger and bitterness had preyed upon me continually for weeks and a deep languor had succeeded this passionate struggle.

From *The Story of My Life* published by Doubleday, a division of Bantam Double Dell Publishing Groups, Inc.

Have you ever been at sea in a dense fog, when it seemed as if a tangible white darkness shut you in, and the great ship, tense and anxious, groped her way toward the shore with plummet and sounding-line, and you waited with beating heart for something to happen? I was like that ship before my education began, only I was without compass or sounding-line, and had no way of knowing how near the harbour was. "Light! give me light!" was the wordless cry of my soul, and the light of love shone on me in that very hour.

I felt approaching footsteps. I stretched out my hand as I supposed to my mother. Some one took it, and I was caught up and held close in the arms of her who had come to reveal all things to me, and, more than all things else, to love me.

The morning after my teacher came she led me into her room and gave me a doll. The little blind children at the Perkins Institution had sent it and Laura Bridgman [the first deaf and blind person to be educated in the United States] had dressed it; but I did not know this until afterward. When I had played with it a little while, Miss Sullivan slowly spelled into my hand the word "d-o-l-l." I was at once interested in this finger play and tried to imitate it. When I finally succeeded in making the letters correctly I was flushed with childish pleasure and pride. Running downstairs to my mother I held up my hand and made the letters for doll. I did not know that I was spelling a word or even that words existed: I was simply making my fingers go in monkey-like imitation. In the days that followed I learned to spell in this uncomprehending way a great many words, among them *pin, hat, cup,* and a few verbs like *sit, stand* and *walk.* But my teacher had been with me several weeks before I understood that everything has a name.

One day, while I was playing with my new doll, Miss Sullivan put my big rag doll into my lap also, spelled "d-o-l-l" and tried to make me understand that "d-o-l–l" applied to both. Earlier in the day we had had a tussle over the words "m-u-g" and "w-a-t-e-r." Miss Sullivan had tried to impress it upon me that "m-u-g" is *mug* and that "w-a-t-e-r" is *water,* but I persisted in confounding the two. In despair she had dropped the subject for the time, only to renew it at the first opportunity. I became impatient at her repeated attempts and, seizing the new doll, I dashed it upon the floor. I was keenly delighted when I felt the fragments of the broken doll at my feet. Neither sorrow nor regret followed my passionate outburst. I had not loved the doll. In the still, dark world in which I lived there was no strong sentiment or tenderness. I felt my teacher sweep the fragments to one side of the hearth, and I had a sense of satisfaction that the cause of my discomfort was removed. She brought me my hat, and I knew I was going out into the warm sunshine. This thought, if a wordless sensation may be called a thought, made me hop and skip with pleasure.

We walked down the path to the well-house, attracted by the fragrance of the honeysuckle with which it was covered. Some one was drawing water and my teacher placed my hand under the spout. As the cool stream gushed over one hand she spelled into the other the word *water,* first slowly, then rapidly. I stood still, my whole attention fixed upon the motions of her fingers. Suddenly I felt a misty consciousness as of something forgotten—a thrill of returning thought; and somehow the mystery of language was revealed to me. I knew then that "w-a-t-e-r" meant the wonderful cool something that was flowing over my hand. That living word awakened my soul, gave it light, hope, joy, set it free! There were barriers still, it is true, but barriers that could in time be swept away.

I left the well-house eager to learn. Everything had a name, and each name gave birth to a new thought. As we returned to the house every object which I touched seemed to quiver with life. That was because I saw everything with the strange, new sight that had come to me. On entering the door I remembered the doll I had broken. I felt my way to the hearth and picked up the pieces. I tried vainly to put them together. Then my eyes filled with tears; for I realized what I had done, and for the first time I felt repentance and sorrow.

I learned a great many new words that day. I do not remember what they all were; but I do know that *mother, father, sister, teacher* were among them—words that were to make the world blossom for me, "like Aaron's rod, with flowers." It would have been difficult to find a happier child than I was as I lay in my crib at the close of that eventful day and lived over the joys it had brought me, and for the first time longed for a new day to come.

Questions for "Everything Has a Name" by Helen Keller

_____1. Based on the first paragraph, what pattern of organization does the author use for this excerpt?

    a. comparison
    b. cause
    c. time sequence
    d. classification

_____2. What is the main idea of the excerpt?

    a. Helen receives and destroys a new doll from the blind children at the Perkins Institute.
    b. Miss Sullivan teaches words to Helen using sign language.
    c. By learning language, people who are deaf and blind can find their life-line to the world.
    d. Helen's dark, shapeless world grows to have meaning and form as she learns how to communicate with words, thanks to her new teacher.

_____3. What "two lives" does Helen Keller refer to in the first paragraph?

    a. Her life at that time vs. her life before her illness
    b. Her life before and after the Civil War.
    c. Her life before and after she learned language.
    d. Her life as a child vs. her life as an adult.

_____4. Helen Keller's writing seems to support the idea that there can be no thought without language. Which of the following quotes does **NOT** support that idea?

    a. "Anger and bitterness had preyed upon me continually for weeks and a deep languor had succeeded this passionate struggle."
    b. "'Light! Give me light!' was the wordless cry of my soul, and the light of love shone on me in that very hour."
    c. "Everything had a name, and each name gave birth to a new thought."
    d. "This thought, if a wordless sensation may be called a thought, make me hop and skip with pleasure."
    e. "That living word awakened my soul, gave it light, hope, joy, set it free!"

_____5. What was Ms. Keller's purpose for her writing?

    a. to persuade
    b. to inform
    c. to entertain

_____6. What is the tone of the piece?

    a. angry, bitter, sarcastic
    b. humorous
    c. ironic, dishonest
    d. hopeful, upbeat

_____7. In paragraph 2, Keller writes, "My fingers lingered almost unconsciously on the familiar leaves and blossoms (of the honeysuckle) which had just come forth to greet the sweet southern spring." Which pattern of organization does this section seem to represent?

    a. comparison
    b. description
    c. generalization and example

8. Find a descriptive phrase that appeals to one of the senses and write it on the line.

_____

_____9. What does Helen Keller mean when she says, "In the still, dark world in which I lived there was no strong sentiment or tenderness?"

    a. She could neither read nor talk, so her life was still, unmoving, and dark.
    b. The "dark world" she inhabited was not illuminated by language or ideas, so she could neither frame nor express her feelings.
    c. Strong feelings were against her natural temperament.

_____10. An "autobiography" is

    a. A fictional account of someone's life.
    b. A biography written by a person other than the person in question.
    c. A biography written by a person about his or her own life.

Learning to Read and Write

Frederick Douglass

Frederick Douglass (1817–1895)—abolitionist, author, and the first black American to become a prominent public figure—was born into slavery near Tuckahoe, Maryland. As a youth, Douglass worked as a household servant, a field hand, and a shipyard apprentice. In 1838, after several failed attempts to escape (for which he received beatings), he successfully reached New York. He took the surname "Douglass" and eventually settled in New Bedford, Massachusetts. In 1841, the Massachusetts Anti-Slavery League, impressed by his great oratory skills, hired Douglass to help promote the abolition of slavery. Douglass bought his freedom in 1847, using money contributed both by Americans and by sympathizers in England, where he had fled to preserve his freedom. For the next 13 years, Douglass edited the abolitionist periodical North Star *(changed to* Frederick Douglass's Paper *in 1851). During the Civil War, Douglass urged President Lincoln to emancipate the slaves and helped recruit black troops. After the war, he held a series of government posts, including Assistant Secretary to the Santo Domingo Commission, Marshall of the District of Columbia, District Recorder of Deeds, and Ambassador to Haiti. This essay, which comes from Douglass's autobiography,* Narrative of the Life of Frederick Douglass, an American Slave *(1845), reveals the guile and determination that Douglass employed to teach himself to read. As you read the words of a former slave, written more than a century ago, think of how closed the world was to Douglass, yet how he recognized that literacy could help open the door.*

1   I lived in Master Hugh's family about seven years. During this time,   1
I succeeded in learning to read and write. In accomplishing this, I
was compelled to resort to various stratagems. I had no regular
teacher. My mistress, who had kindly commenced to instruct me, had,
in compliance with the advice and direction of her husband, not only
ceased to instruct, but had set her face against my being instructed by
any one else. It is due, however, to my mistress to say of her, that she
did not adopt this course of treatment immediately. She at first lacked
the depravity indispensable to shutting me up in mental darkness. It
was at least necessary for her to have some training in the exercise of
irresponsible power, to make her equal to the task of treating me as
though I were a brute.

My mistress was, as I have said, a kind and tender-hearted
woman; and in the simplicity of her soul she commenced, when I first
went to live with her, to treat me as she supposed one human being
ought to treat another. In entering upon the duties of a slaveholder,
she did not seem to perceive that I sustained to her the relation of a
mere chattel, and that for her to treat me as a human being was not
only wrong, but dangerously so. Slavery proved as injurious to her as
it did to me. When I went there, she was a pious, warm, and tender-
hearted woman. There was no sorrow or suffering for which she had
not a tear. She had bread for the hungry, clothes for the naked, and
comfort for every mourner that came within her reach. Slavery soon
proved its ability to divest her of these heavenly qualities. Under its
influence, the tender heart became stone, and the lamb-like disposi-
tion gave way to one of tiger-like fierceness. The first step in her downward course was in her ceasing to instruct me. She now commenced
to practise her husband's precepts. She finally became even more violent in her opposition than her husband himself. She was not satisfied
with simply doing as well as he had commanded; she seemed anxious
to do better. Nothing seemed to make her more angry than to see me
with a newspaper. She seemed to think that here lay the danger. I have
had her rush at me with a face made all up of fury, and snatch from
me a newspaper, in a manner that fully revealed her apprehension. She
was an apt woman; and a little experience soon demonstrated, to her
satisfaction, that education and slavery were incompatible with each
other.

From this time I was most narrowly watched. If I was in a separate room any considerable length of time, I was sure to be suspected

of having a book, and was at once called to give an account of myself. All this, however, was too late. The first step had been taken. Mistress, in teaching me the alphabet, had given me the *inch,* and no precaution could prevent me from taking the *ell.*

The plan which I adopted, and the one by which I was most successful, was that of making friends of all the little white boys whom I met in the street. As many of these as I could, I converted into teachers. With their kindly aid, obtained at different times and in different places, I finally succeeded in learning to read. When I was sent on errands, I always took my book with me, and by going one part of my errand quickly, I found time to get a lesson before my return. I used also to carry bread with me, enough of which was always in the house, and to which I was always welcome; for I was much better off in this regard than many of the poor white children in our neighborhood. This bread I used to bestow upon the hungry little urchins, who, in return, would give me that more valuable bread of knowledge. I am strongly tempted to give the names of two or three of those little boys, as a testimonial of the gratitude and affection I bear them; but prudence forbids;—not that it would injure me, but it might embarrass them; for it is almost an unpardonable offense to teach slaves to read in this Christian country. It is enough to say of the dear little fellows, that they lived on Philpot Street, very near Durgin and Bailey's shipyard. I used to talk this matter of slavery over with them. I would sometimes say to them, I wished I could be as free as they would be when they got to be men. "You will be free as soon as you are twenty-one, *but I am a slave for life!* Have not I as good a right to be free as you have?" These words used to trouble them; they would express for me the liveliest sympathy, and console me with the hope that something would occur by which I might be free.

5   I was now about twelve years old, and the thought of being *a slave for life* began to bear heavily upon my heart. Just about this time, I got hold of a book entitled "The Columbian Orator." Every opportunity I got, I used to read this book. Among much of other interesting matter, I found in it a dialogue between a master and his slave. The slave was represented as having run away from his master three times. The dialogue represented the conversation which took place between them, when the slave was retaken the third time. In this dialogue, the whole argument in behalf of slavery was brought forward by the master, all of which was disposed of by the slave. The slave was made to

say some very smart as well as impressive things in reply to his master—things which had the desired though unexpected effect; for the conversation resulted in the voluntary emancipation of the slave on the part of the master.

In the same book, I met with one of Sheridan's mighty speeches on and in behalf of Catholic emancipation. These were choice documents to me. I read them over and over again with unabated interest. They gave tongue to interesting thoughts of my own soul, which had frequently flashed through my mind, and died away for want of utterance. The moral which I gained from the dialogue was the power of truth over the conscience of even a slaveholder. What I got from Sheridan was a bold denunciation of slavery, and a powerful vindication of human rights. The reading of these documents enabled me to utter my thoughts, and to meet the arguments brought forward to sustain slavery; but while they relieved me of one difficulty, they brought on another even more painful than the one of which I was relieved. The more I read, the more I was led to abhor and detest my enslavers. I could regard them in no other light than a band of successful robbers, who had left their homes, and gone to Africa, and stolen us from our homes, and in a strange land reduced us to slavery. I loathed them as being the meanest as well as the most wicked of men. As I read and contemplated the subject, behold! that very discontentment which Master Hugh had predicted would follow my learning to read had already come, to torment and sting my soul to unutterable anguish. As I writhed under it, I would at times feel that learning to read had been a curse rather than a blessing. It had given me a view of my wretched condition, without the remedy. It opened my eyes to the horrible pit, but to no ladder upon which to get out. In moments of agony, I envied my fellow-slaves for their stupidity. I have often wished myself a beast. I preferred the condition of the meanest reptile to my own. Any thing, no matter what, to get rid of thinking! It was this everlasting thinking of my condition that tormented me. There was no getting rid of it. It was pressed upon me by every object within sight or hearing, animate or inanimate. The silver trump of freedom had roused my soul to eternal wakefulness. Freedom now appeared, to disappear no more forever. It was heard in every sound, and seen in every thing. It was ever present to torment me with a sense of my wretched condition. I saw nothing without seeing it, I heard nothing without hearing it, and felt nothing without feeling it. It looked from every star, it smiled in every calm, breathed in every wind, and moved in every storm.

I often found myself regretting my own existence, and wishing myself dead; and but for the hope of being free, I have no doubt but that I should have killed myself, or done something for which I should have been killed. While in this state of mind, I was eager to hear any one speak of slavery. I was a ready listener. Every little while, I could hear something about the abolitionists. It was some time before I found what the word meant. It was always used in such connections as to make it an interesting word to me. If a slave ran away and succeeded in getting clear, or if a slave killed his master, set fire to a barn, or did any thing very wrong in the mind of a slaveholder, it was spoken of as the fruit of *abolition.* Hearing the word in this connection very often, I set about learning what it meant. The dictionary afforded me little or no help. I found it was "the act of abolishing," but then I did not know what was to be abolished. Here I was perplexed. I did not dare to ask any one about its meaning, for I was satisfied that it was something they wanted me to know very little about. After a patient waiting, I got one of our city papers, containing an account of the number of petitions from the north, praying for the abolition of slavery in the District of Columbia, and of the slave trade between the States. From this time I understood the words *abolition* and *abolitionist,* and always drew near when that word was spoken, expecting to hear something of importance to myself and fellow-slaves. The light broke in upon me by degrees. I went one day down on the wharf of Mr. Waters; and seeing two Irishmen unloading a scow of stone, I went, unasked, and helped them. When we had finished, one of them came to me and asked me if I were a slave. I told him I was. He asked, "Are ye a slave for life?" I told him that I was. The good Irishman seemed to be deeply affected by the statement. He said to the other that it was a pity so fine a little fellow as myself should be a slave for life. He said it was a shame to hold me. They both advised me to run away to the north; that I should find friends there, and that I should be free. I pretended not to be interested in what they said, and treated them as if I did not understand them; for I feared they might be treacherous. White men have been known to encourage slaves to escape, and then, to get the reward, catch them and return them to their masters. I was afraid that these seemingly good men might use me so; but I nevertheless remembered their advice, and from that time I resolved to run away. I looked forward to a time at which it would be safe for me to escape. I was too young to think of doing so immediately; besides, I wished to learn how to write, as I might have occasion to write my own pass. I consoled myself with the hope that I should one day find a good chance. Meanwhile, I would learn to write.

The idea as to how I might learn to write was suggested to me by being in Durgin and Bailey's ship-yard, and frequently seeing the ship carpenters, after hewing, and getting a piece of timber ready for use, write on the timber the name of that part of the ship for which it was intended. When a piece of timber was intended for the larboard side, it would be marked thus—"L." When a piece was for the starboard side, it would be marked thus—"S." A piece for the larboard side forward, would be marked thus—"L. F." When a piece was for starboard side forward, it would be marked thus—"S. F." For larboard aft, it would be marked thus—"L. A." For starboard aft, it would be marked thus—"S. A." I soon learned the names of these letters, and for what they were intended when placed upon a piece of timber in the shipyard. I immediately commenced copying them, and in a short time was able to make the four letters named. After that, when I met with any boy who I knew could write, I would tell him I could write as well as he. The next word would be, "I don't believe you. Let me see you try it." I would then make the letters which I had been so fortunate as to learn, and ask him to beat that. In this way I got a good many lessons in writing, which it is quite possible I should never have gotten in any other way. During this time, my copy-book was the board fence, brick wall, and pavement; my pen and ink was a lump of chalk. With these, I learned mainly how to write. I then commenced and continued copying the Italics in Webster's Spelling Book, until I could make them all without looking on the book. By this time, my little Master Thomas had gone to school, and learned how to write, and had written over a number of copy-books. These had been brought home, and shown to some of our near neighbors, and then laid aside. My mistress used to go to class meeting at the Wilk Street meetinghouse every Monday afternoon, and leave me to take care of the house. When left thus, I used to spend the time in writing in the spaces left in Master Thomas's copy-book, copying what he had written. I continued to do this until I could write a hand very similar to that of Master Thomas. Thus, after a long, tedious effort for years, I finally succeeded in learning how to write.

Mysterious Connections that Link Us Together

Azar Nafisi

Azar Nafisi (1950–) was born in Tehran, Iran. As a teenager, her parents sent her to England to be educated. She attended the University of Oklahoma and Oxford University and has taught at three Iranian universities, including the University of Tehran—from which she was fired in 1981 for refusing to wear a veil. She has been the director of the Dialogue Project, a nonprofit group that brings together Palestinians and Jews for monthly dialogue. Currently, Nafisi teaches at the Johns Hopkins School for Advanced International Studies. She has published articles in The New York Times, The Washington Post, The Wall Street Journal, *and* The New Republic. *She is best known for* Reading Lolita in Tehran: A Memoir in Books *(2003) in which she recounts having secretly taught literature in her home to Iranian women. The following was broadcast on National Public Radio in July 2005 as part of the "This I Believe" series.*

1 I believe in empathy. I believe in the kind of empathy that is created through imagination and through intimate, personal relationships. I am a writer and a teacher, so much of my time is spent interpreting stories and connecting to other individuals. It is the urge to know more about ourselves and others that creates empathy. Through imagination and our desire for rapport, we transcend our limitations, freshen our eyes, and are able to look at ourselves and the world through a new and alternative lens.

Whenever I think of the word empathy, I think of a small boy named Huckleberry Finn contemplating his friend and runaway slave, Jim. Huck asks himself whether he should give Jim up or not. Huck was told in Sunday school that people who let slaves go free go to "everlasting fire." But then, Huck says he imagines he and Jim in "the day and night-time, sometimes moonlight, sometimes storms, and we a-floating along, talking and singing and laughing." Huck remembers Jim and their friendship and warmth. He imagines Jim not as a slave but as a human being and he decides that, "alright, then, I'll go to hell."

What Huck rejects is not religion but an attitude of self-righteousness and inflexibility. I remember this particular scene out of *Huck Finn* so vividly today, because I associate it with a difficult time in my own life. In the early 1980s when I taught at the University of Tehran, I, like many others, was expelled. I was very surprised to discover that my staunchest allies were two students who were very active at the University's powerful Muslim Students' Association. These young men and I had engaged in very passionate and heated arguments. I had fiercely opposed their ideological stances. But that didn't stop them from defending me. When I ran into one of them after my expulsion, I thanked him for his support. "We are not as rigid as you imagine us to be Professor Nafisi," he responded. "Remember your own lectures on Huck Finn? Let's just say, he is not the only one who can risk going to hell!"

This experience in my life reinforces my belief in the mysterious connections that link individuals to each other despite their vast differences. No amount of political correctness can make us empathize with a child left orphaned in Darfur or a woman taken to a football stadium in Kabul and shot to death because she is improperly dressed. Only curiosity about the fate of others, the ability to put ourselves in their shoes, and the will to enter their world through the magic of imagination, creates this shock of recognition. Without this empathy there can be no genuine dialogue, and we as individuals and nations will remain isolated and alien, segregated and fragmented.

5   I believe that it is only through empathy, that the pain experienced by an Algerian woman, a North Korean dissident, a Rwandan child or an Iraqi prisoner, becomes real to me and not just passing news. And it is at times like this when I ask myself, am I—prepared like Huck Finn—to give up Sunday school heaven for the kind of hell that Huck chose?

Mother Tongue

Amy Tan

Amy Tan was born in Oakland, California in 1952, several years after her mother and father immigrated from China. She was raised in various cities in the San Francisco Bay Area. When she was eight, her essay, "What the Library Means to Me," won first prize among elementary school participants, for which Tan received a transistor radio and publication in the local newspaper. Upon the deaths of her brother and father in 1967 and 1968 from brain tumors, the family began a haphazard journey through Europe, before settling in Montreux, Switzerland, where Tan graduated in her junior year in 1969.

For the next seven years, Tan attended five schools. She first went to Linfield College in McMinnville, Oregon, and there, on a blind date, met her future husband, Lou DeMattei. She followed him to San Jose, where she enrolled in San Jose City College. She next attended San Jose State University, and, while working two part-time jobs, she became an English honor's students and a President's Scholar, while carrying a semester course load of 21 units. In 1972 she graduated with honors, receiving a B.A. with a double major in English and Linguistics. She was awarded a scholarship to attend the Summer Linguistics Institute at the University of California, Santa Cruz. In 1973, she earned her M.A. in Linguistics, also from San Jose State University, and was then awarded a Graduate Minority Fellowship under the affirmative action program at the University of California, Berkeley, where she enrolled as a doctoral student in linguistics.

1   I am not a scholar of English or literature. I cannot give you much   1
more than personal opinions on the English language and its variations in this country or others.

I am a writer. And by that definition, I am someone who has always loved language. I am fascinated by language in daily life. I spend
a great deal of my time thinking about the power of language—the
way it can evoke an emotion, a visual image, a complex idea, or a simple truth. Language is the tool of my trade. And I use them all—all
the Englishes I grew up with.

Recently, I was made keenly aware of the different Englishes I do
use. I was giving a talk to a large group of people, the same talk I had
already given to half a dozen other groups. The nature of the talk was
about my writing, my life, and my book, *The Joy Luck Club*. The talk
was going along well enough, until I remembered one major difference that made the whole talk sound wrong. My mother was in the
room. And it was perhaps the first time she had heard me give a
lengthy speech, using the kind of English I have never used with her.
I was saying things like, "The intersection of memory upon imagination" and "There is an aspect of my fiction that relates to thus-and-
thus"—a speech filled with carefully wrought grammatical phrases,
burdened, it suddenly seemed to me, with nominalized forms, past
perfect tenses, conditional phrases, all the forms of standard English
that I had learned in school and through books, the forms of English
I did not use at home with my mother.

Just last week, I was walking down the street with my mother, and
I again found myself conscious of the English I was using, and the
English I do use with her. We were talking about the price of new and
used furniture and I heard myself saying this: "Not waste money that
way." My husband was with us as well, and he didn't notice any switch
in my English. And then I realized why. It's because over the twenty
years we've been together I've often used that same kind of English
with him, and sometimes he even uses it with me. It has become our
language of intimacy, a different sort of English that relates to family
talk, the language I grew up with.

5   So you'll have some idea of what this family talk I heard sounds   5
like, I'll quote what my mother said during a recent conversation
which I videotaped and then transcribed. During this conversation,
my mother was talking about a political gangster in Shanghai who had
the same last name as her family's, Du, and how the gangster in his

early years wanted to be adopted by her family, which was rich by comparison. Later, the gangster became more powerful, far richer than my mother's family, and one day showed up at my mother's wedding to pay his respects. Here's what she said in part:

"Du Yusong having business like fruit stand. Like off the street kind. He is Du like Du Zong—but not Tsung-ming Island people. The local people call putong, the river east side, he belong to that side local people. That man want to ask Du Zong father take him in like become own family. Du Zong father wasn't look down on him, but didn't take seriously, until that man big like become a mafia. Now important person, very hard to inviting him. Chinese way, came only to show respect, don't stay for dinner. Respect for making big celebration, he shows up. Mean gives lots of respect. Chinese custom. Chinese social life that way. If too important won't have to stay too long. He come to my wedding. I didn't see, I heard it. I gone to boy's side, they have YMCA dinner. Chinese age I was nineteen."

You should know that my mother's expressive command of English belies how much she actually understands. She reads the *Forbes* report, listens to *Wall Street Week*, converses daily with her stockbroker, reads all of Shirley MacLaine's books with ease—all kinds of things I can't begin to understand. Yet some of my friends tell me they understand 50 percent of what my mother says. Some say they understand 80 to 90 percent. Some say they understand none of it, as if she were speaking pure Chinese. But to me, my mother's English is perfectly clear, perfectly natural. It's my mother tongue. Her language, as I hear it, is vivid, direct, full of observation and imagery. That was the language that helped shape the way I saw things, expressed things, made sense of the world.

Lately, I've been giving more thought to the kind of English my mother speaks. Like others, I have described it to people as "broken" or "fractured" English. But I wince when I say that. It has always bothered me that I can think of no way to describe it other than "broken," as if it were damaged and needed to be fixed, as if it lacked a certain wholeness and soundness. I've heard other terms used, "limited English," for example. But they seem just as bad, as if everything is limited, including people's perceptions of the limited English speaker.

I know this for a fact, because when I was growing up, my mother's "limited" English limited *my* perception of her. I was ashamed of her English. I believed that her English reflected the quality of what she had to say. That is, because she expressed them imperfectly her thoughts were imperfect. And I had plenty of empirical evidence to support me: the fact that people in department stores, at banks, and at restaurants did not take her seriously, did not give her good service, pretended not to understand her, or even acted as if they did not hear her.

10   My mother has long realized the limitations of her English as well. When I was fifteen, she used to have me call people on the phone to pretend I was she. In this guise, I was forced to ask for information or even to complain and yell at people who had been rude to her. One time it was a call to her stockbroker in New York. She had cashed out her small portfolio and it just so happened we were going to go to New York the next week, our very first trip outside California. I had to get on the phone and say in an adolescent voice that was not very convincing, "This is Mrs. Tan."

And my mother was standing in the back whispering loudly, "Why he don't send me check, already two weeks late. So mad he lie to me, losing me money."

And then I said in perfect English, "Yes, I'm getting rather concerned. You had agreed to send the check two weeks ago, but it hasn't arrived."

Then she began to talk more loudly. "What he want, I come to New York tell him front of his boss, you cheating me?" And I was trying to calm her down, make her be quiet, while telling the stockbroker, "I can't tolerate any more excuses. If I don't receive the check immediately, I am going to have to speak to your manager when I'm in New York next week." And sure enough, the following week there we were in front of this astonished stockbroker, and I was sitting there red-faced and quiet, and my mother, the real Mrs. Tan, was shouting at his boss in her impeccable broken English.

We used a similar routine just five days ago, for a situation that was far less humorous. My mother had gone to the hospital for an appointment, to find out about a benign brain tumor a CAT scan had revealed a month ago. She said she had spoken very good English, her best English, no mistakes. Still, she said, the hospital did not apologize when they said they had lost the CAT scan and she had come for nothing. She said they did not seem to have any sympathy when she told them she was anxious to know the exact diagnosis, since her husband and son had both died of brain tumors. She said they would not give her any more information until the next time and she would have to make another appointment for that. So she said she would not leave until the doctor called her daughter. She wouldn't budge. And when the doctor finally called her daughter, me, who spoke in perfect English—lo and behold—we had assurances the CAT scan would be found, promises that a conference call on Monday would be held, and apologies for any suffering my mother had gone through for a most regrettable mistake.

15   I think my mother's English almost had an effect on limiting my possibilities in life as well. Sociologists and linguists probably will tell you that a person's developing language skills are more influenced by peers. But I do think that the language spoken in the family, especially in immigrant families which are more insular, plays a large role in shaping the language of the child. And I believe that it affected my results on achievement tests, IQ tests, and the SAT. While my English skills were never judged as poor, compared to math, English could not be considered my strong suit. In grade school I did moderately well, getting perhaps B's, sometimes B-pluses, in English and scoring perhaps in the sixtieth or seventieth percentile on achievement tests. But those scores were not good enough to override the opinion that my true abilities lay in math and science, because in those areas I achieved A's and scored in the ninetieth percentile or higher.

This was understandable. Math is precise, there is only one correct answer. Whereas, for me at least, the answers on English tests were always a judgment call, a matter of opinion and personal experience. Those tests were constructed around items like fill-in-the-blank sentence completion, Such as, "Even though Tom was _____, Mary thought he was _____." And the correct answer always seemed to be the most bland combinations of thoughts, for example, "Even though Tom was shy, Mary thought he was charming," with the grammatical structure "even though" limiting the correct answer to some sort of semantic opposites, so you wouldn't get answers like, Even though Tom was foolish, Mary thought he was ridiculous." Well, according to my mother, there were very few limitations as to what Tom could have been and what Mary might have thought of him. So I never did well on tests like that.

The same was true with word analogies, pairs of words in which you were supposed to find some sort of logical, semantic relationship—

for example, "*Sunset* is to *nightfall* as _____ is to _____." And here you would be presented with a list of four possible pairs, one of which showed the same kind of relationship: *red* is to *stoplight, bus* is to *arrival, chills* is to *fever, yawn* is to *boring*. Well, I could never think that way. I knew what the tests were asking, but I could not block out of my mind the images already created by the first pair, "*sunset* is to *nightfall*"—and I would see a burst of colors against a darkening sky, the moon rising, the lowering of a curtain of stars. And all the other pairs of words—red, bus, stoplight, boring—just threw up a mass of confusing images, making it impossible for me to sort out something as logical as saying: "A sunset precedes nightfall" is the same as "a chill precedes a fever." The only way I would have gotten that answer right would have been to imagine an associative situation, for example, my being disobedient and staying out past sunset, catching a chill at night, which turns into feverish pneumonia as punishment, which indeed did happen to me.

I have been thinking about all this lately, about my mother's English, about achievement tests. Because lately I've been asked, as a writer, why there are not more Asian Americans represented in American literature. Why are there few Asian Americans enrolled in creative writing programs? Why do so many Chinese students go into engineering? Well, these are broad sociological questions I can't begin to answer. But I have noticed in surveys—in fact, just last week—that Asian students, as a whole, always do significantly better on math achievement tests than in English. And this makes me think that there are other Asian American students whose English spoken in the home might also be described as "broken" or "limited." And perhaps they also have teachers who are steering them away from writing and into math and science, which is what happened to me.

Fortunately, I happen to be rebellious in nature and enjoy the challenge of disproving assumptions made about me. I became an English major my first year in college, after being enrolled as pre-med. I started writing nonfiction as a freelancer the week after I was told by my former boss that writing was my worst skill and I should hone my talents toward account management.

20   But it wasn't until 1985 that I finally began to write fiction. And   20
at first I wrote using what I thought to be wittily crafted sentences, sentences that would finally prove I had mastery over the English

language. Here's an example from the first draft of a story that later made its way into *The Joy Luck Club,* but without this line: "That was my mental quandary in its nascent state." A terrible line, which I can barely pronounce.

Fortunately, for reasons I won't get into today, I later decided I should envision a reader for the stories I would write. And the reader I decided upon was my mother, because these were stories about mothers. So with this reader in mind—and in fact she did read my early drafts—I began to write stories using all the Englishes I grew up with: the English I spoke to my mother, which for lack of a better term might be described as "simple"; the English she used with me, which for lack of a better term might be described as "broken"; my translation of her Chinese, which could certainly be described as "watered down"; and what I imagined to be her translation of her Chinese if she could speak in perfect English, her internal language, and for that I sought to preserve the essence, but neither an English nor a Chinese structure. I wanted to capture what language ability tests can never reveal: her intent, her passion, her imagery, the rhythms of her speech and the nature of her thoughts.

Apart from what any critic had to say about my writing, I knew I had succeeded where it counted when my mother finished reading my book and gave me her verdict: "So easy to read."

Questions on "Mother Tongue" by Amy Tan

_____1. The phrase "mother tongue" refers to the language to which you were born. What is the other "Mother Tongue" of which Amy Tan speaks?

a. "Mother Tongue" refers to the speech of Tan's mother, which Tan describes as "broken" English.
b. "Mother Tongue" refers to the speech Amy learned in her native country of the United States of America: English.
c. "Mother Tongue" refers to her mother's native country, China.

_____2. What does Tan mean when she says in Paragraph 7, "You should know that my mother's expressive command of English belies how much she actually understands?"

a. She means that her mother understands very little English.
b. She means that her mother understands more than her limited English demonstrates.
c. She means that her mother is a very expressive, understanding person.
d. She means that her mother lies a lot.

_____3. What is the main point of paragraph 9?

a. When Tan was growing up, she believed that her mother's limited English meant her mother's understanding was limited as well.
b. People in department stores or restaurants did not take her mother seriously.
c. Tan grew up ashamed of her mother's English.

_____4. In Paragraph 18, Tan asks, "Why are there few Asian Americans enrolled in creative writing programs? Why do so many Chinese students go into engineering?" What does she think is the answer to these questions?

a. Asian Americans are very good at scientific and math skills.
b. Asian Americans tend to score lower on language tests than math and science tests, so their teachers probably steer them in the direction of their higher test scores.
c. Analogy tests are very difficult.

_____5. How does Tan explain her inability to do analogy questions?

a. She doesn't understand all the vocabulary words used.
b. She simply isn't mentally flexible enough to do them.
c. She see images instead of the relationships of the words..

_____6. See if you can correctly complete this analogy.

Plagiarize is to steal as

a. refute is to agree
b. vivid is to dull
c. cite is to quote
d. coherence is to chaos

_____7. Tan says that she has a "rebellious" nature that made her

a. become an English major, despite her previous test scores.
b. become a pre-med major.
c. reject her mother's language entirely.
d. fight a lot as a child.

_____8. As many writers do, Amy Tan decided to write as though she were writing for a particular reader, a kind of audience. Who was her "reader?"

a. her husband
b. her professors
c. The Joy Luck Club
d. her mother

9-10. How many "Englishes" do you speak, and when do you use them? (two points for two part answer)

_____

_____

The Myth of the Latin Woman: I Just Met a Girl Named María

Judith Ortiz Cofer

Judith Ortiz Cofer (1952–) was born in Hormigueros, Puerto Rico, and emigrated to the United States when she was four. Cofer attended Augusta College and Florida Atlantic University; she was also a Scholar of the English Speaking Union at Oxford University. She has worked as a bilingual teacher in the Florida public schools, and as a visiting writer at Vanderbilt University and the University of Michigan, Ann Arbor. Cofer is currently the Franklin Professor of English and Creative Writing at The University of Georgia. An award-winning poet, Cofer has received grants from the Witter Bynner Foundation and the National Endowment for the Arts. Her books include The Line of the Sun *(1989),* Silent Dancing *(1990),* The Latin Deli *(1993),* Reaching for the Mainland and Selected New Poems *(1995),* The Year of Our Revolution *(1998),* Woman In Front of the Sun: On Becoming a Writer *(2000),* A Love Story Beginning in Spanish: Poems *(2005), as well as a children's book,* Call Me Maria *(2004). Cofer, who has also written for* Glamour *and* The Kenyon Review, *often combines her love of language with her interest in the lives and traditions of Puerto Ricans. In this essay, from* The Latin Deli, *Cofer describes how her Latino ancestry attracts unpleasant stereotyping.*

1   On a bus trip to London from Oxford University where I was earning some graduate credits one summer, a young man, obviously fresh from a pub, spotted me and as if struck by

From *The Latin Deli: Prose and Poetry* by Judith Ortiz Cofer. Published by the University of Georgia Press.

inspiration went down on his knees in the aisle. With both hands over his heart he broke into an Irish tenor's rendition of "Maria" from *West Side Story.* My politely amused fellow passengers gave his lovely voice the round of gentle applause it deserved. Though I was not quite as amused, I managed my version of an English smile: no show of teeth, no extreme contortions of the facial muscles—I was at this time of my life practicing reserve and cool. Oh, that British control, how I coveted it. But "Maria" had followed me to London, reminding me of a prime fact of my life: you can leave the island, master the English language, and travel as far as you can, but if you are a Latina, especially one like me who so obviously belongs to Rita Moreno's gene pool, the island travels with you.

This is sometimes a very good thing—it may win you that extra minute of someone's attention. But with some people, the same things can make *you* an island—not a tropical paradise but an Alcatraz, a place nobody wants to visit. As a Puerto Rican girl living in the United States and wanting like most children to "belong," I resented the stereotype that my Hispanic appearance called forth from many people I met.

Growing up in a large urban center in New Jersey during the 1960s, I suffered from what I think of as "cultural schizophrenia." Our life was designed by my parents as a microcosm of their *casas* on the island. We spoke in Spanish, ate Puerto Rican food bought at the *bodega,* and practiced strict Catholicism at a church that allotted us a one-hour slot each week for mass, performed in Spanish by a Chinese priest trained as a missionary for Latin America.

As a girl I was kept under strict surveillance by my parents, since my virtue and modesty were, by their cultural equation, the same as their honor. As a teenager I was lectured constantly on how to behave as a proper *senorita.* But it was a conflicting message I received, since the Puerto Rican mothers also encouraged their daughters to look and act like women and to dress in clothes our Anglo friends and their mothers found too "mature" and flashy. The difference was, and is, cultural; yet I often felt humiliated when I appeared at an American friend's party wearing a dress more suitable to a semi-formal than to a playroom birthday celebration. At Puerto Rican festivities, neither the music nor the colors we wore could be too loud.

5   I remember Career Day in our high school, when teachers told us to come dressed as if for a job interview. It quickly became obvious that to the Puerto Rican girls "dressing up" meant wearing their mother's

ornate jewelry and clothing, more appropriate (by mainstream standards) for the company Christmas party than as daily office attire. That morning I had agonized in front of my closet, trying to figure out what a "career girl" would wear. I knew how to dress for school (at the Catholic school I attended, we all wore uniforms), I knew how to dress for Sunday mass, and I knew what dresses to wear for parties at my relatives' homes. Though I do not recall the precise details of my Career Day outfit, it must have been a composite of these choices. But I remember a comment my friend (an Italian American) made in later years that coalesced my impressions of that day. She said that at the business school she was attending, the Puerto Rican girls always stood out for wearing "everything at once." She meant, of course, too much jewelry, too many accessories. On that day at school we were simply made the negative models by the nuns, who were themselves not credible fashion experts to any of us. But it was painfully obvious to me that to the others, in their tailored skirts and silk blouses, we must have seemed "hopeless" and "vulgar." Though I now know that most adolescents feel out of step much of the time, I also know that for the Puerto Rican girls of my generation that sense was intensified. The way our teachers and classmates looked at us that day in school was just a taste of the cultural clash that awaited us in the real world, where prospective employers and men on the street would often misinterpret our tight skirts and jingling bracelets as a "come-on."

Mixed cultural signals have perpetuated certain stereotypes—for example, that of the Hispanic woman as the "hot tamale" or sexual firebrand. It is a one-dimensional view that the media have found easy to promote. In their special vocabulary, advertisers have designated "sizzling" and "smoldering" as the adjectives of choice for describing not only the foods but also the women of Latin America. From conversations in my house I recall hearing about the harassment that Puerto Rican women endured in factories where the "boss-men" talked to them as if sexual innuendo was all they understood, and worse, often gave them the choice of submitting to their advances or being fired.

It is custom, however, not chromosomes, that leads us to choose scarlet over pale pink. As young girls, it was our mothers who influenced our decisions about clothes and colors—mothers who had grown up on a tropical island where the natural environment was a riot of primary colors, where showing your skin was one way to keep cool as well as to look sexy. Most important of all, on the island, women perhaps felt freer to dress and move more provocatively since, in most cases, they were protected by the traditions, mores, and laws of a Spanish/Catholic system of morality and machismo whose main rule was: *You may look at my sister, but if you touch her I will kill you.* The extended family and church structure could provide a young woman with a circle of safety in her small pueblo on the island; if a man "wronged" a girl, everyone would close in to save her family honor.

My mother has told me about dressing in her best party clothes on Saturday nights and going to the town's plaza to promenade with her girl-friends in front of the boys they liked. The males were thus given an opportunity to admire the women and to express their admiration in the form of *piropos:* erotically charged street poems they composed on the spot. (I have myself been subjected to a few *piropos* while visiting the island, and they can be outrageous, although custom dictates that they must never cross into obscenity.) This ritual, as I understand it, also entails a show of studied indifference on the woman's part; if she is "decent," she must not acknowledge the man's impassioned words. So I do understand how things can be lost in translation. When a Puerto Rican girl dressed in her idea of what is attractive meets a man from the mainstream culture who has been trained to react to certain types of clothing as a sexual signal, a clash is likely to take place. I remember the boy who took me to my first formal dance leaning over to plant a sloppy, over-eager kiss painfully on my mouth; when I didn't respond with sufficient passion, he remarked resentfully: "I thought you Latin girls were supposed to mature early," as if I were expected to *ripen* like a fruit or vegetable, not just grow into womanhood like other girls.

It is surprising to my professional friends that even today some people, including those who should know better, still put others "in their place." It happened to me most recently during a stay at a classy metropolitan hotel favored by young professional couples for weddings. Late one evening after the theater, as I walked toward my room with a colleague (a woman with whom I was coordinating an arts program), a middle-aged man in a tuxedo, with a young girl in satin and lace on his arm, stepped directly into our path. With his champagne glass extended toward me, he exclaimed "Evita!"

10   Our way blocked, my companion and I listened as the man half-   10
recited, half-bellowed "Don't Cry for Me, Argentina." When he

finished, the young girl said: "How about a round of applause for my daddy?" We complied, hoping this would bring the silly spectacle to a close. I was becoming aware that our little group was attracting the attention of the other guests. "Daddy" must have perceived this too, and he once more barred the way as we tried to walk past him. He began to shout-sing a ditty to the tune of "La Bamba"—except the lyrics were about a girl named Maria whose exploits rhymed with her name and gonorrhea. The girl kept saying "Oh, Daddy" and looking at me with pleading eyes. She wanted me to laugh along with the others. My companion and I stood silently waiting for the man to end his offensive song. When he finished, I looked not at him but at his daughter. I advised her calmly never to ask her father what he had done in the army. Then I walked between them and to my room. My friend complimented me on my cool handling of the situation, but I confessed that I had really wanted to push the jerk into the swimming pool. This same man—probably a corporate executive, well-educated, even worldly by most standards—would not have been likely to regale an Anglo woman with a dirty song in public. He might have checked his impulse by assuming that she could be somebody's wife or mother, or at least *somebody* who might take offense. But, to him, I was just an Evita or a Maria: merely a character in his cartoon-populated universe.

Another facet of the myth of the Latin woman in the United States is the menial, the domestic—Maria the housemaid or counter-girl. It's true that work as domestics, as waitresses, and in factories is all that's available to women with little English and few skills. But the myth of the Hispanic menial—the funny maid, mispronouncing words and cooking up a spicy storm in a shiny California kitchen—has been perpetuated by the media in the same way that "Mammy" from *Gone with the Wind* became America's idea of the black woman for generations. Since I do not wear my diplomas around my neck for all to see, I have on occasion been sent to that "kitchen" where some think I obviously belong.

One incident has stayed with me, though I recognize it as a minor offense. My first public poetry reading took place in Miami, at a restaurant where a luncheon was being held before the event. I was nervous and excited as I walked in with notebook in hand. An older woman motioned me to her table, and thinking (foolish me) that she wanted me to autograph a copy of my newly published slender volume of verse, I went over. She ordered a cup of coffee from me, assuming that I was the waitress. (Easy enough to mistake my poems for menus, I suppose.) I know it wasn't an intentional act of cruelty. Yet of all the good things that happened later, I remember that scene most clearly, because it reminded me of what I had to overcome before anyone would take me seriously. In retrospect I understand that my anger gave my reading fire. In fact, I have almost always taken any doubt in my abilities as a challenge, the result most often being the satisfaction of winning a convert, of seeing the cold, appraising eyes warm to my words, the body language change, the smile that indicates I have opened some avenue for communication. So that day as I read, I looked directly at that woman. Her lowered eyes told me she was embarrassed at her faux pas, and when I willed her to look up at me, she graciously allowed me to punish her with my full attention. We shook hands at the end of the reading and I never saw her again. She has probably forgotten the entire incident, but maybe not.

Yet I am one of the lucky ones. There are thousands of Latinas without the privilege of an education or the entrees into society that I have. For them life is a constant struggle against the misconceptions perpetuated by the myth of the Latina. My goal is to try to replace the old stereotypes with a much more interesting set of realities. Every time I give a reading, I hope the stories I tell, the dreams and fears I examine in my work, can achieve some universal truth that will get my audience past the particulars of my skin color, my accent, or my clothes.

I once wrote a poem in which I called all Latinas "God's brown daughters." This poem is really a prayer of sorts, offered upward, but also, through the human-to-human channel of art, outward. It is a prayer for communication and for respect. In it, Latin women pray "in Spanish to an Anglo God/with a Jewish heritage," and they are "fervently hoping/that if not omnipotent,/at least He be bilingual."

The Myth of the Latin Woman" by Judith Ortiz Cofer

_____1. What was the author doing in England when the "Maria" incident occurred?

   a. She was serving tables at a local restaurant.
   b. She was a graduate student at Oxford on a bus trip to London.
   c. She was a visiting scholar from the United States.

_____2. The author writes in the first paragraph, "...I was at this time of my life practicing reserve and cool. Oh, that British control, how I coveted it." What does she mean?

   a. The British are known for hiding their feelings.
   b. She was trying very hard to keep her feelings under control.
   c. She really wanted to be able to keep her feelings under control, as the British people do much of the time.

_____3. Cofer writes, "But with some people, the same things can make _you_ an island—not a tropical paradise but an Alcatraz, a place nobody wants to visit." Why would people avoid Alcatraz?

   a. It's an island prison, so people would want to stay away.
   b. It's a beautiful, tropical island.
   c. It's a place that can get an island person into trouble.

_____4. Which of the following statements best reveals the author's central point?

   a. "… advertisers have designated "sizzling" and "smoldering" as the adjectives of choice for describing not only the foods but also the women of Latin America."
   b. Women on the island "…were protected by the traditions, mores, and laws of a Spanish/Catholic system of morality and machismo whose main rule was: _You may look at my sister, but if you touch her I will kill you._"
   c. "My goal is to try to replace the old stereotypes…I hope the stories I tell, the dreams and fears I examine in my work, can achieve some universal truth that will get my audience past the particulars of my skin color, my accent, or my clothes."
   d. "Another facet of the myth of the Latin woman in the United States is the menial, the domestic—Maria the housemaid or counter-girl."

_____5. How did the Puerto Rican girls dress "wrongly" for Career Day?

   a. They dressed like professional women, with tailored skirts and silk blouses.
   b. They probably dressed in bright colors, with lots of jewelry.
   c. They dressed like the nuns.

6. What are the **two** stereotypes attributed to Latin women, according to the author?
Circle 2.

   a. lazy; unwilling to work
   b. cheap; stingy with money
   c. sexpot: highly sexual in appearance and actions
   d. stupid; unable to learn
   e. hard-working; studying hard and working long hours
   f. drunk a lot of the time
   g. menial servant: maid, factory worker, or waitress
   h. involved with organized crime

_____7. What is a "cultural clash?"

   a. when someone claps for someone else singing an offensive song in public
   b. when two countries cannot agree on a particular point, and they go to war
   c. when people from various backgrounds have differing expectations of a situation
   d. when people from various backgrounds grow to understand and appreciate each other

8. Have you ever experienced a stereotype or a cultural clash, either as a victim or a witness? Write a few sentences about that experience.

_____

_____

_____

2 more questions!

_____9. Explain what Cofer means in the paragraph that begins, "It is custom, however, not chromosomes, that leads us to choose scarlet over pale pink."

    a. She means that scarlet red is more beautiful than pink on girls from Puerto Rico.

    b. She mans that pale pink is more appropriate for young girls to wear to parties.

    c. She means that the girls from Puerto Rico wore bright colors like their mothers used to wear.

10. Choose one word from the article you are not familiar with, look it up, and write the word and its definition here.

_____

_____

The Perils of Indifference

Elie Wiesel

Elie Wiesel (1928–) was born in the village of Sighet in Romania to a religious Jewish family. In 1944 his life changed when his family was deported by the Nazis to Auschwitz, where his father died in 1945. After the camp was liberated by the Allied forces, Wiesel spent a few years in a French orphanage. In 1948 he entered the Sorbonne and began writing for the newspaper L'arche. *In 1954 he made the decision to write about the Holocaust, which led to the publication of his first book,* Night *(1958), followed by* Jews of Silence *(1966). In 1963 he became a U.S. citizen. In 1978 he was appointed chair of the Presidential Commission on the Holocaust, which led to the American memorial monument to the victims of Nazi oppression during World War II. In 1985 Wiesel received the Congressional Gold Medal of Achievement. The following year he received the Nobel Peace Prize. He has written numerous books dealing with the Holocaust, hatred, racism, genocide, and faith, including* Sages and Dreamers *(1991), and his memoir* All Rivers Run to the Sea *(1995). In the following speech he addresses Congress and the President about the need for vigilance in the face of evil.*

1   Mr. President, Mrs. Clinton, members of Congress, Ambassador Holbrooke, Excellencies, friends:

Fifty-four years ago to the day, a young Jewish boy from a small town in the Carpathian Mountains woke up, not far from Goethe's beloved Weimar, in a place of eternal infamy called Buchenwald. He was finally free, but there was no joy in his heart. He thought there never would be again. Liberated a day earlier by American soldiers, he remembers their rage at what they saw. And even if he lives to be a very old man, he will always be grateful to them for that rage, and also for their compassion. Though he did not understand their language, their eyes told him what he needed to know—that they, too, would remember, and bear witness.

And now, I stand before you, Mr. President—Commander-in-Chief of the army that freed me, and tens of thousands of others—and I am filled with a profound and abiding gratitude to the American people. Gratitude is a word that I cherish. Gratitude is what defines the humanity of the human being. And I am grateful to you, Hillary, or Mrs. Clinton, for what you said, and for what you are doing for children in the world, for the homeless, for the victims of injustice, the victims of destiny and society. And I thank all of you for being here.

We are on the threshold of a new century, a new millennium. What will the legacy of this vanishing century be? How will it be remembered in the new millennium? Surely it will be judged, and judged severely, in both moral and metaphysical terms. These failures have cast a dark shadow over humanity: two World Wars, countless civil wars, the senseless chain of assassinations (Gandhi, the Kennedys, Martin Luther King, Sadat, Rabin), bloodbaths in Cambodia and Nigeria, India and Pakistan, Ireland and Rwanda, Eritrea and Ethiopia, Sarajevo and Kosovo; the inhumanity in the gulag and the tragedy of Hiroshima. And, on a different level, of course, Auschwitz and Treblinka. So much violence; so much indifference.

5   What is indifference? Etymologically, the word means "no difference." A strange and unnatural state in which the lines blur between light and darkness, dusk and dawn, crime and punishment, cruelty and compassion, good and evil. What are its courses and inescapable consequences? Is it a philosophy? Is there a philosophy of indifference conceivable? Can one possibly view indifference as a virtue? Is it necessary at times to practice it simply to keep one's sanity, live normally, enjoy a fine meal and a glass of wine, as the world around us experiences harrowing upheavals?

Of course, indifference can be tempting—more than that, seductive. It is so much easier to look away from victims. It is so much easier to avoid such rude interruptions to our work, our dreams, our hopes.

It is, after all, awkward, troublesome, to be involved in another person's pain and despair. Yet, for the person who is indifferent, his or her neighbor are of no consequence. And, therefore, their lives are meaningless. Their hidden or even visible anguish is of no interest. Indifference reduces the Other to an abstraction.

Over there, behind the black gates of Auschwitz, the most tragic of all prisoners were the "Muselmanner," as they were called. Wrapped in their torn blankets, they would sit or lie on the ground, staring vacantly into space, unaware of who or where they were—strangers to their surroundings. They no longer felt pain, hunger, thirst. They feared nothing. They felt nothing. They were dead and did not know it.

Rooted in our tradition, some of us felt that to be abandoned by humanity then was not the ultimate. We felt that to be abandoned by God was worse than to be punished by Him. Better an unjust God than an indifferent one. For us to be ignored by God was a harsher punishment than to be a victim of His anger. Man can live far from God—not outside God. God is wherever we are. Even in suffering? Even in suffering.

In a way, to be indifferent to that suffering is what makes the human being inhuman. Indifference, after all, is more dangerous than anger and hatred. Anger can at times be creative. One writes a great poem, a great symphony. One does something special for the sake of humanity because one is angry at the injustice that one witnesses. But indifference is never creative. Even hatred at times may elicit a response. You fight it. You denounce it. You disarm it.

10   Indifference elicits no response. Indifference is not a response. In-   10
difference is not a beginning; it is an end. And, therefore, indifference is always the friend of the enemy, for it benefits the aggressor—never his victim, whose pain is magnified when he or she feels forgotten. The political prisoner in his cell, the hungry children, the homeless refugees—not to respond to their plight, not to relieve their solitude by offering them a spark of hope is to exile them from human memory. And in denying their humanity, we betray our own.

Indifference, then, is not only a sin, it is a punishment.

And this is one of the most important lessons of this outgoing century's wide-ranging experiments in good and evil.

In the place that I come from, society was composed of three simple categories: the killers, the victims, and the bystanders. During the darkest of times, inside the ghettoes and death camps—and I'm glad that Mrs. Clinton mentioned that we are now commemorating that event, that period, that we are now in the Days of Remembrance— but then, we felt abandoned, forgotten. All of us did.

And our only miserable consolation was that we believed that Auschwitz and Treblinka were closely guarded secrets; that the leaders of the free world did not know what was going on behind those black gates and barbed wire; that they had no knowledge of the war against the Jews that Hitler's armies and their accomplices waged as part of the war against the Allies. If they knew, we thought, surely those leaders would have moved heaven and earth to intervene. They would have spoken out with great outrage and conviction. They would have bombed the railways leading to Birkenau, just the railways, just once.

15   And now we knew, we learned, we discovered that the Pentagon   15 knew, the State Department knew. And the illustrious occupant of the White House then, who was a great leader—and I say it with some anguish and pain, because, today is exactly 54 years marking his death—Franklin Delano Roosevelt died on April the 12th, 1945. So he is very much present to me and to us. No doubt, he was a great leader. He mobilized the American people and the world, going into battle, bringing hundreds and thousands of valiant and brave soldiers in America to fight fascism, to fight dictatorship, to fight Hitler. And so many of the young people fell in battle. And, nevertheless, his image in Jewish history—I must say it—his image in Jewish history is flawed.

The depressing tale of the *St. Louis* is a case in point. Sixty years ago, its human cargo—nearly 1,000 Jews—was turned back to Nazi Germany. And that happened after the Kristallnacht, after the first state sponsored pogrom, with hundreds of Jewish shops destroyed, synagogues burned, thousands of people put in concentration camps. And that ship, which was already in the shores of the United States, was sent back. I don't understand. Roosevelt was a good man, with a heart. He understood those who needed help. Why didn't he allow these refugees to disembark? A thousand people—in America, the great country, the greatest democracy, the most generous of all new nations in modern history. What happened? I don't understand. Why the indifference, on the highest level, to the suffering of the victims?

But then, there were human beings who were sensitive to our tragedy. Those non-Jews, those Christians, that we call the "Righteous Gentiles," whose selfless acts of heroism saved the honor of their faith. Why were they so few? Why was there a greater effort to save SS murderers after the war than to save their victims during the war? Why did some of America's largest corporations continue to do business with Hitler's Germany until 1942? It has been suggested, and it was documented, that the Wehrmacht could not have conducted its invasion of France without oil obtained from American sources. How is one to explain their indifference?

And yet, my friends, good things have also happened in this traumatic century: the defeat of Nazism, the collapse of communism, the rebirth of Israel on its ancestral soil, the demise of apartheid, Israel's peace treaty with Egypt, the peace accord in Ireland. And let us remember the meeting, filled with drama and emotion, between Rabin and Arafat that you, Mr. President, convened in this very place. I was here and I will never forget it.

And then, of course, the joint decision of the United States and NATO to intervene in Kosovo and save those victims, those refugees, those who were uprooted by a man, whom I believe that because of his crimes, should be charged with crimes against humanity.

20 But this time, the world was not silent. This time, we do respond. 20 This time, we intervene.

Does it mean that we have learned from the past? Does it mean that society has changed? Has the human being become less indifferent and more human? Have we really learned from our experiences? Are we less insensitive to the plight of victims of ethnic cleansing and other forms of injustices in places near and far? Is today's justified intervention in Kosovo, led by you, Mr. President, a lasting warning that never again will the deportation, the terrorization of children and their parents, be allowed anywhere in the world? Will it discourage other dictators in other lands to do the same?

What about the children? Oh, we see them on television, we read about them in the papers, and we do so with a broken heart. Their fate is always the most tragic, inevitably. When adults wage war, children perish. We see their faces, their eyes. Do we hear their pleas? Do we feel their pain, their agony? Every minute one of them dies of disease, violence, famine.

Some of them—so many of them—could be saved.

And so, once again, I think of the young Jewish boy from the Carpathian Mountains. He has accompanied the old man I have become throughout these years of quest and struggle. And together we walk towards the new millennium, carried by profound fear and extraordinary hope.

"The Perils of Indifference" by Elie Wiesel

_____1. This essay was first

    a. in a book
    b. delivered in a speech
    c. written in the New York Times

_____2. Who, besides President and Mrs. Clinton, heard this speech?

    a. Congress
    b. Prisoners at a concentration camp
    c. The Commander-in-Chief

_____3. Why would Weisel have been "grateful for" the rage of the soldiers who freed him?

    a. He wasn't grateful. He wishes he had been allowed to die.
    b. Weisel was grateful for the soldiers' compassion toward him.
    c. He knew that they were so horrified and angered by what they saw at the camp that they would tell the world what had happened there.

4. Name two of the "failures" that Weisel speaks of in paragraph 4.

_____

5. Are there any you hadn't heard of before? Which ones? _____

_____

_____6. Weisel says that indifference can be more than tempting, that it can be seductive. What does he mean?

    a. He means that indifference makes no difference.
    b. He means that to fight an injustice involves taking caring to the next level: action.
    c. He means that it is easier to not fight injustice because to do so requires a person to be involved in another person's pain and despair.

_____7. According to Mr. Wiesel, why is indifference more dangerous than anger and hatred? (see Paragraphs 9-10)

    a. Indifference is never creative.
    b. Since indifference is not a response, indifference is always the friend of the enemy.
    c. Indifference is a sin.

_____8. Wiesel's society was made up of three categories. What were they?

    a. the killers, the victims, and the bystanders
    b. the good, the bad, and the ugly
    c. the Nazis, the Jews, and the Gentiles

_____9. The point that Wiesel makes about indifference and President Franklin Delano Roosevelt is:

    a. Roosevelt was a great leader, but not tuned into the problems of his people.
    b. By turning away a ship of 1000 Jews escaping Nazi Germany, Roosevelt demonstrated indifference on the highest level.
    c. Wiesel had believed that if the leader of the free world knew about Auschwitz and Treblinka, the President "would have moved heaven and earth to intervene."

10. Of all the good things Wiesel says have happened during the 20th Century (see paragraph 19), name **one** you have heard of before, **and one** you never heard of. See if you can find out about it.

_____

_____

The Lottery

Shirley Jackson

Shirley Hardie Jackson (1919-1965) was born in San Francisco. She received her B.A. from Syracuse University in 1940, then married literary critic Stanley Edgar Hyman, settling in North Bennington, Vermont, where they raised four children. Both parents continued vigorous literary careers. Jackson published the light and charming works Life among the Savages *(1953) and* Raising Demons *(1957) out of her experiences as a parent. At the same time, she was writing more disturbing works of horror and moral criticism,* The Lottery and Other Stories *(1949) and* The Haunting of Hill House *(1959). She said of "The Lottery" that she was hoping to force readers to see that their own lives contained inhumanity and cruelty.*

1 The morning of June 27th was clear and sunny, with the fresh warmth of a full-summer day; the flowers were blossoming profusely and the grass was richly green. The people of the village began to gather in the square, between the post office and the bank, around ten o'clock; in some towns there were so many people that the lottery took two days and had to be started on June 26th, but in this village, where there were only about three hundred people, the whole lottery took less than two hours, so it could begin at ten o'clock in the morning and still be through in time to allow the villagers to get home for noon dinner.

The children assembled first, of course. School was recently over for the summer, and the feeling of liberty sat uneasily on most of them; they tended to gather together quietly for a while before they broke into boisterous play, and their talk was still of the classroom and the teacher, of books and reprimands. Bobby Martin had already stuffed his pockets full of stones, and the other boys soon followed his example, selecting the smoothest and roundest stones; Bobby and Harry Jones and Dickie Delacroix—the villagers pronounced this name "Dellacroy"—eventually made a great pile of stones in one corner of the square and guarded it against the raids of the other boys. The girls stood aside, talking among themselves, looking over their shoulders at the boys, and the very small children rolled in the dust or clung to the hands of their older brothers or sisters.

Soon the men began to gather, surveying their own children, speaking of planting and rain, tractors and taxes. They stood together, away from the pile of stones in the corner, and their jokes were quiet and they smiled rather than laughed. The women, wearing faded house dresses and sweaters, came shortly after their menfolk. They greeted one another and exchanged bits of gossip as they went to join their husbands. Soon the women, standing by their husbands, began to call to their children, and the children came reluctantly, having to be called four or five times. Bobby Martin ducked under his mother's grasping hand and ran, laughing, back to the pile of stones. His father spoke up sharply, and Bobby came quickly and took his place between his father and his oldest brother.

The lottery was conducted—as were the square dances, the teenage club, the Halloween program—by Mr. Summers, who had time and energy to devote to civic activities. He was a round-faced, jovial man and he ran the coal business, and people were sorry for him, because he had no children and his wife was a scold. When he arrived in the square, carrying the black wooden box, there was a murmur of conversation among the villagers, and he waved and called, "Little late today, folks." The postmaster, Mr. Graves, followed him, carrying a three-legged stool, and the stool was put in the center of the square and Mr. Summers set the black box down on it. The villagers kept their distance, leaving a space between themselves and the stool, and when Mr. Summers said, "Some of you fellows want to give me a hand?" there was a hesitation before two men, Mr. Martin and his oldest son, Baxter, came forward to hold the box steady on the stool while Mr. Summers stirred up the papers inside it.

5   The original paraphernalia for the lottery had been lost long ago, 5
and the black box now resting on the stool had been put into use even
before Old Man Warner, the oldest man in town, was born. Mr. Summers spoke frequently to the villagers about making a new box, but
no one liked to upset even as much tradition as was represented by the
black box. There was a story that the present box had been made with
some pieces of the box that had preceded it, the one that had been
constructed when the first people settled down to make a village here.
Every year, after the lottery, Mr. Summers began talking again about
a new box, but every year the subject was allowed to fade off without
anything's being done. The black box grew shabbier each year; by now
it was no longer completely black but splintered badly along one side
to show the original wood color, and in some places faded or stained.

Mr. Martin and his oldest son, Baxter, held the black box securely
on the stool until Mr. Summers had stirred the papers thoroughly
with his hand. Because so much of the ritual had been forgotten or
discarded, Mr. Summers had been successful in having slips of paper
substituted for the chips of wood that had been used for generations.
Chips of wood, Mr. Summers had argued, had been all very well when
the village was tiny, but now that the population was more than three
hundred and likely to keep on growing, it was necessary to use something that would fit more easily into the black box. The night before
the lottery, Mr. Summers and Mr. Graves made up the slips of paper
and put them in the box, and it was then taken to the safe of Mr. Summers' coal company and locked up until Mr. Summers was ready to
take it to the square next morning. The rest of the year, the box was
put away, sometimes one place, sometimes another; it had spent one
year in Mr. Graves's barn and another year underfoot in the post office, and sometimes it was set on a shelf in the Martin grocery and left
there.

There was a great deal of fussing to be done before Mr. Summers
declared the lottery open. There were the lists to make up—of heads
of families, heads of households in each family, members of each
household in each family. There was the proper swearing-in of Mr.
Summers by the postmaster, as the official of the lottery; at one time,
some people remembered, there had been a recital of some sort, performed by the official of the lottery, a perfunctory, tuneless chant that
had been rattled off duly each year; some people believed that the official of the lottery used to stand just so when he said or sang it, others

believed that he was supposed to walk among the people, but years and years ago this part of the ritual had been allowed to lapse. There had been, also, a ritual salute, which the official of the lottery had had to use in addressing each person who came up to draw from the box, but this also had changed with time, until now it was felt necessary only for the official to speak to each person approaching. Mr. Summers was very good at all this; in his clean white shirt and blue jeans, with one hand resting carelessly on the black box, he seemed very proper and important as he talked interminably to Mr. Graves and the Martins.

Just as Mr. Summers finally left off talking and turned to the assembled villagers, Mrs. Hutchinson came hurriedly along the path to the square, her sweater thrown over her shoulders, and slid into place in the back of the crowd. "Clean forgot what day it was," she said to Mrs. Delacroix, who stood next to her, and they both laughed softly. "Thought my old man was out back stacking wood," Mrs. Hutchinson went on, "and then I looked out the window and the kids were gone, and then I remembered it was the twentyseventh and came a-running." She dried her hands on her apron, and Mrs. Delacroix said, "You're in time, though. They're still talking away up there."

Mrs. Hutchinson craned her neck to see through the crowd and found her husband and children standing near the front. She tapped Mrs. Delacroix on the arm as a farewell and began to make her way through the crowd. The people separated good-humoredly to let her through; two or three people said, in voices just loud enough to be heard across the crowd, "Here comes your Missus, Hutchinson," and "Bill, she made it after all." Mrs. Hutchinson reached her husband, and Mr. Summers, who had been waiting, said cheerfully, "Thought we were going to have to get on without you, Tessie." Mrs. Hutchinson said, grinning, "Wouldn't have me leave m'dishes in the sink, now, would you, Joe?" and soft laughter ran through the crowd as the people stirred back into position after Mrs. Hutchinson's arrival.

10   "Well, now," Mr. Summers said soberly, "guess we better get   10 started, get this over with, so's we can go back to work. Anybody ain't here?"

"Dunbar," several people said. "Dunbar, Dunbar."

Mr. Summers consulted his list. "Clyde Dunbar," he said. "That's right. He's broke his leg, hasn't he? Who's drawing for him?"

"Me, I guess," a woman said, and Mr. Summers turned to look at her. "Wife draws for her husband," Mr. Summers said. "Don't you have a grown boy to do it for you, Janey?" Although Mr. Summers and everyone else in the village knew the answer perfectly well, it was the business of the official of the lottery to ask such questions formally. Mr. Summers waited with an expression of polite interest while Mrs. Dunbar answered.

"Horace's not but sixteen yet," Mrs. Dunbar said regretfully. "Guess I gotta fill in for the old man this year."

15 "Right," Mr. Summers said. He made a note on the list he was holding. Then he asked, "Watson boy drawing this year?"

A tall boy in the crowd raised his hand. "Here," he said. "I'm drawing for m'mother and me." He blinked his eyes nervously and ducked his head as several voices in the crowd said things like "Good fellow, Jack," and "Glad to see your mother's got a man to do it."

"Well," Mr. Summers said, "guess that's everyone. Old Man Warner make it?"

"Here," a voice said, and Mr. Summers nodded.

A sudden hush fell on the crowd as Mr. Summers cleared his throat and looked at the list. "All ready?" he called. "Now, I'll read the names—heads of families first—and the men come up and take a paper out of the box. Keep the paper folded in your hand without looking at it until everyone has had a turn. Everything clear?"

20 The people had done it so many times that they only half listened to the directions; most of them were quiet, wetting their lips, not looking around. Then Mr. Summers raised one hand high and said, "Adams." A man disengaged himself from the crowd and came forward. "Hi, Steve," Mr. Summers said, and Mr. Adams said, "Hi, Joe." They grinned at one another humorlessly and nervously. Then Mr. Adams reached into the black box and took out a folded paper. He held it firmly by one corner as he turned and went hastily back to his place in the crowd, where he stood a little apart from his family, not looking down at his hand.

"Allen," Mr. Summers said. "Anderson . . . Bentham."

"Seems like there's no time at all between lotteries any more," Mrs. Delacroix said to Mrs. Graves in the back row. "Seems like we got through with the last one only last week."

"Time sure goes fast," Mrs. Graves said.

"Clark . . . Delacroix."

25   "There goes my old man," Mrs. Delacroix said. She held her   25
breath while her husband went forward.

    "Dunbar," Mr. Summers said, and Mrs. Dunbar went steadily to
the box while one of the women said, "Go on, Janey," and another
said, "There she goes."

    "We're next," Mrs. Graves said. She watched while Mr. Graves
came around from the side of the box, greeted Mr. Summers gravely,
and selected a slip of paper from the box. By now, all through the
crowd there were men holding the small folded papers in their large
hands, turning them over and over nervously. Mrs. Dunbar and her
two sons stood together, Mrs. Dunbar holding the slip of paper.

    "Harburt . . . Hutchinson."

    "Get up there, Bill," Mrs. Hutchinson said, and the people near
her laughed.

30   "Jones."   30

    "They do say," Mr. Adams said to Old Man Warner, who stood
next to him, "that over in the north village they're talking of giving up
the lottery."

    Old Man Warner snorted. "Pack of crazy fools," he said. "Listen-
ing to the young folks, nothing's good enough for *them*. Next thing
you know, they'll be wanting to go back to living in caves, nobody
work any more, live *that* way for a while. Used to be a saying about
'Lottery in June, corn be heavy soon.' First thing you know, we'd all
be eating stewed chickweed and acorns. There's *always* been a lottery,"
he added petulantly. "Bad enough to see young Joe Summers up there
joking with everybody."

    "Some places have already quit lotteries," Mrs. Adams said.

    "Nothing but trouble in *that*," Old Man Warner said stoutly.
"Pack of young fools."

35   "Martin." And Bobby Martin watched his father go forward.   35
"Overdyke . . . Percy."

    "I wish they'd hurry," Mrs. Dunbar said to her older son. "I wish
they'd hurry."

    "They're almost through," her son said.

    "You get ready to run tell Dad," Mrs. Dunbar said.

    Mr. Summers called his own name and then stepped forward pre-
cisely and selected a slip from the box. Then he called, "Warner."

40   "Seventy-seventh year I been in the lottery," Old Man Warner   40
said as he went through the crowd. "Seventy-seventh time."

"Watson." The tall boy came awkwardly through the crowd. Someone said, "Don't be nervous, Jack," and Mr. Summers said, "Take your time, son."

"Zanini."

After that, there was a long pause, a breathless pause, until Mr. Summers, holding his slip of paper in the air, said, "All right, fellows." For a minute, no one moved, and then all the slips of paper were opened. Suddenly, all the women began to speak at once, saying, "Who is it?" "Who's got it?" "Is it the Dunbars?" "Is it the Watsons?" Then the voices began to say, "It's Hutchinson. It's Bill," "Bill Hutchinson's got it."

"Go tell your father," Mrs. Dunbar said to her older son.

45 People began to look around to see the Hutchinsons. Bill Hutchinson was standing quiet, staring down at the paper in his hand. Suddenly, Tessie Hutchinson shouted to Mr. Summers, "You didn't give him time enough to take any paper he wanted. I saw you. It wasn't fair."

"Be a good sport, Tessie," Mrs. Delacroix called, and Mrs. Graves said, "All of us took the same chance."

"Shut up, Tessie," Bill Hutchinson said.

"Well, everyone," Mr. Summers said, "that was done pretty fast, and now we've got to be hurrying a little more to get done in time." He consulted his next list. "Bill," he said, "you draw for the Hutchinson family. You got any other households in the Hutchinsons?"

"There's Don and Eva," Mrs. Hutchinson yelled. "Make them take their chance!"

50 "Daughters draw with their husbands' families, Tessie," Mr. Summers said gently. "You know that as well as anyone else."

"It wasn't *fair*," Tessie said.

"I guess not, Joe," Bill Hutchinson said regretfully. "My daughter draws with her husband's family, that's only fair. And I've got no other family except the kids."

"Then, as far as drawing for families is concerned, it's you." Mr. Summers said in explanation, "and as far as drawing for households is concerned, that's you, too. Right?"

"Right," Bill Hutchinson said.

55 "How many kids, Bill?" Mr. Summers asked formally.

"Three," Bill Hutchinson said. "There's Bill, Jr., and Nancy, and little Dave. And Tessie and me."

"All right, then," Mr. Summers said. "Harry, you got their tickets back?"

Mr. Graves nodded and held up the slips of paper. "Put them in the box, then," Mr. Summers directed. "Take Bill's and put it in."

"I think we ought to start over," Mrs. Hutchinson said, as quietly as she could. "I tell you it wasn't *fair*. You didn't give him time enough to choose. *Every*body saw that."

Mr. Graves had selected the five slips and put them in the box, and he dropped all the papers but those onto the ground, where the breeze caught them and lifted them off.

"Listen, everybody," Mrs. Hutchinson was saying to the people around her.

"Ready, Bill?" Mr. Summers asked, and Bill Hutchinson, with one quick glance around at his wife and children, nodded.

"Remember," Mr. Summers said, "take the slips and keep them folded until each person has taken one. Harry, you help little Dave." Mr. Graves took the hand of the little boy, who came willingly with him up to the box. "Take a paper out of the box, Davy," Mr. Summers said. Davy put his hand into the box and laughed. "Take just *one* paper," Mr. Summers said. "Harry, you hold it for him." Mr. Graves took the child's hand and removed the folded paper from the tight fist and held it while little Dave stood next to him and looked up at him wonderingly.

"Nancy next," Mr. Summers said. Nancy was twelve, and her school friends breathed heavily as she went forward, switching her skirt, and took a slip daintily from the box. "Bill, Jr.," Mr. Summers said, and Billy, his face red and his feet over-large, nearly knocked the box over as he got a paper out. "Tessie," Mr. Summers said. She hesitated for a minute, looking around defiantly, and then set her lips and went up to the box. She snatched a paper out and held it behind her.

"Bill," Mr. Summers said, and Bill Hutchinson reached into the box and felt around, bringing his hand out at last with the slip of paper in it.

The crowd was quiet. A girl whispered, "I hope it's not Nancy," and the sound of the whisper reached the edges of the crowd.

"It's not the way it used to be," Old Man Warner said clearly. "People ain't the way they used to be."

"All right," Mr. Summers said. "Open the papers. Harry, you open little Dave's."

Mr. Graves opened the slip of paper and there was a general sigh through the crowd as he held it up and everyone could see that it was blank. Nancy and Bill, Jr., opened theirs at the same time, and both beamed and laughed, turning around to the crowd and holding their slips of paper above their heads.

70 "Tessie," Mr. Summers said. There was a pause, and then Mr. Summers looked at Bill Hutchinson, and Bill unfolded his paper and showed it. It was blank.

"It's Tessie," Mr. Summers said, and his voice was hushed. "Show us her paper, Bill."

Bill Hutchinson went over to his wife and forced the slip of paper out of her hand. It had a black spot on it, the black spot Mr. Summers had made the night before with the heavy pencil in the coal-company office. Bill Hutchinson held it up, and there was a stir in the crowd.

"All right, folks," Mr. Summers said. "Let's finish quickly."

Although the villagers had forgotten the ritual and lost the original black box, they still remembered to use stones. The pile of stones the boys had made earlier was ready; there were stones on the ground with the blowing scraps of paper that had come out of the box. Mrs. Delacroix selected a stone so large she had to pick it up with both hands and turned, to Mrs. Dunbar. "Come on," she said. "Hurry up."

Mrs. Dunbar had small stones in both hands, and she said, gasping for breath, "I can't run at all. You'll have to go ahead and I'll catch up with you."

75 The children had stones already, and someone gave little Davy Hutchinson a few pebbles.

Tessie Hutchinson was in the center of a cleared space by now, and she held her hands out despertely as the villagers moved in on her. "It isn't fair," she said. A stone hit her on the side of the head.

Old Man Warner was saying, "Come on, come on, everyone." Steve Adams was in the front of the crowd of villagers, with Mrs. Graves beside him.

"It isn't fair, it isn't right," Mrs. Hutchinson screamed, and then they were upon her.

Index